# NASD
# Exam

SERIES **6**

PREPARATION GUIDE

**THOMSON**

™

**SOUTH-WESTERN**

Australia · Canada · Mexico · Singapore · Spain · United Kingdom · United States

**THOMSON**
™
**SOUTH-WESTERN**

# NASD Exam, Series 6

## Preparation Guide
Greensward Publications

**VP/Editorial Director:**
Jack W. Calhoun

**VP/Executive Publisher:**
Dave Shaut

**Sr. Acquisitions Editor:**
Scott Person

**Developmental Editor:**
Sara Froelicher

**Marketing Manager:**
Mark Linton

**Production Editor:**
Robert Dreas

**Media Development Editor:**
Timothy Morley

**Media Production Editor:**
Edward Stubenrauch

**Manufacturing Coordinator:**
Charlene Taylor

**Production House:**
Shepherd Incorporated

**Printer:**
West
Eagan, Minnesota

**Design Project Manager and Internal Designer:**
Chris A. Miller

**Cover Designer/Illustrator:**
Chris A. Miller

# Contents

# 2 Investment Companies, Taxation, and Customer Accounts

# 3 Variable Contracts and Retirement Plans  140

# 4 Securities Industry Regulations      170

# Preface

## Welcome to South-Western's NASD Series 6 Exam Prep Guide

Congratulations, you have taken an important step toward achieving success on the NASD Series 6 exam. You have selected one of the most innovative certification exam prep tools engineered around the identical structure of the actual Series 6 exam from NASD.

As one of the most respected providers of business learning solutions worldwide, South-Western is committed to meeting the learning needs of professionals like you to reach their career goals and to achieve business success. The *Series 6 Exam Prep Guide* is one part of the new COMPASS Learning System from South-Western—designed unlike any other program to deliver highly targeted and streamlined instruction that leads quickly to success on the NASD Series 6 exam.

## NASD's Series 6 Exam

The Investment Company/Variable Contracts Licensure Exam 6 from NASD is required of individuals soliciting the purchase or sale of redeemable securities (mutual funds), variable contracts (variable annuities), and insurance premium funding programs (variable life) issued by insurance companies.

The NASD Series 6 examination is administered by the National Association of Securities Dealers (NASD) and is proctored at 380 Prometric testing centers throughout the United States and Canada. To obtain an admission to the Series 6 exam, your firm will submit your application along with the processing fees. Upon receipt of valid enrollment, register immediately to take the exam at a local Prometric Testing Center. Call 1-866-PROMETRIC for more information or visit *www.prometric.com/nasd* to schedule your Series 6 exam at Prometric.

The NASD Series 6 exam consists of 100 multiple-choice questions based on the following four sections:

▷ Securities and Markets; Investment Risks and Policies (23 questions)
▷ Investment Companies, Taxation, and Customer Accounts (36 questions)
▷ Variable Contracts and Retirement Plans (16 questions)
▷ Securities Industry Regulations (25 questions)

There are no prerequisite exams you must pass before taking the Series 6 exam. The questions on the actual exam do not appear in any particular order. Each test candidate will receive a randomized set of 100 multiple-choice questions based on the present topic weights of the exam.

▷ You will have 135 minutes of testing time to complete the Series 6 exam.
▷ You must correctly answer 70 percent of the questions in order to earn a passing grade.
▷ The Series 6 is a closed book examination.
▷ Scratch paper will be provided by the proctor at the testing center.
▷ Candidates will not be allowed to use their personal calculators. At your request, the testing center staff will provide a calculator.

# South-Western's COMPASS Series 6 Learning System

Built on a highly successful class-tested instructional test-prep model that has helped thousands of professionals pass certification exams, South-Western's COMPASS Learning System delivers focused instruction targeting the core content areas critical for you to pass the Series 6 exam from NASD. Unlike the topical approaches of other Series 6 test-prep materials, each of the learning tools from South-Western aligns directly with the four sections of the actual Series 6 Exam.

In addition to this Series 6 Exam Prep Guide, stay on track toward your success by using one of the most advanced and fully integrated learning technologies available today. The Prescriptive and Practice CD-ROM applications (powered by SmartLink™) provide you with reinforcing instruction and diagnostic feedback customized to your individual needs. South-Western's COMPASS Learning System for the NASD Series 6 exam includes:

▷ NASD Series 6 Exam Prep Guide     0-324-18696-7
▷ NASD Series 6 Exam Prep Drill & Practice CD-ROM     0-324-20335-7
▷ Success on the NASD Series 6 Exam Prescriptive CD-ROM     0-324-20179-6
▷ NASD Series 6 Exam Prep Online Course     0-324-20334-9

# Track Your Individual Progress

The self-paced instructional design of this Series 6 Exam Prep Guide provides you with the tools you need to take charge of your exam preparation.

▷ **Success Tips.** Abundant tips and valuable insights to passing the Series 6 exam are found throughout each chapter helping you zero in on the key elements of the exam and build your confidence each step of the way.

▷ **Comprehensive Summaries and Reviews.** Each chapter provides a quick overview and direct application of the essential knowledge and concepts you need to pass the Series 6 Exam—to stay on target.

▷ **Two Practice Final Exams.** Test your mastery of the content by completing the two practice final exams that mimic the actual Series 6 exam. These practice exams include the same proportion of questions per topic established by NASD.

▷ **Test Answer Keys and Rationale.** Check your understanding with the detailed explanations provided for each practice final exam question. This valuable self-paced feature enables you to immediately determine your mastery of the exam content and provides you with insights to the logic of each answer.

# Navigate Your Own "Learning Path"

Accelerate your exam preparation with interactive and diagnostic electronic test-prep tools (both online and CD-ROM). These innovative SmartLink™ tools streamline your preparation time for success on the Series 6 exam by providing you with immediate reinforcement and a direct roadmap for review specific to your individual study needs. Features include:

▷ **Pre-Exam**—used to access your specific learning needs. An individualized learning path is created based on your level of mastery of topics.

▷ **"My Learning Path"**—an individualized, prescriptive learning path based on the results and evaluation of your Pre-Exam scores. By using "My Learning Path," you can easily review areas where more study is needed.

▷ **Chapter Exams**—deliver four self-paced exams based on each of the four sections of the NASD Series 6 exam.

▷ **Vocabulary Drills**—tests your knowledge of terminology essential for success on the exam. Two types of drills test your understanding by *term* and by *definition*.

▷ **Course Exam**—simulates the actual Series 6 exam with 100 multiple-choice questions with a time limit of 135 minutes for completion.

▷ **Customized Exams**—allow you to create customized exams for additional practice by selecting the desired number of questions from each chapter.

▷ **Vocabulary Exam**—tests your knowledge on words and terms used in the securities market.

▷ **Progress View**—tracks your progress through detailed progress reports each step of the way, from start to finish.

# Good Study Methods—The Basics

If you haven't taken an exam in several years, you are probably feeling a little anxious. Let's review some good study habits that may add 10–15 points to your score.

▷ Study at a time of day that is comfortable for you. Everyone is different, but it should be a time of day that you are alert and focused.

▷ Get rid of distractions! This means NO TV, food, children, or spouses. Try to stay off a bed or couch because you are more likely to fall asleep.

▷ Do not cram the night before the exam. You will retain information effectively by studying regularly.

▷ To improve your success and streamline your exam preparation schedule, use one of South-Western's CD-ROM learning tools to take additional computerized practice tests, identify areas you have mastered and target specific content you may need to review further to ensure your success on the exam.

▷ READ THE QUESTION. READ THE QUESTION. READ THE QUESTION. Read the question at least three times before you look at the answer, and then read the answers at least two times before selecting the best one. Understand what the question is asking and catch key words like *except* and *only*.

▷ Know definitions by studying the glossaries in this prep guide. If you don't, you are doing yourself a grave injustice because more than 70% of the exam is definitions.

▷ Sleep well the night before the exam. Try to have your exam scheduled first thing in the morning so you are alert and refreshed.

▷ Be positive and have confidence in yourself. Starting today, tell yourself "I'm going to pass one time—the FIRST time!"

# Successful Test-Taking Techniques

▷ If you tell your friends and family when you are taking your exam, it may place pressure on you by setting up expectations. Instead of worrying about everyone's expectations, try to keep your exam date a secret and then surprise them after you pass!

▷ Don't spend too much time on one question. If you don't know the answer to a question, mark it and come back to it later. You may think of the answer later or you might even find it in another question later on in the exam.

▷ During the exam, you may lose your train of thought. When this happens, stop, relax, and take a deep breath. Return your focus to the exam and proceed.

▷ Remember that two of the four answers are often not worth considering. Pick one of the two remaining answers when guessing.

▷ Please remember that your first answer is usually the right one, so do not change it unless you are sure.

▷ Answers with absolutes such as *must, always, greatest, never,* and *has to be* generally are not the correct answers.

▷ Above all, do not panic! Stop! Take a moment. Reorganize the material. You know more than you think you do. Relax and let it become clear.

# Reaching Your Goal

Achieving success is not by chance; it requires solid commitment, targeted strategy, and superior resources. You have shown your commitment to passing the Series 6 exam by selecting South-Western's COMPASS Learning System that provides the most targeted and streamlined instructional resources available. Chart your way to success by becoming a Limited Representative.

PROFESSIONAL
*Portfolio*

The COMPASS Learning System is part of the South-Western **Professional Portfolio,** covering advanced business topics that deliver real business solutions for real business problems. For over 100 years, South-Western has provided time-tested and market-leading learning materials for business success. South-Western, a Thomson Learning business, is the leading learning solutions provider of business learning materials worldwide. Turn to South-Western as you continue on your path to career success in financial services.

# 1

# Securities and Markets; Investment Risks and Policies

*In order for you to make suitable recommendations and give clients the advice they need, you as a Limited Representative must have a good grasp of the various securities, markets, and investment vehicles available. Even though you will be limited in the types of securities that you may sell, many of these securities still form the foundation of the mutual funds and other investment products that you will sell.*

*When you have finished studying this chapter, you should be able to fully describe the characteristics, advantages and disadvantages, risks and rewards of various securities. This will ensure that the customer is provided with the pertinent information for a particular investment. This chapter will also give you an understanding of the primary and secondary securities markets, and discuss the relevance of economic factors, helping you explain those events as they affect the markets and investments. But the key in all of this is listening to clients, assisting them with determining goals and objectives, and showing them which investment strategies are suitable for their financial situation, investment experience, and risk tolerance.*

*As you study this textbook to prepare for the Series 6 exam (which you must pass to become a Limited Representative), be aware that the exam requires knowledge of many topics and types of securities that you will not be able to sell. Furthermore, this book does not necessarily represent the order in which these topics will be covered on the test, but much of the material in this chapter will help form a basis of understanding for concepts in subsequent chapters. Finally, this first chapter ("Securities and Markets; Investment Risks and Policies") represents about 23% of the total test: approximately 23 questions of the total 100 questions on the Series 6 exam.*

## This chapter will be broken up into six sections:

**1.1 Investment Securities.** This first section looks at corporate securities (common stock, preferred stock, bonds), then various types of government bonds and securities (Treasuries, agency issues, municipals), and finally other money market instruments. The features, rights, and characteristics of each are also examined.

**1.2 Securities Markets.** This section explores how the securities markets work. The exchange auction markets (e.g., New York Stock Exchange [NYSE]) are discussed first, followed by negotiated markets (e.g., NASDAQ, over-the-counter [OTC]), then new issue markets and the role of investment bankers in primary offerings. Market terms and prices round out this section.

**1.3 Economic Factors.** This section discusses various economic factors that affect prices in the economy as a whole, and the markets in particular. Inflation and monetary policy are the focus of the discussion, but with a mention of fiscal policy and taxes as domestic factors, as well as exchange rates as an international factor.

**1.4 Investment Risk Factors.** This section details different risks associated with various investments, the risk/reward concept, and importance of diversification.

**1.5 Suitability Factors.** This section explains some typical client objectives, financial considerations of clients when choosing suitable investments, and various risk tolerance concerns that must be discussed with the client.

**1.6 Investment Company Portfolio Risk Characteristics.** This section goes through a brief description of various investment company product objectives and risk considerations for income products, growth products, specialized and more.

## key terms

**Aggressive investments:** stocks of rapidly growing companies that have prospects for above-average growth, but with prices that are highly volatile over time when compared with the broader market. (e.g., high-tech companies and start-ups)

**Defensive investments:** high-grade bonds and stocks with prices that are more stable over time than the broad market. (e.g., utilities, certain blue-chip stocks, and some high-grade preferred stock)

**Inflationary risk:** chance that the value of assets or income will decline relative to the prices of other goods and services. Also called **purchasing power risk.**

**Interest rate risk:** chance that changes in interest rates will adversely affect the value of an investment.

**Liquidity:** the ease with which assets can be converted into cash (at full value).

**Portfolio diversification:** spreading out risk by holding investments in varying types, amounts, and asset classes.

**Preservation of capital:** ensuring that the original amount of money invested is as safe as possible.

**Primary market:** sale of new securities issues directly by the issuer to investors.

**Primary offering:** sale of stock in the primary market, with the proceeds from the sale of stock going into the company treasury.

**Secondary market:** place where securities are bought and sold after original issue, with proceeds going to the investor selling the security.

**Secondary offering:** sale of stock in the primary market, with the proceeds from sale of stock going to present shareholders.

**Securities:** any investment relationship with a company or government, and the instruments which represent that investment. Securities can be equity in a company (stock), debt with a company (bond), a pooling of investment instruments (mutual fund), or any instrument transferring a future right (option).

# 1.1

# Investment Securities

**Investment** is the use of capital to create money via an income-producing instrument, or the use of capital to create capital appreciation from a risk-oriented venture. In other words, investing is using money to try and make more money. **Securities** are any investment relationship with a company or government, and the instruments that represent that investment. An investment security, therefore, can be equity ownership in a company (stock), debt with a company or government (bond), a pooling of investment instruments (mutual fund), or any instrument that transfers a future right (option). Let's look at various corporate and government securities.

# 1.1.1

# Corporate Securities

**Corporate securities** are an investment relationship with a company. The most common of these are equity ownership (stock) and debt obligations (bonds). We will discuss variations of these two main types, as well as other special securities.

## 1.1.1.1 Equity Securities

**Equity** is an ownership interest in a company. Thus, **equity securities** are the instruments that signify ownership interest in a company, commonly called **stock.**

Think: "stock" equals "ownership." There are actually many kinds of stock, and other instruments that represent rights to buy stock which are also referred to as equity securities. The four broad classifications of stock are authorized, issued, outstanding, and treasury. Sometimes, stock starts in one classification and moves to another. Let's explain the classifications, then discuss movement and value.

**AUTHORIZED. Authorized stock** is stock originally approved by a corporation in its Articles of Incorporation. This is the maximum number of shares the company may create, but the company does not have to issue or sell all of the shares at once. In fact, a company will usually only sell enough shares to raise the money it needs in its initial stages and will save shares for future needs. The decision to sell shares up to the maximum number of authorized stock shares is made by the board of directors, but if the company wants to sell more stock than the original number of authorized shares, it must put the matter to a vote of current shareholders.

**ISSUED. Issued stock** is stock that has been distributed by the corporation. This can be the result of stock sold to investors, stock distributed to the founders of the company, or stock given to employees as incentives, bonuses, or for retirement plans. Stock that has been authorized, but not yet issued, is referred to as **unissued stock.** This is stock held back for future needs and does not have voting privileges nor count when doing calculations for capitalization, earnings per share, or dividends.

**OUTSTANDING. Outstanding stock** is stock presently held by shareholders. Again, this could be investors, founders, or employees. The difference, though, between *issued* and *outstanding* stock, is that shares may have been issued but subsequently reacquired by the corporation and thus are no longer outstanding.

**TREASURY. Treasury stock** is stock reacquired by the corporation. It is issued, but not outstanding. Treasury stock may be held to resell at a future date, or reissued for incentives, bonuses, or retirement plans. The company can also retire the shares. Like unissued stock, treasury stock does not have voting privileges nor count when doing calculations for capitalization, earnings per share, or dividends.

Since a company's earnings and capitalization figures are based only on the number of outstanding shares, an important formula to remember is

**Issued Stock – Treasury Stock = Outstanding Stock**

There will likely be a Series 6 exam question asking you how much stock a company has outstanding. You will likely be given several figures (perhaps even some extraneous ones), and you will need to know this formula.

Exam Topic
Alert

**How Stock Classifications Change.** It is easy to understand why companies authorize shares—they want to distribute ownership shares to founders, and they want to raise money. Some of the other mechanics may be a little less clear. Once stock has been authorized in the original Articles of Incorporation or charter of the company, it's available to the company for any purpose the board of directors sees fit.

It can be sold to raise money, or it can be given to employees as incentives, it can be kept by the company for future use. But once stock is authorized, the stock does not become unauthorized. Instead authorized stock either is used—and thus becomes issued stock—or it remains unused—and thus it remains unissued stock.

Issued stock is outstanding stock unless and until it is reacquired by the company. Once it has been reacquired by the company, it is treasury stock until it is retired or reissued. Remember, treasury stock does not have voting rights and is not eligible to receive a share of any dividends declared by the company.

**How Stock Value Is Determined.** There are actually three different stock values that can be discussed: **par value, book value,** and **market value.** All three values are usually *very* different. Note that when stock starts out as authorized, but unissued, it has no market value. The company may assign an arbitrary value to the stock (called **par value**), it may assign no par value to the stock, or it may give the stock a stated value. This value may or may not appear on the stock certificates, but is largely irrelevant (except with preferred stock, as we shall see). The difference between par value and the money a company receives for selling the stock is referred to as paid-in capital. **Paid-in capital** is money received from investors, as opposed to money actually earned by the company. Paid-in capital is an asset to the company.

A company that is a going concern regularly acquires assets and incurs liabilities. An important formula is Assets – Liabilities = Net Worth. If we take the net worth figure for a company and divide it by the number of shares outstanding, we get the **book value** of the company. This value represents an estimate of what the company would be worth in a liquidation sale. It is useful to analyze the company and make comparisons with other companies in its sector, but not for much else. If you are asked to calculate a company's book value per share, you will need to know the net worth formula. The question will be rather basic. Here's an example.

## EXAMPLE

A company has $30 million in assets and $18 million in liabilities. If there are 4 million shares outstanding, what is the book value?

**Assets – Liabilities ÷ Shares = Book Value (per Share)**

**$30 million – $18 million ÷ 4 million = $3 per Share**

Exam Topic Alert

Stock only acquires a true value once it has been issued. At that point, *the stock price is driven by supply and demand,* based on what investors will pay for it in the marketplace. This is referred to as **market value.** This is the price (minus commissions, etc.) at which an investor could expect to buy or sell the stock. For most purposes, this is the most relevant value.

**How a Stock Split Affects Market Value.** A **stock split** is an attempt to adjust the price of a stock downward by increasing the number of outstanding shares without changing the percentage of company ownership held by each stockholder, and without changing the total market value of all outstanding shares. In other words, as of the date of the stock split, the stockholders all own the same proportionate share of the company as they did before, and the total value of their stock holdings is also the same. Let's look at an example.

## EXAMPLE

Pat owns 1000 shares of ABC, value is $100 each before the split.
Pat's total stock value is 1000 x $100 = $100,000
ABC Corp. announces a 2 for 1 stock split, so every one share of stock Pat owns
    is now split into two shares.
Pat owns 2000 shares of ABC, value is $50 each after the split.
Pat's total stock value is 2000 x $50 = $100,000

A company usually does this when it feels that its share price is too high. Investors like to see high prices, but that can also keep the stock out of the hands of smaller investors and result in less trading activity. Conversely, if the company worries that its stock price is too low, it may do a reverse split.

A **reverse split** is an attempt to adjust the price of a stock upward by decreasing the number of outstanding shares without changing the percentage of company ownership held by each stockholder and without changing the total market value of all outstanding shares. Companies worry that low share prices will not attract institutional investors or "sophisticated" investors because the stock price makes the company look like a "penny stock." Furthermore, if the share price drops too low for an extended period of time, some exchanges will delist the stock.

Remember that share price and number of shares go in opposite directions for either split, and that total ownership *percentage* and total stock *value* don't change. Also, if a split would increase the authorized shares, the shareholders must vote.

Exam Topic Alert

**Other Important Points about Stock.** Remember, only stock that is issued *and* outstanding can convey rights to the shareholder. These rights depend on what type of stock is held, and even within these types there can be different subclasses of stock (e.g., Class A, Class B) that convey different stockholder rights.

For the Series 6 exam, you should know that the *two primary types of equity securities are common stock and preferred stock.* Let's examine each of these more closely.

Exam Topic Alert

## Common Stock

**Common stock** is an ownership interest in a corporation that conveys to the holder certain rights, including the right to vote for the board of directors and certain other issues, and the right to receive a proportionate share of any declared dividend. Common stockholders also enjoy the benefits of company ownership, without the potential liability that could befall owners of a business that was not incorporated. This limited liability is a big advantage. The investor is insulated from being responsible for the company's debts or other obligations (although there are some exceptions for closely held corporations). The most that a typical common stockholder can lose is the amount he or she invested to buy the stock. The other two main advantages to common stock ownership are the potential for unlimited capital appreciation and the possibility of income from dividends.

**RIGHT TO EARNINGS.** When investors buy a stock, they not only buy a piece of the company, but they also buy a right to share in the company's future earnings. In theory, stock prices are the present discounted value of expected future earnings and profits. Although stock prices can fluctuate for reasons other than changes in profitability, in general this principle is sound. Expectations of future profits reflect the level and growth of profits in the recent past, so current stock prices are trying to anticipate the level and growth of profits in the future.

This leads to the use of a company's price-to-earnings (PE) ratio as a way to compare companies across an industry. This also explains why at times a company's stock price will drop even if it is profitable and sometimes even when it beats analysts' expectations. In these situations, investors have determined that even though a company is doing well now, its current profit numbers do not warrant such a high valuation for the expected future earnings of the company. In other words, the expectations of future company profits are not as high as once thought, or the stock price was already high because better growth expectations were already figured into the price, so the current stock price has changed based on new expectations.

**RIGHT TO DIVIDENDS. Dividends** are a distribution of company earnings to stockholders as voted on by the board of directors. A shareholder only has the right to receive a dividend if it is declared by the board of directors. (Shareholders do NOT vote on dividends.) Some companies (particularly high-growth companies) choose not to declare a dividend, and instead invest the money in research and development.

Once a dividend has been declared, the stockholders have the right to receive it. Each stockholder of record as of a certain date (more on this in a future chapter) is sent a check, or the check is sent to the brokerage house if stocks are held in the firm's name. Dividends are paid out to shareholders on a *pro rata* basis, based on the percentage of stock ownership in the company. The dividends are usually paid in cash, but they can also be paid out in stock or even sometimes with company products (this is rare, but actually anything of value can be distributed as a dividend). Dividend payments are made quarterly, and create a taxable event that must be declared as ordinary income in the year received—even if the money is reinvested. (Note, though, that U.S. corporations get a **dividend exclusion,** whereby they don't pay tax on 70% of the dividend income they receive from other U.S. companies.)

**VOTING RIGHTS.** Voting is one of the most important rights that a common stockholder has, because it is one of the few ways that the investor can exert some measure of control over what happens at the corporation.

There are four main areas where common stockholders are permitted to vote:

> ▷ electing the board of directors
> ▷ dilution issues (e.g., authorizing stock, issuing convertible bonds)
> ▷ changes in business direction of the company (e.g., mergers, buyouts)
> ▷ stock splits

Note that stockholders do *not* vote on dividends, pay increases, new product introductions, or other day-to-day management items.

Here are some other important key terms and points you need to know about voting:

a. **statutory:** This is a type of voting that follows the one share, one vote rule, whereby stockholders get a single vote on each issue or each board member.

b. **cumulative:** This is a type of voting whereby stockholders receive a total number of votes equal to their total number of shares of stock, then the stockholders may place all of those votes for a single board member or issue, or divide the vote any way they want. (This gives minority stockholders more voting influence.)

c. **proxies:** This is a kind of absentee ballot, whereby the stockholder can vote on matters without having to attend the annual stockholder's meeting. Proxy solicitations must be sent to the Securities and Exchange Commission (SEC) for approval before the company can send them to stockholders. Proxy fights, which attempt to alter control of a company, must have all parties register with the SEC or risk criminal penalties.

d. **nonvoting:** Corporations may decide to issue subclasses of common stock (e.g., Class A, Class B) that do not carry voting rights. Although unusual, this can be done to raise capital without fear of losing management control.

**OTHER RIGHTS OF COMMON STOCKHOLDERS.** In addition to these benefits, investors who hold common stock enjoy other rights and privileges. These include:

**Preemptive Rights. Preemptive rights** are the right of existing stock holders to buy, in proportion to their current holdings, additional shares of a new issue by the company before the stock is offered to the public. This is often referred to as an **antidilution provision** because it allows current shareholders the right to maintain their present proportionate control over the company in voting matters, and their present share of declared dividends.

Remember that this is a right, not a requirement. The current stockholders get a first right of refusal to buy new shares up to their present proportion, but they may choose not to do so. Also note that these rights vary based on state law or corporate charter provisions, and either of these may also permit the corporation to pay existing shareholders in lieu of offering them stock from the new issue.

**Access to Corporate Books.** All stockholders have the right to inspect the books of the corporation in which they hold stock. This is usually interpreted to mean that stockholders have the right to receive all financial statements of the company, annual statements, list of stockholders, and other corporate communications. This is not meant to include detailed financial records, internal memos, or other confidential documents. Notes and minutes from the board of directors meetings are also off-limits. Of course, shareholders who own a substantial position in the company's stock may be afforded more access. Requests for information must be made during normal business hours.

**Residual Claim on Corporate Assets.** In a bankruptcy, the common stockholders are the last in line to recoup any money. After all creditors and lien holders have been satisfied, though, the common stockholders do have a claim on whatever assets, if any, are left. (The chart below shows the payout order if a company liquidates. This chart will likely contain the answer to a question or two on the Series 6 exam. Note that common stockholders are last in line.)

---

chart 1.1.1.1

**ORDER OF PAYOUT IF A COMPANY LIQUIDATES**
*(This may be on Series 6 exam.)*

**Highest Claim, Paid First- - - -** 1. wages

2. taxes

3. secured debt (bonds)

(Remember: **WTSeGSuPC**) 4. general creditors (includes debenture holders)

1 2 3 4 5 6 7 5. subordinated debt (junior debentures)

6. preferred stockholders

**Lowest Claim, Paid Last- - - -** 7. common stockholders

To remember the order of payout, think: **W**hen **T**he **S**hip **G**oes, **S**ip **P**iña **C**oladas.

---

## Preferred Stock

**Preferred stock** is an ownership interest in a corporation that pays a specified dividend rate. Like common stock, owners of preferred stock have limited liability when it comes to corporate obligations—the most the preferred stockholder can lose is the original investment. (Par face value of preferred stock is $100 per certificate.)

Preferred stock, though, has some disadvantages when compared with common stock. One disadvantage is that preferred stockholders usually do not receive the voting rights that common stockholders have. Preferred stock usually does not have pre-emptive rights either. Another important disadvantage is that preferred stockholders do not get to share in the capital appreciation of the company like common stockholders do. This is because preferred stockholders are guaranteed a certain rate of return on their investment. Since they have less risk, they get less reward.

**LIQUIDATION PREFERENCE.** Preferred stockholders have an important advantage because they can recoup assets in a liquidation before common stockholders. Preferred stockholders must wait until after all creditors and lien holders have been satisfied, but preferred stockholders have a **liquidation preference** over common stockholders. (See Chart 1.1.1.1.) Because of this, common stock is a *junior security* vis-à-vis preferred stock, which here is a *senior security*. But preferred stock is a junior security vis-à-vis debt—it's all relative.

**DIVIDEND PREFERRED.** Preferred stock has another advantage over common stock: preferred stockholders get paid dividends before common stockholders. To make it more attractive for investors, companies have created a number of different preferred stock variations with different dividend payout methods. These include:

**Cumulative. Cumulative preferred stock** allows dividends to accrue so that in the event that dividends cannot be paid, the unpaid dividends become a liability. All back dividends must be paid in full, and there must be enough to pay current preferred stock dividends, *before* any regular dividends can be paid to common stockholders. This feature is typical of preferred stock today.

**Noncumulative. Noncumulative preferred stock** does not have dividends that accrue, so any unpaid dividends will likely never be paid. This type of straight preferred stock is rather unusual today since most issue cumulative.

**Participating. Participating preferred stock** pays its stated dividends and allows preferred stockholders the chance to receive certain extra bonus payments, which may be made to all common *and* preferred shareholders after regular dividends are paid. It's rare for preferred stock to have this provision.

**Nonparticipating. Nonparticipating preferred stock** pays only its stated dividends and does not have any provisions for extra payments. It is typical for preferred stock issued today to be nonparticipating.

**CONVERTIBLE. Convertible preferred stock** has the added feature that the stockholders can trade in the convertible preferred stock for common stock in the company at a preset price. This allows preferred stockholders to have a chance to share in the capital appreciation of the underlying company's stock. Because of this feature, the price of convertible preferred stock may fluctuate in line with the common stock. The dividend paid on convertible preferred stock is usually *lower* since investors will accept this in exchange for a chance to convert to common stock and enjoy capital appreciation at a future date.

When an investor is deciding whether or not to convert the preferred stock to common stock, there are several factors that must be considered. These include the conversion price (price at which a preferred stockholder can buy the common stock) and the conversion ratio (how many shares would be received for converting). Both of these are set when the preferred stock is issued and normally stated on the face of the preferred stock certificate. Another factor that must be considered is the future prospects of the company. Let's run through a quick example that introduces the conversion concept.

## EXAMPLE

If preferred stock is currently trading at $26.75, with a conversion price of 20, and the current market value of the common stock is $6, should the preferred stockholder convert to common stock?

To answer this question, ignore "future prospects of the company," and focus on the number and value of common shares the investor gets for converting.

**Step 1:** Since the preferred stock certificate or contract is always worth 100 at par, and we know the conversion price is 20, we can figure out that the investor would get 5 shares of common stock for converting. (100 ÷ 20 = 5)

**Step 2:** Since converting will give us 5 shares of stock, at the current market value of $6, those 5 shares are worth $30. (5 × $6 = $30)

**Step 3:** To get a final answer, compare the result of Step 2 with the current value of the preferred stock. Since preferred stock is trading at $26.75, but converting would get the investor $30 worth of common stock, the investor would be better off to convert and take the more valuable common stock.

**OTHER TYPES OF PREFERRED STOCK.** Other types of preferred stock also exist. Some of these features may also be combined with those we just mentioned.

**Callable. Callable preferred stock** is redeemable by a company at a preset price. Usually there is an initial period during which the company cannot exercise this right, but after that date it can be done at any time the company feels it is advantageous to do so. This may be because interest rates have fallen and so the preferred stock can be replaced with cheaper debt, or the company wants to change its debt-to-equity ratio. Quarterly dividends paid on callable preferred stock are usually *higher* since investors expect to be compensated for the added risk that their source of income could be terminated at any time.

**Sinking Fund. Sinking fund preferred stock** is preferred stock with a special provision stating that the issuer will regularly pay money into a separate account, thus giving investors some assurance that dividends will be paid in a timely fashion. The dividend paid on sinking fund preferred stock is usually *lower* since investors feel that dividend payments are more secure.

**Adjustable-rate. Adjustable-rate preferred stock** has the dividend rate adjusted to mirror market conditions based on some index. The adjustments usually occur quarterly, and the rate is pegged to a widely used index, such as the Treasury Bill rate. The price for this type of preferred stock is less volatile than it would otherwise be, because having the rate adjust to match market conditions has a stabilizing effect.

Exam Topic
Alert

For the Series 6 exam, it is important to remember the differences between common stock and preferred stock. Like common stock, preferred stock represents ownership in the company and affords the investor the protection of limited liability. But unlike common stock, preferred stock usually does *not* confer voting rights or preemptive rights on the stockholder. Also, with preferred stock, the investor does not have the opportunity to share in capital appreciation of the company (unless the preferred stock is convertible).

There are two main advantages that preferred stock has over common stock. First, preferred stockholders get preference over common stockholders if the corporation files bankruptcy. Remember from our chart that common stockholders get paid last; preferred stock is a senior security to common stock, but junior to debt. Second, preferred stockholders are paid their quarterly dividends before common stockholders. Dividends are never guaranteed, but must be declared by the Board of Directors.

With cumulative preferred stock, all past-due dividends must be paid to preferred stockholders, *plus* the currently declared dividend, before dividends can be paid to common stockholders. Watch this on the Series 6 exam. For example, if $12 is past due from 2 prior years dividends that were not paid, and the current dividend is $6, then cumulative preferred stockholders must be paid a total of $18 before common stockholders could receive their dividend. On the other hand, if the preferred stock is noncumulative, then only the current $6 must be paid to non-cumulative preferred stockholders before a dividend is paid to common stockholders. Any excess dividends or profit participation paid to shareholders cannot be paid until after all preferred shareholders are paid in full, and all common stockholders have received the current dividend.

# 1.1.1.2 Debt Securities

When we talk about debt securities, we are usually talking about bonds. A **bond** is a security that pays interest, and returns the principal investment amount upon maturity. Bonds are a loan representing debt. Originally, all bonds were bearer **bonds,** meaning the person who held the bond was the owner. The bond had coupons that were detached and submitted to collect interest payments. To this day, the interest rate is still often referred to as the **coupon** rate, even though most bonds now are registered bonds where the name of the owner is recorded with the company-designated registrar with interest payments sent automatically or paid electronically. Corporate bonds are issued as bearer bonds, registered bonds, registered coupon bonds, or book entry bonds.

**BEARER BONDS.** **Bearer bonds** are bonds where the person who holds the bond is the owner, and coupons must be submitted to collect interest payments.

**REGISTERED BONDS.** **Registered bonds** are bonds where the name of the bond owner is recorded on the face of the bond and with the registrar of the issuing company. With these bonds, semiannual interest payments and the final principal payment are automatically sent to the person of record. Transfer occurs by proper endorsement of the bond certificate with notification to the registrar.

**REGISTERED COUPON BONDS.** **Registered coupon bonds** or **registered as to principal only** are bonds that have the name of the bond owner recorded on the face of the bond and with the registrar of the issuing company. Here only the final principal payment is automatically sent to the person of record. To collect the interest payments, the coupons must be presented.

**BOOK ENTRY BONDS.** **Book entry bonds** are the same as registered bonds, except that no certificate is issued. Instead, all transactions are handled by the registrar based on owners named in the bond records. All payments are automatic, and all transfers must go through the registrar. (Most corporate and government bonds issued today are book entry.)

**Interest Payment Periods.** Corporate bonds pay interest semiannually. The issuer pays the final interest payment along with the return of the principal on the date that the bond matures. When the bond is traded, the buyer of the bond pays the bond price "and interest" that has accrued since the last interest payment was made.

**Maturities.** Corporate bonds are issued for anywhere from 1 to 20 years and have what are called term maturities. **Term maturity** means that the bonds all come due at once. This is much different than the staggered (**serial**) maturities that government issued securities have. Because corporations must repay a significant amount of debt in one big chunk, they establish a sinking fund that they pay into regularly so that the bonds' principal amounts can be paid when the bonds come due.

**Trust Indenture Act of 1939.** The Act requires corporate bonds to have an indenture agreement. The **indenture agreement** provides for appointment of a qualified, independent trustee; protective clauses for, and list of promises to, bondholders; semiannual financial reports to bondholders; and periodic SEC filings to show compliance.

**Exam Topic Alert**

*Note that although the indenture agreement is designed to protect bondholders, it is a contract between the corporation and trustee—**not** between the company and bondholder.* This may be a trick question on the Series 6 exam.

**Bond Ratings. Bond ratings** are values on a scale that represent the likelihood the issuer will default on a debt obligation. They are, in essence, the credit rating of the entity issuing debt securities. The ratings are done by one of several agencies who assess the issuer's previous debt repayment history, current debt load, and prospects for future revenue stability and growth. The higher the bond rating, the more marketable the bond is, but sometimes small bond issues are not rated.

Two bond rating agencies you should know are Moody's and Standard & Poor's (S&P). Moody's and S&P use different, but similar, scales to rate the quality of corporate and municipal bonds. Moody's highest bond rating is "Aaa" while S&P's is "AAA", meaning the issuer is highly unlikely to default on the debt. You can remember which agency uses which rating scale rather easily: *S&P is in all capital letters, and their ratings are in all capital letters; Moody's uses upper- and lowercase letters, as does their name.*

Moody's top four ratings are Aaa, Aa, A, and Baa. S&P's top four ratings are AAA, AA, A, and BBB. The top four bond ratings by both agencies are considered **investment grade bonds.** To further distinguish bonds in a group, Moody's can assign a 1, 2, or 3 to modify a rating, such as Baa3 for the lowest in a group. S&P uses + or - to modify some ratings. Although lower grade bonds have higher yields, they're often referred to as **junk bonds.** Bonds with a D rating are in default.

Ratings are important to the issuer. Many institutional investors (e.g., pension plans, insurance companies) only buy investment grade bonds. Some states mandate that fiduciaries who invest money on behalf of other people can't buy bonds below investment grade. Since Federal Reserve/FDIC rules state that banks can only use reserves to buy investment grade bonds, they're often called **bank grade bonds.**

**Other Important Points about Corporate Bonds.** Corporate bonds (often referred to as **corporates**) are backed by the issuing corporation and may or may not have collateral associated with them. The bond, though, is merely a promise by the issuer to repay a fixed sum of money with interest—it does not confer any rights of ownership in the corporation like stock does. Bondholders are creditors of the corporation; stockholders are owners of the corporation. Since bondholders are credi-

| BOND RATING TABLE FOR CORPORATE AND MUNICIPAL BOND ISSUES | | |
|---|---|---|
| **Rating Explanation** | **Moody's** | **S&P** |
| Investment Grade | Aaa, Aa, A, Baa | AAA, AA, A, BBB |
| Medium Grade | Ba, B | BB, B |
| Highly Speculative | Caa, Ca, C | CCC, CC, C |
| In Default | D | DDD, DD, D |

chart 1.1.1.2

tors of the corporation that issued the debt, corporate bondholders have a claim on the assets of a corporation should the company be liquidated.

Corporate bonds have a par value of $1000. (**Par** for a bond is equal to the face value of the security.) This amount is used for figuring interest and calculating quotes, and is the amount paid out at maturity to the holder of the bond. Like stocks, bonds are actively traded in the secondary market. Any interest and capital gains from corporate bonds are fully taxable at all levels of government.

Because the interest rate paid by a bond provides a fixed rate of return, bonds are also called **fixed-income securities.** Although bonds are a "security," many bonds are unsecured debt. Another name for an unsecured bond is a **debenture.** A debenture does not have any collateral backing up the debt. Instead, the holder relies on the full faith and credit of the issuer. Let's look at some specific bond types.

## Secured Bonds

**Secured bonds** are backed by specific collateral named in the bond indenture. The collateral can be a mortgage, equipment, or other assets. Upon default of a secured bond, the bondholders have the right to foreclose on the asset stated in the bond indenture and liquidate it to satisfy the debt. The secured bondholders, however, are not permitted to liquidate any other assets. If the sale of the specified asset does not satisfy the claim in full, then the bondholders become general creditors of the corporation as a means to recover the rest of the money owed. Here are some specific types and features of the most commonly issued secured bonds:

### MORTGAGE BONDS
▷ type of collateral: mortgage issued on the corporation's real property
▷ priority of claim: first mortgage bonds are paid first, then lien order
▷ unique characteristics: mortgage bonds can be issued as open-end (meaning more bonds may be issued) or closed-end (meaning no more bonds may be issued below the mortgage bondholders); if sale of real estate does not satisfy all mortgage bond claims, then mortgage bondholders are general creditors of company.

### EQUIPMENT TRUST CERTIFICATES
▷ type of collateral: equipment bought with proceeds of bond sale
▷ priority of claim: first right to seize equipment if bond is not paid
▷ unique characteristics: often used by transportation companies; equipment is held in trustee's name until bond is repaid.

## Unsecured Bonds

**Unsecured bonds** are debentures that are not backed by any specific collateral, but instead have the bondholder rely on the full faith and credit of the issuer for repayment. Upon default of the unsecured bond, the bondholders become general creditors of the corporation to recover the money owed. Here are some specific types and features of different unsecured bonds:

### DEBENTURES

▷ type of collateral: none—unsecured debt; full faith and credit of issuer

▷ priority of claim: paid after secured bonds, but before stockholders

▷ unique characteristics: debentures are backed by full faith and credit of the issuer only; if more debentures are issued at a later date, they would be subordinate to (put under, paid after) prior issued debentures; debenture holders are general creditors of corporation.

### INCOME BONDS (ADJUSTMENT BONDS)

▷ type of collateral: none—unsecured debt

▷ priority of claim: paid after secured bonds, but before stockholders

▷ unique characteristics: interest payment is contingent on earnings of the company; often used when company faces bankruptcy; adjustment bonds are traded for other bonds; bonds trade flat, meaning no accrued interest is figured since it may not be paid.

### GUARANTEED BONDS

▷ type of collateral: none—unsecured debt; full faith and credit of issuer and also guaranteed by full faith and credit of another company

▷ priority of claim: paid after secured bonds, but before stockholders

▷ unique characteristics: the other company guaranteeing the bond is usually related to the issuing company, such as a parent company guaranteeing a bond for a subsidiary; this may be needed to improve the bond's credit rating; guarantee could be interest-only.

## Zero Coupon Bonds

**Zero coupon bonds** are bonds sold at a deep discount from par because they do not make periodic interest payments, but instead pay the full face amount at maturity. The investor receives a rate of return by the gradual appreciation (**accretion**) of the bond from the purchase date until maturity. Since interest received on corporate bonds is an immediate taxable event, the Internal Revenue Service (IRS) views zero coupons as paying **imputed interest** to the bondholder. Thus taxes must be paid on interest that accrues in the investment each year, even though the bondholder does not receive any money until the bond matures. (This is why zero coupons are often held in retirement accounts.)

Exam Topic Alert

Zero coupon bonds are the only investment with *no* reinvestment risk, because there is no advantage for companies to pay them off early. (This may be on the Series 6 exam.)

Zero coupon bonds are good for companies that don't want to make regular interest payments. They are also good for investors who want to have a fixed sum of cash at some point in the future (such as for college expenses), without having to worry about the bond being called early and having to find another investment offering the same rate of return on investment (reinvestment risk).

## Other Features of Bonds

Unlike stock, which exists as long as the company is in business, bonds must at some point be repaid. This is often referred to as **retiring** the bonds. Corporate bonds are retired in one of three ways. The bonds can be redeemed by paying them off, converted by the bondholder into common stock (if they're convertible), or called early by the company and replaced with lower yielding bonds. Let's look at these.

**REDEMPTION. Redemption** is repayment of a debt obligation at maturity, or earlier. If done at maturity, the final interest and principal payment are made to the bondholder or holder of record, and the debt is thus retired. Regardless of the price at which the bond may have been bought or sold in the past, the day that the bond comes due, the corporate issuer of the bond is liable for payment of the par value of the bond (usually $1000). If bonds are redeemed before they mature, they must have a call provision allowing the issuing company to redeem the bonds early in exchange for payment of principal, interest owed, and often a call premium. If an entire issue is not called, the trustee randomly chooses the bonds that will be redeemed.

Since most corporate bonds have term maturities (meaning they all come due at once), companies often set up a sinking fund. A **sinking fund** is a special account that is paid into on a regular basis and saved for a specific purpose. Here the company would put away some revenue each year to redeem the bonds when they come due (or to call them early or to buy them back in the open market). The interest rate paid on sinking fund bonds is usually *lower* since investors feel the interest is more secure.

**CONVERSION. Conversion** is exchanging bonds for a fixed number of shares of common stock. This can be done if bondholders own convertible bonds. **Convertible bonds** are corporate debt securities that may be traded for common stock in the company at a predetermined price. This gives the bondholder the safety of guaranteed interest payments and status as a creditor, with a chance to share in the capital appreciation of the underlying company's stock if it goes above the conversion price. The price for convertible bonds is usually *higher,* and the interest paid is usually *lower* than standard bonds issued by the company, but investors accept this in exchange for a chance to convert to common stock and enjoy capital appreciation at a future date.

Companies issue convertible bonds because they can be sold for more money and pay a lower interest rate. Sometimes a conversion option is needed to get investors to buy the issue. Of course, there are downsides to convertible bonds: if too many investors convert, then the company can face lower earnings per share as the amount of outstanding stock increases, greater dividend payouts which aren't tax deductible like interest payments, and potential for less management control as dilution occurs.

**Conversion Privilege.** Since convertible bonds may be exchanged for a fixed number of common stock shares, this is referred to as a **conversion privilege.** If the bondholder elects to convert to common stock, this can be done for a fixed number of shares, or for a variable number of shares based on a specific ratio or formula. The method for deciding the conversion amount is determined when the bond was originally issued. This conversion number is usually adjusted for stock splits, stock dividends or new issues, depending on the terms stated in the bond's trust indenture.

**Conversion Price and Ratio.** The conversion price tells you at what price the stock should trade before the bondholder considers conversion. If the bond was issued with a conversion price of $50, then once the stock reaches $50 or above, it would be advantageous to do the conversion (if the bond was purchased at face value). Figuring the conversion ratio tells you how many shares the bondholder would receive for converting. To calculate the number of shares, take the par face value of the bond and divide by the conversion price, as shown in the following example.

## EXAMPLE

Face Value ÷ Conversion Price = Number of Shares

$1000 (Face Value) ÷ $50 (Conversion Price) = 20 Shares

The bondholder would receive 20 shares of stock when converting the bond.

**Calculation of Parity.** Although the convertible bond price often fluctuates in line with the common stock price, they do not always move in tandem. Upward movements tend to go together, but when the company's stock falls, the bond will usually not fall as much since the bond payments are fixed. At times when the value of a convertible bond and the stock intersect, this is referred to as **parity** because the convertible bond can be exchanged for stock of equal value. Let's revisit our example:

**$1000 (Face Value) ÷ $50 (Conversion Price) = 20 Shares**

So if the bondholder bought the bond at par (face value), conversion parity would be $50. When the stock price is above $50, then it makes sense to convert the bond because the stock is worth more at any price above $50. (For purposes of this discussion, we'll ignore other risk factors of stock ownership, such as falling prices.)

Remember, we said earlier, that convertible bonds often trade at a premium (price over par) because of their conversion feature. This means the parity price will need to be higher than if the bond was bought for face value. Let's say the bond quote is 120, or $1200 (par of $1000 × 120% quote). The conversion price is still $50, and we still get 20 shares of stock because the conversion ratio doesn't change. Since we paid a premium for the bond, however, the conversion parity price is higher.

**$1200 (Bond Price) ÷ 20 Shares = $60 (Conversion Parity Price)**

Because the bondholder paid a premium for the bond, but still would receive only 20 shares of stock when converting the bond, the conversion parity price of the underlying stock must go above $60 (not $50) for conversion to benefit the bondholder.

Remember, the conversion price is only used for figuring the number of shares the bondholder will receive. The conversion parity price moves up and down with the actual bond price. Figuring conversion parity price takes four steps:

1. find par (always assume $1000 for bonds unless told otherwise)
2. calculate how many shares you would get:
   Face Value ÷ Conversion Price = Number of Shares
3. get the current bond price (CMV = current market value): Par × Quote = CMV
4. figure the conversion parity price:
   Current Bond Price ÷ Number of Shares = Conversion Parity Price

You may also be asked to reverse the logic. For example, a question might say: If the stock price increases by 20%, what happens to the bond price? In this case, look for an answer where the bond price also rises 20% because in theory these two should move up in tandem. *If the question asks about a falling stock price, though, be careful.* If a stock only falls a little, the bond price usually falls by an equal amount; but if a stock drops dramatically, then in theory the bond price should not drop as much since it still has the guaranteed interest payments to help support its price in line with other bonds offering similar returns. Read all answers carefully and choose wisely.

Exam Topic
Alert

**Factors Influencing Conversion.** There are several things that a bondholder must consider when deciding whether or not to convert a bond into common stock. First is the prospects of the company. Even if the stock price rises above the parity price, if there is no substantive reason for the movement, it is possible the stock price might come back down. Second, if the company is about to be acquired or merged, the conversion option may be erased. Third, a company may do a **forced conversion** by calling the bond so that it is more advantageous for the bondholder to convert than to surrender the bond. Finally, the bondholder may decide to take advantage of the price differential between the trading price of the convertible bond and the stock, convert, and then sell the stock and profit from this **arbitrage** transaction.

**CALL PROVISIONS.** Corporate bonds often have a call feature that allows the issuer to redeem the bond earlier than its stated maturity date. The terms and conditions under which a call can be exercised are spelled out in the indenture agreement when the bonds are originally issued. The corporation may redeem the bonds early in exchange for payment of principal, interest owed, and often a **call premium** paid by the company to the bondholder for the right to repay the debt early. The only other protection that a bondholder has is that some bonds are issued with a **call protection** period during which time the bond may not be called early.

It can be a big advantage for the issuer to be able to call bonds early if interest rates fall significantly, because then the corporation can issue new debt at the lower interest rates. **Refunding** is replacing a debt obligation with another debt security that has different terms, such as a lower interest rate. Calling bonds also allows the corporation to change the terms of its debt, change its debt repayment schedule, or change its debt-to-equity ratio in its financial statements.

If there are no call provisions in a bond, the corporation can approach current bondholders and offer to buy their bonds. This **tender offer** may be at current market value or it may be at a premium. It is the bondholder's option whether or not to accept a tender offer. The company can also go into the secondary market and buy back its bonds to retire the debt. This is referred to as **tendering.** If the company is in financial trouble, bondholders may also allow refunding even without a call provision in the bonds as a way to help the company avoid bankruptcy.

# 1.1.1.3 Special Securities

Although stocks and bonds are the two main types of securities, there are other securities that can be bought and sold. Some of these other securities are referred to as derivative securities. A **derivative security** is an instrument whose value is dependent on the value of another underlying security. By itself, the derivative security is worthless; but it derives its value from the fact that it gives the holder the right to buy (or sell) another security or investment.

Derivative securities may be traded in the secondary market (but their value is largely determined by the value of the underlying security on which they are based). The main derivative securities we will look at are rights, warrants, and options. We will also look at mortgage-backed (pass-through) securities, collateralized mortgage obligations (CMOs), and American Depository Receipts (ADRs).

## Rights

**Rights** are a special benefit given to existing common stockholders that allows them to buy additional shares of newly issued stock before it is offered for sale to the general public. This special **rights offering** is done to honor the preemptive rights that the existing common stockholders have, giving them the opportunity to buy enough shares to maintain their present proportionate ownership in the company. Current shareholders get one right for each share of stock owned, as do new investors who quickly buy stock "cum" rights (with the rights still attached—because after the ex-date, no rights transfer with the stock).

When current stockholders are given notice of a rights offering, they have three choices. They can exercise their rights and opt to buy more stock; they can sell their rights to other interested parties since it is a derivative security; or they can do nothing and allow the rights to expire. Typically, rights have a very small window—usually 30 to 45 days. Within that time frame, the current stockholder must choose one of the three courses of action just described. Usually the price at which the rights holder can buy the new issue is less than the current market price of the stock. The price for the rights is referred to as the **subscription price,** and it must be lower than the market price to absorb the new shares into the marketplace. If the price was the same as the current market price, there would be no incentive for investors to buy the new shares. Furthermore, the price that is offered to existing stockholders in the rights offering is even lower than the anticipated offering price of the new issue.

A more favorable price is offered to existing shareholders as an incentive to get them to make a quick buying decision. The investment banking firm that is selling the new issue for the company wants to ensure that as much of the new issue as possible is sold (or presold) because typically the investment banking firm does the new issue as a standby underwriting.

---

### COMPARISON OF RIGHTS AND WARRANTS
*(This may be on Series 6 exam.)*

| Comparison Points | Rights | Warrants |
|---|---|---|
| Time: | short—usually 30 to 25 days | long—usually at least 5 years |
| Money: | subscription price is lower than current market price | exercise price is higher than current market price |
| Associated Key Term: | standby underwriting | sweetener |

chart 1.1.1.3

---

A **standby underwriting** means that the investment banking firm guarantees the issuing company that the firm will buy all shares that are not bought as part of the rights offering. This definition will likely appear somewhere on the Series 6 exam. Remember, *when you see "rights offering" in a question, look for "standby underwriting" in the answer (and vice versa).*

Exam Topic Alert

## Warrants

**Warrants** are an additional security offered along with the sale of another security. Warrants usually allow the warrant holder to buy shares of common stock at some point in the future at a predetermined price. Warrants are typically offered with bonds and preferred stock as an incentive, or **sweetener.** A warrant can entice investors to buy the underlying bond or stock when it is less attractive for some reason, or adding a warrant as a sweetener may allow a company to offer a lower interest rate for the bond or preferred stock. Warrants may also be offered to an investment banking firm if they agree to do an offering for the company.

Like rights, warrants are a derivative security. Warrants may or may not be sold separately. If the warrants are **detachable,** then the investor may sell them separately to anyone. If the warrants are **nondetachable,** then they can only be transferred with the bond, preferred stock, or other security they were sold with.

---

A question about warrants will likely appear somewhere on the Series 6 exam. Remember, *when you see "warrants" in a question, look for "sweetener" in the answer (and vice versa).*

Exam Topic Alert

When investors are given a warrant, they have two or three choices. They can exercise their warrant and buy the stock at the predetermined price; if the warrants are detachable, they can sell their warrants to other interested parties since it is a derivative security; or they can do nothing and allow the warrants to expire. Typically, warrants have a very long window—usually at least five years, and sometimes they do not expire. Within that time frame, the warrant holder must choose one of the courses of action we just described.

Unlike rights offerings, the price at which the warrant holder can buy stock in the future is usually much higher than the current market price of the stock. This is because the company does not want the warrants exercised right away. In fact, if the market value of the stock does not get above the price in the warrant, the warrant will likely never be exercised. Given that fact, you can see that the warrant becomes more valuable as the market value of the stock gets closer to (or rises beyond) the price in the warrant.

## Options

**Options** are the right, not the obligation, to buy or sell something at a predetermined price and under predetermined conditions (usually conditioned by a time limit, but they can have other conditions as well). The advantage of options is leverage. They allow an investor to control a large block of securities for a relatively small investment. The disadvantage of options is that they expire. They are a wasting asset because if they are not exercised the investor loses the **premium** (amount paid to buy the option contract).

If an investor **buys** an option, he or she is the **owner** of the option. You can also say that the investor is the **holder** of the option, or is **long** the option. So all of these terms are synonymous: **buyer = owner = holder = long.** An investor can also **sell** an option. You can also say that the investor is the **writer** of the option, or is **short** the option. (Note that this is NOT the same as selling stock short.) So all of these terms are synonymous: **seller = writer = short.** (Actually, all these terms are used with stock ownership as well as with options.) Option strategies can either be **bullish** (positive outlook, think markets will rise), **bearish** (negative outlook, think markets will decline), or neutral. There are two basic types of options: calls and puts.

**CALL DEFINED.** A **call** is the right to buy a certain number of shares of a security, at a predetermined price (**strike price** or **exercise price**), before a certain date (**expiration date**). The person who buys the call has the *option* to buy the stock; the person who sells the call has the *obligation* to sell the stock at that price if the buyer exercises the option. If the buyer of the call option is correct, the actual market price of the stock should go higher than the strike price in the option. When that happens, the person who bought the call option can buy the stock from the call seller at the agreed-upon lower price stated in the option contract, then resell the stock at the higher market price to make a profit. (The call buyer can also make a profit by selling the call option contract, giving someone else the right to buy the stock cheaper).

**PUT DEFINED.** A **put** is the right to sell a certain number of shares of a security at a predetermined price (strike price or exercise price), before a certain date (expiration date). The person who buys the put has the *option* to sell the stock; the person who sells the put has the *obligation* to buy the stock at that price if the buyer exercises the option. If the buyer of the put option is correct, the actual market price of the stock should go lower than the strike price in the option. When that happens, the person who bought the put option can sell his or her stock to the put seller at the agreed-upon higher price stated in the option contract, then the buyer of the option contract doesn't lose as much money compared with selling the stock in the market. (The put buyer can also make money selling the put option contract to someone else).

---

### BASIC OPTIONS POSITIONS

| BULLISH: | LONG CALL (Buy a Call) | SHORT PUT (Sell a Put) | (same side of the market) |
|----------|------------------------|------------------------|---------------------------|
| BEARISH: | LONG PUT (Buy a Put) | SHORT CALL (Sell a Call) | (same side of the market) |

dia 1.1.1.3

---

## Mortgage-Backed (Pass-Through) Securities

**Mortgage-backed securities** are bonds, notes, or other securities that have a pool of mortgage loans behind them to give them underlying value. These are also referred to as **pass-through securities** because the monthly principal and interest payments "pass through" directly to the investors who hold the security. Thus investors receive a monthly income stream from these investments, but they do not get any capital appreciation.

Mortgage-backed securities are offered by various government agencies (GNMA, FNMA, FHLMC) and as private investment vehicles (CMO, REMIC). We'll look at GNMA and CMO because those are the two that you are most likely to see on the Series 6 exam.

**GNMA.** Mortgage-backed securities offered through the **Government National Mortgage Association (GNMA)** are commonly referred to as "Ginnie Maes." **Ginnie Maes** are special securities based on a pool of insured mortgages (FHA, VA) backed by the full faith and credit of the U.S. government. The security passes through monthly principal and interest payments to investors. Although there is almost no repayment risk or default risk since they are guaranteed by the U.S. government, Ginnie Maes are subject to interest rate risk (if rates go higher, you're locked in) and reinvestment risk (if rates go lower, people will refinance their homes, and these will get paid off early so investors must find other investments with similar returns).

---

Ginnie Maes are *not* bonds. They are pass-through certificates that offer investors a monthly income stream. Ginnie Maes are also the only mortgage-backed securities backed by the full faith and credit of the U.S. government. The biggest risk associated with Ginnie Maes is reinvestment risk.

Exam Topic
Alert

**CMO.** A **Collateralized Mortgage Obligation (CMO)** is a vehicle for issuing mortgage-backed securities, separated into different groups (called **tranches**) based on maturity dates. Like Ginnie Maes, CMOs pass through monthly principal and interest payments to investors. With the separation into different tranches, CMOs can offer staggered maturity dates that offer different rates of return, different payment schedules, and different levels of risk. For example, an investor might buy a CMO now but doesn't need the income stream to start for several years. By buying a CMO with payments starting later, the investor could get a higher rate of return, but the investor is taking a chance because the mortgages backing the security might be paid off early and end the income stream.

CMOs share the same interest rate risk and reinvestment risk as Ginnie Maes, but because CMOs are not backed by the government, they also have extension risk (if homeowners are late paying their mortgages, payments are delayed) and repayment risk (if homeowners default, investors do not receive their money). Because of these added risks from not being government guaranteed, CMOs offer a better rate of return than Ginnie Maes. CMOs are not for everyone, however, and are considered a high-risk investment.

Exam Topic Alert

Remember, CMOs are pass-through certificates backed by a pool of mortgages, which offer investors a monthly income stream. CMOs are not backed by the U.S. government, so their risks and rewards (yields) are higher than Ginnie Maes. *If you see "tranches" in a question, look for "CMOs" in the answer (and vice versa).*

## American Depository Receipts (ADRs)

**American Depository Receipts (ADRs)** are a U.S. substitute for foreign common stock. Investors can hold ADRs instead of trying to obtain stock in a foreign country. With ADRs, foreign companies can sell shares to U.S. investors without having to go through the lengthy and expensive SEC registration process. ADRs allow investors in the United States to collect dividends and enjoy the capital gains of the foreign stock, but they do not usually come with voting rights or preemptive rights.

Although ADRs trade in the secondary market, they are not very liquid—and are often less liquid than the underlying foreign stock because ADRs have less trading volume. ADRs are typically held in the vault of a commercial bank, so the bank will collect dividend payments in the foreign currency and convert them into U.S. dollars. (Of course, there's risk of foreign currency fluctuations for these dividend payments.)

1.12

# U.S. Government Securities

**U.S. Government securities** are debt obligations of the U.S. government issued by the U.S. Treasury; hence, they are sometimes referred to as **Treasuries.** Treasuries are debentures, backed by the full faith and credit of the U.S. government—but nothing else. Still, they are considered the most risk-free investment that money can buy. Because of this, though, they have lower yields than corporate bonds. Investors are willing to accept this because of the safety of principal they afford, and because the interest is free from state income tax (but not federal income tax).

# 1.1.2.1 Marketable Issues

**Marketable issues** are securities that are easily sold. This implies that they can be bought and sold between investors in the open exchange markets. There are three main types of marketable securities sold by the U.S. Treasury: U.S. Treasury bills (T-bills), U.S. Treasury notes (T-notes), and U.S. Treasury bonds (T-bonds). We will also mention U.S. Treasury receipts (and STRIPS), before moving on to U.S. government agency bonds. We will discuss characteristics of each.

### TREASURY BILLS

▷ maturities are short-term, 1 year or less (3 months, 6 months, 1 year)

▷ denominations are $10,000 minimum face value

▷ issue form is book entry—registration of owner's name

▷ quotations have "bid" and "ask" numbers that are a discount from par, so if the Bid is 3.00 and Ask is 2.75 for $100,000: $100,000 − 3% = $97,000 Bid; $100,000 − 2.75% = $97,250 Ask (these calculations are probably not on the test, but know *bid quote is higher than ask quote here*—opposite of most!)

▷ pricing is done at a discount from par and written as a decimal bid/ask discount from face value (see example above)

▷ interest is NOT paid on T-bills; since the investor buys them at a discount, the rate of return is the gradual appreciation of the T-bill, which pays full face value when it matures

### TREASURY NOTES

▷ maturities are intermediate-term, 1 to 10 years (but are callable)

▷ denominations are $1000 minimum face value

▷ issue form is book entry—registration of owner's name

▷ quotations are done as a percentage of par and written as 97.01 or 97-01, where 01 = 1/32 of a percentage point, so a quoted spread might be Bid 97.04, Ask 97.26, meaning that the Bid is 97 4/32%, and Ask is 97 26/32%

▷ pricing is done as a percentage of par in 1/32 increments, with the numbers after the point signifying the number of 32nd increments—not a decimal! Here's an example: Bid 97.04 = 97 4/32% × $1000 (face value), so Bid = $971.25

▷ interest payments are made every six months (semiannual)

### TREASURY BONDS

▷ maturities are long-term, 10 years or more (but are callable)

▷ denominations are $1000 minimum face value

▷ issue form is book entry—registration of owner's name

▷ quotations are same as Treasury notes

▷ pricing is same as Treasury notes

▷ some Treasury bonds are callable (with 4 months notice)

▷ interest payments are made every six months (semiannual)

▷ T-bonds are *not* the same as government savings bonds

Treasury receipts and STRIPS are special securities. Treasury receipts are actually created by broker-dealer (B-D) firms and do not represent direct obligations of the U.S. government. The B-D buys T-notes and T-bonds and separates the interest payments and the final principal payment. The B-D then sells "receipts" to investors, allowing them to buy, at a discount, any particular future payment they choose. The investor can choose to buy only one future interest payment, a series of future interest payments, or the investor can buy the future principal payment. Again, all of these trade at a discount based on the time value of money paid now for payments in the future. That represents the interest rate return on the investment.

**STRIPS** stands for **S**eparate **T**rading of **R**egistered **I**nterest and **P**rincipal of **S**ecurities. They are essentially a zero coupon bond. STRIPS are a product of the U.S. Treasury that mirrors what the broker-dealers do with Treasury receipts.

*Exam Topic Alert*

*STRIPS are backed by full faith and credit of U.S. government, but T-receipts are not.* Instead, with T-receipts, investors are relying on the B-D who has stripped the Treasury securities, and the bank or other entity holding the Treasury securities in a trust account until payments are due.

**AGENCY BONDS.** U.S. government **agency bonds** are debt issued by U.S. government sponsored entities and other federally related institutions. There are several agencies involved with the issuance of U.S. government agency bonds. **Government sponsored entities (GSE)** are privately owned, but publicly chartered entities created by the government to help farmers, students, homeowners, and others by lowering borrowing costs. The GSEs sell securities to investors, then take the investors' money and use the funds to buy mortgages or provide low-interest loans to people in targeted groups who meet certain criteria. Some GSEs include Federal Farm Credit Consolidated Bank, Federal Home Loan Bank, Student Loan Marketing Association (Sallie Mae), Federal National Mortgage Association (FNMA or Fannie Mae), and Federal Home Loan Mortgage Corporation (FHLMC or Freddie Mac). Most GSE securities are backed by the agency issuing them, and are *not* backed by the full faith and credit of the U.S. government.

**Federally related institutions** are arms of the U.S. government that have the authority to issue securities for the needs of their agency. These include the Government National Mortgage Association (GNMA or Ginnie Mae), Small Business Administration, General Services Administration, and many others. In reality, though, few of these institutions issue their own securities today because the Federal Financing Bank, which is owned by the U.S. government, coordinates and consolidates all borrowing activities in an effort to reduce borrowing costs. Most federally related securities are backed by the full faith and credit of the U.S. government. You can expect most questions in this area to be about Ginnie Maes, so let's review those.

### GINNIE MAES: (GNMA, GOVERNMENT NATIONAL MORTGAGE ASSOCIATION)
▷ characteristics:
  1. securities are based on a pool of insured mortgages (FHA, VA, etc.)
  2. security is NOT a bond—it's a pass-through certificate

3. backed by full faith and credit of U.S. government

4. interest is fully taxable (all government levels—fed, state, local)

▷ maturities: based on a quoted 12-year planned repayment, but often mature early as homeowners refinance loans

▷ denominations: minimum $25,000 face value

▷ risks:

1. interest rate risk (if rates go higher, you're locked in)

2. reinvestment risk (if rates go lower, get paid off early so need to find other investment with similar return)

3. almost NO repayment risk—guaranteed by U.S. government

▷ principal and interest payments: paid monthly

---

Here are some points to remember for the Series 6 exam. Securitized mortgages, such as Ginnie Maes, are pass-through certificates (*not* bonds). They are for investors who want an income stream but aren't concerned with capital appreciation. When monthly principal and interest payments are received, the interest portion of the payment is an immediate taxable event—fully taxable at all levels of government. Yields on government agency securities are higher than yields on Treasuries because there is more risk of repayment. Ginnie Maes are the only mortgage-backed security backed by the full faith and credit of the U.S. government. Interest rate risk exists, but reinvestment risk is the greatest for Ginnie Maes/mortgage-backed securities.

Exam Topic
Alert

# 1.1.2.2 Nonmarketable Issues

**Nonmarketable issues** are securities that cannot be easily sold. They do not trade on any exchange and cannot be sold by investors, but must be redeemed through the issuer—here, the U.S. Treasury. Three types of nonmarketable securities issued by the U.S. Treasury are Series EE bonds, Series HH bonds, and Series I bonds.

**SERIES EE BONDS. Series EE bonds** are U.S. government savings bonds, sold in amounts of $25 to $10,000. The bonds are sold at a discount of 50% of face value and mature at the face amount. All interest is paid at maturity, and federal tax due on the interest can be deferred until maturity. The federal tax due can be deferred beyond the 30-year maturity of the bond by exchanging the mature Series EE bond for a Series HH bond. The Series EE bonds are exempt from state and local taxes.

**SERIES HH BONDS. Series HH bonds** are U.S. government savings bonds, issued in amounts of $500 to $10,000. The bonds are only available by trading in Series EE bonds at maturity. Interest on Series HH bonds is paid semiannually until they mature in ten years. Federal tax is due on the interest, but Series HH bonds are exempt from state and local taxes.

**SERIES I BONDS. Series I bonds** are U.S. government savings bonds sold in eight denominations, $50, $75, $100, $200, $500, $1000, $5000, and $10,000. The bonds are sold at face value and pay an interest rate that is adjusted for inflation every six months. All interest is paid at maturity, and federal tax due on the interest can be deferred until maturity. Series I bonds are exempt from state and local taxes.

# State and Municipal Bonds

**State and municipal bonds** are debt obligations of state and local governments. They are sometimes referred to as **municipals** or **munis.** Although there are many types of municipal securities, they can be divided into two broad categories: public purpose bonds and private purpose bonds. **Public purpose bonds** benefit the general public and are afforded **tax-exempt** status. **Private purpose bonds** are those that are more than 10% beneficial to private parties, and as such they are generally **taxable.** Most of our focus in this section will be on tax-exempt bonds.

There are many types of municipal bonds. Some are backed by specific tax revenue, others by the faith and credit of the issuer. Different types have different characteristics also. Let's look at general obligation, revenue, and industrial bonds.

**GENERAL OBLIGATION BONDS (GOS).** GOs are bonds paid for out of the general revenue of the municipality, which may also use additional tax revenues or borrow funds to cover any shortfall. These tax-backed bonds offer a high level of safety to investors. Taxes can be levied on income, on property, as sales tax, or other user fees. In fact, the more sources of tax revenue the issuer has, the safer the issue.

GO bonds are backed by the full faith and credit of the issuer. Most GO bond issues, however, require voter approval to be enacted, especially if the bond issue will raise taxes. Some jurisdictions also have laws in place that restrict the amount of debt that a municipality can incur, or may have limitations on the tax rates that can be imposed on its citizens.

**REVENUE BONDS. Revenue bonds** are bonds paid for from the income (revenue) generated by a specific project. These are usually used to pay for public works projects, such as roads or water plants. The revenue bonds are backed by the tolls or user fees from the project. Revenue-backed bonds are less secure than GO bonds, so yields are generally higher here. Unless specifically stated, revenue bondholders do not have a claim to other revenue sources or general tax collections to pay the debt.

Because revenue bond issues do not use tax revenue, they usually do not require voter approval. Furthermore, there are usually no restrictions on the amount of debt that a municipality can incur because revenue bonds are supposed to be self-supporting. In fact, municipalities will conduct a **feasibility study** to demonstrate to investors the economic soundness of the proposal and usually will provide a **"flow of funds"** resolution that details how revenues will be used and how the debt will be repaid.

For the Series 6 exam remember that *when you see "feasibility study" or "flow of funds" in a question, look for "revenue bond" in the answer (and vice versa).*

**INDUSTRIAL REVENUE BONDS. Industrial revenue bonds** or **industrial development bonds (IDBs)** are bonds used to finance fixed assets, which are then leased to private corporations. These are a type of revenue bond, but are usually NOT tax exempt because they are designed to help private parties, so an investor must read the official statement carefully. These are the most risky of the municipal bonds because repayment is dependent on lease payments from the corporate tenants. Furthermore, the IDB bonds carry the debt rating of the corporation, not the municipality. IDBs can be used to help revive an area, such as through the financing of an industrial park that the municipality hopes will bring high-paying jobs to the area.

**TAX IMPLICATIONS.** Municipal bond issues will often include a legal opinion to assure investors that the bonds are eligible for tax-exempt status. An **unqualified legal opinion** states that the attorney has researched the contemplated bond issue and that the municipality has the legal authority to issue the bonds. The legal opinion will also state if the bonds are eligible for tax-exempt status. This is made part of the official statement for the bond issue. The legal opinion is also distributed with the bonds and may even be printed on the face of the bond. Smaller issuers or "obvious" tax-exempt issues (e.g., public school bonds) may choose not to have a legal opinion done to save the expense; thus, **"ex-legal"** is stamped on the bond documents.

Bonds issued within the client's state of residence, and territorial bonds (Puerto Rico, Guam, U.S. Virgin Islands), normally offer tax-free interest income at the state and local level as well. Of course, capital gains made when selling municipal bonds for a profit are still fully taxable at all levels of government.

**Taxable Equivalent Yield.** If the municipal bond issue is tax exempt, then interest paid is tax free at the federal level. This allows municipal bonds to offer lower interest rates and still be an attractive investment. **Taxable equivalent yield** is the yield that would have to be paid out on a taxable bond in order for it to equal the yield paid out on a tax-free bond. In other words, what yield on a corporate bond would give an investor the same yield as a tax-free municipal bond, if the tax savings were included. The muni bond will usually have a lower yield. This formula tells the investor how much less of a yield is acceptable on the municipal bond.

**Municipal Bond Yield ÷ (1 – Investors Tax Bracket) = Taxable Equivalent Yield**

The number varies by investor, based on the person's tax bracket.

## EXAMPLE

An investor is considering a municipal bond that pays 4%. If the investor is in a 36% tax bracket, what is the equivalent corporate bond yield?

**Municipal Bond Yield ÷ (1 – Investors Tax Bracket) = Taxable Equivalent Yield**
**4 ÷ (1 – .36) = 6.25**

So for our investor, a muni bond paying 4% is equal to a corporate bond paying 6.25%.

# Money Market Instruments

**Money market instruments** are short-term debt obligations that are due and payable in 12 months or less. Money market instruments can only be debt securities with short-term maturities. They are highly liquid and generally considered safe. Let's look at a few of these instruments and some of their characteristics.

**TREASURY BILLS. Treasury bills (T-bills)** are debt securities issued by the U.S. Treasury. Because they mature in one year or less, they trade in the secondary markets as money market instruments. Face value is a minimum of $10,000, and price is quoted at a discount from par (e.g., bid price of 3 is $100,000 – 3% = $97,000).

**CERTIFICATES OF DEPOSIT (CDs). Certificates of Deposit (CDs)** are debt securities, usually issued by a financial institution. Negotiable CDs have a minimum face value of $100,000 and are offered by commercial banks to investors as a time deposit. Since these so-called "jumbo" CDs are negotiable, they are considered a money market instrument. (These negotiable CDs should not be confused with the "standard" CDs offered by neighborhood banks to depositors. Standard CDs are available in much smaller face amounts and are not negotiable, so they are not considered money market instruments.)

**COMMERCIAL PAPER. Commercial paper** is short-term debt issued by corporations to finance inventories, accounts receivable, and other obligations. Maturities range from 2-270 days to avoid registration requirements. Commercial paper issued by corporations is typically unsecured, although it is often backed by bank lines of credit. Corporations prefer commercial paper because they can get better rates than using their bank lines, plus the repayment terms can be negotiated so they're more flexible. Such debt is rated by the rating agencies discussed before, but some money market managers will not buy commercial paper since it's unsecured.

On the Series 6 exam, *if you see an answer to a question stating that commercial banks issue commercial paper, it is most likely a trick and probably the wrong answer.*

**BANKERS' ACCEPTANCES (BAs). Bankers' acceptances (BAs)** are a time draft drawn on a particular bank, whereby the bank accepts responsibility for payment. The **time draft** designates the date on which payment will be made. BAs are a tool for handling the extension of credit. Essentially, BAs work like a letter of credit and are often used for import-export financing or the purchase of goods and services when doing international business. Because of the bank's backing, BAs are often used as money market instruments.

For the Series 6 exam remember that *when you see "time draft" in a question, look for "banker's acceptances" in the answer (and vice versa).*

# 1.2 Securities Markets

**Securities markets** are where securities and security instruments are bought and sold. This can occur on a formal exchange (such as the NYSE) or in a computer-based setting (such as the OTC market). Sales of securities can also take place in the primary, secondary, third, or fourth markets.

The **primary market** is where new securities issues are sold directly by the issuer to investors. Some examples are Initial Public Offerings (IPOs) when companies sell new stock, or a new bond issue is sold by a municipality. What distinguishes a primary offering transaction is that the sale proceeds from the securities go to the issuer. This is much different than the secondary marketplace, where stocks change hands between investors. **Secondary markets** are the exchanges and OTC markets where investors buy and sell securities after the initial offering. This is also called the **resale market.** Here, proceeds from the sale of stock go to the investor selling the securities—the issuing company gets none of the money! The secondary market for equities consists of several exchanges, including NYSE. Equities are also traded on the NASDAQ and in the OTC markets.

The **third market** is the buying and selling of exchange listed stocks in the over-the-counter market by nonexchange members and institutional investors. Here large orders are made off the exchange floor so that large institutional investors (such as pension funds, insurance companies, mutual funds, banks, etc.) can save commissions. The **fourth market** is the direct trading of large blocks of securities between institutional investors using a computerized system called **Instinet,** an acronym for Institutional Networks Corporation, owned by Reutters. Instinet is registered with the SEC as a stock exchange. All members are linked directly by computer, without broker-dealers or commissions. Trades can take place any time.

For the Series 6 exam, you will need to know more about how the secondary exchange auction markets work, how the negotiated NASDAQ and OTC markets work, and more about the market for new issues. Let's briefly look at each of these.

# Exchange/Auction Markets

There are reasons why companies want to be listed on a major exchange, such as the NYSE. One of the big advantages is that exchanges provide a centralized trading floor that offers immediate access to buyers and sellers.

Exam Topic Alert

You may see a question on the Series 6 exam asking what is the primary role of the NYSE. It is NOT buying and selling stocks from the American public. The NYSE only provides the trading floor and a centralized location that provides a forum for the buying and selling. The NYSE approves companies and traders, and monitors trading activities for fraud, but that is the extent of its involvement. Watch this on the exam.

Another big advantage is the double auction mechanism for pricing securities. This coupled with the instant reporting of trades leads to a true up-to-the-minute gauge of market value based on supply and demand. Other reasons companies list on exchanges include lower cost of capital, ready access to capital, availability of institutional investors, greater liquidity, and higher visibility and prestige.

**NATURE OF AUCTION MARKETS.** Exchanges act as a centralized trading floor where listed securities can be bought and sold using a **double auction** pricing mechanism. What this means is that the markets are constantly getting pricing information from buyers and sellers. The instant reporting of trades provides for a true free market, where supply and demand dictate the price of a particular stock issue. All of this is made possible by floor brokers who try to get the best possible prices for clients, and the **specialist** who ensures that orders are matched up in a fair and orderly process.

The specialist is a member of a stock exchange given authority to act as broker and dealer (agent and principal) for other brokers. The specialist must be ready to buy and sell from the firm's own account to stabilize the market when there's a supply and demand imbalance. Specialists conduct auctions between buyers and sellers, acting in the capacity of an agent when there is sufficient market activity. When there is little or no trading volume, specialists act in the capacity of principal and trade from their own account. In this respect, the specialist is a market maker.

# NASDAQ/NNOTC/Negotiated Markets

There are several reasons why companies want to be listed on NASDAQ. NASDAQ provides increased secondary market liquidity for smaller companies. While the disclosure and accounting norms required for getting listed on the NASDAQ are very stringent, company size and capitalization requirements are not as high as the NYSE. NASDAQ also offers an exchange with high efficiency, good settlement processes, and low cost of operation. This is enhanced by the large capital commitment from market makers and increased competition, which provides very competitive bid and ask prices for securities. There's also the reputation, prestige, and visibility of being on an exchange recognized for its high-growth companies. Companies that do not have sufficient capitalization or stock price to be listed on NASDAQ often use the OTC or other negotiated markets to gain access to capital.

**NATURE OF A NEGOTIATED MARKET.** NASDAQ and the OTC markets are a decentralized trading environment that relies on negotiated bid and ask (buy and sell) prices between investors and market makers. A **market maker** is a brokerage firm that has taken a position (built up an inventory) in a certain stock and is ready to honor quoted bid and ask prices for round lots. Market makers help maintain stability in the negotiated market and are the reason these markets can function.

The market maker acts as a principal dealer for the stocks in which the firm has taken a position, buying and selling from the firm's own inventory in the stock. This gives the negotiated markets much-needed liquidity so that investors know they will always have a means to sell their shares. Every stock must have at least two market makers. Market makers must meet NASDAQ minimum net capital requirements and must demonstrate that they are willing to execute trades for minimum lots of 100 shares at the firm bid and ask quotes that they provide.

**Quotes.** The market maker is the one who gives quotes. Sometimes they are based on the most recent transaction; other times the quote represents the firm's bid and ask prices. There are actually several different types of quotes, but two of the more common ones are firm quote and subject quote. **Firm quotes** mean that the broker-dealer is willing to sell or buy at least one round lot (100 shares of stock or 5 bonds) at that price. But a firm quote is only good for the number of shares quoted; if more are needed, you must ask for a new firm quote. **Subject quotes** mean that the quote must still be verified or confirmed, and the market maker is not ready to trade right away at that price. Subject quotes are not firm. Other terms are **nominal quotes** (price quote for informational purposes only—must be confirmed like subject quotes), **workout quotes** (approximate quote that must still be negotiated, depending on order size), **bid wanted** (no activity in a stock, but the dealer wants to sell some and wants traders to submit a bid), and **offer wanted** (there is no activity in a stock, but the dealer wants to buy some and wants traders to submit an ask price).

**NASDAQ STOCK MARKET.** The NASDAQ stock market is a decentralized trading environment that relies on negotiated bid and ask (buy and sell) prices between investors and market makers. NASDAQ stands for National Association of Securities Dealers Automated Quotations Service. The NASDAQ system links broker-dealers by telephone and computer to facilitate trades. The service has three levels:

> **Level 1:** This shows *only* the highest bid price and lowest ask price (the **"inside quote"**) for any NASDAQ stock that has at least two active market makers. These quotes, though, aren't firm until confirmed by another broker-dealer. Reps have access to this level but can't use it to guarantee any prices.

**Level 2:** This provides quotes from *multiple market makers,* showing the current firm quote (good for a minimum of 100 shares) and the quote size available. This level of access is primarily for institutional investors.

**Level 3:** This has the same info as levels 1 and 2, but also lets market makers *update or change their stock quotes.* This level is for market makers only.

Note: The NASDAQ system only provides a stock's trading volume at the end of the day.

Automated execution systems are used by NASDAQ to handle small market orders more quickly and efficiently. NASDAQ uses the Small Order Execution System (SOES), which aggregates small market orders of less than 1000 shares and executes them using firm quotes from that stock's market makers who put quotes on the NASDAQ system.

**NON-NASDAQ OVER-THE-COUNTER (NNOTC).** The over-the-counter (OTC) market consists of broker-dealers trading in unlisted securities. These are securities not listed on the NASDAQ exchange either because they do not qualify or because they have chosen to trade OTC. For trading information, the OTC market relies on a number of different systems, depending on the trading volumes of the securities.

**NASDAQ National Market Issues.** Stock issues that are actively traded OTC are listed on this electronic system that quotes up-to-the-minute prices as trades occur. These are generally large, easily identifiable stocks, with high volume and/or national interest, but which are not listed on the NASDAQ system for some reason.

**OTC Bulletin Board.** This is an electronic listing of bid and ask quotes for OTC stocks not meeting the minimum net worth (or other) requirements of NASDAQ. This is a step up from the pink sheets, where pricing info is only updated once daily.

**Pink Sheets.** This is the name of the daily publication of the National Quotation Bureau showing wholesale interdealer listings of bid and ask prices of OTC stocks not listed on the NASDAQ. The pink sheets get their name from the color of paper they are printed on. There are three things you should know about the pink sheets:

1. They are interdealer quotes only, and not for public consumption.
2. Stocks are usually at low end of price scale. (under $5 = **penny stocks**)
3. Pink sheets are *never* firm quotes, because they may not be two-sided. Of course, dealers must be ready to quote a firm price when called upon to do so, but on the Series 6 Pink Sheet, prices are NOT firm quotes.)

1.2.3

# New Issues Market

The new issues market is also referred to as the primary market or **primary market-place.** This is where new securities issues are sold. Some examples are IPOs where companies sell new stock, or a new bond issue sold by a municipality. This is much different than the secondary marketplace, where stocks change hands between investors. With the primary marketplace, there are many additional rules and regulations that must be followed. For example, a **prospectus** (document that details many aspect of a company, its history, its finances, and its management) must be given out to investors with all primary issues.

**PRIMARY OFFERING.** There are actually two types of stock issues and two types of offerings. A company that is going public for the first time sells new shares is a **new issue** stock offering. This is what is commonly referred to as an **initial public offering,** or **IPO.** A company that is already public but wants to sell more stock can do an **additional issue** stock offering.

With either of these types of issues, there can be a primary offering or a secondary offering. In a **primary offering,** the proceeds from the sale of stock go into the company treasury. In a **secondary offering,** the proceeds from the sale of stock go to present shareholders. This is one way that founders and employees can take money out of the company. The offering can also be a **combined offering,** where some of the proceeds go to the company and some go to current shareholders.

Do not confuse secondary *offering* with secondary *market*. The only similarity is that present stockholders receive money from the sale of stock. But a secondary offering for company insiders must be done through an investment banker following the SEC rules for stock issues, whereas stock sold in the secondary market is an investor-to-investor transaction that takes place on an exchange.

Exam Topic Alert

**ROLE OF INVESTMENT BANKER.** When companies or municipalities want to raise money, one way is to contact an investment banker and try to sell stock or bonds to the public. The investment banker is not a typical banker and does not loan out money. An investment banker is a broker-dealer that specializes in underwriting new securities issues. The underwriter works on behalf of the company or municipality to sell securities to the investing public. The investment banker makes a spread between the price charged to the public (public offering price) and the money given to the issuer selling the securities. Companies usually select an investment banking firm, decide on whether the securities will be sold as stocks or bonds, and then negotiate the underwriting size, price, and other details. Municipalities usually have underwriting firms compete through the competitive bid process to ensure taxpayers get the best deal.

During this negotiated or competitive bid process, the investment banking firm is fulfilling its first function as advisor, helping the issuer determine the best means of raising capital, determining the issue price for the securities, and advising on compliance with securities laws. The investment banker's second function is distribution, finding the best way to get the securities into the hands of investors. The investment banker will study the new issue and the market, then come up with a distribution plan. Some of the decisions will be whether the investment banker will work alone or put together a team **(syndicate),** and if the investment banker will guarantee a sell out of the issue **(firm commitment)** or work on a **best efforts** basis.

# Market Terms

There are several terms you will hear used with reference to stock trades in the various exchange markets or OTC trades. Some of these will be on the Series 6 exam.

**TRADE DATE.** The **trade date** is the actual date that a buy or sell order is authorized and executed. For tax purposes, the holding period for a security begins (or ends) on the trade date. (The holding period is used to determine, among other things, if an investment was held long enough to qualify for capital gains treatment.)

**SETTLEMENT DATE.** The **settlement date** is the date by which an executed order must be completed, either with the buyer delivering money to pay for the securities or the seller delivering the securities. There are several different settlement dates.

**Reg. T. Regulation T** is a section of the Federal Reserve Board rules governing the extension of credit from broker-dealers to their clients. You might think that this covers margin accounts—and it does—but it also covers transactions where securities are bought and not immediately paid for in cash. In essence, if a client orders a trade and does not pay for the securities in full in cash that day or from a balance in an existing brokerage account, the client has been extended credit. Reg. T requirements call for settlement to occur within five business days from the date of the trade. This is often abbreviated as Trade + 5, or T + 5. In some cases, clients and brokerage firms can agree on an extension before the expiration, but if any balance is still outstanding after 20 business days, the account may be restricted. The brokerage firm also has the option of selling out the position. This results in the account being frozen for 90 days. **(Key: Reg. T = T + 5)**

**Regular Way. Regular way** is the way most corporate and municipal securities settle, based on rules established by the NYSE and NASD Uniform Practice Code. These bodies have adopted the more stringent standard of having the client settle a securities transaction within three business days from the date of trade (T + 3). Since Federal Reg. T requirement is five days, this gives broker-dealers some extra time to ensure compliance with Reg. T. So if the client or broker-dealer is not able to comply with the three-day settlement rule, the parties still have two more days to try to rectify the situation before they run afoul of Reg. T rules. **(Key: for corporates and municipals, Regular Way = T + 3)**

Exam Topic Alert

On the Series 6 exam, if a question asks about settlement, *assume they're talking about "regular way" T + 3 settlement* unless the question mentions Reg. T, U.S. Treasury securities, or cash settlement.

**U.S. Securities.** U.S. Treasury securities always settle a securities transaction within one business day from the trade date (T + 1). Note that this is still often referred to as a regular way settlement, but if you are talking about U.S. Treasuries, settlement

| SETTLEMENT DATES COMPARED | | | | |
|---|---|---|---|---|
| **Settlement** | **Reg. T** | **Corporate** | **Municipals** | **U.S. Treasuries** |
| Cash | — | same day | same day | same day |
| Regular Way | T + 5 | T + 3 | T + 3 | T + 1 |

chart 1.2.4

must occur within one business day. This should be fairly easy to remember since the federal government doesn't like to wait to get its money. Agency issues, however, still settle T + 3. **(Key: Treasuries = T + 1; Agency Issues = T + 3)**

**Cash.** Cash settlements occur on the same day as a trade. Clients have until 2:30 P.M. to deliver the cash (or 30 minutes after a trade after 2:00 P.M.). **(Cash = same day)**

**GOOD DELIVERY. Good delivery** means that securities have the necessary requirements to be transferred when sold. These include good physical condition of the securities, proper endorsement of the securities, and physical delivery by the settlement date. If the securities are being held by the brokerage firm in street name, then there should be no problems. If the firm is holding the securities for a customer, but they are in the customer's name, then the firm must have a valid, executed stock power allowing the firm to endorse the securities on behalf of the client.

If customer-held securities are damaged, missing coupons, or soiled enough to obscure the writing on the face, then the issuer's transfer agent will need to be notified to rectify the situation. The transfer agent may issue new certificates, or require a surety bond if the authenticity of the certificate is in question.

Also, to be considered good delivery, stock certificates must be in round lots of 100 shares, or separate certificates that can be combined to create 100 share round lots. For bonds, good delivery is bearer bonds in face value denominations of $1000 or $5000. Registered bonds are only acceptable for good delivery if they are cleared beforehand and deemed acceptable by the receiving party.

Finally, two points of "good delivery" unique to bonds are also important for you to know. First, if a bond is a bearer bond, then a signature endorsement is not necessary. Second, municipal bond issues must have the legal opinion attached or be stamped "ex-legal" to be considered good delivery.

**DECLARATION DATE.** The **declaration date** is the date on which a company's board of directors announces a stock dividend. At the same time as the company declares the dividend, it also sets the record date, often a few days or more later to give investors some time to buy the stock and still qualify for the dividend.

**RECORD DATE.** The **record date** is the cut-off date for an investor to be considered the owner of record and eligible to receive rights, dividends, etc. (Also called **date of record.**) An investor, though, cannot typically buy a stock right up until the record date to receive the dividend. Remember, the trade date and the settlement date are only the same for cash transactions. The investor is not considered the owner of record and is not entitled to any rights or dividends until the settlement date.

**EX-DIVIDEND DATE.** The **ex-dividend date** (or **ex-date**) is the last date that a person can buy a stock and still have time to settle the transaction and be the owner of record to receive rights or dividends. Typically, trades must occur three business days before the date of record so that the new owner will settle in time to be the owner of record and qualify for the rights or dividend. Stocks trading before the record date but after the ex-date are said to trade "ex-rights" or "ex-dividend." This means that the stock that is being sold no longer gives the new owner the right to receive the rights or dividends that have been declared. In this situation after the ex-date, the stock typically trades at a lower price to reflect the "lost" dividend. This is why it is considered unethical to "sell dividends." **Selling dividends** is telling clients to buy stocks right before the ex-date so as to capture the dividend. This is usually not in the client's best interests because after the ex-date, the client can buy more stock at the cheaper price with the same total investment, plus the client does not have the immediate taxable event that is incurred as a result of a dividend payment.

**PAYMENT DATE.** The **payment date** is the date on which a declared stock dividend or scheduled bond interest payment is to be made. Checks are automatically sent to the stock owners of record or to registered bond holders.

1.25

# Price and Yield Terms

There are several price and yield terms associated with various securities. We have mentioned some previously. Let's review those and introduce some others that you will see in your career—and on the Series 6 exam.

**MARKET VALUE.** **Market value** is the price that investors are willing to pay for a security. Market value is driven by supply and demand. This is the price (minus commissions, etc.) at which an investor could expect to buy or sell the stock. For most purposes, this is the most relevant value.

**BID.** The **bid** is an offer to buy a security at a specified price. To have a price quote, you actually need to know the bid *and* ask price. Since the bid price is an offer to buy a security, from the broker-dealer's perspective, this would be equivalent to a wholesale price. This is also the price that an investor could expect to sell securities. (**BID = WHOLESALE = SELL**)

**ASKED or OFFERING.** The **asked** (or **offering**) is an offer to sell at a specified price. Typically, the term *asked* is used in the OTC market, and *offering* is used in the exchange markets. To have a price quote, you actually need to know the bid *and* ask price. Since the asked price is an offer to sell a security, from the broker-dealer's perspective, this would be equivalent to a retail price. This is also the price that an investor could expect to buy securities. (**ASKED = RETAIL = BUY**)

**NET ASSET VALUE (NAV).** **Net asset value (NAV)** is the value of a mutual fund and its shares, derived by taking the funds' assets minus liabilities, then dividing that result by the number of outstanding shares. NAV is the "bid" price at which mutual fund shares are redeemed. (**BID = NAV = INVESTOR SELLS BACK / REDEEMS**)

**Public Offering Price (POP).** The **public offering price (POP)** is the price of buying a mutual fund share, derived by taking the NAV and adding the sales charges. POP is the "ask" price at which mutual fund shares are sold to the public. (**ASK = POP = INVESTOR BUYS**)

**PREMIUM, PAR, DISCOUNT.** These three terms go together when discussing bond pricing, but they also have additional unrelated meanings. Premium is the price an investor pays to buy an option contract (or insurance contract). Par is the arbitrary value assigned by a company to its authorized stock. Discount is when something is reduced in price. Now let's look at these three terms as they relate to bond pricing.

**Premium.** Premium is the amount above par that an investor pays for a bond, preferred stock, or other security.

**Par.** Par is the face amount value of a bond, preferred stock, or other security.

**Discount. Discount** is the amount below par that an investor pays for a bond, preferred stock, or other security. **Original issue discount (OID)** bonds are sold below par value when they are first issued.

**NOMINAL YIELD.** **Yield** is the rate of return earned on an investment, expressed as a percentage. **Nominal yield** is the interest rate that the issuer will pay on a security, expressed as a percentage. In other words, the nominal yield is the coupon rate (often stated on the face of the security). Since security prices fluctuate in response to supply and demand in the marketplace and investors often buy bonds for prices other than par value, the nominal yield is rarely equal to a bond's actual yield. Instead, it is useful to evaluate current yield and yield to maturity.

**CURRENT YIELD.** **Current yield (CY)** is the coupon rate of the bond divided by the purchase price paid: **Current Yield (CY) = Coupon ÷ Price.** CY is a relative price that depends on the price you actually pay to acquire the bond. Let's assume you buy a bond with a face value of $1000 and a coupon rate of 10%. If you paid $1000 for the bond, your coupon rate is 10% and your current yield is 10%. If you could buy the same bond at a discount for $500, your current yield is 20%.

**YIELD TO MATURITY (YTM).** **Yield to maturity (YTM)** is the total rate of return that an investor will receive by holding a bond to maturity. YTM gives the discounted price the bond should trade at, so the present value of all future payments equals the current price of the bond.

**Bond Price Relationships.** Bond price relationships are the same for corporate bonds (corporates), U.S. government bonds (Treasuries), and municipal bonds (munis). Bond price has an inverse relationship with yield. If the bond is bought at par, then the coupon rate is equal to the yield. If a bond is bought at a discount, the current yield is higher than the coupon rate of the security. If a bond is bought at a premium, the current yield is lower than the coupon rate. The best way to illustrate this is to use balance diagrams:

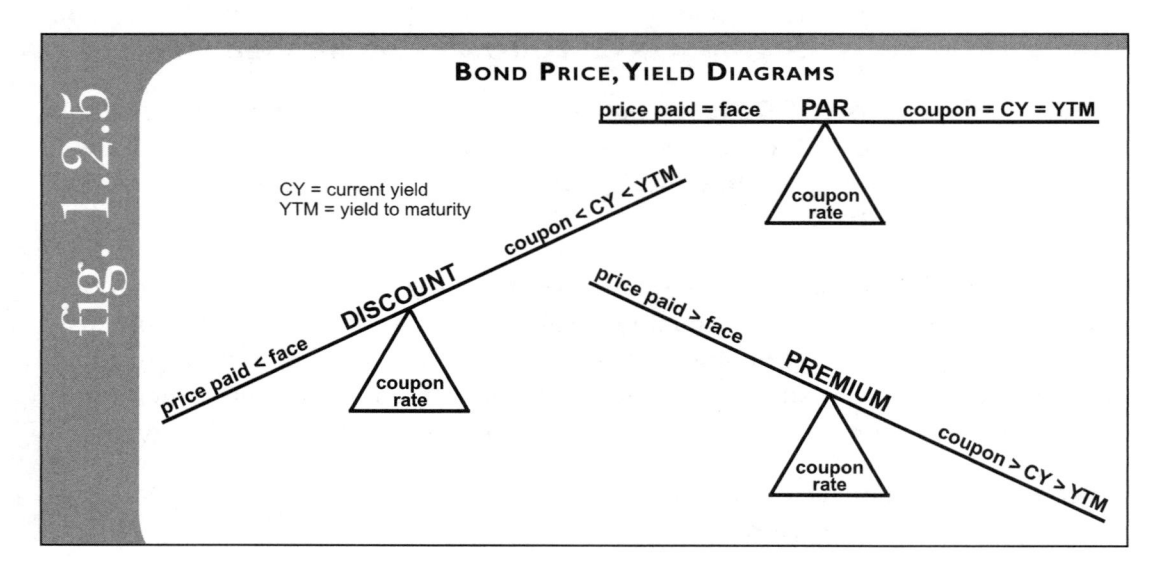

fig. 1.2.5

**BOND PRICE, YIELD DIAGRAMS**

price paid = face   **PAR**   coupon = CY = YTM

CY = current yield
YTM = yield to maturity

coupon < CY < YTM

DISCOUNT

price paid < face

coupon rate

coupon rate

price paid > face

PREMIUM

coupon rate

coupon > CY > YTM

Exam Topic Alert

**Remember:** Yield, CY, and YTM have an inverse relationship with bond price. When bond price is high, CY and YTM are low. When bond price is low, CY and YTM are high.

Be aware that the coupon rate is always the fulcrum on which the balance hinges. The coupon rate stays constant as the current yield (CY) and bond price paid move up and down.

# 1.3 Economic Factors

Aside from all of the market factors that we have discussed in an effort to explain how securities rise and fall in value, we also need to consider business cycles, the economy, and other principal business factors that affect the securities markets and securities prices. All of these securities are issued by companies or municipalities or the U.S. government. Since the values of the securities are based on the strength of the issuing entities, we need to look at how their strength is affected by business cycles and the economy.

**BUSINESS CYCLE.** The **business cycle** is general swings in business activity, going through periods of **e**xpansion, **p**eak, **c**ontraction, and **t**rough during different phases of the cycle, then repeating. (EPCoT can help you remember the four phases of the business cycle in order.) Cycles last for varying lengths of time.

Expansions in the economy are generally accompanied by increases in industrial production, consumers who are eager to buy more goods and services, increased demand for housing (especially more new home permits), and a rising stock market.

Contractions in the economy are generally accompanied by decreases in industrial production, falling consumer demand, heavy debt loads for consumer and businesses, increases in bankruptcies (personal and corporate), rising unemployment, and a falling stock market.

Here are some economic terms you should be familiar with:

**Expansion** is a period of business activity marked by rising production, which is growing to help supply keep up with growing demand.

**Peak** is the top of a business cycle, where expansion begins to level off as demand catches up with supply. From this point, production and prices will begin to fall.

**Contraction** is a period of business activity marked by falling production, which is slowing down until demand catches up with the supply.

**Trough** is the bottom of a business cycle, where contraction begins to stop its decent and turn upward. Supply no longer exceeds demand, so from this point, production and prices begin to rise.

**Depression** is a severe economic downturn caused by excess supply and rising unemployment that leads to falling demand, reduced purchasing power, and deflation of prices. Depressions are characterized by dramatic rises in unemployment and acute public caution and fear.

**Recession** is a less severe economic downturn, characterized by two consecutive quarters of decline in the country's level of business activity as defined by the gross domestic product (GDP).

**Recovery** is a period of business activity marked by increasing production as supply is trying to catch back up to increasing demand. This is the precursor to an expansion phase of the business cycle and growth for the economy.

Measuring business cycles and the level of business activity is a constant challenge. One measurement that analyzes current business output and compares it with past statistics to determine if business activity is rising or falling is GDP.

**Gross domestic product (GDP)** measures the value of all goods and services produced within the United States. This includes consumer spending, government spending, and the net value of exports. (On the test you may also see the gross national product [GNP], but this measure is not used as frequently since it also includes net foreign investments in its total.)

Note that GDP figures are adjusted for inflation. That is, the comparisons between the current number and previous numbers use constant dollars, so comparisons represent the true core value of output without inflation.

1.3.1

# Price Changes in the Economy

Economic theory says that supply and demand always seek to balance each other; thus, the market responds with price changes and economic activity. When demand for a product exceeds supply, the price for that product will rise, thereby stimulating more production (expansion). As production increases, more of the demand is satisfied until eventually the supply outstrips demand. At that point, prices will fall and production will slow until demand catches up with supply (contraction), then the cycle starts over.

The business cycle affects corporate cash flow and profits (a consideration for dividend payouts and bond payments), tax revenue and project revenues (a consideration for muni bonds), and the inflation rate (a consideration for U.S. Treasuries). The rate of inflation also affects the relative rate of return on all investments.

**INFLATION. Inflation** is an increase in the cost of goods or services. This is also called cost inflation because it's the result of manufacturers and others passing along to the consumer increases in their costs. Inflation is also defined as too much money chasing too few goods. This is also called **demand inflation** because it's driven by demand where too many people want to buy something in limited supply.

**Deflation. Deflation** is a decline in the cost of goods or services. This is a real decline in prices, not merely a slowed rate of growth (which is disinflation). Also keep in mind that some prices cannot decline in this environment (such as contract union wages), so a company's stock can get hurt as profitability is squeezed.

One measurement that analyzes past and current inflation as a means of forecasting the future direction and rate of inflation is the consumer price index (CPI). The CPI can help gauge if price levels in the economy are generally rising or falling.

> **Consumer Price Index (CPI)** measures the fixed cost of a market basket of goods and services. CPI includes components from the food, transportation, energy, housing, and clothing sectors, as well as other items. The figure is published monthly and used as an inflation adjuster for such things as Social Security benefits, union wage contracts, and other cost-of-living adjustments.
>
> Note that CPI figures are often quoted two ways: one with the complete theoretical market basket of goods and one that excludes the volatile food and energy sectors. Also note that taxes are not part of the CPI.

**EFFECTS ON BOND MARKETS.** Inflation and the perception of inflation have a direct impact on bond yields. During expansion periods in the business cycle, inflation tends to creep upward. As inflation rises, interest rates tend to rise as well. When interest rates go up, bond prices fall making bonds a less attractive investment vis-à-vis stocks.

During contraction periods in the business cycle, there is more of a deflationary tendency as prices drop to attract more spending. As business and economic activity fall, interest rates tend to fall as well. When interest rates go down, bond prices rise, making bonds a more attractive investment compared to stocks.

**EFFECTS ON EQUITIES MARKETS.** Inflation and the perception of inflation have a direct impact on stocks, but so do business cycles and expectations of future profits. During expansion periods in the business cycle, inflation tends to creep upward. As inflation rises, interest rates tend to rise as well. As business expands and profits rise, buying stocks is more attractive because of their high potential returns. This can also be a double-edged sword, because as inflation rises, new issues of fixed-income securities (bonds) are also offering higher yields, making them an attractive alternative with less risk than stocks.

During contraction periods in the business cycle, there is more of a deflationary tendency as prices drop to attract more spending. As business and economic activity fall, interest rates tend to fall as well. As businesses struggle and profits decline, buying stocks is less attractive because of their lower potential returns than the fixed-income securities (bonds), which are seeing their prices rise.

Some investors believe that deflation is beneficial because it helps maintain moderate economic growth, with falling real wages and raw material costs, which theoretically should lead to higher corporate profits. In reality, though, deflation can keep businesses from raising prices or passing on cost increases, and falling wages tend to decrease consumption, all of which make it hard to maintain or grow profits.

**Sensitive Stocks. Interest-rate-sensitive stocks** are stocks that are affected greatly by changes in interest rates. Some examples of these are bank stocks, which feel the effects of any move by the Federal Reserve to adjust interest rates, and utility stocks, which are highly leveraged and must pay out more in debt service. **Cyclical stocks** are common stocks that generally rise and fall quickly in response to economic conditions. Some examples of cyclical stocks are automobile stocks and housing-related stocks. **Countercyclical stocks** are common stocks that generally rise when economic conditions worsen. The best example of a countercyclical stock is the food sector (because demand is constant regardless of economic conditions, so the relative performance of these stocks is better than the overall market).

1.3.2

# Monetary Policy

**Monetary policy** is the government's mechanism through which it can exert control over the supply and cost of money. Monetary policy also has the goals of economic growth, full employment, and international balance of payments, plus monetary policy tries to maintain stability in prices, interest rates, and financial markets. The Federal Reserve is directly involved with the physical money supply of the United States in two ways. First, the Federal Reserve oversees the printing of more currency by the U.S. Treasury (but the Treasury does the actual printing!). Second, the Federal Reserve Board acts as an agent of the U.S. Treasury when it sells and buys Treasury securities.

**ROLE OF THE FEDERAL RESERVE.** The Federal Reserve Board plays a large role in controlling the level of business activity through interest rates and other means. **The Federal Reserve Board** (also referred to as **the Fed**) is responsible for U.S. monetary policy, maintaining economic stability, regulating commercial banks, and setting margin requirements. The Fed uses monetary policy to make more or less money available for banks to lend, in effect raising or lowering interest rates for business and consumers. Higher interest rates mean tougher credit, and lower interest rates mean easier credit. By making credit easier or tougher, the Fed also controls the level of economic activity (for businesses and consumers).

**CHANGING INTEREST RATES AND THE MONEY SUPPLY.** The Fed affects changes in interest rates and the money supply through the use of five different monetary policy tools (remembered easily as the acronym **DORMM**):

1. Discount rates
2. Open market operations
3. Reserve requirements
4. Margin requirements
5. Moral suasion

**1. Discount rates** or **federal discount rates** are the interest rates charged by Federal Reserve Banks on loans to member commercial banks. This is one way the Fed can change interest rates—and it's easy to remember. If Federal Reserve Banks charge higher discount rates when they lend money to commercial banks, then the banks will pass along those higher costs to their customers as higher interest rates. A cut in the discount rate also filters down to the loans banks make to their customers (but usually not as fast).

Exam Topic Alert

An increase in the discount rate equals an increase in interest rates to customers; a decrease in the discount rate equals a decrease in interest rates to customers. (**Note:** This is the only rate that the Fed directly sets!)

Now, though, the discount rate is less of a policy tool. The Fed discourages banks from borrowing funds directly from the Fed, unless they are in financial trouble and not able to borrow from other banks on the open Fed funds market. The discount rate is still important, however, because money managers watch the discount rate. If the Fed adjusts the discount rate in line with the Fed funds rate, this is seen as confirmation of the Fed's true long-term outlook and bias for future monetary policy decisions.

**2. Open market operations** are when the Fed sells or buys government securities (bonds) as a means of controlling the supply of, and demand for, money. Interest rates are affected because when the Fed buys and sells securities, it makes more or less money available for banks to lend.

To accomplish the Fed's goals, the Federal Open Market Committee (FOMC) meets regularly to discuss the present and future state of the economy, including where interest rates should ideally be to accomplish the Fed's long-term objectives of economic growth and stability with minimal inflation. One of the things the Fed does at its FOMC meeting is to exert indirect influence over long-term interest rates by establishing a target Fed funds rate. The **Fed funds rate** is the short-term interest rate that commercial banks charge each other when they borrow money in the Fed funds market (usually short-term loans for one to two days to help banks cover reserve requirements caused by normal daily fluctuations in their deposits).

The Fed does NOT set the Fed funds rate. Instead, the Fed will sell or buy securities to hit its target Fed funds rate. When the Fed *sells* securities, it increases its stockpile of cash and takes money out of circulation. Since the banks have less money available to lend out, this raises interest rates. (Part A below) Conversely, if the Fed *buys* securities, it decreases its stockpile of cash and puts more money into circulation. When banks sell securities that they own or hold, they have more money available. The banks want to quickly relend the money somewhere so that they can earn interest on the money instead of just letting it sit in their banks. Since the banks have more money to lend, they will lower interest rates (a loan sale!—Part B below).

Keep in mind, though, that other factors, such as inflation, may be applying upward pressure on interest rates at the same time that an increase in money supply is exerting downward pressure. The Fed can only influence (not set!) short-term Fed funds rates, and the Fed also has no direct affect (and does not set!) the **prime rate** (the lowest interest rate that banks charge their best commercial customers). Long-term interest rates usually follow the lead of Fed funds rate movements, but there are times when long-term interest rates don't follow short-term interest rates. This may occur if there are other perceived long-term risks, such as fear of future inflation.

(The Fed can also buy and sell U.S. dollars as part of its open market operations if there's an imbalance in international supply and demand for U.S. dollars. Although this can also affect inflation and interest rates, it is beyond the scope of this text.)

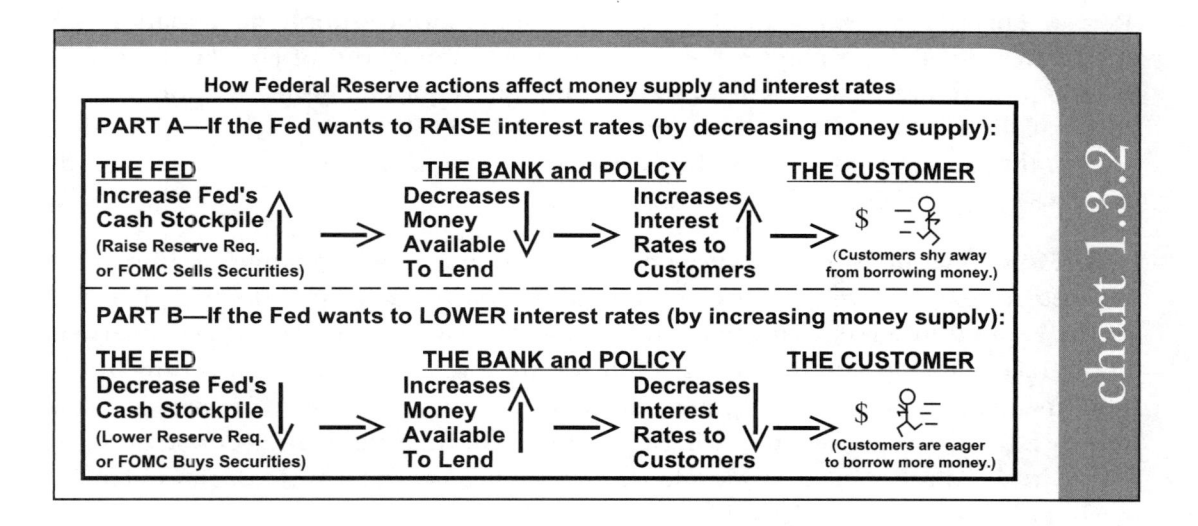

**3. Reserve requirements** are the percentage of deposits that commercial banks are required to keep on deposit, either on hand at the bank or in the bank's own accounts—in other words, money the bank can't lend to customers. The original purpose of reserve requirements was to help avert financial panic by giving depositors some confidence that their deposits were safe and accessible. Reserve requirements, however, have also become a policy tool.

By raising or lowering reserve requirements, the Fed controls the supply and cost of money, and the quality of credit. If you wanted to raise interest rates, make credit tougher to get and/or improve the quality of credit, then you'd raise the reserve requirements because raising reserve requirements decreases the money supply available for banks to loan. When there's a smaller supply of money, you can be more selective about who borrows it and thus improve the quality of loans (and hopefully have less bad debt losses). When there's a smaller supply of something, you want to decrease demand—and higher interest rates should decrease demand! (See Chart 1.3.2)

Conversely, if you wanted to lower interest rates or make credit easier to get, then you'd lower the reserve requirements. Lowering the reserve requirements increases the money supply available for banks to loan out to businesses and consumers. When there's a larger supply of money, you can be less selective about who borrows it. You also want to increase demand—and lower interest rates should increase demand! (Part B in chart)

Using reserve requirements to adjust interest rates and control inflation has become a less important near-term Fed tool. This is because of the "multiplier effect." Changing reserve requirements has a rather large effect on the money supply since it affects *all* of the deposit assets of banks. Instead, the Fed is able to have a similar outcome but on a smaller, more manageable, scale with FOMC open market operations. Now reserve requirement changes are mostly used as a policy tool in the face of a severe recession or severe inflation.

**4. Margin requirements** are the amount of money that an investor must deposit in a margin account before buying stock on credit or selling short, as required by Reg. T. This is another way the Fed can control the money supply since margin is a form of credit. Raising margin requirements takes money out of circulation, which should push interest rates higher. Lowering margin requirements leaves more money in circulation, which should push interest rates lower. Changes in margin requirements, though, are not seen as effective a policy tool as the others we've discussed, because margin affects less people and less money.

**5. Moral Suasion** is trying to use persuasive influences on the public and financial markets so that they will perceive credit in a specific way. For example, the chairman of the Federal Reserve Board may make a speech stating that the Fed is concerned about rising stock prices fueling inflation. Even though there may not be any intention of actually raising interest rates, the chairman's statement may nevertheless still produce the desired effect of having the public and financial markets do less speculating in the market for *fear* of higher interest rates—without interest rates actually having to be raised to achieve this result.

**RELATION TO THE LEVEL OF ECONOMIC ACTIVITY.** The Fed actively tries to manage the economy through the use of monetary policy. Interest rates have a direct affect on economic activity, and the Fed tries to control this with changes in the money supply. Since higher interest rates mean tougher credit and lower interest rates mean easier credit, the Fed is able to discourage or encourage economic activity. During expansion periods in the business cycle, the Fed is generally worried about inflation, so by using monetary policy to lower the money supply and increase interest rates, the Fed can curtail business and consumer spending to try to keep inflation in check.

Conversely, during contraction periods in the business cycle, the Fed is generally trying to stimulate the economy to avoid recession, so by using monetary policy to increase the money supply and lower interest rates, the Fed can encourage borrowing to spur business and consumer spending. The balancing efforts of the Fed are directed toward managing the growth of the money supply to allow adequate growth of the economy at reasonable interest rates, without fueling inflation or fears of inflation, which could lead to higher interest rates.

Part of the Fed's role in managing interest rates is to deal not only with actual inflation, but also with anticipated inflation. In recent years, the Fed has adopted a policy of trying to anticipate future economic conditions rather than simply reacting to them as it had in the past. This has also involved trying to further reduce the size and impact of swings in the business cycle. Most economists and businesses watch the Fed's actions when the FOMC meets to see if they will raise interest rates to reduce growth and head off inflation, or lower rates in an effort to spur economic growth and head off recession. Although many believe that inflation is less of a threat in our current global economy, the Fed still plays an important role in managing economic growth and business activity, as well as money supply and interest rates.

**RELATION TO PRICES AND THE RETURN ON SECURITIES INVESTMENTS.** Interest rates and the business cycle have many direct effects on the securities markets. As business cycles go through different phases, investors constantly shift money back and forth between the bond market and the stock market as they seek the best rate of return given current and future economic conditions.

If business is doing well and the business cycle is in an upswing, then it is expected that increased demand will lead to increases in spending and credit, which will lead to increased interest rates. Conversely, when business is not doing well and the business cycle is in a downswing, there is falling demand, less spending, and less borrowing. When this happens, investors expect future interest rates to be lower. As a result, disintermediation occurs. **Disintermediation** is when funds flow out of banks and financial institutions and into other investments seeking higher yields.

Here are a few things to remember for the Series 6 exam. First, the Fed does **not** set the prime rate nor the Fed funds rate. Instead, the Fed influences these with its open market operations of buying and selling securities. The Fed sets the discount rate, margin, and reserve requirements. Reserve requirements cause the largest change (because of the multiplier effect), margin requirements cause the smallest change (because fewer people affected). Monetary policy is the Fed influencing interest rates by various means; fiscal policy is government taxes and spending.

Exam Topic Alert

1.3.3

# Fiscal Policy of the Federal Government

**Fiscal policy** is the government's plan for spending, taxation, and debt management. The legislative and executive branches of government enact fiscal policy by passing legislation that sets the government's priorities for how much money will be collected, who it will be collected from, and how it will be spent. The ultimate goals of fiscal and monetary policies are supposed to be economic growth, full employment, and international balance of payments. Unfortunately, there's much debate over which policies actually promote those results. Worse yet, the government's fiscal policy is subject to tremendous political pressure.

The **U.S. Treasury Department** is part of the executive branch of the federal government. As fiscal manager of the nation, the Treasury is responsible for carrying out the nation's fiscal policy by doing the actual spending, taxing, and debt financing through an account it keeps with the Federal Reserve. Treasury funds come from a number of sources, but the largest source is personal and business income taxes. The Treasury issues all government checks, uses the IRS to collect taxes and enforce tax laws, issues securities to cover any spending deficits, and prints more currency as needed.

**Taxation** and **spending** are the two main policy tools that the Treasury Department can and does use to implement fiscal policy. Both of these are a means of controlling the supply of money in circulation, thus, these policy tools also indirectly affect interest rates.

**FEDERAL TAXES.** Taxes have a direct impact on the spending habits and abilities of all businesses and individuals. Lower taxes mean taxpayers have more funds for spending or investing. Higher taxes mean that they will not only have fewer funds to spend or invest, but they will be more likely to invest in tax-exempt securities or other investments that help to defer or avoid taxes. While some would argue that government spending is necessary and has the same net result on economic activity, higher taxes result in people having less money to spend or invest.

Taxation can also have direct and deliberate secondary effects on economic activity. Along with raising revenue, tax provisions are used to implement social policies by encouraging or discouraging certain behaviors or activities. This is done through tax deductions, exemptions, or other tax law provisions. For example, the deduction for mortgage interest from taxable income effectively stimulates housing and encourages home ownership. Tax code changes also affect investments in other ways. For example, provisions of the Tax Reform Act of 1986 limited or eliminated tax benefits previously available. The capital gains exclusion for long-term capital gains was eliminated, accelerated cost recovery methods were eliminated, and straight-line cost recovery periods for income and investment property were increased. The ability to offset passive losses against income from wages and salaries was also restricted for many taxpayers. All of these made certain types of investments less attractive (such as limited partnerships).

**FEDERAL SPENDING.** Federal spending is how the government distributes the money it collects in taxes. The goods and services purchased by the government represent a sizeable portion of economic activity that can have a stimulative effect on the economy. Certainly, some stocks, such as defense contractors, are helped when the government increases spending. On the other hand, lack of fiscal discipline can lead to inflation if the government spends too freely without regard to cost (e.g., defense items purchased for more than the same item costs at a hardware store), without competitive pressures (e.g., the post office), or without forcing suppliers to feel competitive pressures (e.g., continual increases in health care costs).

**Deficit spending** is when the government spends more money than it takes in from tax revenue. When federal income is less than federal expenditures, a shortfall called a **federal budget deficit** results. Until recently, a deficit occurred in most years since the Great Depression. When a deficit occurs, the Treasury obtains funds to cover the shortfall by issuing interest-bearing securities to investors. Depending on their term, these securities are referred to as Treasury bills or T-bills (1 year or less), **Treasury notes** (1 to 10 years) or **Treasury bonds** (10 years or more). In issuing these securities, the federal government is borrowing from the private sector and accumulating debt. When the government borrows money to cover deficits or debt, less money is available for private borrowers.

While some economists believe that federal deficits and debt have little impact on interest rates, other believe that large-scale federal borrowing can have a dramatic effect on interest rates as private borrowers compete for limited funds remaining. If the government spends too much money, then there's less money available for people to borrow—which could push up interest rates.

1.3.4

# International Economic Factors

International economic factors can play an important role in our domestic securities markets and our business cycles. This is true not only because many U.S. companies are international in scope and depend on foreign manufacturing subsidiaries and export sales, but also because of competition in the marketplace. We are not only talking about competition between companies offering similar goods and services, but also competition for the limited dollars that consumers have to spend. Competition also exists for investment dollars staying in the U.S. securities markets or flowing to other countries to obtain better returns.

These same international factors also affect money coming into the United States from other countries. The U.S. **balance of payments** measures money flowing into or out of the U.S. economy. This is somewhat dependent on foreign exchange rates, which affect the purchasing power people have to buy goods and make investments.

For the Series 6 exam, know that a rise in foreign exchange rates leads to a depreciation of the U.S. dollar relative to the foreign currency. This reinforces the fact that a weak dollar makes U.S. investments less attractive to foreigners, and it makes foreign imports expensive while making U.S. goods cheaper in other countries. Also know that a strong dollar attracts deposits and foreign investment money into the U.S. markets, and it makes foreign imports cheaper while making U.S. goods more expensive in other countries.

Exam Topic
Alert

**CURRENCY EXCHANGE RATES.** The **exchange rates** are the price at which one country's currency can be converted into another country's currency. Talking about the strength or weakness of a currency is relative, depending on whether the country is talking about their own currency or that of another country. Let's use the dollar as an example. A **weak dollar** is when the dollar can be exchanged for less of a foreign currency. This makes foreign imports expensive, but it encourages other countries to buy more U.S. goods. A **strong dollar** is when the dollar can be exchanged for more of a foreign currency. This makes foreign imports cheaper, but it makes it more expensive for other countries to buy U.S. goods. Also, a strong dollar attracts deposits and foreign investment money into the United States. Their investment dollars don't buy as much initially, but foreign investors want their investment to enjoy capital appreciation (income or interest) in the stronger U.S. dollar so they can get more of their own currency later when the investment matures or is liquidated.

# 1.4 Investment Risk Factors

All investments have some element of risk. When most people hear the term *risk,* they associate that with risk of principal. **Risk of principal** is the chance that invested capital will decrease in value. Here one thinks of the investor who buys a stock that becomes worthless, but this is hardly the only risk that an investor faces. **Investment risk** is the chance that adverse conditions will cause the value of an investment to drop. The important difference is that we are speaking about the investment value in relative terms. Furthermore, these "adverse conditions" may or may not be directly related to the investment itself.

Suppose your client buys a bond paying 6% interest. That may sound like a good return, but there are other factors to consider. What if inflation rises to 8%? The investor did not lose any principal and may still collect all the interest that's owed. What once may have been a "good" investment is not anymore—even if the bond is repaid in full—because the investor *did* lose money vis-à-vis inflation. What if that same investor bought the bond because it was a tax-free municipal issue, but the tax status of the bond or tax laws change? This could effectively reduce the investor's net return on the investment. These are just two of the many investment risks that must be considered when advising clients about what investments to make when putting together a diversified portfolio.

# Kinds of Investment Risk

In the prior section, we briefly mentioned two ways that an investor can actually lose money without any adverse condition being directly attributable to the underlying investment. There are many more kinds of risks. Each must be fully understood by you as advisor and by your client as investor if suitable recommendations and investments are to be made for your client's portfolio.

**BUSINESS/CREDIT RISK. Business risk** is defined as risk that a company will go out of business or not be able to meet its debt obligations. This term is closely associated with credit risk. **Credit risk** is defined as the risk that an investment will lose money because it is not repaid. This is also referred to as **repayment risk** or **financial risk.** Here the default of the issuer of the debt is borne by the person holding the bond or other debt instrument. Of course, bondholders do have some recourse in a bankruptcy proceeding, but they are not likely to recover the full amount owed if they must go this route. This type of risk can be minimized by the quality of debt instruments chosen for investment, but at the trade-off of lower returns. Federal government securities are the safest but offer lowest returns. Some corporate bonds offer very attractive returns, but their credit ratings must be examined carefully so that the investor understands the risks.

**INTEREST RATE RISK. Interest rate risk** is the risk that changes in interest rates will adversely affect the value of an investment. As interest rates rise, the value of bonds falls. This is part of the inverse relationship illustrated earlier with the balance diagrams. Bonds with long-term maturities are hit the hardest because they are typically locked in at lower interest rates. To make matters worse, interest rates typically rise as inflation rises. Not only is the investment worth less because of the lower coupon rate, it also has less purchasing power because of higher inflation. The effect on bonds with short-term maturities can be more pronounced, because short-term interest rates usually move in bigger swings than long-term interest rates.

The stock market is also affected by interest rate risks. As interest rates rise, money will move out of stocks and into bonds seeking those new higher interest rates (which are perceived to be safer than stocks). Also, since utility companies are highly leveraged, utility company stocks also take a hard hit in value as interest rates rise, because as utilities devote a higher portion of their revenue to pay debt service, their bottom-line profitability suffers. This is true for all highly leveraged companies.

**PURCHASING POWER RISK. Purchasing power risk** is the chance that the value of assets or income will decline relative to the prices of other goods and services, thus resulting in less purchasing power (also called **inflationary risk**). Inflation is one of the most important investment risks that must be considered since it exerts great force on the markets. Inflation can be bad for current bondholders who are receiving a fixed rate of return. Long-term bondholders are hit the hardest because they are typically locked in at a lower interest rate. Retirement investments especially must be structured to minimize the effects of inflation.

Inflation is also bad for the stock market, not only because it can hurt the bottom-line performance of companies, but also because as inflation rises, money will move from stocks and into the bond market seeking those new higher (and safer?) returns.

**LIQUIDATING AT INAPPROPRIATE TIMES. Timing risk** is the danger that an investor will not pick the best time to buy or sell an investment and thus not maximize his or her gain. Timing risk actually involves four risks rolled into one: getting in, getting out, transaction costs, and tax consequences. Buy low and sell high is not as easy as it sounds. Certainly, getting in and out at the right time is important, but no one truly knows which way the market is going or when a particular investment has peaked or bottomed out. The investor must also figure the transaction costs of continually trying to get in and out to beat the market. This is especially true for day traders. Finally, tax consequences can affect timing decisions. Selling early to move taxable gains to an earlier year can result in a sale too early; delaying a sale to have it taxed as a capital gain instead of higher tax rates could also result in a missed opportunity to sell higher.

**MARKETABILITY/REDEEMABILITY RISK.** These risks are synonymous with liquidity risk. **Liquidity risk** is the chance that an investor may not be able to convert an investment, security, or asset into cash when needed. This can be because the asset is stock in a privately held company, shares in a limited partnership, or real estate. Even regional stocks and some thinly traded over-the-counter shares may not be able to be sold easily. If one of these investments is sold, the investor may have to accept less than market price because there is limited demand for it. This is an important consideration in recommendations you make to clients.

Exam Topic
Alert

This is a good place to reiterate an important point about the Series 6 exam: *Never ignore liquidity considerations of a client on the test!* If a test question says your client needs money soon or in less than six months or some other short period of time, look for an answer that talks about you recommending money market investments, regular bank CDs, or some other short-term investment that is very liquid.

**TAXABILITY. Taxability risk** refers to the risk of a change in the tax law that adversely affects an investment. Sometimes these new laws can have unintended consequences beyond the scope of their original intent. Take as an example tax law changes in 1986 that changed the deductibility of passive losses. This certainly had a direct affect on values of limited partnerships, but it was also a contributing factor to the devaluation of some real estate investments and the Savings and Loan crisis.

**MARKET RISK. Market risk** is risk that is common to all investments of the same type or classification, owing more to broad market conditions or investor sentiment toward a particular sector of stocks or bonds. This is also referred to as **systematic risk** that can't be eliminated through diversification, although it can be lowered by adding more types of securities to a portfolio. The narrower the focus of investments in the portfolio (e.g., emphasis on certain sector funds), the more pronounced the risk.

**SOCIAL/POLITICAL RISK. Social risk** is the risk of adverse affects on an investment from a change in the law or a change in social acceptance. For example, new clean air laws affect utilities, transportation, and other related investments. An example of social risk is cigarette company investments. Not only is smoking declining because it is looked upon unfavorably by society, but these companies are also bearing the brunt of lawsuits stemming from current social attitudes.

Political risk is closely associated with legislative risk, but the two are not the same. **Political risk** is the risk of a change in government policy that adversely affects an investment. This usually refers to a foreign country, such as when an industry is nationalized or protectionist measures are adopted that affect specific import or export products. **Legislative risk** is the risk of a change in the law that adversely affects an investment. This usually refers to domestic policies, such as new clean air requirements or tax law changes.

**CURRENCY EXCHANGE RISK. Currency exchange risk** is the chance of foreign exchange loss because of fluctuations in the value of foreign money vis-à-vis the dollar. (This is also called **currency risk** or **exchange risk.**) At first glance, this may only seem to affect speculators who trade in foreign currency markets, or those who invest in foreign companies. In reality, any multinational corporation which has profits from foreign subsidiaries, companies who manufacture products in other countries, or any entity that imports or exports goods or services is susceptible to this risk. Of course, there are ways to minimize this risk (e.g., hedging with foreign currency options and futures contracts), but good investment advice must consider this risk to ensure that appropriate steps are taken to protect the investor, or make sure the companies he or she is investing in have taken steps to protect themselves.

1.4.2

# Concept of Risk/Reward

Risk tolerance and investment experience of the client will likely influence all investment decisions. Of course, the more risky an investment is, the greater the payoff will be if it succeeds, but high risk should only be a small portion of the client's portfolio. You may be surprised to learn that even within investment product types there are varying degrees of risk. (We have seen this with some of the investments we have discussed thus far and will continue to point this out where appropriate.)

Some risks may or may not be appropriate given an investor's situation. For example, an elderly couple that just entered retirement should not gamble their entire nest egg in a risky investment. On the other hand, a young couple who has 100% of their retirement money invested in bank CDs should probably try and get a better return elsewhere since they are far from retiring and inflation will eat up a good portion of

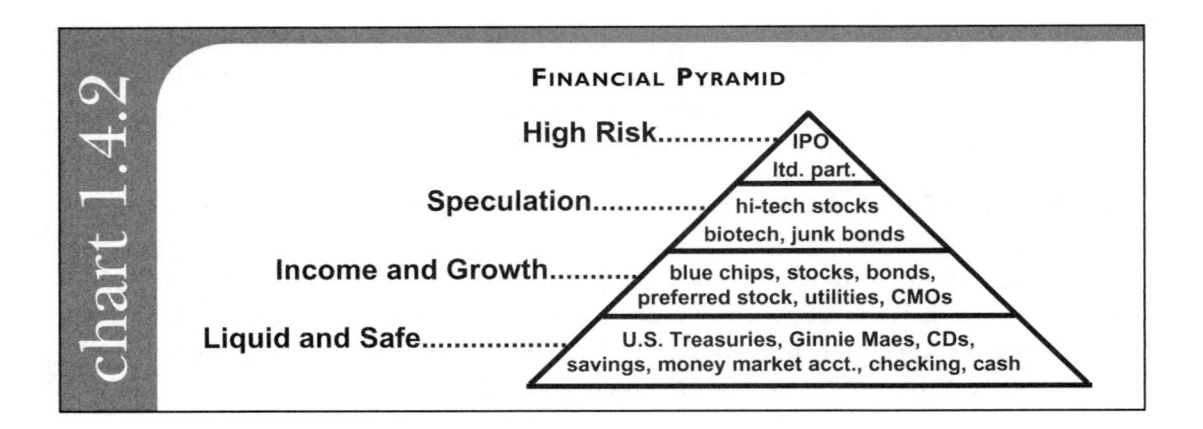

**chart 1.4.2**

**FINANCIAL PYRAMID**

High Risk.............. IPO / ltd. part.

Speculation............. hi-tech stocks / biotech, junk bonds

Income and Growth.......... blue chips, stocks, bonds, preferred stock, utilities, CMOs

Liquid and Safe................ U.S. Treasuries, Ginnie Maes, CDs, savings, money market acct., checking, cash

the return from the CDs. Diversification of an investor's portfolio tailored to his or her unique situation and goals is important. The financial pyramid (chart 1.4.2) illustrates risk-reward trade-offs and their relative place in a portfolio.

**DEGREES OF RISK RELATIVE TO RETURN ON INVESTMENT.** As you can see in the Financial Pyramid chart in the previous section, liquid and safe low-return investments should be a large part of an investor's portfolio to form a solid foundation, with high-risk high-return investments forming the smallest part of a portfolio. Along with the different types of investments, another consideration is the length of time that an investment will be held by the investor.

When considering risk relative to return on investment, the investor must balance long-term versus short-term risks as part of the overall risk-reward ratio of investments in the portfolio. This risk analysis recognizes that ALL investments have some element of risk. Thus, one consideration and possible objective for portfolio diversification is balancing these investment risks within the portfolio.

Let's illustrate this with some examples. Investing in bank CDs and government securities may appear to be low risk, but their low risk of principal loss must be balanced against the relatively high risk that their small returns on investment will not keep pace with inflation. Stocks that historically have a moderate risk of capital loss over the long term have the short-term market risk that the overall broad market (and perhaps the individual stock value) may be down at the time a client needs to sell a stock and get money out. The more diversified a portfolio is, the less any one type of risk can affect the overall value and performance of the entire portfolio. Having too much of one kind of investment does not lower risk as much as it shifts risk from one type to another. That's where diversification comes in.

**IMPORTANCE OF DIVERSIFICATION. Portfolio diversification** is spreading out risk by holding investments in varying types and amounts. Investors need to understand the merits of a diversified investment portfolio. This would entail spreading the clients risk over the entire financial pyramid, having most of his or her money in the bottom safety portion and the smallest amount invested in high-risk investments at the top of the pyramid. Of course, different clients will have different risk tolerances and want more money put into different areas, depending on their investment needs. Portfolio diversification will likely be an important goal, though, for clients who have recently received a large amount of money, perhaps through an inheritance, or who have all of their money tied up in one investment or one type of investment, perhaps all in a savings account or retirement account. Having a diverse portfolio can be a hedge against a downturn in a particular sector of the economy, as well as being a good means of keeping pace with inflation.

As we discuss the various investment risks that an investor must consider, we also periodically mention some things that could be done to offset those risks. In the end, though, the only true way to mitigate investment risks is for the investor to have a diversified portfolio. Still, within the framework of a diversified portfolio there is room for different strategies to help clients achieve other investment objectives as well. As discussed, these objectives might include safety or moderate growth through defensive investments, speculation or high growth using aggressive investments, or a combination of these.

Safety entails preservation of capital. The investor may also desire to generate some income. Safety and moderate growth are best achieved through the use of defensive investments. Speculation, on the other hand, entails greater accepted risk. Investors who want to maximize their return on investment understand that the greater the risks, the greater the potential rewards. Speculation and high growth are best achieved through the use of aggressive investments. In reality, most investment portfolios fall somewhere between these two extremes. This is at the heart of diversification.

**DEFENSIVE AND AGGRESSIVE INVESTMENT STRATEGIES. Defensive investments** include high-grade bonds and stocks with prices that are more stable over time than the broad market and are more likely to perform consistently through all parts of the economic cycle. Some stocks that would be part of a typical defensive investment strategy are utilities, certain blue-chip stocks, and some high-grade preferred stock. The blue chips would allow for some moderate growth and may even pay a dividend, while maintaining the safety component that the investor requires. A defensive investment strategy would also hold debt securities as a larger portion of the overall portfolio. These bonds would be government issued, or high-grade corporate bonds from companies that have an excellent debt rating.

**Aggressive investments** are stocks of rapidly growing companies that have prospects for above-average growth, but with prices that are highly volatile over time when compared with the broader market. Some stocks that would be part of a typical aggressive investment strategy would be high-tech companies and other start-ups. These stocks are generally relied upon solely for capital appreciation since they usually offer no dividend income. An aggressive investment strategy would have very little in the way of investments with fixed returns, such as bonds (although zero coupon bonds are one way to speculate on interest rates because the zero coupon prices are very volatile). An aggressive investment strategy would also have a portion of securities bought on margin to gain maximum leverage with its funds and perhaps even delve into options.

# 1.5 Suitability Factors

When evaluating various suitability factors for your investment clients, one of the best methods is to examine the investment profile of a customer. This investment profile consists of many elements but can be broken down into several categories: investment objectives, financial status, risk tolerance, and other nonfinancial investment considerations. Once there is a good understanding of an investor's suitability factors and investment profile, then attainable investment objectives can be identified along with ways to achieve those goals.

An investor's financial needs must also take into account the investor's available investment capital, current investment holdings, risk tolerance, and investment experience in order to get a complete picture of the situation. This is important because your securities license means that you pledge to "know your customer."

## 1.5.1

# Investment Objectives of Clients

After a thorough analysis of a client's investment profile, it is time to choose a course of action based on the investment objectives the client has laid out. The client's investment objectives may include any number of potential investment strategies, or a combination of these. As we focus on three key objectives that many investor's have, we will mention where they fall on the financial pyramid and also give an example or two of an investment type that would fit the criteria for that investment objective. (Don't worry if you don't know all of the investment products mentioned as examples. They will be explained in detail in upcoming chapters.)

Exam Topic Alert

An important point to keep in mind (and this may appear on the test) is that *one cannot assume that every investor has the same objectives for his or her portfolio.* Everyone is unique and has different objectives.

**PRESERVATION OF CAPITAL. Preservation of capital** is ensuring that the original amount of money invested is as safe as possible. No one likes to lose money, and everyone who invests hopes to make money. But clients who tell you that preservation of capital is their prime objective are a special case. They are telling you that safe investments are more important than trying to get larger returns on their money. They would want most of their money (if not all of it) in the bottom of our financial period, invested in "safe" investments, such as CDs, money market funds, fixed annuities, and perhaps some high-grade bonds or government securities. People at or near retirement age often have this as their main investment objective.

**CURRENT INCOME. Current income** is trying to generate an immediate cash flow from a portfolio of investments. This is a common investment objective that can certainly be done through some of the "safe" investments mentioned previously, but now the client may be giving you a little more latitude. Bonds, of course, are a good source of income, but the rating of the company (or municipality) issuing them must be balanced against the returns offered. Investing in mortgage-backed securities can also be a relatively safe way to generate income (especially safe are the Ginnie Maes), although there are other risks associated with these (interest rate risk, reinvestment risk, etc.). Preferred stock and even some utility stocks, while slightly higher on the risk scale than bonds, can also be a source of income. Real estate investment trusts (REITs) can also pass through rental and other income with less risk than a client actually owning and managing the piece of real estate directly.

**GROWTH OF INVESTED CAPITAL. Capital growth** is trying to make the original amount of invested money appreciate over the long term. Here we are higher in our financial pyramid as the client has defined a new objective that is less compatible with the first two. The best way for a client's money to grow over time is to have it invested in stock. Common stock in corporations is an excellent way to achieve growth, but the potential risk of principal must always be in the back of the investor's mind. Of course, this risk can be mitigated somewhat by the type of stocks chosen for the portfolio: blue chip stocks of well-established companies are safer, but the trade-off is lower, more moderate capital growth; biotech or high-tech stocks offer the potential of high, more aggressive growth, but they are much higher on the financial pyramid in the speculative to high-risk range. Mutual fund investing and other sector funds are another way to achieve growth while mitigating risk through the diversification of stocks that a fund has invested in. Still the risk of loss is there. Direct investment in real estate offers growth potential but entails additional risk.

1.5.2

# Financial Status of Clients

In examining the financial status of a client, there are several items that must be gathered and analyzed. Most of the information needed can be obtained from a typical new account form. It contains lots of questions for the client to answer about income, expenses, assets, liabilities, current investment holdings, etc. From this information, you can assemble a simple balance sheet and income statement to get a clearer picture of the client's current holdings, net worth, and cash flow. Let's take a look at some of these concepts and define some of the terms. (These are likely to appear in one form or another on the Series 6 examination).

**PERSONAL FINANCIAL INFORMATION.** When examining a client's personal financial information, it is important to keep in mind other aspects of the client's situation. This includes nonfinancial considerations, as well as relatives and home life circumstances. Still, the best place to start is with an analysis of the numbers.

**Income, Expenses, Discretionary Income.** All three of these items are easily extracted from the new account form we mentioned earlier, but to get a really clear picture of the client and make this data useful, it is best to construct a simple income statement. An **income statement** is a financial report that summarizes an entity's income and expenses over a given period of time. Typically, an income statement is done for a corporation (where it is also referred to as a **profit and loss statement**), but this is, nevertheless, a good exercise to help you understand your customer's financial situation. By creating an income statement that details a client's income and expenses, you can clearly see the amount of discretionary income available for investing. This **discretionary income,** arrived at by subtracting expenses from income, is sometimes referred to as **net spendable income** or **liquid net worth** because it is readily accessible. Let's look at a sample personal income statement.

**chart 1.5.2a**

| SIMPLE INCOME STATEMENT | |
|---|---|
| Chris Smith 12-01 thru 12-31 | |
| **INCOME** | |
| Salary | $55,000 |
| Interest/Investments | 8,000 |
| Other | 3,000 |
| **Total Income** | **$66,000** |
| **EXPENSES** | |
| Housing (mortg., prop. tax) | $14,000 |
| Other Debt (car, VISA, etc.) | 9,000 |
| Food | 2,700 |
| Utilities | 1,800 |
| Other | 1,000 |
| **Total Expenses** | **$27,500** |
| **Total Tax Payments** | **$20,500** |
| **NET SPENDABLE INCOME** (Income − Expenses − Tax) | **$18,000** |

Note that the income statement covers a certain period of time, not just a single date. By looking at different lines, you can perform different analysis of the client's financial situation. For example, by looking at the client's income before taxes and after taxes and doing some calculations, you can determine whether or not the client would benefit from investments that are tax-free or tax-deferred. Another thing that can be learned is how much income the client receives from a job versus how much income is received from current investments. Looking at this information in conjunction with the assets listed on a balance sheet may help you recommend investments that have the potential for better returns.

Again, remember that our example is a simple one. A company's income statement has much more detail, and it often shows income monthly or quarterly. Nevertheless, our simple example shows how analysis of a client's financial situation can reveal information to help you make suitable recommendations.

**Assets and Liabilities.** These items can be extracted from the new account form mentioned earlier and used to construct a simple balance sheet. A **balance sheet** is a financial report that shows the financial status of an entity with regard to assets, liabilities, and net worth as of a particular date. Although typically done for a company (in greater detail), nevertheless, this is a good exercise to help you understand your customer's financial situation. On one side of the page, assets are listed. **Assets** are things of value that are owned or in ones possession. Assets would include such things as cash, stocks, or real estate. On the other side of the page, liabilities are listed. **Liabilities** are any debt, financial obligation, or claim that another has on the ownership of an asset. Liabilities would include such things as credit card bills, installment loans, home mortgages, or taxes due but unpaid.

Often, though, the claim that another has on the ownership of an asset is only a partial claim. A good example of this is when a down payment is made on a house or mortgage payments have been made for a time. In both of these cases, it is likely that the person who owns the asset has some equity (ownership interest in something). Here, equity is the difference between what has been paid on an obligation and the value of the asset. So if a home is worth $100,000, but you made a down payment of $20,000 and borrowed $80,000, then we would say that the asset is worth $100,000 but the owner has a liability of $80,000 and thus has equity of $20,000. Making additional mortgage payments could increase the owner's equity. If the owner can take advantage of the equity (e.g., by taking out a home equity loan), then the owner has access to the equity. Typically, though, an asset must be sold to convert it to cash **(liquidated)**. **Liquid assets** are any assets that can be easily converted to cash. If the asset is not owned free and clear, the owner will only receive the net equity.

| SIMPLE BALANCE SHEET | |
|---|---|
| *for Chris Smith as of 12-31-02* | |
| **ASSETS** | |
| House | $175,000 |
| Car | 25,000 |
| Stocks | 75,000 |
| Checking Account | 5,000 |
| Retirement/Savings | 45,000 |
| **Total Assets** | **$325,000** |
| **LIABILITIES** | |
| Mortgage (on home) | $100,000 |
| Installment loan (car) | 20,000 |
| Credit Cards | 15,000 |
| **Total Liabilities** | **$135,000** |
| **TOTAL NET WORTH** (Assets – Liabilities) | **$190,000** |

chart 1.5.2b

While we talk about the net value of a particular asset in terms of equity, when we look at the entire financial situation of an individual or a company we use the term *net worth*. **Net worth** is the value left over after adding up all assets and subtracting all liabilities from that total. We can write the net worth formula as: **assets – liabilities = net worth.** In short, assets are what you have; liabilities are what you owe; net worth is what you own. Of course, the net worth figure could be a negative number, meaning that the person or company owes more money than it has in assets; thus, it really doesn't own anything.

Note that our sample balance sheet covers one specific date only. New assets may have been acquired or more debt may have been incurred since the date the statement was prepared. Also, remember that our example is a very simple one. A personal balance sheet would include more detail, and more items would be classified under assets, such as marketable securities (e.g., Treasury bills, CDs close to maturity, etc.) and deferred assets (e.g., annuities, retirement accounts, etc.).

Balance sheets are most helpful when they are compared with balance sheets from prior years. This gives a better picture of the trend of the person's or company's financial situation. Are they in a better or worse position now than they were a year ago? This is a good financial profile tool, and when used with an income statement, it can be helpful in determining what types of investments are suitable for a customer, what they still need to meet their objectives, and what they can afford.

**Liquidity. Liquidity** is the ease with which assets can be converted into cash. Although much investing is done for retirement or to fill other future needs, most clients will need to get to their money at one time or another before that. How often this occurs will depend on the client's job status, family situation, and lifestyle. Clients who know that their income situation is unstable, or who are close to a major purchase or expense, will likely want to have a specific amount of money readily available in liquid investments. These include regular CDs, marketable securities, money market funds, and bonds close to maturity. Stocks that trade on the major exchanges are also fairly liquid because they can be readily sold, but they carry with them some market risk because their value may be down when the client needs to sell them and get his or her money out. Highly illiquid investments would include such things as limited partnerships (because there is no secondary market for them), real estate (because of the time and expense involved in selling it), and annuities or other retirement accounts (because of the penalties for early withdrawal of funds).

Exam Topic Alert

An important point about the Series 6 exam is *never ignore liquidity considerations of a client on the test!* For example, if a test question says that your client needs money soon, or your client will need money in less than six months or in some other short period of time, look for an answer that talks about you recommending money market investments, regular bank CDs, or some other short-term investment that is not speculative and is very liquid to meet your customers needs. Any other answer would be a bad recommendation not in the best interests of your customer.

**Insurance Needs.** Insurance is also an important component of a client's overall financial plan. Unexpected disabilities can derail retirement investment plans, so disability insurance can help offset that risk. Life insurance is needed so that loved ones can continue the lifestyle they are used to without having to sell assets or cash in investments to cover expenses or pay estate taxes.

**Participation in Retirement Programs, Participation in Benefit Plans.** Most investors have two goals: save money for retirement and avoid as much taxation as possible. Many retirement plans help achieve both goals. Good retirement planning, though, requires you to know what investments clients already have and which plans they may be eligible for based on age, income, and employment status. You also need to know which individual retirement account (IRA) might be right for them, or if an annuity fits into their retirement plans. (Proper estate planning and a will are also essential so that as much as possible of an investor's money passes on to heirs instead of the government. Advise clients to seek professional advice here.)

**Tax Status.** Knowing the client's tax status is also important if you are to give suitable advice on what types of products would make good investments. An investment objective that a client wants to pursue might involve investing money in structured ways or in particular kinds of investments to minimize taxes, defer taxes, or avoid taxes altogether. Clients who wish to reduce their tax liability or offset gains in other areas have a few options at their disposal. These investment choices range from rather safe, like municipal bonds, to fairly risky, like limited partnerships. All have different tax implications. For example, municipal bonds pay interest that is free from federal income tax; IRAs (individual retirement accounts) allow pretax contributions that lower current tax liability and defer the taxes until retirement; and limited partnerships allow write-offs of only certain kinds of losses. Indexed funds, annuities, and several other kinds of IRAs beyond the standard IRA all offer different tax advantages and incentives.

An important point about the Series 6 exam is *watch the tax status of customers in test questions!* You should not recommend the sale of municipal bonds or other tax advantaged investments to clients who would not benefit from the tax savings. This is considered a violation of the "know your customer" rules. For example, if a test question talks about a client in the lowest tax bracket or who is low income, look for answers that **do not** include municipal bonds. You can only sell these types of "low tax" clients a municipal bond if the client already has a specific bond purchase in mind, gives you the specific purchase information, and explicit instructions to buy.

Exam Topic Alert

1.5.3

# Risk Tolerance of Clients

The final piece that makes up the investment profile of a customer is also perhaps one of the most important when considering what suitable recommendations to make to the client: risk tolerance and investment experience of the client. The client must fully understand the risks and be prepared to take them. Part of your job is giving advice on what risks may be appropriate given an investor's situation. But situations can and do change, so you need to continually ask questions of clients to make sure that the client's investment objectives haven't changed. Asking questions is the most important thing you can do. Let's review some of the issues and risk factors that need to be considered—and some questions you might ask to help understand the client's attitude toward risk tolerance.

**SHORT- AND LONG-TERM LIQUIDITY NEEDS.** You need to find out the client's investment goals. What is your current situation? Are your goals long-term or short-term? How liquid do you want your investments to be? What are some upcoming expenses you know you will need to take care of? What are your future plans, goals, dreams? Are you depending on these investment dollars for retirement?

**FLUCTUATIONS IN THE VALUE OF INVESTED CAPITAL.** In addition to these long-term versus short-term considerations from the client's perspective, there may also be other family considerations and situations that are important. The value of the investment could be down at a time when an emergency comes up. Does the client have adequate cash reserves to weather a storm without having to dip into this investment money? As dependents get older they require more financial assistance, is the client prepared for that? The client's goals and objectives will likely be shaped by these things and more. It is your job to understand these possibilities and help the client to have a plan in place should a need for money arise when the value of the investment is down. This could be reserves, liquid investments, or diversification, but it must be a risk consideration that is discussed, and prepared for, with the client.

**INCOME LEVEL CHANGES.** The employment status of the client and other family members also brings up important considerations. Does the client have a steady job with a regular paycheck that allows for periodic payment investments, or is the client self-employed and receives large but sporadic checks for consulting services? Are other family members dependent on the client, or are they employed and making additional income which could help pay expenses or contribute to a retirement account (or other investment)? Each of these situations would require a different investment strategy. They might also affect the client's goals. For example, the client with the steady job may want to max out retirement contributions because he is not worried about meeting monthly expenses, while the client with the consulting business may want more liquid investments so that she has ready access to cash between consulting contracts.

**PURCHASING POWER OF INCOME AND/OR PRINCIPAL.** Knowing things such as the client's age, marital status, and number of dependents is important in assessing the current and future financial needs of the client. Although purchasing power risk can't be avoided, it helps to discuss the possibilities with your clients. Let them make an informed choice about ways to invest for retirement. For example, with IRAs, tax-deferred isn't always the way to go. The longer the client has until retirement, the more aggressive the client may choose to be with a portion of the investment portfolio to try to beat inflation by a wide margin.

**ATTITUDE TOWARDS RISK.** You can get some idea of a client's risk tolerance and investment experience by looking at current investment holdings on the balance sheet. Asking clients what they have invested in before is also an important gauge of their experience. Then you can dig deeper with more questions. How much can you afford to invest? Is this money risk capital? Do you have other investments earmarked for retirement? What will you do if an investment doesn't pan out?

# 1.6 Investment Company Profile/Risk Characteristics

**Investment companies** are firms that assemble a pool of funds from small investors, invest those funds for the group, and collect a management fee for services. Investment companies are formed like any other corporation, with shares available to investors. Investors who own shares in the investment company, also own part of the large joint investment account created by the pool of money from all the investors.

**Mutual funds** are a pooled investment, managed by an investment company, offering an undivided interest in the portfolio to holders of shares in the fund. The three main advantages to a mutual fund are liquidity, diversification, and professional management. Mutual fund objectives can range from very aggressive growth funds to income funds to more conservative funds that have capital preservation as their main objective. Mutual fund types can also be segregated by portfolio composition. Sometimes the composition of the portfolio is set up to mirror an objective. Other times, maintaining the unique composition of the portfolio is the objective. Let's look at a few of these.

# 1.6.1 Money Market

**Money market funds** invest in money market instruments, such as short-term notes, commercial paper, banker's acceptance, repurchase agreements, government securities close to maturity, and T-bills trading in the secondary market. Money market funds serve as a good way to preserve capital while providing liquidity. Often fund-holders can write checks against their money market fund accounts (but usually with restrictions as to number, frequency, or amount).

# Income

**Income funds** invest primarily in preferred stocks and bonds. Generally, if income potential is preferred by an investor, then there is less potential for growth of capital. By looking to acquire high-yielding stocks and bonds, utility company stocks, and blue chips that consistently pay dividends, the fund can meet its objectives of providing income. This type of fund is best suited for investors who need cash flow or near-term funds, perhaps for retirement.

# Growth

**Growth funds** invest a greater portion of their assets in higher risk company stocks, such as high-tech, or in other industries that appear poised for growth. Growth companies often do not pay dividends because they reinvest profits in R and D to fuel their growth. Growth funds are also sometimes referred to as **diversified common stock funds** because of their emphasis on stocks to achieve the fund's primary objective of capital growth. This type of fund is best suited for money that will not be used for retirement or other expenses until well into the future so that the money has time to grow.

# Growth/Income

**Balanced funds** seek to have the areas of growth *and* income covered by investing in common stock, preferred stock, bonds, and cash in order to achieve the highest returns with high stability. A typical structure would be about half stock and half bonds, with perhaps 5% of the assets in cash. This allocation would be adjusted as market conditions change, based on a preset formula. These funds try to balance growth and income by diversifying the portfolio not only with different investment vehicles, but also across different industries, and in various regions of the country.

# Aggressive Growth

**Aggressive growth funds** invest most (if not all) of their assets in stocks of rapidly growing companies. These funds have capital appreciation as their sole goal. Because of the composition of their investment portfolio, the fund is more risky and share prices are very volatile. Aggressive growth funds are also sometimes referred to as **capital appreciation funds** because of their emphasis on stocks that have the potential to rise rapidly ahead of the broad market.

1.6.6

# Bonds

**Bond funds** invest in various types of bonds that have different maturities to meet the objectives of the fund. Certainly, income is one objective, but there can be others. Funds investing in **corporate bonds** can seek different yields based on bond quality. Funds investing in **U.S. government bonds** exclusively can offer safer income, with staggered maturities to offer different payout schedules to investors. Funds investing in **tax-exempt municipal bonds** can offer tax-free income, because tax advantages flow through to the investors.

1.6.7

# Specialized

**Specialized mutual funds** invest in only one industry, type of company, or other unique category. Although shares tend to be very volatile, they offer investors a high-risk high-reward opportunity. They are a "pure play" that offers investors a chance to get into a specialized investment area with the benefit of professional management. A myriad of specialized categories exist. Here are a few examples.

> ▷ **Industry sector funds** invest in companies that are in a particular industry or "sector" of the economy. A sector could be chosen because it is thought to have high growth potential (e.g., high-tech), or a sector may be chosen because it is a cyclical or countercyclical sector (e.g., energy, gold).

Although sector funds offer the potential of high returns or can act as a hedge for other investments, *on the Series 6 exam, do not put beginning investors into a sector fund.*

Exam Topic Alert

> ▷ **Geographic concentration funds** invest in company stocks or muni bonds that are from a certain area of the country. A region could be chosen because it is thought to be going through a period of high growth, to take advantage of tax incentives, or for other reasons. These are also called **regional funds.**

> ▷ **Special situation funds** invest in common stocks that are undervalued for a short time but are about to rise significantly because of an upcoming event. This could be a pending merger or acquisition, new management team, or a new product introduction. Usually these situations are short-lived since it's difficult to get in early, and investors reacting to the news drive the stock price up. Special situation funds are risky also—the news could drive the stock price down if it's received unfavorably by investors or the event doesn't occur.

> ▷ **Asset allocation funds** are balanced funds that have multiple asset classes. This type of fund not only invests in different kinds of stocks (e.g., small cap, large cap),

but also will tilt its asset balance between stocks, bonds, and cash much more heavily (perhaps as high as 80% stock at one time, 80% bonds another) depending on market conditions, but without a preset formula.

▷ **International funds** invest in companies from a certain area of the world. A region is chosen for the type of industries or growth potential.

▷ **Mortgage-backed security funds** are funds devoted to investing in various types of mortgage-backed securities to generate income. Fund assets may consist of Ginnie Maes, CMOs, etc. The fund shares the same risk as the underlying security, but the impact is lessened via diversification of holdings.

# 1.X Summary

**1.1** Investing is using money to make money. Securities are investment relationships with company or government; instruments representing an investment. Can be stock (ownership), bond (debt), mutual fund (pool), option (future right).

**1.1.1** Equity = ownership. Stock can be authorized, issued, outstanding, treasury. Treasury stock can't vote or get dividends. Issued – Treasury = Outstanding. Stock price is driven by supply and demand (market value). Stock split: adjust stock price downward by increasing outstanding shares—current stockholders keep same ownership percentage: more shares, less money per share. Reverse split: decrease shares to raise price (so they won't get delisted).

Common stock is company ownership, limited liability. Rights: earnings, dividend, voting, preemptive (antidilution), access to books, residual claim to assets. Dividends: distribution of company earnings to stockholders by board vote. Voting: board of directors, dilution issues, change in company direction, splits. Voting can be statutory (1 share = 1 vote), or cumulative (total shares voted for one director); proxies (absentee voting); nonvoting classes of stock exist.

Preferred stock is company ownership that pays a specified dividend rate. Limited liability, no voting, no preemptive rights, no capital appreciation. Has priority over common stock for dividends and asset claims in bankruptcy. Kinds of preferred: cumulative (unpaid is future liability), noncumulative, participating (bonuses), nonparticipating, convertible (trade for common stock at fixed price), callable (can redeem early), sinking fund, adjust. rate.

Debt securities are mainly bonds. Can be bearer or registered. Bearer have coupons, so interest rate is called coupon rate (or nominal rate or stated rate). Corporate bonds, backed by issuer, par = $1000. Ownership: bearer, registered, registered coupon, and book entry. Interest paid semiannually, redeemable at par at maturity. Corporate bonds have term maturities (all due at once). Need indenture agreement: between corporation and trustee, *not* corporation and bondholder.

Corporate bonds rated by Moody's, S&P. Investment grade (a.k.a., bank grade) are four highest ratings for each. S&P = all capital letters; Moody's = upper, lowercase. Bonds also called fixed-income securities. Secured bonds are mortgage bonds and equipment trust certificates. Unsecured bonds are also called debentures, and include income/adjustment bonds and guaranteed bonds. Zero coupons sold at discount, pay no interest, redeem at face value—no reinvestment risk.

Redeeming bonds: at maturity, calling, tender offer, refunding, conversion. Convertible bonds can be exchanged for common stock at preset price. Parity is when bond value = stock price. Convertible bond and stock usually move in tandem, but stock can drop lower since bond has yield value to support price. If callable, company may pay call premium; holder may get call protection period.

Derivative security has value dependent on underlying security (e.g., option). Rights offering: offer new shares to existing stockholders before public (due to preemptive rights); subscription price is usually lower than price to public; standby underwriting—guarantee to company, underwriter buys all unsold shares). Warrants are future right to buy stock at preset price; given as a sweetener.

**1.1.1+**  Options give holder the right, but not obligation, to do something (buy or sell). Call buyer has option to buy; put buyer has option to sell. Strike price is price holder can exercise option. Exercise means make use of right before it expires. Option price called premium. buyer = owner = holder = long; seller = writer = short.

Mortgage-backed securities pass through principal and interest payments o investors. Ginnie Maes are mortgage-backed, pass-through certificates, backed by U.S. government. Reinvestment risk is high. CMOs (collateralized mortgage obligations) pass through principal and interest payments. CMOs put into tranches (groups), offer staggered maturity dates. CMOs have four risks: interest rate (lower rates = refinance), prepayment (if paid off early need replacement investment), extension (late payments), and repayment (default). CMO is rather safe because backed by mortgages but not backed by U.S. government ADRs are foreign stock sold in United States—no SEC, banks hold, no voting, less liquid.

**1.1.2**  U.S. government bonds are called Treasuries. All kinds use book entry registration. T-bills: 1 year or less, $10,000 face, quoted at a discount from par (no interest); bid price is higher than ask price because quoted at a discount from par. T-notes: 1-10 years, $1000 face, quoted as percent of par, 1/32 increment. T-bonds: 10+ years, $1000 face, quoted as percent of par, 1/32 increment. STRIPS are U.S. government backed zero coupon bonds; T-receipts not government backed.

U.S. government agencies, entities issue debt to help certain groups lower borrowing costs (e.g., farmers, students). Ginnie Maes are pass-through certificates, securitized by mortgages, backed by U.S. government. Reinvestment risk is high. Nonmarketable securities include Series EE savings bonds (sold at discount, all interest paid at maturity, federal tax due can be deferred till maturity); Series HH bonds (get by trading in EE bonds, interest paid semiannually, federal tax due on interest); Series I bonds (interest paid at maturity, rate adjusted for inflation every six months, can defer federal tax due till maturity).

**1.1.3**  Municipal securities: debt of state or local governments. Most are tax exempt. Municipal issuers (but not dealer) are exempt from SEC rules (except fraud). Muni interest rates are usually lower because they offer tax advantages.

General obligation (GO) bonds are repaid with tax dollars; backed by full faith and credit of issuer; voter approval may be needed, legal limits on indebtedness must be observed; safest because of municipality's taxing authority. Revenue bonds repaid from project revenues (income), not taxes; feasibility study needed; may have indenture agreement with flow of funds statement. Industrial revenue bonds paid by company lease payments, not taxes (so have company's credit rating); feasibility study needed; most risky muni bond; not tax exempt.

Unqualified legal opinion tells investor that bonds are eligible for tax exempt. Taxable equivalent yield is formula that shows investor how much less of a rate is acceptable on tax-exempt muni bonds compared to taxable corporate bonds.

**1.1.4**  Money market instruments are short-term debt obligations (1 year or less): T-bills (when trading in the secondary market), CDs (only jumbo $100,000+ face value are negotiable), commercial paper (issued by corp., NOT banks), banker's acceptances (time drafts, used like a letter of credit for exports).

**1.2**  Primary market is for new issues. Primary offering: money goes to company; secondary offering: money goes to shareholders (company founders, insiders). Secondary market for equities is exchange or OTC. Third market is OTC by nonmembers—usually large institutional investors to save commissions. Fourth market is Instinet—direct computerized trades among institutional investors. Instinet is registered with SEC as an exchange.

**1.2.1**  Exchange markets are double auction (constantly get buy and sell price information). NYSE specialist keeps orderly market; buys/sells from own account if needed. NYSE is centralized trading floor, approves members, watches for fraud.

**1.2.2**  NASDAQ, OTC are negotiated markets (bid and ask prices are negotiated between investors and market makers). Market maker must be ready to give firm quote to buy/sell round lots (100 shares). Can do subject quotes, workout. Markets are decentralized. NASDAQ computerized market has three levels.

**1.2.3**  Sale of a new stock issue (in the primary market) uses investment bankers, underwriters. Investment banker is broker-dealer who underwrites new issues. New stock issue is an initial public offering (IPO). Primary offering: money to company; secondary offering: money to shareholders (company founders, insiders). Syndicate is a purchase group of underwriters. Commitments for the sale of the securities can be firm (guaranteed) or best efforts.

**1.2.4** Various market terms are used for exchange and OTC trades. Trade date is the day a trade is authorized and executed. Settlement date is when securities are paid for or securities are delivered to the broker-dealer to complete a trade. Settlement rules: Reg. T is T+5, so NASD, NYSE are T+3 to give two day cushion to catch and fix problems. Cash settlement is same day; regular way is T+3 (except government securities—regular way is T+1). Delivery can be delayed, seller's option, buyer's option, as mutually agreed—need written contract.

Good delivery: good physical condition, proper endorsement, timely delivery. Proper endorsement includes all signatures, power of attorney, other documents. Stocks must also be round lots of 100 shares; bonds need $1000 or $5000 face. Ex-date is last day one can buy stock with time to settle transaction and be owner of record to receive dividends. Payment date is the day dividend is paid.

**1.2.5** Securities price can be market value (determined by supply and demand on an exchange), or bid/ask (negotiated between buyer and seller for NASDAQ, OTC). Bid = wholesale = investor sells; Ask = offer price = retail = investor buys. Mutual funds use NAV (net asset value—value of all assets, minus liabilities, divided by number of outstanding shares). NAV = Bid = investor sells back/redeems. POP (public offering price is NAV + sales charges). POP = Ask = investor buys.

Can buy bonds at par (face value), premium (above face), discount (below face). OID (original issue discount) bond is sold below par when new. Bond price has inverse relationship with bond yield. Nominal yield is interest rate (coupon rate) on bond's face. Current yield (CY) is coupon rate divided by bond price. Yield-to-maturity (YTM) is total return to investor if bond is held to maturity. High bond price (premium) = low CY,YTM; low bond price (discount) = high CY,YTM.

**1.3** Business cycle is swings in the economy: expansion, peak, contraction, trough. (Remember: EPCoT). Supply and demand seek balance. Expansion is rise in production, demand, prices, stocks. Contraction is fall in demand, production. Recession is two consecutive quarters of declining GDP. Gross Domestic Product (GDP) is value of all goods and services produced in United States (may also see GNP on test, which includes net foreign investment).

**1.3.1** Inflation can be cost (passing along price increases) or demand (too much money, too few goods). Consumer Price Index (CPI) is an inflation adjuster. CPI measures fixed cost of market basket of goods: includes food, transportation, energy, housing, clothing.

Bond prices affected by business cycle due to inflation, interest rates, yields. Expansion = rates rise, bond prices fall. Contraction = rates fall, bonds rise. Equities prices are affected by business cycle because expansion equals rising profits, which equals rising stock prices. Contraction equals falling profits, which equals falling stock prices. Some stocks are very sensitive to cycles (e.g., autos), others are countercyclical because demand is constant (e.g., food). Interest-rate-sensitive stocks include banks and utilities. Stock price = present discounted value of expected future profits.

**1.3.2** Monetary policy: government mechanism to control supply and cost of money. Federal Reserve (Fed) affects interest rates by adjusting money supply through open market operations (buy and sell securities to hit target Fed funds rate), discount rates (rate charged for member bank loans), reserve requirements (money banks must keep in their accounts), margin requirements (Reg. T.). If more money is available, rates should fall; if less money, rates should rise. Fed does not set prime rate. Reserve require = largest effect, margin = smallest.

**1.3.3** Fiscal policy: government plan for spending, taxation, and debt management. Taxes can affect investment decisions—sometimes having unintended consequences (e.g., Tax Reform Act of 1986 devalued some real estate). Deficit is federal spending exceeding revenue—Treasury issues bonds to cover.

**1.3.4** International economic factors include balance of payments (difference between all goods and services sold); exchange rates (weak dollar helps foreign countries buy exports, strong dollar makes imports cheaper and attracts foreign investment); interest rates can bring in investment money but is offset by exchange rates.

**1.4** Risk of principal is the chance that invested capital will decrease in value. Investment risk is chance that adverse conditions will affect relative value.

**1.4.1** Credit risk = repayment risk = financial risk—company fails, can't pay debts. Interest rate risk—changes in interest rates will adversely affect investment. Inflationary risk = purchasing power risk—chance that value of asset will decline, relative to other goods or services (i.e., not keep pace with inflation). Timing risk—investor may need cash when value is down. (Never ignore liquidity concerns on exam!) Taxability risk—risk of changes in tax law. Market risk = systematic risk—drop in value due to broad market conditions. Political risk—foreign (e.g., nationalization); Legislative risk—domestic laws. Currency risk = exchange risk—foreign currency price fluctuations.

**1.4.2** Risk tolerance: greater risk = greater reward. Diversification is important. Financial pyramid: safety at base (biggest part), high risk on top (smallest). Cannot assume every investor has same objectives for his or her portfolio. Long versus short risk, balance of risk-reward: all investments have risk. Safe short-term investments (e.g., CDs) have risk of low return. Safe long-term investments (e.g., stocks) have market risk (low price when need to sell).

Portfolio diversification spreads risk over entire financial pyramid. Defensive investing: bonds, blue chip, utilities. Aggressive: high-tech, margin.

**1.5** Client profile is financial and nonfinancial. Must consider client's available capital, current holdings, risk tolerance, investment experience. Making unsuitable recommendations is violation of NASD rules.

**1.5.1** Client's investment objectives are learned by listening and analyzing data. Preservation of capital requires safety: CDs, money market funds, fixed annuities, high-grade bonds, government securities. (e.g., for people near retirement) Current income to generate cash now: bonds (watch ratings), mortgage-backed securities (Ginnie Maes), preferred stock, utility stock, REIT (risky). Capital growth for long-term appreciation: common stock (blue chips), mutual funds (can spread risk), direct real estate investment (more risky).

**1.5.2** Financial considerations: income, debt, own home, insurance, taxes, credit. Nonfinancial considerations: age, marriage, dependents, job, tax status, will.

Personal financial information includes income, expenses, discretionary income. Income statement summarizes income and expenses over a period of time; thus, it shows net spendable income (liquid net worth) available for investing. Balance sheet shows assets, liabilities, net worth as of a certain date. Assets − Liabilities = Net Worth. Equity is difference between value of asset and what is owed. Don't put clients in munis if client is in low tax bracket.

**1.5.3** Client's family situation is most likely to change, necessitating a change in investment strategy. As client gains investing experience, they can try new things. Portfolio diversification spreads risk over entire financial pyramid. Need to consider client's short-term and long-term liquidity needs. Liquidity is ease of converting assets to cash: money market investments, CDs, short-term investments. Never ignore liquidity needs in test questions.

Must ensure that fluctuations in the value of investments won't interfere with client's needs (i.e., don't put retirement money in volatile investments). Also, purchasing power of income is more important closer to retirement.

**1.6** Investment companies are firms that assemble a pool of funds from small investors, invest those funds for the group, and collect a management fee. Mutual funds are a pooled investment, managed by an investment company, offering an undivided interest in the portfolio to holders of shares in the fund. Three main advantages to a mutual fund are liquidity, diversification, and professional management. Mutual fund objectives can range from very aggressive growth funds to income funds to more conservative funds.

**1.6.1** Money market funds invest in money market instruments—short-term notes, commercial paper, banker's acceptance, repurchase agreements, T-bills. Preserves capital, provide liquidity—client can write checks against account.

**1.6.2** Income funds invest in preferred stocks and bonds, with some utility stocks or blue-chip stocks paying dividends. For investors who need cash flow.

**1.6.3** Growth funds invest in higher risk company stocks, such as high-tech or other growth industries. Companies reinvest in R&D, so often no dividends.

**1.6.4** Growth and income funds allocate the portfolio between stocks, bonds, and cash. Diversification of the portfolio changes with market conditions. These are called balanced funds if they have a preset formula for the asset composition of the portfolio, or called asset allocation funds if there's no preset formula.

**1.6.5** Aggressive growth funds invest in stock of rapidly growing companies. Often referred to as capital appreciation funds.

**1.6.6** Bond funds have debt securities with different objectives. Their portfolio may focus on corporates (with different yields), U.S. government bonds (with staggered maturities), or munis (with income exempt from federal taxes).

**1.6.7** Specialized funds invest in only one industry, type of fund, or other category. Industry sector funds specialize in an industry (e.g., high-tech, cyclical, etc.). Geographic funds focus on one area of country or high-growth region. Special situation funds buy undervalued stock (e.g., merger target, etc.) Asset allocation fund has multiple asset classes; tilt heavily based on market. International funds look for growth industries or regions in the world. Mortgage-backed security funds diversify with many different types of CMOs and Ginnie Mae investments.

# Chapter 1 Review Quiz

1. Market value of stock is determined by
   a. the issuing company.
   b. the underwriter.
   c. supply and demand.
   d. par value listed on the certificate.

2. Which of these risks refers to a decline in the value of assets relative to prices?
   a. capital risk
   b. purchasing power risk
   c. interest rate risk
   d. systematic risk

3. Which of the following types of stock is NOT eligible to vote?
   a. authorized and outstanding
   b. issued and outstanding
   c. outstanding
   d. treasury

4. Which of the following would be voted on by shareholders?
   a. decision on stock buy-back
   b. merger and acquisition activity
   c. dividend payments
   d. board of directors' salaries

5. Which of the following helps a company fulfill its preemptive rights obligation?
   a. warrants
   b. standby underwriting
   c. preferred stock
   d. banker's acceptance time draft

6. An example of countercyclical stock would be
   a. IPO stocks.
   b. housing stocks.
   c. high-tech stocks.
   d. food stocks.

7. Preferred stock
   a. pays a dividend.
   b. confers preemptive rights.
   c. gives stockholder voting rights.
   d. all of the above

8. The value of a derivative security is dependent on all of the following, EXCEPT
   a. value of the underlying security.
   b. market conditions.
   c. expiration of the derivative.
   d. interest rate paid on bonds.

9. Which of the following are NOT backed by the full faith and credit of U.S. government?
   a. T-bills
   b. U.S. Treasury notes and Treasury bonds
   c. Treasury Receipts
   d. STRIPS

10. When bonds are purchased at a discount, this means that
    a. the investor paid a premium price for the bond.
    b. the purchase price is the same as the face amount.
    c. the purchase price is more than the face amount.
    d. the purchase price is less than the face amount.

11. Which of the following bonds are backed by the full faith and credit of U.S. government?
    a. Sallie Maes
    b. Ginnie Maes
    c. Freddie Macs
    d. Fannie Maes

12. A collateralized mortgage obligation is
    a. backed by a pool of mortgages.
    b. is divided into tranches.
    c. both a and b.
    d. neither a nor b.

13. An indenture agreement is required for which of the following?
    a. corporate bonds
    b. municipal bonds
    c. both a and b.
    d. neither a nor b.

14. Calculating conversion parity is important for corporate bonds because
    a. investors want to know when the call protection period has expired.
    b. investors need to know if they should convert the bond to common stock.
    c. investors need to watch for interest rate fluctuations.
    d. investors know a falling stock price moves in tandem with bond prices.

15. What does it mean when a bond is stamped ex-legal?
    a. the issue is not legal to buy
    b. the interest is definitely tax-exempt
    c. the issuer chose not to have a legal opinion done for the bond
    d. the previous lawyer who reviewed the documents approved them

16. Whose highest bond rating is Aaa?
    a. Moody's
    b. S&P's
    c. Fitch's
    d. Washington, D.C.

17. Which of the following is NOT a money market instrument?
    a. repurchase agreement
    b. commercial paper
    c. banker's acceptance
    d. standard CDs

18. Diversification in bond holdings could entail
    a. buying bonds from different parts of the country.
    b. buying some revenue bonds and some GO bonds.
    c. buying different bond maturity dates.
    d. all of the above

19. When the price of a bond is higher than the coupon rate, then the bond is
    a. trading at a premium.
    b. trading at a discount.
    c. trading at par.
    d. trading flat.

20. Taxable equivalent yield tells an investor
    a. how much higher of a yield is required on municipal bonds.
    b. how much lower of a yield is required on corporate bonds.
    c. how much tax the investor will pay on municipal bonds.
    d. how much lower of a yield is acceptable with tax-exempt bonds.

21. A recession is defined as
    a. two consecutive years of decline in GDP.
    b. increase in business activity following a recovery period.
    c. the part of the business cycle that immediately follows expansion.
    d. two consecutive quarters of decline in GDP.

22. The Consumer Price Index
    a. measures housing starts.
    b. measures the fixed cost of a market basket of goods.
    c. is a good indicator of future gasoline prices.
    d. is a direct function of the GDP.

23. The method most used by the Fed to adjust interest rates is
    a. open market operations.
    b. adjustment of discount rates.
    c. reserve requirements.
    d. margin requirements.

24. Which of the following is best for U.S. exports?
    a. negative balance of trade
    b. capital account surplus
    c. strong dollar
    d. weak dollar

25. A balance sheet
    a. is good for one full year from the date it was prepared.
    b. covers the date it was prepared for only.
    c. tells about the year preceding the date it was prepared.
    d. is good for the month or year stated only.

26. An income statement
    a. is good for one full year from the date it was prepared.
    b. covers the date it was prepared only.
    c. tells about the future income potential.
    d. is good for the time period stated at the top only.

27. A client you've been advising has done very well with a high-tech stock fund that you recommended. The client refers some friends to invest with you. You should
    a. immediately put them in the same investments as the client who referred them.
    b. advise them to put money in cash because they look like older people who want safe investments for retirement.
    c. have them fill out a new client form and ask them questions about their investment objectives and experience.
    d. turn away the business because it is a conflict of interest.

28. When advising a client, which investment objective is the most important?
    a. preservation of capital (safety of principal)
    b. current income
    c. capital growth
    d. whichever the client tells you is most important

29. A client comes in and complains that he doesn't like to pay taxes and does everything in his power to pay as little of his money to the government as possible. The client tells you that he is in the lowest tax bracket, then says he wants to buy Missouri dam project bond fund because he's familiar with the issue. You should
    a. put all of the clients money into tax-exempt municipal bond funds since he doesn't like to pay taxes.
    b. help the client buy the Missouri dam project bond fund because he asked for it by name, but also explain to him that his tax situation does not necessarily warrant buying additional tax-exempt mutual funds.
    c. avoid recommending Treasury funds of any kind since the client doesn't like to give any of his money to the government.
    d. recommend that the client instead put his money into risky tax-sheltered limited partnerships so he can avoid taxes.

30. A client tells you that she will begin studying for her Ph.D. in six months and will need to pull her money out then, but in the meantime, she wants to make her investment grow as much as possible. You should
    a. immediately put the client's money into a high-growth stock fund.
    b. tell the client that she is best off keeping her money in cash.
    c. recommend that a portion of the funds go into money market funds and that some of the money should go into other liquid investments.
    d. advise the client to put money into long-term Treasury fund so the money will be safe and she can get higher yields than short-term securities.

# 2

# Investment Companies, Taxation, and Customer Accounts

*This chapter focuses on some of the products you will sell as a Limited Representative. Investment companies offer many different products, and you will need to have comprehensive knowledge of what is available so that you can make sound recommendations to clients. Most of this chapter is devoted to mutual funds, because that is where the greatest variety of products is available—and where the largest sales volume comes from for a typical Limited Representative.*

*When you have finished studying this chapter, you should have a good understanding of how investment companies work, as well as the various products they offer. Along with this knowledge, you will learn some basic tax issues and customer account handling. You will certainly not become a tax expert (and you should never pass yourself off as such), but there is a certain level of background information that you need to talk intelligently with clients—and know when to advise them to seek professional help. Finally, customer account basics are important for the Series 6 exam, although be aware that your employing member firm will likely have additional or different policies and procedures for you to follow.*

*As you study this chapter, keep in mind that mutual funds are the most heavily tested topic on the Series 6 exam. This chapter ("Investment Companies, Taxation, and Customer Accounts") represents about 36% of the total test: approximately 36 questions of the total 100 questions on the Series 6 exam.*

## This chapter will be broken up into four sections:

**2.1 Investment Companies.** This first section introduces the three basic types of investment companies, before explaining the differences between closed-end and open-end management companies. The rest of this section goes into much detail about mutual funds, their structure, functions, types of funds, characteristics, policies, requirements, purchasing, redemption and other mutual fund issues.

**2.2 Federal Income Tax Regulations for Mutual Funds.** This section looks at various tax issues. Some are specific to mutual funds, while others apply to many types of investments. These comparisons and contrasts are important test topics.

**2.3 Customer Accounts.** This section discusses the mechanics of customer accounts—opening accounts, documentation, ownership—providing a solid foundation for specific broker-dealer policies that will be encountered in the real world.

**2.4 Contractual Plan, Periodic Payment Plan.** This section explains characteristics of contractual plans, their requirements (including prospectus issues), and how they operate. Periodic payment plans offered by mutual funds are also mentioned, pointing out similarities and differences with contractual plans.

**Load:** a sales charge added to the price of an investment. Also called **sales charge.** Can be a front-end load, back-end load, or one of several other load options. Load is the cost of buying a fund. Compare: **expense ratio.**

**Mutual fund:** a pooled investment, managed by an investment company, offering an undivided interest in the portfolio to holders of shares in the fund.

**Net asset value (NAV):** the value of a fund and its shares, derived by taking a fund's assets minus liabilities, then dividing that result by the number of outstanding shares. Formula: NAV = (Fund Assets − Fund Liabilities) ÷ Number of Outstanding Shares. NAV is the bid price at which mutual fund shares are redeemed. ("wholesale") Compare: **public offering price.**

**Public offering price (POP):** the price of buying a mutual fund share, derived by taking the NAV and adding sales charges. Formula: POP = NAV + Sales Charges. POP is the ask price at which mutual fund shares are purchased. ("retail") Compare: **net asset value.**

# 2.1

# Investment Companies

**Investment companies** are firms that assemble a pool of funds from small investors, invest those funds for the group, and collect a management fee for services. Investment companies are formed like any other corporation, with shares available to investors. Investors who own shares in the investment company, also own part of the large joint investment account created by the pool of money from all the investors.

# 2.1.1

# Types of Investment Companies

The **Investment Company Act of 1940** divides the various types of investment companies into three groups: unit investment trusts, face amount certificates, and management companies. Management companies are the most common of the three, and we will spend a good deal of time analyzing these. The main distinguishing feature, as the name implies, is that management companies have a manager responsible for actively managing the company's investment portfolio. Mutual funds fall into this group. Unit investment trust companies, on the other hand, have a fixed portfolio that investors put their money into, so there is no need for a portfolio manager. Face amount certificate companies are the least diversified of the three, because their portfolio of investments contains debt instruments only, with shares in the pool issued by the face amount certificate company. Let's look at all three.

## 2.1.1.1 Unit Investment Trust

A **unit investment trust (UIT)** is an investment company that invests in a fixed portfolio of securities. If the securities are bonds, then usually the UIT will dissolve when the bonds mature. If the securities are stocks, then the UIT dissolves on a specified date. Holders of a UIT own an undivided interest in the investment portfolio of the company.

**Fixed Portfolio.** Having a fixed portfolio means that UIT companies do not actively trade the securities in their portfolio. Because of this, UITs do not have a need for Investment Advisors, resulting in no management fees and low sales charges. UITs also do not have a board of directors. Instead, matters are voted on by shareholders.

**Redeemability.** The Investment Company Act of 1940 requires UITs to redeem shares from investors at current NAV. This is important for investors since there is *no secondary market trading* of UIT shares. UITs are good vehicles for investors who want to use a periodic payment plan to withdraw funds on a regular schedule.

## 2.1.1.2 Face Amount Certificate

A **face amount certificate** is a debt instrument representing a share in the pool of bonds and debt securities the face amount certificate company holds in its portfolio. Only a face amount certificate company may issue these certificates. This type of investment was authorized by the Investment Company Act of 1940, but few exist today because tax law changes made them less attractive.

**Debt Instrument.** The shares issued by a face amount certificate company are obligations to pay a fixed amount on a specific date. As such, the certificates are usually bought at a discount from their par face value and appreciate until maturity. *Deposits in periodic installments or single payment* can be used to purchase the face amount certificates from the investment company. The investor receives a *predetermined rate of interest* by getting the certificate's face value at maturity, but no periodic interest payments. Still, the investor owes tax each year on the imputed interest (the increase in value of the investment each year from the discounted price up to full maturity value.)

## 2.1.1.3 Management Companies: Closed-End

**Closed-end investment companies** are management companies that offer a fixed number of shares to investors and use the funds raised to operate a packaged security. Shares of the closed-end fund trade on an exchange, and this serves as the vehicle for investors to buy and sell their positions after the initial offering. Closed-end investment companies operate just like any other company, except that the company's business is to make money through investments rather than products or services.

**Capitalization.** A closed-end investment company is usually capitalized through a **one-time public offering of shares.** The company issues stock to raise capital and then hires a money manager to manage the company's investments. The company is considered "closed-end" because after the initial offering of shares to the public, the fund is closed out and no further investments are accepted. After the initial offering, *the value of shares fluctuate with market demand.* Investors who want to invest in the company do so by buying shares of the fund in the open market; investors who want to cash out their position do so by selling their shares in the open market.

**Trading in shares takes place on an exchange or OTC.** Only full shares may be bought and sold. This is all very different from open-end management companies, as we will see in the next section. Also, a closed-end company may issue additional common stock, preferred stock, or bonds at some point in the future, but it must go through the SEC registration process again. This is because the closed-end company *does not continuously redeem shares held by investors.* Remember, shares are traded in the open market after the initial offering. By contrast, open-end investment companies only have one kind of stock which is part of a continuous stock offering.

# 2.1.1.4 Management Companies: Open-End

**Open-end investment companies** are management companies that continually offer shares to investors and use the funds raised to operate a packaged security, such as a mutual fund. The goals of open-end companies are similar to those of closed-end companies: raise capital through an offering, hire a money manager to manage the company's investments, and make money through investments.

**Continuous Offering of Shares.** Because an open-end investment company does a continuous offering of shares, it must always use a prospectus when selling shares. This is much different than the requirement for shares of a closed-end fund, which

---

**chart 2.1.1**

**COMPARISON OF CLOSED-END VS. OPEN-END MANAGEMENT COMPANIES**

| Closed-End | Open-End |
|---|---|
| • fixed number of shares | • variable number of shares (no limit) |
| • can issue more stock, bonds, etc., but need to reregister with SEC | • only one type of stock permitted because it's a continuous primary offer |
| • only give out prospectus at initial offering | • must always give out prospectus |
| • buy and sell on exchange (after offering) | • can only buy from, and redeem through, issuer |
| • can only purchase whole shares | • partial shares can be purchased |
| • price is supply and demand (after offering) | • public offering price (NAV + sales charge) |

trade in the secondary market with no prospectus. Another important difference is that because the open-end company does a continuous offering, the fund can continue to grow over time. In other words, the number of shares in an open-end investment company varies. As the fund sells more shares, it absorbs this new money and puts it to work to buy more assets for the benefit of everyone in the fund.

**Redeemability.** Shares of the open-end fund can only be sold and redeemed by the particular fund that issued them. The open-end structure allows investors to buy partial shares, since they are only offered by the fund itself. Since the open-end company is the only outlet for selling the shares, the Investment Company Act of 1940 dictates that an open-end investment company must redeem shares within seven calendar days after they are tendered by the investor.

## 2.1.1.5 Diversified and Nondiversified Companies

Under the Investment Company Act of 1940, a **diversified investment company** is defined as an investment company that has no more than 5% of its assets in any one company or bond, no more than 10% of the voting shares of any one company, and 75% or more of its total assets must be invested. This 5-10-75 standard applies to open-end or closed-end companies. Also, an investment company that specializes in one sector or industry is still considered "diversified" if it meets the 5-10-75 standard. Any investment company that does not meet this standard is considered nondiversified.

2.1.2

# Open-End Mutual Funds

The most common open-end investment company vehicle is the mutual fund. **Mutual funds** are a pooled investment managed by an investment company offering an undivided interest in the portfolio to holders of shares in the fund. We'll explore the structure and characteristics of mutual funds in the next few sections.

## 2.1.2.1 General Concept

Investment companies offer many different kinds of **packaged securities** created by combining several other investments One of the most popular packaged securities is the mutual fund. It's a good way for small investors to pool their money and benefit from a larger, more diversified, and professionally managed portfolio.

For the Series 6 exam, you should know *the three main advantages of mutual funds are liquidity, diversification, and professional management.*

Exam Topic Alert

**Investment Portfolio.** The investment portfolio of a mutual fund is what gives the fund its diversification. Mutual funds offer an **undivided interest** in the portfolio to holders of shares in the fund. In fact, this undivided interest is where the name *mutual* fund comes from. Mutual funds, like mutual insurance and other mutual companies, have shared ownership with profits distributed among the members. Investment companies are set up to offer direct returns to investors, allowing them to share in the gains and losses of the portfolio.

**Diversification** within the investment portfolio can be very broad or very narrow depending on the objectives of the fund. A mutual fund can be diversified by:

▷ industry (e.g., high-tech stocks)
▷ type of investment instruments (e.g., only bonds)
▷ issuers (e.g., various corporate securities)
▷ geographic areas (e.g., one city or region)

A fund can also choose to be nondiversified by holding a heavy concentration of investments in a certain company or keep too large a portion of its portfolio in cash.

**Professional Management.** Professional management is an advantage of mutual funds because it offers small investors access to money managers and experts specializing in different types of investments. Fund managers are hired to help reach *investment objectives of the mutual fund,* from very aggressive growth funds to income funds to more conservative funds with capital preservation as their main objective. In each case, the fund manager not only looks at having the correct mix of securities in the portfolio to achieve the objective, but also the timing of the investment decisions to try and maximize the fund's effectiveness.

**Timing of investment decisions** is more than just buying low and selling high. Getting in and out at the right time is important, but even a professional manager can't know for certain when a particular investment has peaked or bottomed out. Nevertheless, professional fund managers are relied upon to make informed decisions about which way the market is going, the future outlook for an entire industry, and the outlook for a particular company. All of these analyses depend on knowledge and research by a full-time professional manager with experience in a given area.

Exam Topic
Alert

**Tax status of fund distributions** must also be considered by the fund manager when making buy or sell decisions for the investment portfolio. The sale of a fund's holdings generates a taxable event. Too much portfolio turnover can eat into the total return an investor receives from the fund, because determining whether an investor gets a long-term or short-term capital gain depends on how long the fund held the investment—*not* how long the shareholder held the mutual fund shares. If a fund held a certain company's shares for 18 months before selling them, but the investor just got into the fund last month, any capital gains on the sale are still considered a long-term capital gain for the investor. Conversely, if the investor has held a mutual fund for three years, but the fund keeps buying and selling stocks after only holding them for six months, the capital gains from those sales are all considered short term.

**Financial and economic research and analysis** are also important. As we said, investors rely upon the professional fund manager in these areas because the average investor does not have the time or resources to conduct extensive research. It is assumed by the investor that the professional manager is not only conducting the research, but is able to make good use of the information obtained.

**Fund Shares.** With mutual fund shares, there are four points to remember:

▷ **full and fractional shares** are possible: less than one full unit can be purchased since shares are only offered by the fund itself;

▷ **continual offering:** open-end structure allows a fund to constantly sell new issue shares and so must always use a prospectus;

▷ **redemption of shares:** since the mutual fund is the only outlet for the shares, the law says they must be redeemed within seven days;

▷ **voting rights:** the shareholders of a mutual fund vote for the fund's board of directors and are permitted by law to have final say (by majority vote) over changes in a fund's direction or objective.

It's important to note that when mutual fund shares are redeemed, no one else gets them. Unlike company shares of stock that trade hands, mutual fund shares are cancelled when redeemed. When clients invest money, they always get newly issued shares—that's why mutual funds are considered open-end investment companies. They must always use a prospectus since they're always doing a primary offering.

Exam Topic
Alert

# 2.1.2.2 Structure and Operation

A mutual fund is a collage of different persons, groups, and organizations interacting in their respective roles to make the open-end investment company operate successfully. There is a board of directors, investment advisor, and custodian. The underwriter helps market and sell the fund. Other important role players are the transfer agent, accounting firm, and legal advisors. All of these groups work together to reach the fund's objectives, balanced by shareholder rights in the mutual fund.

**Function of Board of Directors.** The board of directors establishes the investment policies of the mutual fund by choosing the direction of the fund, specifying the type of fund it will be, and determining the objectives of the fund. After that, the board's primary responsibility is engaging the services of the investment advisor, as well as deciding who to use as custodian and transfer agent. The board of directors can enter into contractual arrangements with the underwriter, who will act as sponsor and distributor for the mutual fund. It is also the board's job to establish the dividend and capital gains policy of the fund. Note that the Investment Company Act of 1940 requires at least 40% of the board members to be noninterested parties, who are not connected with the mutual fund in any way.

**Approve 12b-1 Plans.** 12b-1 fees are special assessments that allow mutual funds to collect money to reimburse marketing and distribution expenses. This was originally done as a way for no-load mutual funds to raise money to promote their fund, but load funds also have ways to collect these charges. The fee is figured on an annual basis but charged quarterly to each customer's account. The fee is not paid for investment advice. It is only for distributing and promoting the fund. A 12b-1 fee must be approved annually by:

1. a majority vote of fund shareholders, *and*
2. a majority vote of the board of directors, *and*
3. a majority vote of the noninterested board members.

Termination of the 12b-1 fee can be done by a majority vote of either 1 or 3.

**Functions of Investment Advisor.** The **investment advisor** is the one responsible for carrying out the goals and objectives of the fund on a daily basis. The investment advisor's primary job is to try to make the mutual fund's investments grow. The investment advisor has direct supervision over the investment portfolio and thus is also referred to as the **portfolio manager.** This individual or firm (as is usually the case) is charged with carrying out the investment policies described in the fund's prospectus and registration letter filed with the SEC. Other duties of the investment advisor/portfolio manager include providing investment advice, helping the fund conform with federal securities and tax law, researching and analyzing financial and economic trends, and conforming to the investment objectives and policy decisions of the mutual fund's board of directors.

Exam Topic
Alert

Additional points you should know are that an investment advisor:

▷ may not delegate or subcontract any duties without the fund's okay
▷ can invest only in securities a fund permits (can't change objectives)
▷ gets a two-year contract, then renewed annually by shareholder vote
▷ is paid a percentage of the portfolio assets under management (This is the largest expense incurred by the mutual fund!)

## 2.1.2.3 Cost of Operation of Mutual Fund

Costs associated with mutual funds can come in a variety of forms. Ultimately, these are borne by the shareholders, whether through direct sales charges, or indirectly through a reduction in the assets of the fund's investment portfolio. The expense ratio is the amount of expenses that a fund charges its shareholders each year for running the fund. The **expense ratio** is the cost of owning a fund (as opposed to the sales charge which is the cost of buying a fund). The expense ratio is charged as a percentage of the fund's assets.

**Sales Expenses.** Mutual fund sales charges can come in a variety of forms. Even so-called "no-load" funds that don't have sales charges, can charge "marketing fees." (Keep in mind, though, that these sales charges and fees are *not* part of the expense ratio calculation. Also, sales charges only apply to open-end mutual funds. Closed-end funds are purchased OTC so they have brokerage commissions or markups instead.)

▷ **No-load** means that there are no sales charges to fundholders for buying the mutual funds. No-load funds are usually purchased directly from the fund company. For no-load funds, the POP (public offering price, or retail price), and NAV (net asset value, or wholesale price) are the same, since no sales charges are added.

▷ **Load** is the sales charge added to the price of an investment. A load fund is sold by a broker-dealer or registered representative to investors. The sales charge (load) is added to the NAV (wholesale) to get the POP (retail) cost of the fund. With that added sales charge comes investment advice on what to buy, when to buy, and when to sell. Load charges can be front end (paid when the fund is bought) or back end (paid when the fund is sold).

By NASD rule, the sales charges cannot exceed 8.5%, and this 8.5% maximum can only be charged if three conditions are met:

1. breakpoint pricing is offered
2. automatic reinvestment of distributions is allowed
3. rights of accumulation are permitted

These will be explained shortly, but essentially, they are ways for investors to save sales charges later. If these three conditions are not met, then the maximum sales charge permitted is 6.25%. The NASD does not want firms charging clients excessive fees, then adding more fees at every opportunity. In reality, though, most sales charges are much lower because of competition.

*(Note that out of all the mutual fund players—board of directors, financial advisor, custodian, etc.—only the distributor/wholesaler/sponsor/underwriter gets paid from the sales charges. The rest are paid from the fund's net assets.)*

Exam Topic Alert

**Management Fees.** Management fees are paid to the financial advisor and others responsible for managing the mutual fund portfolio. These fees are figured as a percentage of the fund's net asset value. Management fees are also paid for administration and other functions within the fund. Management fees are usually an annual amount deducted from the gross assets. Typical management fees are in the 0.5% to 2.0% range, but may be higher, and often have performance incentives built in. The total amount of management fees and expenses is usually limited to a certain maximum amount. All fees must be disclosed in the prospectus.

**Other Expenses.** We already mentioned the 12b-1 fee, which is a special assessment that allows mutual funds to collect money to reimburse marketing and distribution expenses. This was originally done as a way for no-load mutual funds to raise money to promote their fund, but load funds also have ways to collect these charges. The fee is figured on an annual basis, but it is charged quarterly to each customer's account. The fee can be no more than 0.75% for load funds and no more than 0.25% for no-load funds. The fee is not paid for investment advice, but is only for distributing and promoting the fund. A 12b-1 fee must be approved annually.

One other fee that you may see mentioned on the Series 6 exam is called a distribution fee. **Distribution fees** are the compensation paid to the distributor (wholesaler, sponsor, underwriter) out of the mutual fund's sales charges. This is *not* a separate or additional expense, but instead is part of the sales charge. Remember, by NASD rule, total sales charges cannot exceed 8.5%.

Exam Topic Alert

## 2.1.2.4 Functions of Underwriter (Distributor)

The underwriter is also referred to as the sponsor, distributor, or wholesaler because it acts in these capacities at various times in the process. The mutual fund may not act as its own underwriter or distributor unless it is a no-load fund.

**Wholesale marketing of the mutual fund shares to securities dealers** is one of the main jobs of the underwriter. These retail broker-dealer firms enter into a selling agreement with the wholesale sponsor to resell shares to the investing public.

**Direct sales to the public** by the underwriter may also occur, but the customer always pays the POP (public offering price) no matter where the shares are purchased.

**Preparation of sales literature** is another function performed by the underwriter. The fund's sales literature must be filed with the NASD within ten days of first use.

Exam Topic Alert

**Compensation to dealers** is part of the total sales charge of a mutual fund. The broker-dealer's part of the sales charge is called **dealer's concession.** The underwriter also receives a part of the sales charge as a fee for selling and marketing the fund, called **underwriter's concession.** *Neither is paid from the fund's assets!*

## 2.1.2.5 Functions of Custodian

The custodian cannot be owned or controlled by the mutual fund. It must be an independent trust organization and is often a bank.

**Safeguarding the physical assets of the fund** is the custodian's primary job. The custodian's official duties include:

▷ physically securing (locking up) securities owned by the mutual fund
▷ maintaining a restricted admissions list so that not just anyone can enter the place where the securities are held
▷ only allow authorized access and withdrawal of the securities
▷ admit independent auditors authorized to check on the securities
▷ keep a records handling system that is approved by the NYSE

**Payable/receivable functions of securities transactions** is another responsibility of the custodian. Money in and out of the fund account goes through the custodian. **Receipt of interest and dividends** paid by securities in the fund portfolio also goes through the custodian, with the money being held until the declared distribution date.

## 2.1.2.6 Functions of Transfer Agent

The transfer agent for a mutual fund performs similar functions as the transfer agent for a corporation. The transfer agent can be the same entity as the custodian, or the agent can be a different party. The duties include:

▷ issuance of physical shares or book entry

▷ cancellation of redeemed shares

▷ disbursements of dividend and capital gains distributions to shareholders of record

All of these bookkeeping-type functions are ultimately the responsibility of the transfer agent. All sales and redemptions are recorded, so distributions, notices, and tax forms can be sent out correctly and efficiently.

## 2.1.2.7 Rights of Shareholders

Rights of shareholders hold the structure and operation of the mutual fund in check. Certainly, the largest power the shareholders have is to vote with their money—if they don't like what the fund is doing, they will redeem their shares and invest elsewhere. Some power is wielded by shareholders within the mutual fund structure, however. Shareholders are given the right to vote and other rights by the Investment Company Act of 1940. Shareholders:

▷ have voting rights/proxies on important issues affecting the fund

▷ must approve changes in investment objective, policy (majority vote)

▷ must approve investment advisory agreements (majority vote)

▷ elect directors (majority vote)

▷ receive semiannual reports from the fund (at least one audited)

# 2.1.3

# Types of Fund Distributions

There are several ways investors can receive cash or other distributions from a mutual fund investment. We will discuss the tax implications of these in a future section, but for now just know that the fund sends each investor a 1099 tax form detailing the tax liability owed. Here we will briefly introduce you to some terms.

## 2.1.3.1 Net Investment Income

**Net investment income** is the income received by the mutual fund investment company from stock dividends, bond interest, and other payouts from investments in the fund's portfolio, minus management fees and administrative expenses. The investment company divides this total net income figure by the number of outstanding mutual fund shares and distributes a proportionate amount to each shareholder as a dividend. Dividends may be paid out by the mutual fund as often as the fund chooses.

## 2.1.3.2 Capital Gains

**Capital gains** are the increase in value realized when an asset is sold. Every time the fund manager sells a stock, bond, or other security, a capital gain or loss is realized, and these gains or losses are passed through to the fund's shareholders. The length of time the fund held the investment determines whether the capital gain is short-term (and taxed as ordinary income) or long-term (and taxed at a more favorable rate). Note, though, that fluctuations in the value of assets in the portfolio **(paper gains)** do not have tax implications until the assets are sold (and thus become **realized gains** or losses). Capital gains distributions are usually only made once a year by the mutual fund.

## 2.1.3.3 Return of Capital

**Return of capital** is a distribution of cash from a mutual fund investment company because of a sale of a portfolio asset. Many times when an asset is sold, the fund manager will reinvest the money. The shareholders still have a taxable event from the capital gain, even if they don't get the reinvested money. There are situations when money may be returned to shareholders, such as when a bond matures near the predetermined termination date of the fund. The amount of capital returned to each investor is considered part of the original investment (cost basis) first before any money is considered a capital gain (with tax consequences).

## 2.1.3.4 Distribution Alternatives

Any time the investor has a chance to receive cash distributions from the fund, the investor has a taxable event. This is true whether the investor takes the cash out or chooses to reinvest the money to buy more shares of the mutual fund. Once the asset has been sold (or other event takes place), the tax liability is incurred and must be reported. The investor's decision to take the distribution as cash or to reinvest the money has no impact on the tax consequences.

# Conveniences and Services Provided to Investors

Mutual funds offer a number of conveniences and advantages for investors. We have already discussed the three main advantages: liquidity, diversification, and professional management. You may see these on the Series 6 exam. Others mentioned below can also be a real advantage to customers. Some of the ones listed here are less likely to appear on the exam; others are related to the three main ones we've discussed. You should keep these in mind to help you as a sales tool with clients.

## 2.1.4.1 Day-to-Day Investing Decisions Made by Portfolio Manager

Leaving the decisions in the hands of professional managers can be a big relief to some investors. It can also allow them to focus on long-term objectives, rather than get nervous about daily fluctuations in the markets.

## 2.1.4.2 Safekeeping of Portfolio Securities

There is comfort for many investors in knowing that there is a system of checks and balances in place helping to safeguard the assets of the mutual fund (such as a custodian watching the assets).

## 2.1.4.3 Exchange Privileges within Families of Funds

Investors may want to cash in one fund and use the proceeds to buy a different fund within the same family of funds offered by an investment company. If completed within a certain time frame, the exchange will often qualify for reduced or waived sales charges.

This **conversion privilege** lets investors change investment objectives (e.g., growth versus income), depending on their needs and perception of market conditions. (Selling a fund is a taxable event, even if the proceeds are used right away to buy another fund.)

Exam Topic Alert

## 2.1.4.4 Ability to Invest Sums in Full and Fractional Shares

Because the fund is the only source and outlet for the mutual fund shares, investors can buy as many or as few shares as they want—even fractional shares. This is important for investors who invest using dollar cost averaging. **Dollar cost averaging (DCA)** is an investment method whereby a set dollar amount is invested at regular intervals. We will do the calculations in an upcoming section. For now, just know that DCA lends itself well to mutual funds because investors can buy full or fractional shares, whereas with regular stocks an investor would be forced to buy round lots (or at least full shares), so it's unlikely the same amount of money could be invested each time.

## 2.1.4.5 Can Liquidate Part of Investment and Keep Diversification

Diversification is maintained by an investor because even after selling some mutual fund shares, the remaining shares held still have the same diverse balance and proportionate representation of investments as the mutual fund portfolio. This would not be possible with a small individual portfolio because selling off part of ones holdings would entail sacrificing one part or one sector of the portfolio.

## 2.1.4.6 Fund Shares Provide Collateral for Loans

Although an investor must buy mutual fund shares with cash (no margin!) because they are a primary offering, after the shares have been held for 30 days, they can be used as collateral for a margin account or for other loans. (Banks regard fund shares as good collateral.)

## 2.1.4.7 Simplified Recordkeeping

Having the mutual fund keep track of all the different investments in the portfolio is certainly easier than an individual investor monitoring multiple buy and sell transactions in a portfolio. Furthermore, the fund manager at the end of the year sends a statement to each shareholder detailing how much of the distributions made were considered income, and how much were capital gains. An IRS form 1099 sent by the fund details each person's tax liability, which the investor then reports when filing a federal tax return. Investors should also keep their annual statements from the mutual fund for as long as they own the fund and beyond, to help figure out their cost basis (Original Cost + Fees) for the investment.

## 2.1.4.8 Ease of Diversification

There are many facets to the ease of diversification that investors enjoy with mutual funds. One is the ability to change to a different fund objective within the same family. Another is the ability to buy and sell fractional shares without altering the diversification of the investor's holdings. A third one that we have not talked about is related to the professional management advantage that mutual funds have. Even if an investor knew that he or she wanted to invest the bulk of their money in a particular sector or industry, there is still the problem of trying to pick the right investment. The lone investor would likely only have enough money to buy a few stocks, so it's a gamble. With a mutual fund, the professional fund manager picks a variety of securities from a range of companies (some safe, some high risk) to balance the portfolio, then monitors and changes the portfolio mix as needed.

## 2.1.4.9 Ease of Account Inquiry

With a single phone call, it's possible for an investor to find out information about his or her mutual fund account. Maintaining a personal portfolio would require much more information and time to determine the status of the investments and to have questions answered.

## 2.1.4.10 Ease of Purchase and Redemption of Shares

Mutual fund shares must be redeemed within seven calendar days to comply with the Investment Company Act of 1940. As you can imagine, it is even easier to buy the shares with a phone call. The only caveat with buying or selling mutual fund shares is that an investor will not know the buy or sell price when the trade order is placed. That's because the redemption price (or purchase price) is based on the NAV (net asset value) of the fund, which is only calculated at the end of the day. Since the buy and sell orders for mutual fund shares are placed before a final price is known, this is **forward pricing.** The investor will not know exactly how many shares he or she will get or how much money will be received until after the fund has calculated its NAV. We'll do the calculations in a future section.

## 2.1.4.11 Automatic Reinvestment of Dividends and Capital Gains

Many funds offer the option of automatic reinvestment of dividends and capital gains. Funds do this to qualify for higher sales charge rate (8.5%), and also because of competition in the market. It's an advantage for investors because it reduces the amount of effort they need to put into the investment, and often may be done by the investor at a discounted price, provided that certain conditions are met:

▷ fund's prospectus must allow reinvestment of dividends/capital gains

▷ fund holders all have an equal opportunity to do a reinvestment

▷ fund holders are notified annually of their right to reinvestment

▷ reinvestment program must not place a financial burden on the fund

The fund may impose a handling charge for providing the reinvestment service, but it must be reasonable and can't equal the regular sales charge. Also, even if dividends or capital gains are reinvested, they're still a taxable event to the investor. Taxes are due on the reinvested amount, then the investor adds that amount to the cost basis.

*For the Series 6 exam, know that reinvested dividends and capital gains are taxed.*

Exam Topic Alert

## 2.1.4.12 Systematic Withdrawal Plans

Withdrawal (or payout) plans are a means of mutual fund redemption where the investor receives fixed payments on a regular basis. Payments can be interest only, dividends only, or part of an investor's shares can be liquidated on a regular schedule. Payments are usually made monthly or quarterly. Once clients start to redeem shares, they should not put any money back in so as not to waste sales charges. Here are a few other points to consider.

**Minimum Investment.** To be eligible for a systematic withdrawal plan, most funds require that the investor's shares be worth a certain minimum amount, which varies by fund. Otherwise, cash redemption in a lump sum is the only option available.

**Potential Exhaustion of Principal.** Mutual fund withdrawal plans are not designed to guarantee a lifetime of income. Market fluctuations can reduce the payout and funds can be exhausted. (So never show clients payout projections!)

**Types of Withdrawal Payouts.** There are three main ways payouts are structured:

▷ fixed dollar amount (paid quarterly or monthly until funds are exhausted)
▷ fixed percentage (percentage of shares are redeemed on a regular schedule)
▷ fixed shares (fixed number of shares are redeemed on a regular schedule)

**Liquidation Over Fixed Time.** Investors can also take the value of their shares, divide it by a chosen period of time, then redeem on that schedule in even payments.

## 2.1.4.13 Check-Writing Privileges

Some funds offer accounts similar to money market accounts, so that an investor can write checks against his or her mutual fund account balances. The checks can be treated as a loan or cause shares to be sold.

## 2.1.4.14 Telephone Exchanges and Services

Just as a phone call can be used to get information about an investor's account, many funds also accept buy, sell, and exchange orders over the phone. There is often a floor limit on how large a telephone redemption request can be. Other phone services may also be offered by a fund.

## 2.1.4.15 Simplified Tax Information

As we mentioned before, each year the fund sends out tax information to investors on an IRS Form 1099, detailing the investor's tax liability for dividends and capital gains. Investors can also use annual statements from the mutual fund to figure out their cost basis for the investment.

# Types of Mutual Funds, Characteristics, Investment Policies

Mutual funds come in many different types. They can be categorized by the fund's objectives (e.g., growth, income, etc.), portfolio (e.g., stocks, bonds, etc.), or any other areas of specialization (e.g., sector, geographic, etc.). Let's look at some of the more common types of funds, first by objective, then by investment type.

## 2.1.5.1 By Objective

Mutual fund objectives can range from very aggressive growth funds to income funds to more conservative funds that have capital preservation as their main objective. Let's look at a few of these.

▷ **Growth funds** are sometimes called **diversified common stock funds** because of their emphasis on stocks to achieve the fund's primary objective of capital growth. This type of fund is best suited for money that will not be used for retirement or other expenses until well into the future so that the money has time to grow. Growth funds can be either aggressive or conservative.

    **Aggressive growth funds** focus on small cap (under $5 billion market capitalization) or mid cap ($5 to 10 billion market cap) company stocks in higher risk industries (e.g., high-tech) that appear poised for growth. Growth companies don't pay dividends, instead reinvesting profits in R and D to fuel growth.

    **Conservative growth funds** invest in stocks but buy the stock of established large cap (over $10 billion market cap) companies with growth prospects instead of high-risk, high-reward stocks. For example, conservative funds invest in software companies as a leading edge industry that still has growth potential, but stick with companies that have a history of earnings.

▷ **Income funds** invest primarily in preferred stocks and bonds. Generally, if income potential is preferred by an investor, then there is less potential for growth of capital. By looking to acquire high-yielding stocks and bonds, utility company stocks, and blue chips that consistently pay dividends, the fund can meet its objectives of providing income. This type of fund is best suited for investors who need cash flow or near-term funds, perhaps for retirement.

▷ **Growth and income funds** are sometimes referred to as **balanced funds.** These funds seek to have all areas covered by investing in common stock, preferred stock, bonds, and cash in order to achieve the highest returns with high stability. A typical structure would be about half stock and half bonds, with perhaps 5% of the assets in cash. This allocation would be adjusted as market conditions change, based on a preset formula. These funds balance growth and income by diversifying the portfolio with different investment vehicles, across different industries, and in various regions of the country.

▷ **Specialized funds** seek a market niche they can offer to investors. Some examples might be a sector fund or a special situation fund.

    **Sector funds** invest in companies in a particular industry or "sector" of the economy. A sector could be chosen because of its high growth potential (e.g., high-tech), or because it is a cyclical or countercyclical sector (e.g., energy, gold).

*On the Series 6 exam, never put a novice investor in a sector fund!*

Exam Topic Alert

    **Special situation funds** invest in stocks that are undervalued for a short period of time but are about to rise significantly because of an upcoming event. This could be a pending merger or acquisition, a new management team or new product introduction. These funds are high-risk, high-reward.

▷ **Asset allocation funds** are balanced funds that have multiple asset classes. Like the growth and income funds, these funds cover all areas by investing in common stock, preferred stock, bonds, and cash in order to achieve the highest returns with high stability. An asset allocation fund not only invests in different kinds of stocks (e.g., small cap, large cap), the fund also tilts its asset balance of stocks, bonds, and cash much more (maybe up to 80% stock one time, 80% bonds another) depending on market conditions, with no preset formula.

▷ **Tax-exempt funds** are funds that focus on various tax-free bonds. Funds that invest in municipal bonds can offer tax-free income, because tax advantages flow through to investors.

Other bond funds are structured to minimize the tax burden to investors as well, but tax is always due on capital gains.

Exam Topic Alert

## 2.1.5.2 By Underlying Investment

Mutual fund types can also be segregated by the underlying investments that make up the portfolio. Sometimes the composition of the portfolio is set up to mirror an objective. Other times, maintaining the unique composition of the portfolio is the objective. Here are a few examples.

▷ **Money market funds** invest in money market instruments—commercial paper, government securities close to maturity, T-bills trading in the secondary market, and other short-term notes (maturing in 90 days or less as required by the SEC). Money market funds are a good way to preserve capital while providing liquidity. Often, fund holders can write checks against their money market fund accounts (but usually with restrictions as to number or amount). Target NAV price is $1 per share, and SEC requires the fund to be no-load.

▷ **Bond and preferred stock funds** invest in various types of debt securities with different maturities to meet the objectives of the fund. Certainly income is one objective, but there can be others. **Municipal bond funds** can offer tax-free income, because tax advantages flow through to the fund's investors. **U.S. government securities funds** can offer safer income, whereas funds investing in **corporate bonds** can seek different yields based on bond quality.

▷ **Ginnie Mae funds** invest in relatively safe Ginnie Mae pass-through certificates; thus, it is considered a type of **capital preservation fund.** Ginnie Mae mortgage-backed certificates pass through income to investors and are backed by the U.S. government against default so they are a safe, conservative fund.

▷ **Common stock funds** focus on a sector, geographic area, etc. One common type of stock fund that focuses on composition of the portfolio is an index fund. **Index funds** track a recognized index and match its portfolio composition and movements. Rather than trying to "beat" the market, the index fund follows along and shares the same capital growth over time. Some recognized indices include S&P's 500 and Wilshire 5000.

Exam Topic Alert

On the Series 6 exam, know that *index fund portfolio managers try to **match** the index, not beat it.*

▷ **Other types** of mutual funds with focused portfolio investments include **option funds** (generate income from option contracts), **precious metal funds** (everything precious metal-related, from mining stocks to bullion), and **foreign securities funds** (which can include anything from American Depository Receipts to mirroring an index like the Morgan Stanley Europe-Asia-Far East Index).

2.16

# Important Factors in Comparison of Mutual Funds

Mutual funds have a number of factors that need to be compared when deciding which one best fits a particular client's financial objectives. A fund's characteristics and philosophy are important but so are the fees and returns. Let's look at some of the different criteria that can be used when making mutual fund comparisons.

# 2.1.6.1 Basis of Comparison

There are several bases of comparison that can be used. Here we'll mention some of the nonstatistical means that can be used to compare the advantages and disadvantages of various mutual funds. Even though numbers are not involved, it is important that the comparisons be made as objectively as possible.

**Investment Objectives and Policies.** When looking at mutual funds, one of the first decisions must be what type of mutual fund is right for the client. There are mutual funds that invest solely in stocks, some that only invest in bonds, and others that use a balanced approach to investing. Even within these broad categories, there are different choices. Stock funds can be growth funds, income funds, hybrid funds, or specialized funds. Bond funds can invest in U.S. government bonds, municipal bonds, corporate bonds, or preferred stock. Within each of those groups, the funds can emphasize growth, income, safety, or any of these in varying combinations. Investors should read the fund's prospectus carefully to determine the fund's objectives, then the investor should look at the fund's portfolio to see if the objectives are being met.

**Quality of Management.** The quality of management at a mutual fund has many components that can be evaluated. Of course, the most important is statistical—how much was the return on investment for the mutual fund. There are other nonstatistical factors that can be important as well. How long has the fund manager been managing the fund? What is the fund manager's background? What is his or her previous experience? What about other members of the management team? How long have they worked together? These and other questions can help put the numbers in context when evaluating a mutual fund. Past performance of the fund means nothing if the management is new. Investors need to know about the team.

**Risk Factors.** Mutual funds have the same risk factors as other investments, so investors need to research the underlying investments and objectives of the fund. A cautious investor who is risk averse has no more business being in a high-tech sector fund than buying high-tech company stocks. Most of the same theory applies here. You will likely see some questions on the Series 6 exam where you are told about an investor coming to you for advice on buying a mutual fund, and you need to recommend one. Here are some sample pairings:

▷ investors just starting out → put them in stock funds, index funds, or conservative growth funds

▷ investors nearing retirement → put them in income or bond funds

▷ investors with near-term expense → put them in money market funds

▷ investors worried about taxes → put them in tax-exempt, muni funds

▷ investors looking for safety → put them in Ginnie Mae funds, government funds, or capital preservation funds

▷ investors looking for high returns → put them in aggressive growth funds

For the Series 6 exam, never put beginning investors in sector funds, option funds, foreign securities funds, or other high-risk investments. Never put novice investors in a hedge fund. This is *not* a type of mutual fund. A **hedge fund** is a limited partnership that invests in highly speculative strategies (e.g., selling short).

Exam Topic Alert

Also, if there is a question on the Series 6 exam that suggests mutual funds are a good investment because of their tax advantages, that is usually a trick question or an incorrect answer. The mutual fund itself benefits by not having to pay taxes and instead passes the tax liability directly to individual shareholders. Although many investors may put mutual fund shares into IRAs or other retirement plans that shelter or defer taxes, *mutual funds in and of themselves are **not** tax shelters*. Mutual funds can be good investments, but investors should not enter them to gain any tax advantages.

## 2.1.6.2 Performance Statistics

The bottom line with any investment is making money, so a comparison of mutual funds must also include a comparison of returns, expense ratios, etc. in order to make an informed choice. These objective numbers can be used to get a better picture of which mutual fund is right for a client.

**Total Return.** A mutual fund's **total return** is the annual return of the fund, including appreciation, capital gains, and dividends, minus any fees paid. The total return for a mutual fund assumes reinvestment of all distributions to buy additional fund shares. Total return reflects changes in a fund's net asset value. From an investment standpoint, total return should be one of the first considerations. Growth and income are also important points of comparison among mutual funds, but the total return an investor gets to keep is the ultimate measure of success. If fees are high, then the performance of the fund (growth and/or income) needs to be that much better to compensate. Of course, past performance does not guarantee future results, but assessing the fund's performance over time can give some indication.

**Standardized Yield.** In order to make comparisons between mutual funds more informative and relevant for investors, the SEC requires a standard computation of a fund's yield that must be used for advertising purposes. The SEC formula for **standardized yield** is calculated as dividends plus interest paid by the fund, divided by the maximum offering price of shares (*no* capital gains are included). This calculation uses the fund's net income over the past 30 days, then makes a projected annualized yield based on that number. In other words, by looking at the past month, the formula extrapolates what an investor might receive if the rate continued for the next 12 months. Although that scenario is unlikely, it gives a consistent basis of comparison between mutual funds, since they must all use the same formula.

**Current Distribution Rate.** The **current distribution rate** indicates what the fund's yield would be if you only used the most recent distribution and the month-end POP (public offering price). This number is calculated by annualizing the last distribution (last distribution × 12) and dividing by its offer price. This number may appear to be the same as standardized yield (above), but even though the two calculations cover the same time period, the numbers are often not the same. That's because while the SEC mandates how the standardized yield calculation is done, the current distribution rate calculation can vary somewhat by fund. Also, some classes of securities (such as preferred stock and mortgage-backed securities) are all handled differently by each calculation.

**Expense Ratio.** The **expense ratio** is the amount of expenses that a fund charges its shareholders each year for running the fund. A mutual fund's expense ratio is calculated by adding up all of the fund's operating expenses and management fees for the year, and dividing by the fund's total net assets. **(Expenses ÷ Fund's Net Assets)** This number is expressed as a percentage. The expense ratio is the cost of owning a fund (as opposed to the sales charge which is the cost of buying a fund). The expense ratio is charged as a percentage of the fund's assets.

The expense ratio includes all the various costs and expenses (investment advisory fee, administrative costs, 12b-1 distribution fees, and other operating expenses) into one number. A typical expense ratio is about 1.5% for an actively managed mutual fund. This amount is paid regardless of the fund's performance. With indexed funds and other funds that are not actively managed, the expense ratio is typically around 0.25%. (We will discuss sources for performance stats shortly.)

# 2.1.6.3 Other Factors

Other factors to consider when comparing funds include:

**Convenience and Services.** Mutual funds have many different levels of service and offer different conveniences to attract investors. For example, we discussed redemption of mutual fund shares with a simple telephone call, but this convenience is not offered by all funds. The same goes for checking privileges with a mutual fund. Beyond these conveniences, services might include investment advice or knowledgeable staff who are available to answer questions over the phone. Investors need to consider what's important to them before making an investment decision.

**Special Features.** Some mutual funds offer features to make them more appealing to investors, others do not. These features include **conversion privileges,** which allow customers to exchange mutual fund within the same family of funds without sales charges; **combination privileges,** which allow customers to combine mutual fund purchases across the same family of funds to reach breakpoints and receive sales charge discounts; and **withdrawal plans,** which allow systematic redemption of shares by investors over a period of time. Not all of these features are offered by all funds, so they must be investigated before a mutual fund is purchased.

**Minimum Purchase Requirements.** This is an important consideration for many investors. Some mutual funds have a minimum amount that must be invested with each purchase; others allow investors to contribute any amount they want after making the initial purchase. Some require scheduled periodic investment payments. Also, some allow **letters of intent** (commitment by an investor to invest a certain amount of money within 13 months, to receive breakpoint sales charge rates now), or **rights of accumulation** (breakpoint sales offered at a future time once the total amount of money invested has reached the breakpoint); some funds don't allow these.

**Sales and Distribution Charges.** Mutual fund sales charges are called **loads.** Sales charges can be collected as a **front-end load,** where a commission is paid when the mutual fund is purchased; or as a **back-end load,** where a commission is paid when the fund is sold. Back-end loads are sometimes referred to as **contingent deferred sales loads (CDSL)** when the percentage of load decreases the longer the fund is held, and usually reaches 0% after about the fifth year. A third fee option is a small **level load** charged yearly for the life of the fund, similar to the 12b-1 fee of up to 1% charged by **no-load** funds for marketing expenses. We'll go do some calculations in an upcoming section, but for now know that this is an important comparison.

# Sources of Mutual Fund Performance Statistics

There are several good sources of information on mutual funds and their performance. Most of these sources are even free for the asking.

**PROSPECTUS.** A mutual fund prospectus must be given out to all prospective investors before they put any money into the fund. The **prospectus** gives detailed information about the investment company, management team (including the name of the primary fund manager), fund objectives, investment policies, and all sales charges and management fees. A mutual fund prospectus must show the formula used to compute NAV (net asset value), sales charges added, and the final POP. The prospectus must also state the performance history of the fund over the past 1 year, 5 years, and 10 years (if the fund has been around that long).

**SHAREHOLDER REPORTS.** This is the semiannual report made by the fund to shareholders. Included in the report are a balance sheet and income statement from the fund, a list of all securities in the portfolio and their values, a statement of all portfolio transactions, and details of the compensation paid to all management personnel and the board of directors. The financials in at least one of the semi-annual reports must be audited as per the Investment Company Act of 1940. This detailed financial information is a good place to research performance of the fund.

**INFORMATION SERVICES.** Various investment advisory services stand ready to provide investment research information for a fee. Some specialize in certain investment areas, while other offer broad research capabilities. Some also offer additional services, such as targeted research information, custom analysis, publications, and credit ratings. One independent company that specializes in mutual fund research and information is Morningstar. They offer reports and on-line information.

Financial newspapers, such as *Wall Street Journal*, magazines, such as *Kiplinger's*, and hybrids, such as *Barron's*, provide information on popular mutual funds on a regular basis. Other more specialized publications also have detailed information on mutual funds, as do a myriad of on-line resources.

**ADVERTISING AND SALES LITERATURE.** Mutual fund-related advertising, sales literature, marketing literature, and research reports must be sent to the NASD no later than 10 days after first being used or being made available to the public. This requirement is waived if the material has already been filed by another member firm. This is often the case with mutual funds, which are the primary type of investment company products you will likely deal with. With mutual funds, there is a sponsoring broker-dealer (also referred to as the underwriter or distributor) whose primary responsibility is to market the fund and create the collateral sales literature. As other broker-dealers begin selling the fund, they are not required to submit sales literature to the NASD if they are using the same materials already submitted by the sponsor. These rules also apply to other investment company products, such as variable annuity contracts.

Note that the requirement for investment company products is different than that for first-year broker-dealers: first-year broker-dealers must submit advertising *before* first use; investment companies can submit materials *after* use. The NASD does not "approve" materials, but collects them to perform compliance spot checks. Broker-dealers must keep all advertising and sale literature on file for three years.

**Using Charts and Graphs.** The NASD requires that broker-dealers use charts and graphs with mutual fund ads and sales literature to show the fund's performance over the past 10 years. Longer time periods can be used, but shorter periods should not be used as they may not show a fund's performance in varying market conditions. Furthermore, the charts and graphs can't be misleading, and may not skip over time periods where the fund's performance was lagging. Finally, the advertising or sale literature must state the source of the information depicted in the charts and graphs.

**Showing Returns.** If mutual fund ads show returns, they must be calculated using the SEC method, which assumes reinvestment of all dividends, capital gains, and other fund distributions. Also, when calculating the return, all sales charges, management fees, and other such charges are not included. The SEC calculation for fund performance must be explained if returns are advertised, and figures must show 1-year, 5-year, 10-year returns or average life-of-fund returns. SEC rules also say any mention of current yield must be based on income distributions over past 12 months.

**Other Rules.** Additional NASD rules for investment company product ads are:

▷ ads may not state that mutual funds are safer than other investments,
▷ ads must show the highest possible sales charges (without breakpoints), and
▷ ads that state cash returns must combine dividends and capital gains.

# 2.18

# Methods by Which Fund Shares Are Purchased by the Public

There are many ways that mutual funds can be sold. In addition to the fund itself, usually a distributor and/or a broker-dealer are part of a transaction. No matter where a customer ultimately buys mutual fund shares, the investor is always charged the POP. This is an NASD rule. Only NASD members may buy fund shares at a discount. Investors may only receive sales charge reductions (not discounts!) for quantity purchases. Here are three paths mutual fund sales can follow.

**FUND TO UNDERWRITER TO DEALER TO INVESTOR. Underwriters** have the job of marketing the mutual fund to retail broker-dealers and to the investing public. The underwriter also acts as the sponsor, distributor, or wholesaler at various times in the process. Retail broker-dealers enter into a selling agreement with the wholesale underwriter to resell shares to the investing public. The difference between what the investing public pays and what the mutual fund receives makes up the fund's sales charges. Sales charges are also referred to as the **load** or **spread.** The part of the spread paid to the sponsor/wholesaler/distributor is called the **underwriter's concession.** Retail broker-dealers also get part of the spread, called the **dealer's concession.** Remember, by NASD rule, total sales charges can't exceed 8.5%.

**FUND TO UNDERWRITER TO INVESTOR.** Although the underwriter may not buy excess shares to keep in its inventory, the underwriter may act as a distributor and sell shares directly to the public. The customer always pays the POP no matter who the shares are purchased from. Here the underwriter receives the entire sales charge spread as a fee for selling and marketing the fund but pays part of that out in commission to its licensed representative who made the sale.

**FUND TO INVESTOR.** The fund may only act as its own underwriter or distributor and sell shares directly to the public if it is a no-load fund. In this case, the fund is only collecting the 12b-1 fee, and there are no distribution or sales charges involved.

2.1.9

# Prices of Mutual Fund Shares

We said that when investors buy mutual fund shares, the price they pay is the POP. The POP the customer pays is actually a combination of the net asset value (NAV) of the fund plus the sales charges. When a customer sells shares back to the fund, the redemption price is always the NAV. (Remember: POP = retail; NAV = wholesale.) Let's discuss NAV, sales charges and distribution fees.

## 2.1.9.1 Net Asset Value (NAV) Per Share

A mutual fund's **NAV** is the value of the fund and its shares, derived by taking the fund's assets minus liabilities, then dividing that result by the number of outstanding shares.

**How Determined.** The formula is for calculating NAV is:

**(Fund Assets – Fund Liabilities) ÷ Number of Outstanding Shares = NAV Per Share**

**When Determined.** Unlike a stock, which is actively traded in the secondary market and can have different prices from minute-to-minute, mutual funds are priced only once a day (usually at the end of the day). After the markets close, the fund adds up the value of all its stocks and other assets, and calculates its NAV. This figure is then used to fill buy or sell orders that have been received. NAV is the bid price at which fund shares are redeemed, and NAV plus the sales charges is the POP, or ask price, at which fund shares can be purchased. Since the buy and sell orders for mutual fund shares are placed before the final price is known, this is called **forward pricing.** In fact, investors buying mutual fund shares don't even know how many shares they will get until the end of the day when the NAV is calculated.

A popular topic on the Series 6 exam is what affects NAV. Lots of money going in and out of the fund to buy shares or redeem them does *not* change the NAV because they offset each other: more money coming in to buy shares equals more outstanding shares to divide the total by; money going out to redeem shares equals less shares to divide the total by. The primary affect on NAV is the market value of the stocks owned by the fund. Corporate dividends paid into the fund from stocks in the portfolio and reinvestment of dividends can also affect NAV. This is because these actions affect the asset value in the fund without changing the number of shares. Interest rates can also affect NAV if bonds are part of the fund.

Exam Topic Alert

**Ex-Dividend.** Dividend payments go to owners of record as of a certain date (called the **record date**). **Ex-dividend** means a security no longer gives the holder the right to collect the dividend that was announced. With mutual funds, the ex-dividend date is the day after the record date. The fund's board of directors specifies a record date during each distribution period. If an investor owns mutual fund shares on or before the record date, then the investor qualifies for the dividend. If an investor buys shares the day after the record day (the ex-dividend date), then the dividend amount is subtracted from the fund's net asset value (NAV) per share because on the ex-dividend date the fund's net asset value drops by the amount of dividends paid.

**Redemption Fees.** These are fees charged by a mutual fund if shares are redeemed too soon after being acquired. The length of time that incurs a fee and the amount of the fee varies by fund, but the idea is to discourage constant turnover of shares.

## 2.1.9.2 Sales Charges

Mutual fund sales charges are called **loads.** These loads are the cost of buying a fund (as opposed to the expense ratio which is the fees and other total costs of owning a fund). Sales charges can be computed one of several ways.

**Front-end loads** are commissions paid when the mutual fund is purchased. These can range up to an average of 5% and come off the top of the investor's investment dollars. Spending $10,000 on a mutual fund with a 5% front-end load means that the investor is really only buying $9,500 worth of mutual fund shares. (Mutual funds with front-end loads are often referred to as **Class A shares.**)

**Back-end loads** are commissions paid when the fund is sold. The lure of a back-end load is that the entire investment amount goes to buy mutual fund shares. Of course, this means that the load percentage is taken off of a larger amount if the mutual fund grows while the investor owns it. One feature of back-end loads, though, is that the percentage of load often decreases the longer the fund is held, and usually reaches 0% after about the fifth year. We will compare load charges over time shortly. (Back-end loads are sometimes called **CDSLs,** and mutual funds with back-end loads are often referred to as **Class B shares.**)

**Level loads** are small fees charged yearly for the life of the fund, similar to the 12b-1 fee of up to 1% charged by funds (including **no-load** funds) for marketing expenses. If a fund is held for a long period of time, a level load can be a significant cost concern. (Mutual funds with level loads are often referred to as **Class C shares.**)

**Combination loads** are funds with fees that start out with internal fees similar to a back-end load (like a Class B), but after a certain amount of time, the fees change to a level load (like a Class C). (Funds with hybrid loads are **Class D shares.**)

**Prospectus.** The prospectus that must be distributed as part of the mutual fund offering is required by the SEC to include a **standardized table of fees and expenses.** The table must be in the beginning part of the prospectus, along with an executive summary of the table and a risk/reward analysis of the fund in plain English. This table of expense disclosures is submitted to the SEC when mutual funds file registration form N-1A. The idea of putting the table in the prospectus is so investors can easily understand the fees and make comparisons between funds since all tables must use the same uniform, tabular presentation of fees and expenses associated with the mutual fund investment.

The fees in the table include charges paid directly by shareholders from their investment money, such as sales loads, as well as recurring charges deducted from fund assets, such as management fees. The table also has an example that shows the total dollar amount investors could expect to pay on a $10,000 investment if they got a 5% annual return and held the fund for various lengths of time.

**Newspaper Quotes.** The newspapers and other financial publications that publish prices for mutual funds typically list the NAV price per share for the fund. This is the same as the **bid price** for the fund. The NAV plus the sales charges equals the POP. The POP is the same as the **asked or offering price.** If a newspaper quote has a small "NL" in the "offer price" column, then the fund is a no-load fund, which means that the NAV and the POP are the same.

**Compute Offering Price.** We have gone through the calculations of the NAV and talked about the various sales charges. Now it's time to put it all together and work some computations of the POP.

You will probably see one or more variations of this on the Series 6 exam, so let's take a look at some different formulas. The one you need to use will depend on what figures you are given in the question and which number you need to solve for.

**Net Asset Value + Sales Charge = Public Offering Price**

**POP – NAV = Sales Charge**

**$ Sales Charge ÷ POP = Sales Charge %**

**NAV ÷ (1 – Sales Charge %) = POP**

The first two equations are the easiest and more likely for the Series 6 exam, but even problems with the other two are not difficult. Let's do an example.

## EXAMPLE

A mutual fund has a per share net asset value of 19 and a sales charge of 5%. What is the public offering price?

Since we are given the NAV and sales charge %, the best formula to use is:

$$\text{NAV} \div (1 - \text{Sales Charge \%}) = \text{POP}$$

$$19 \div (1 - 5\%) = \text{POP}$$

$$19 \div (1 - .05) = 20$$

So, the public offering price is $20 per share.

For the Series 6, remember: **POP is the same as asked or offering price; NAV is the same as bid price;** sales charges may not exceed 8.5% per NASD rules, and for no-load funds, the POP and NAV are the same. Also, when doing calculations, *POP is always greater than or equal to NAV, never less than.*

Exam Topic
Alert

**Contingent Deferred Sales Charges.** Back-end loads are higher initially to discourage investors from exiting the investment too soon. Which option if best for an investor, front or back loads? That depends on how long the investor plans to hold the fund. In fact, this can have a serious impact on total return. Here's a comparison.

| | Front-End Sales Charges | | | |
|---|---|---|---|---|
| Year | Annual 12b-1 | Cumulative 12b-1 Fees | Entrance Fee | Total Fees |
| 1 | 1% | 1% | 1.5% | 2.5% |
| 2 | 1% | 2% | 1.5% | 3.5% |
| 3 | 1% | 3% | 1.5% | 4.5% |
| 4 | 1% | 4% | 1.5% | 5.5% |
| 5 | 1% | 5% | 1.5% | 6.5% |
| 6 | 1% | 6% | 1.5% | 7.5% |
| 7 | 1% | 7% | 1.5% | 8.5% |
| 8 | 1% | 8% | 1.5% | 9.5% |
| 9 | 1% | 9% | 1.5% | 10.5% |
| 10 | 1% | 10% | 1.5% | 11.5% |

| | Back-End Sales Charges | | | |
|---|---|---|---|---|
| Year | Annual 12b-1 | Cumulative 12b-1 Fees | Exit Fee | Total Fees |
| 1 | 1% | 1% | 5% | 6% |
| 2 | 1% | 2% | 4% | 6% |
| 3 | 1% | 3% | 3% | 6% |
| 4 | 1% | 4% | 2% | 6% |
| 5 | 1% | 5% | 1% | 6% |
| 6 | 1% | 6% | 0% | 6% |
| 7 | 1% | 7% | 0% | 7% |
| 8 | 1% | 8% | 0% | 8% |
| 9 | 1% | 9% | 0% | 9% |
| 10 | 1% | 10% | 0% | 10% |

As you can see in the comparison chart, our sample 1.5% front-end sales charge seems much lower than the 5% back-end charge. But when total fees are compared, the front-end load is only a better deal if the fund is held for less than 5 years.

# 2.1.9.3 Distribution Plans, SEC Rule 12b-1

SEC Rule 12b-1 allows mutual funds to use the fund's assets to finance the distribution of shares. **12b-1 fees** are special assessments that allow mutual funds to collect money to reimburse marketing and distribution expenses. This was originally done as a way for no-load mutual funds to raise money to promote their fund, but load funds also have ways to collect these charges. The purpose of 12b-1 fees is to increase fund assets by attracting more investors into the fund, then using economies of scale to reduce the relative expenses of the fund when figured on a per investor basis.

12b-1 fees are figured on an annual basis, but charged quarterly to each customer account. The fee can be no more than 0.75% for load funds and no more than 0.25% for no-load funds. The fee is not paid for investment advice, but is only for distributing and promoting the fund. Remember, 12b-1 fees must be approved annually by:

1. a majority vote of fund shareholders, and
2. a majority vote of the board of directors, and
3. a majority vote of the noninterested board members.

Termination of the 12b-1 fee can be done by a majority vote of either 1 or 3.

# 2.1.10

# Reduced Sales Charges, Quantity Discounts

Sales charge reductions are often offered to clients for quantity purchases. In fact, this is the only way investors can reduce the cost of a mutual fund since investors must always pay the POP. (Remember, only NASD member broker-dealers are permitted to buy mutual funds at a discount.) Let's look at different methods of qualifying for sales charge reductions and examine how rights of accumulation work.

## 2.1.10.1 Qualifying for Reduced Sales Charges

Although mutual funds are not required to offer sales charge reductions, many do. This is usually done because it encourages more investment and often is needed in a competitive marketplace.

**Breakpoint. Breakpoints** are the investment dollar levels at which investors are eligible for a reduced sales charge. Breakpoints can usually be achieved by combining the investment amounts of married couples, or parents and their minor children, but not for adult children, unrelated people, etc.

**Exam Topic Alert**

Firms must do what they can to help clients reduce sales charges. Some funds allow investments across their family of funds to count toward breakpoints, others do not. **Breakpoint selling,** always keeping clients' trades just below breakpoints so that they can't qualify for reduced sales charges, **is a violation of NASD rules.**

**Letter of Intent (LOI).** A **letter of intent** is a nonbinding commitment by an investor to invest a certain amount of money within 13 months, in exchange for being entitled to receive breakpoint sales charge rates now.

**Backdating the letter 90 days** is usually permitted to encompass previous investments by that person. If the investor cannot follow through on the LOI, the **effect of an incomplete investment** is that the sales charge reductions must be repaid in cash, or some shares can be sold to cover the money due. In fact, the LOI usually authorizes the custodian to escrow enough shares to cover these fees, with the shares being liquidated to cover the extra sales charges if the investor can't come up with the money. The money needed to reach the breakpoint must be a **cash contribution** by the investor; account **appreciation** and reinvestment of dividends and capital gains do *not* count toward the investor's total investment commitment.

## 2.1.10.2 Rights of Accumulation

**Rights of accumulation** are breakpoint a future time once the total amount of money invested has reached the breakpoint. From that point forward, all newly invested money qualifies for the reduced sales charges. Again, mutual funds aren't required to offer this, but many do.

**Valuation Methods.** Account valuation methods are different when investors try to reach breakpoint targets using rights of accumulation compared to other methods. Rights of accumulation don't count the initial investment and are not retroactive, but these rights do accumulate indefinitely as the account grows in value until the breakpoint goal is reached. With rights of accumulation, appreciation of fund shares and reinvestment of dividends or capital gains *do* count toward the accumulation total.

**Combining accounts** (also called **linking**) to reach rights of accumulation breakpoints is usually allowed for married couples or parents and their minor children, but not for adult children, unrelated people, etc. Qualifying for a reduction in sales charges is based on the combined account value of all eligible accounts. Accounts that are eligible for combining are husband and wife, immediate family members, or multiple corporate accounts. Investment club accounts are not eligible.

# 2.1.11

# Dollar Cost Averaging (DCA)

**Dollar cost averaging (DCA)** is an investment method whereby a set dollar amount is invested at regular intervals. Even though the investor buys fewer shares when the price is high, since he or she can buy more shares when the price is low, this produces a lower average price per share, and a lower total investment cost, than could be achieved by buying a set number of shares at those same intervals. Furthermore, the average DCA price per share is lower than the average share price.

**CALCULATION.** Let's look at a sample calculation to illustrate how DCA works.

Using dollar cost averaging, so investing the same $ amount at each interval:

| Interval | $ Invested | $ Per Share | # Shares Bought |
|---|---|---|---|
| March 31 | $300 | $10 | 30 |
| June 30 | $300 | $7.5 | 40 |
| Sept. 30 | $300 | $10 | 30 |
| Dec. 31 | $300 | $15 | 20 |
| | Total $1200 | ave. $10.63 | total 120 |

So average cost to investor was only $1200 ÷ 120 shares = $10 per share ave.

Without using dollar cost averaging, so buying same # of shares at each interval:

| Interval | $ Invested | $ Per Share | # Shares Bought |
|---|---|---|---|
| March 31 | $300 | $10 | 30 |
| June 30 | $225 | $7.5 | 30 |
| Sept. 30 | $300 | $10 | 30 |
| Dec. 31 | $450 | $15 | 30 |
| | Total $1275 | ave. $10.63 | total 120 |

Without using dollar cost averaging, the investor must spend more money to get the same number of shares and pays a higher average cost per share ($10.63).

Of course, if the market keeps heading in one direction, DCA really doesn't help. This method certainly does not guarantee profits or a certain rate of return. It is merely a method to help investors maximize their investment dollars. DCA lends itself well to mutual funds because investors can buy full or fractional shares, whereas with regular stocks an investor would be forced to buy round lots (or at least full shares), so it's unlikely the same amount of money can be invested each time.

2.1.12

# Redemption of Mutual Fund Shares

Redemption of mutual fund shares is the process by which investors cash in their shares. Essentially, the investor is selling the shares back to the fund. Although there are several ways that the shares can be redeemed, it is important to note that when mutual fund shares are redeemed, no one else gets them. Unlike company shares of stock that trade hands, mutual fund shares are cancelled when redeemed.

Restrictions on share redemptions may be imposed by the fund as long as they do not violate the Investment Company Act of 1940, and such restrictions must be detailed in the fund's prospectus. Some restrictions may require that share redemptions must be done in writing or that certain requests need a guaranteed signature. Setting floor limits on the size of a telephone redemption request is also fairly standard. Finally, many redemption restrictions involve minimum holding periods for shares in order to avoid redemption fees or qualify for reduced back-end loads. Let's look at some redemption methods and other considerations, as well as the basis of redemption pricing and requirements for when the fund must remit payment.

When clients invest money, they are always getting newly issued shares—that's why mutual funds are considered open-end investment companies (and why mutual funds must always use a prospectus—they're always doing a primary offering).

Exam Topic Alert

## 2.1.12.1 Methods

We have touched upon some of the methods for redemption in previous sections. Here we will review the four main methods and mention some additional points that need to be discussed.

**Written Request.** Written requests are a common way for fund shares to be redeemed, especially when liquidating or closing an account. The fund may also require in its prospectus that a redemption be done in writing. A written request typically consists of a letter of instruction that details what the investor wants done with the account. The fund may require that this letter have a signature guarantee. (This will be explained shortly.) If the investor holds the physical fund shares, the certificates to be redeemed must also be included with the written request.

All written requests must be in "good order," meaning that all details about the account are clearly and correctly stated, a transaction request is complete including a statement of the number of shares to be sold, all certificates being sold are sent in by the investor (if being held by them), and all required documents are included with signatures exactly as they're registered in the account (with guarantees, if required).

**Telephone.** Telephone redemption requests are a common convenience offered by many funds. There is usually a floor limit as to how much can be redeemed with a phone order, and there are usually other restrictions placed on using this service as detailed by the fund in the prospectus. For example, the fund may state that it will not close out an account with a phone request or will not process requests over the phone if the transaction has funds being sent to a new address not on file at the fund.

**Check Writing.** Check writing privileges as a means of redeeming mutual fund shares is also quite common, particularly with money market mutual funds. Some funds allow shares to be transferred from a regular mutual fund account to a money market fund account to cover checks written. Overdraft rules apply as with a regular bank checking account. Only checks printed and issued by the fund are acceptable.

There are rules on check writing, often with a minimum and maximum amount for which checks may be written. Many times, only one authorized signature is required on the checks (even with joint accounts). Checks written may act as a loan against the investor's fund shares or cause shares to be sold to cover the amount of the check. Finally, a common restriction is that the fund will not allow an account to be liquidated or closed just by writing a check.

**Through a Dealer.** If an investor chooses to redeem shares through a broker-dealer, the procedures are similar to a written request made to the fund. The broker-dealer must receive a request during normal business hours, with the NAV for the end of the day's business used to calculate the share redemption price. The broker-dealer will make sure that all required documents (and certificates) are assembled to execute the order. This may include trust documents or a corporate resolution authorizing a trade. The broker-dealer can also give any signature guarantees that are required.

## 2.1.12.2 Considerations

Here are two important considerations for mutual fund share redemption: Is a signature guarantee required? Who's holding the share certificates?

**Signature Guarantee.** A **signature guarantee** is written authentication by a broker-dealer firm, bank, or other accepted guarantor, that a person's signature is genuine.

A notary public may *not* guarantee a signature.

Exam Topic Alert

The idea behind the signature guarantee is to avoid misunderstandings and minimize incidents of fraud with the account. A signature guarantee can be required for many reasons, such as:

▷ money is to be paid to someone who is not listed as an owner of the account;
▷ money from the redemption is supposed to go to an address or bank account that is not listed on the account;
▷ the investor's address or bank account has been recently changed; or
▷ the shares to be redeemed are over a certain dollar amount.

The fund also requires additional documentation and signatures when the account is that of a corporation, trust, etc. In such cases, the fund needs a certified copy of the corporate resolution authorizing the sale, trust documents showing the fiduciary's power of attorney over the account, or other authorizing legal document.

**Outstanding Certificate.** Any certificate in the hands of an investor is considered outstanding. Here, though, an important consideration is whether the investor has taken physical possession of the share certificates. If so, then the certificates must be properly endorsed and submitted to the fund for redemption. If the certificates are not received by the fund within a certain time period following a customer's sell order (stated in the prospectus, usually no more than ten business days), then the fund may cancel the redemption order. If certificates are held by the fund or a broker-dealer, then the investor needs to submit a valid stock power or power of attorney in lieu of submitting the certificates (unless one is already on file).

## 2.1.12.3 Basis of Redemption Price

The redemption price for mutual fund shares is the net asset value (NAV) of the mutual fund. Remember, our formula for NAV is:

**(Fund Assets – Fund Liabilities) ÷ Number of Outstanding Shares = NAV Per Share**

**NAV Computed.** NAV is usually only calculated once at the end of the trading day. In order for an investor to get that day's NAV pricing, the redemption order must be submitted before the end of the trading day. Since mutual fund buy and sell orders are placed before a final price is known, this is **forward pricing.** The investor will not know how much money will be received until after the fund calculates its NAV.

**Redemption Fee.** Some mutual funds also impose a redemption fee, primarily when shares are not held long enough. This fee combined with all others still can't exceed 8.5% per NASD rules.

## 2.1.12.4 Fund Required to Remit Timely Payment

Redemption of mutual fund shares must take place within seven calendar days to comply with the Investment Company Act of 1940. This is designed to protect investors since the fund is the only market for the fund shares. There are very few conditions under which the fund may not have to redeem the shares within seven days, such as trade restrictions on the NYSE, a redemption suspension ordered by the SEC, or other declared emergency.

## 2.1.13

# Prospectus and Statement of Additional Information (SAI)

The **prospectus** is a formal written document that gives comprehensive information about the investment company, management team (including name of the fund manager), mutual fund objectives, investment policies, and all sales charges and expenses. The **statement of additional information (SAI)** is a mutual fund disclosure document that gives more detailed information than the mutual fund prospectus. The SAI is often referred to as Part B of the prospectus. Let's look at when these documents must be given out, their purpose, and examine their contents.

# 2.1.13.1 Registration Requirement

The Securities Act of 1933 requires that all securities must first be registered with the SEC before they can be sold to the public. The act also requires the use of a prospectus to provide full disclosure of all pertinent information. Once the registration statement and preliminary prospectus are filed with the SEC disclosing all required information about the company and the proposed offering, then the SEC imposes a **cooling off period.** During this time, the company may only get general indications of interest in a new offering and is prevented from sending any materials other than the **preliminary prospectus.** (This is also called a **red herring** because it must state on the cover—often printed in red ink—that "This prospectus is not an offer to sell securities nor solicit orders.") There's also a **quiet period** that lasts concurrently with the cooling off period, then the quiet period continues for an additional 25 days after a stock starts trading. This means that a company is prevented from promoting the issue and must let the final prospectus be the vehicle to explain and sell the issue.

Once the registration has been cleared by the SEC, this is considered the **effective date** of registration. From that point on, the underwriters may advertise and solicit orders to sell securities as long as the final prospectus is also sent to investors. The fund underwriters are required to file updated prospectus materials with the SEC no later than 16 months after the end of the mutual fund's fiscal year. (In reality, most funds refile an updated prospectus annually.)

The SAI also contains information that is part of the registration filing with the SEC. The SAI is legally considered part of the prospectus. The SEC created the separate SAI document to remove some of the complexity from the prospectus and make it easier for investors to understand. For example, the SAI now contains all technical explanations and calculations regarding fees. All changes and amendments to the SAI must be filed with the SEC at least 60 days prior to usage.

Recently, the SEC has created a profile document, which is more simplified than the prospectus. The **profile document** must contain specific information about the mutual fund in clear, concise, plain English and be presented in a standardized format. The profile document must be filed with the SEC at least 30 days prior to first use and within 5 days of first use after substantive changes. The profile document does not replace the prospectus but may precede it as we'll see in the next sections.

**Prospectus.** A full mutual fund prospectus must be delivered to all prospective investors upon request, before they put any money into the fund, or no later than with the confirmation of sale if the investor sends money after reviewing the profile statement. A prospectus can be obtained by contacting the fund, or an underwriter or broker-dealer firm representing the fund. A prospectus must be sent within three days of a request. The same information can be obtained on-line at the fund's website, or through SEC filings on-line at http://www.sec.gov/edgar/searchedgar/webuser.htm or http://www.10kwizard.com.

**Statement of Additional Information.** The SAI can be obtained by contacting the company or through the same on-line resources as the prospectus. The difference is that the SAI is only sent upon special request. Although it is assumed that an investor has read the SAI because it is legally considered to be part of the prospectus, it's *not* mandatory nor automatic that the SAI is sent with a prospectus.

**Profile.** A profile statement may be sent to an investor who requests more information on a mutual fund. The fund may also send out the profile statement with a purchase application in lieu of the prospectus, provided that the application explains that a complete prospectus is available upon request and states that the investor can and should review the full prospectus before making an investment decision. If a client sends in money based solely upon review of the profile statement, then the full prospectus must be sent with the confirmation of sale at the latest. (Note that although profile statements may be sent without a prospectus, SEC rules state that supplemental sales literature must still be sent to investors with a full prospectus.)

## 2.1.13.2 Purpose of Prospectus

A prospectus is required for full disclosure of all pertinent information related to an investment, so that investors can make an informed investment decision. The SEC only clears a registration and prospectus, allowing a public offering to take place. It is unlawful to state, imply, or represent that the prospectus, or any other documents, materials, etc., are somehow approved by the government, the SEC, or any other oversight body.

**SEC "No Approval" Clause.** To avoid any potential confusion by investors, the law states that a prospectus used for the sale of securities must contain a disclaimer on its cover that says, "These securities have not been approved by the SEC."

## 2.1.13.3 Contents

Although the order of items may vary slightly in a prospectus, all points must be included to comply with federal law and SEC regulations. As stated before, the SAI includes much of the same information as the prospectus, albeit in greater detail. The main thrust of this section will be to go over points covered in a prospectus, but specific details in the SAI will be referenced where appropriate.

**Investment Objectives, Policies, and Restrictions.** This part of a prospectus explains the philosophy of the fund, its objectives (income, growth, etc.), and the strategy the fund uses to achieve its objectives. This section will likely include a list of the types of securities in which the fund invests and state if there are any restrictions on the portfolio (such as types of securities the fund will not buy).

**Sales Loads and Fees.** The fund is required to list all transaction expenses (loads) first before listing the fund's operating expenses (management fees). Details, such as any temporary fee reductions, should be read carefully because expenses can rise significantly once the temporary period is over. The total annual expense figure must be listed, along with an example of fees paid on a theoretical $10,000 investment that is held for various time periods. Finally, brokerage arrangements, commission breakdowns, and other financial agreements of fees for services (called **soft dollar arrangements** when insiders are involved) must be detailed here and/or in the SAI.

Additional information that typically appears in the SAI includes calculations of these fees, formulas used to derive the fees and expenses, and a breakdown of how the fees and expenses are spent by the mutual fund.

**Front-end loads** are explained along with their calculations, if applicable. **Contingent deferred** loads (back-end loads) are detailed, if used, along with a table that shows how the fee is reduced over time. **12b-1 fees** used for distribution and advertising must also have a technical disclosure (usually in the SAI) that explains the fee in detail. The prospectus and/or SAI must also include a list of the types of persons that qualify for reduced or waived sales charges, along with other dealer re-allowance information that affects the fees charged and collected by the fund. **Redemption fees** must also be included if charged by the fund, along with an explanation of what they are, when they are collected, and how they are calculated. **Management fees** charged by the fund are also detailed, including which company or person is charging the fund and for what services. These, along with **other expenses** incurred by the fund for day-to-day operations, are in a list of the fund's annual operating expenses. All of these expenses affect the fund's expense ratio.

**Expense Table.** An expense table appears near the beginning of the prospectus. The expense table has a detailed list of all expenses associated with owning the fund. Three main groups of expenses include sales loads, expense ratio, and any 12b-1 fees. (Note that loads, 12b-1 fees, and redemption fees are not part of the expense ratio.) If there is a 12b-1 fee, the amount will also be listed in the table (usually 0.25% to 1%). This is important because the 12b-1 fee is paid directly from fund assets so an investor doesn't directly see this fee. The expense table is also where you will find the example we talked about previously where the expenses are broken down, showing how they affect the value of a theoretical $10,000 investment held for various periods of time, assuming the fund returns 5% a year. As a point of reference, the average expense ratio for all equity funds is a little under 1.5%, but this figure can vary greatly depending on the specific fund category.

The expense table that appears in the prospectus (or a variation of that table) will also likely reappear in the SAI. Most funds, however, have moved many of the figures, calculations, and detailed explanations of the various numbers to the SAI.

**Breakpoints, Rights of Accumulation, Combining Accounts, Letter of Intent.** The prospectus includes information about any breakpoints that the fund offers, along with specific details explaining how investors can take advantage of them. This would include a discussion of whether or not backdating is allowed, whether or not appreciation or reinvestment is considered, and the procedures that are used in the event that an investor is not able to follow through with an investment commitment.

**Exchange Privileges within Family of Funds.** The prospectus details what exchange privileges or conversion privileges are available to investors. Typically, this involves trading in or selling one fund and acquiring another in the same family of funds offered by the investment company. Remember, though, that any redemption is a taxable event even if mutual fund shares are purchased with the proceeds. The prospectus and/or SAI will discuss tax consequences associated with the fund.

**Per-Share Income and Capital Changes.** This discusses the fund's payout policy and frequency of dividends, capital gains, and the impact on income per-share. Information will also be included about NAV calculations and events that affect the net asset value of the fund (although some or all of these may be shifted to the SAI).

**Methods of Sale.** This information would include such things as where shares can be purchased, the procedure for purchasing shares (and opening an account, if needed), and an explanation of how the share purchase price is calculated. Actual calculations showing how to determine NAV, sales charges, and POP would likely be contained in an SAI. Also, breakpoint sales and exchange privileges would be stated.

**Methods of Redemption.** This information would include such things as where shares can be redeemed, the procedure for selling shares (e.g., if telephone redemption is allowed), and an explanation of how the buy back price is calculated. Actual calculations showing how to determine NAV and any back-end loads or redemption fees would likely be in the SAI. Also, withdrawal plan options would be listed.

**Investment and Withdrawal Plans.** A prospectus is the main source of information on what is permitted by the fund. This would include details of any regularly scheduled investment plans that might be available (e.g., minimum amounts that can open an account or be contributed on a regular basis). Conversely, the prospectus would also indicate what withdrawal plans are available and the minimum value of shares that must be owned before a plan can be chosen. Automatic checking deposits or withdrawals, check writing privileges, and retirement accounts are just some of the other available services that the prospectus and/or SAI may describe.

**Financial Statements.** The prospectus shows the fund's annual performance for the past ten years, including the value of fund's portfolio assets. Other financial highlights included in the prospectus are tables that show all of the money that has gone into and out of the mutual fund each year, affecting the NAV. Also shown are expense ratios and turnover ratios (how often the fund bought and sold securities). Additional details, information, and calculations appear in the SAI.

*Note:* Information contained in the profile statement is essentially a synopsis of the prospectus. The contents of the profile statement are not currently a tested topic, but your instructor will indicate if/when this changes. Still, let's list them for your own information, as you will likely see profiles when you sell mutual funds. After the cover page, the following nine topics (only!) must be presented in this order:

(1) fund objectives and goals, (2) principal investment strategies, (3) principal risks of investing in the fund, (4) fees and expenses, (5) investment advisor and portfolio manager, (6) procedure for buying fund shares, (7) procedure for selling fund shares, (8) fund distributions and tax information, and (9) other services provided by the fund.

# 2.2 Federal Income Tax Regulations for Mutual Funds

There are many tax laws specific to mutual funds. These include tax laws that deal with the consequences of investment company activities and tax consequences for individual investors who buy and sell mutual fund shares. Let's examine these, as they will affect a client's investment—and likely will appear on the Series 6 exam.

## 2.2.1 Tax Consequences of Investment Company's Activities

For registered investment companies to receive favorable tax treatment, they must qualify as a **regulated investment company** under the Internal Revenue Service tax code and must meet minimum requirements for capital gains and income distributions. If they qualify, regulated investment companies receive special tax considerations. Let's look at these regulations.

### 2.2.1.1 Regulated Investment Company

Under Regulation M of the IRS code, mutual fund companies can avoid double taxation by distributing at least 90% of the dividends they receive and at least 90% of net income from capital gains. This is referred to as the **conduit theory, Subchapter M theory,** or **pipeline theory.**

**Conduit Theory. Conduit theory** says that a regulated investment company that meets IRS guidelines is merely a conduit for passing through capital gains, dividends, and interest directly to fund shareholders. This allows taxes to be paid only once at the shareholder level. If the fund doesn't pass through 90% as required, then the fund must pay taxes on 100% of its income. This threat of double taxation virtually forces the fund to pass through dividends and other gains to shareholders.

As long as the fund makes the **required distribution of income and realized capital** gains to shareholders (currently at 90% or higher), then the fund pays no federal tax on the money that is distributed to shareholders. The fund also sends an IRS Form 1099 to shareholders each year, detailing the individual investor's share of dividends and capital gains that must be declared, including the **identification of the tax category** of the distributions (e.g., long-term or short-term capital gains).

## 2.2.1.2 Tax Treatment of Capital Gains Distributions

Most mutual funds distribute 90% of their capital gains to shareholders to avoid taxation at the fund level. Still, there are other tax considerations. The tax treatment of capital gains distributions to shareholders (i.e., whether or not a capital gain is long term or short term) depends on how long the fund held the investment—not how long the shareholder held the mutual fund shares. This is why **portfolio turnover** is important.

**Portfolio Turnover.** Mutual funds buy and sell their holdings at varying paces. Turnover is expressed as a percentage of a fund's portfolio that's sold during the year.

**Annual Portfolio Turnover Rate = Gross Proceeds From Sales ÷ Total Assets**

Average turnover rate for managed mutual funds is about 85% per year. Indexed and nonactively managed funds are significantly less. There are two reasons why turnover is important from an investor's standpoint. First, more turnover of funds means the fund is paying more in sales commissions that can eat into a fund's assets. Second, the sale of a fund's holdings generates a taxable event for shareholders.

Remember, it's a short-term capital gain for the shareholder if the asset was held for less than 12 months—by the fund, not the shareholder. If the fund held a certain company's shares for 18 months before selling them, but the investor just got into the fund last month, any capital gains on the sale is still considered a long-term capital gain for the investor. Conversely, if the investor has held a mutual fund for three years, but the fund keeps buying and selling stocks after only holding them for six months, the capital gains from those sales are all considered short-term.

## 2.2.1.3 Tax Treatment of Income Distributions

Most mutual funds distribute at least 90% of their income from dividends and interest to shareholders to avoid taxation at the fund level. Dividends and interest are taxed as short-term capital gains to shareholders—whether the shareholder takes the cash or reinvests the distributions—unless the mutual fund shares are held in an individual retirement account (IRA) or other tax-deferred account. There is another concern for the fund, though, dealing with the short-short rule (also called the **30% rule**).

**Short-Short Rule.** The **short-short rule** is an IRS tax code rule that disqualifies an investment company's status as a regulated investment company and cancels its ability to pass through gains and income to avoid double taxation, if more than 30% of the fund's gross income (i.e., before deductions) comes from trades where the asset was held for less than three months. This is done to discourage funds from active trading.

# Tax Consequences of Mutual Fund Investor's Activities

Individual investors in a mutual fund have two sets of tax considerations. The first is related to the mutual fund's handling of its portfolio investments, as we saw in the previous section. The investor also has to consider the standard tax laws that apply to all types of investments (mutual funds and otherwise). Let's look at these.

## 2.2.2.1 Shareholder Responsibility

Shareholders are responsible for reporting all dividend and capital gains distributions to the IRS, as well as state and local tax authorities. The fund will send an IRS Form 1099 to each shareholder at the end of the year detailing the dividends and capital gains distributions made. This is true regardless of whether or not the investor has supplied a valid Social Security or other tax ID number to the fund. (If the investor does not supply the fund with a Social Security number, then the fund must withhold 31% of all distributions. We'll discuss this shortly.) Ultimately, the duty to report falls on the shoulders of the investor.

## 2.2.2.2 Tax Treatment of Securities Transactions

The investor who buys and sells mutual fund shares has to consider the individual tax treatment of securities transactions, the same as for all other investments that are traded. This involves understanding the definitions and computations of capital gains and losses.

**Definitions.** A **capital gain** is the increase in value above the adjusted cost basis realized by an investor when an asset is sold. A **capital loss** is the decrease in value below the adjusted cost basis realized by an investor when an asset is sold. Note that these definitions do not use the purchase or sale price of the security. Price is only one component involved when computing gains or losses.

**Computation.** Normally, you would think that a gain or a loss would be calculated by comparing the prices at which you bought something and then sold it. Instead, IRS rules use an **adjusted cost basis,** which is the original price, plus any commissions or allowable expenses. The sale price, minus the adjusted cost basis, is the amount of the gain or loss used for tax calculations.

**TAX TREATMENT OF REALIZED CAPITAL GAINS / LOSSES.** Tax treatment of capital gains varies depending on how long the investor held the shares before selling. If shares were held for less than 12 months, then any gain is treated as ordinary income and taxed at the investor's marginal tax rate. If shares were held for at least 12 months, then the gain is treated as a long-term capital gain and taxed at a lower rate.

Tax treatment of capital losses is a bit more complicated. The investor must first separate out all taxable events as being a short-term gain or long-term gain, short-term loss or long-term loss. As with gains, 12 months is the cutoff: losses on assets held for less than 12 months are short-term losses; losses on assets held for 12 months or

Note here we're talking about how long the *investor* held the shares. When an investor sells shares, it doesn't matter how long the fund held anything.

Exam Topic Alert

more are considered long-term losses. Short-term losses are offset against short-term gains; long-term losses are offset against long-term gains. Capital losses are deducted first against capital gains, and if there is any additional loss, then up to $3000 of the capital loss may be deducted against ordinary income. Capital losses over the $3000 limit may be carried forward indefinitely to subsequent years, but the maximum capital loss that may be claimed is still $3000 per year.

Another important point is that this entire discussion only deals with *realized* capital gains and losses. In other words, real losses that the investor incurs as a result of the sale of mutual fund shares. There is no capital gain or loss incurred simply because the value of the shares (or the value of the mutual fund portfolio) goes up and down. You only pay taxes on income you take in or money you make from selling something, and the IRS only lets you take a deduction for actual losses.

Exam Topic Alert

**EXCHANGES AS A TAXABLE EVENT.** We said that investors only pay taxes on money they actually make. Once a security is sold and money is made, taxes are owed no matter how quickly the money passes through the investor's hands. Thus, if an investor sells mutual fund shares with the intention of exchanging the shares, the sale is a taxable event, and taxes are due on the gain even if the money is used right away to buy more shares in a different fund. Of course, if the shares are sold at a loss in order to make an exchange, then the investor gets to claim the loss.

Interestingly, some funds (mostly money market mutual funds) endeavor to maintain a stable share price, usually around $1 per share. The idea is that the stable share price in effect makes exchanges and redemptions virtually tax-free events. If you buy shares at $1 and sell them at $1, you would not owe tax on the sale or exchange. Of course, there's no guarantee the share price will stay at $1 or be at $1 when you need to sell, but the goal is to keep it as close to that level as possible. That way, when investors write checks to sell shares from their account, they do not incur any significant tax consequences. Instead of share appreciation, investors are interested in liquidity and convenience, and they also make money from dividends and interest payouts, which money market mutual funds are able to make somewhat regularly.

## 2.2.2.3 Tax Basis of Securities

Thus far, we've talked about the tax consequences of securities transactions as if the investor is always the original purchaser of the shares from the fund. Certainly, there are other ways that shares can be acquired, and different considerations when determining the cost basis. Let's look at these.

**Offering Price.** The public offering price that investors pay for mutual fund shares is not the only component of their cost basis. Any additional fees paid may get added to the cost basis, and any back-end loads and redemption fees paid when the shares are sold are added to the investor's cost basis as well. Remember, too, that forward pricing is used when shares are bought and sold, so the basis isn't known until after the NAV is calculated at the end of the day.

**Exchange of Securities.** Exchanges are a taxable event for the investor, which may generate a capital gain or loss. The gain or loss is reportable in the year of the exchange, and the tax is due, even if the investor complied with all fund rules and made a successful exchange that avoided sales charges. Any sales charges or exchange fees incurred are added to the investor's cost basis.

**Gifts of Securities.** If securities are passed on during a person's lifetime, they are considered a gift. The gift recipient's cost basis for tax purposes is based on the fair market value (FMV) of the shares, according to the following rules:

> If the FMV of the shares is *less* than the donor's basis at the time of the gift:
> > Your cost basis for gain is the same as the donor's adjusted basis.
> > Your cost basis for loss is the FMV at the time of the gift.
> If the FMV of the shares is *more* than the donor's basis at the time of the gift:
> > Your cost basis is the same as the donor's adjusted basis.

Also, if the donor was required to pay a gift tax, the recipient's cost basis is increased by the amount of gift tax paid that is attributable to that gift of securities.

**Inheritance of Securities.** If mutual fund shares are received as an inheritance, the cost basis is stepped up to the FMV of the shares on the date the deceased passed away. With inheritances, any gain or loss when the shares are sold is always considered long term, regardless of the actual holding period (length of time an investment was owned) by the deceased or the person who inherited them.

**Reinvested Dividends and Capital Gains.** Reinvestment of capital gains and dividends is still a taxable event for the investor. Once the gain is realized, the taxes are owed. If the money is reinvested, then that adjusts the cost basis upward for the investor. That is, once the investor has paid taxes on the money (e.g., realized capital gains from the mutual fund), then taxes are not paid on it a second time when shares are redeemed. So the investor's adjusted cost basis equals the original amount invested, plus allowable fees, plus reinvested dividends and capital gains.

## 2.2.2.4 Holding Periods of Securities

When we talk about holding periods for securities, we're referring primarily to the 12-month cutoff that has been discussed in previous sections. This is used to determine if a gain or loss is long-term or short-term.

**Acquisition.** When shares are purchased or acquired at various times, the holding periods are different for each group of shares. (This is important when we discuss redemption and tax consequences.) Different rules apply to gifts and inheritances.

Exam Topic Alert

For tax purposes, the holding period begins at the **trade date** (when you authorize the trade), not the settlement date (when you pay for the trade).

For securities received as a gift, the start of the holding period depends on the intent of the giver. If the person giving the securities is donating them in exchange for a tax write-off (as when securities are given to charity), then the holding period starts on the day after the gift was given. If, on the other hand, the person is giving the securities as a personal gift and not seeking a tax deduction, then the holding period starts on the day the donor's holding period started.

For inherited securities, any future gain or loss is treated as a long-term capital gain—regardless of how long the deceased person or the recipient actually held the asset. So holding periods don't come into effect here, since all inheritances are treated as if the 12-month period has already elapsed.

**Redemption.** If an investor does not sell all of his or her shares in a particular fund, then there may need to be some analysis to determine which shares to sell first to minimize tax consequences. Of course, if given a choice, it would be to the investor's advantage to sell shares that have already been held for more than 12 months, but there are other considerations (such as figuring the cost basis). For our discussion about holding periods, just know that one of the redemption methods an investor can choose is called identified shares.

**Identified shares** is the best of both worlds for the investor. By keeping good records of when shares were acquired and what was paid for each lot of shares purchased, the investor can use the most favorable holding period and cost basis for his or her current tax situation. The investor can identify which shares are being sold when filing taxes with the IRS and might be able to show losses when needed or take a larger tax hit in years when it would not result in being bumped into a higher marginal tax bracket. (If the investor does not identify shares, then the IRS uses the First In, First Out (FIFO) method. **FIFO** assumes that the shares being sold are the earliest ones purchased. These shares will likely have the lowest cost basis and result in a larger tax liability for the investor.)

## 2.2.2.5 Wash Sale Rule

**Wash sales** are when the same securities (or substantially similar securities) are bought and sold simultaneously or within a short period of time. The IRS has established that wash sales that occur within 30 days before or 30 days after a transaction are not eligible for use as a capital loss. This creates a 61-day window within which substantially similar activity may not occur, or any resulting losses are not deductible by the investor. This is to avoid the situation where an investor attempts to create a loss when a fund is down by selling it, realizing the loss, and then buying back the same security so that the investor's position did not change (i.e., the investor owns the same number of shares as before, but now also has a capital loss to claim on his or her taxes).

Note that IRS wash sale rules also don't allow investors to buy options or other derivative securities from the same company during the 30-day window before or after the trade date establishing a loss. This does not typically apply, though, to fund exchanges—even within the same family of funds—as long as the fund is a different fund, with a different name, a different portfolio, and a separate SEC registration. The only other exception is bond swaps. **Bond swaps** are when investors buy bonds from a different issuer, or buy bonds from the same issuer with two or more different characteristics (e.g., new maturity date and interest rate) to get around wash sale rules.

# 2.3 Customer Accounts

When opening new customer accounts, there are many documents to fill out and procedures to follow. All new accounts require a new account form. There are other items that the broker-dealer may need in order to set up and handle the account properly. Some of these items depend on what kind of account will be opened, who will own the account, and who is authorized to trade for the account. These choices may entail additional restrictions or require more documentation, which we will mention as we discuss each topic. (Remember, too, that because mutual fund shares are always done as a primary offering, they may only be purchased in a cash account.)

## 2.3.1

# Open Account Characteristics

Once an account has been opened, there are a number of rules and regulations that must be followed. In addition to securities laws and SEC rules, broker-dealer firms will have their own procedures in place which must be followed. Most of these rules have to do with ensuring that the client's interests are protected. When dealing with customer accounts, it is very important to follow all rules and procedures put in place by your broker-dealer. These are designed to ensure compliance with the securities laws and regulations. Customer complaints and violations in dealing with customer accounts are taken very seriously.

## 2.3.1.1 Required Minimum Investment

Most mutual funds have a minimum investment amount that must be made in order to open a new account. Also, if the investor is participating in some type of periodic payment plan or periodic investment plan, then the mutual fund will likely have a set amount that must be contributed on a set schedule. Of course, some plans allow investments of any amount at any time, but investors must observe minimums put in place by the fund.

## 2.3.1.2 Dividend/Capital Gains Election

When opening a new account, it is typical for the investor to be asked how he or she wants dividend payments and capital gain distributions to be paid out. If the investor chooses the **cash** option, then checks will be sent to the address on record every time a distribution is declared. If the investors chooses **automatic reinvestment,** then the fund will take any distributions and buy additional full or fractional shares for the investor with that money.

2.3.2

# Account Documentation

Most brokerage firms have special forms that new clients must fill out as a means of gathering the necessary information. Much of this information is standard, but we will make comments where appropriate.

> It is interesting to note that the new customer is not required to sign the new account form for mutual funds, since he or she is opening a cash account. (The authorized sales representative and branch manager or other principal of the firm must sign the form for the broker-dealer.)

Exam Topic
Alert

## 2.3.2.1 Customer Name and Residence

In addition to the customer's legal name and residence address, it's also important to get a customer's residency information (i.e., the customer's citizenship). If the customer is not a citizen of the United States, then the person's residency status must be noted (resident alien with a green card or visa status). Persons who are nonresident aliens are subject to 31% tax withholding requirements. For joint accounts, you must get this information for all persons.

## 2.3.2.2 Whether of Legal Age

Although customers are not required to reveal their age, this is still a concern for the account representative and broker-dealer firm. Since minors cannot legally enter into binding contracts, the age of the customer must be estimated. If there is some question as to whether or not the customer is of legal age, the broker-dealer may require proof of age before allowing the account to be opened. (Check with your broker's policies.) Also, knowing the age of a client (or at least an estimate of the client's age) is important for planning retirement accounts.

## 2.3.2.3 Reasonable Efforts to Obtain Other Information

There are a few other important items that should be part of a new account record. Many of these are required to help you comply with rules and regulations. These include:

**Tax ID Number (TIN) or Social Security Number.** Obtaining the Social Security number of a client (or TIN for a business account) is important. By law, shareholders are required to certify that the Social Security number they give is correct and that they're not subject to back-up withholding. If the client declines to give a Social Security number or sign the certification, then the fund must withhold 31% of all dividends and capital gains distributions to cover federal tax liability.

**Occupation of Customer and Name, Address of Employer.** When a new account is opened, the representative must make every effort to obtain accurate information about the client's occupation and get the employer's name and address for verification. The brokerage firm needs to know whether or not the customer is an employee of another member broker-dealer firm and whether or not the customer is an officer, director, executive, or shareholder (10% or higher) of any publicly traded company. This is to monitor potential conflicts of interest, insider trading, or illegal activity.

**Whether Person Is Associated with Another NASD Member.** The new account form asks if a client works for another broker-dealer firm because NASD broker-dealers must be given written notice before an employee opens an account with another broker-dealer. The NASD firm also has the option of requesting duplicate trade confirmations for all trading activity. (NYSE members require written permission before the account is opened and require duplicate trade confirmations.)

**Discretionary Account Data.** Discretionary accounts give the licensed representative authority to make trades on behalf of the client, without the client's prior knowledge. Just because you decide at what price to buy or sell a security for the client does not mean you have made a discretionary trade. It would only be a discretionary trade if you chose the **security,** and the **amount** of shares, and whether to **buy or sell.** All three elements are necessary (picked by you) for a trade to be considered discretionary.

**Name and Signature of Person(s) with Account Authority.** Only persons named on the account may authorize trades or perform other actions related to the account, unless the client executes a valid power of attorney. A **power of attorney** is an instrument that authorizes one person to act on behalf of another. The document details exactly what authority the person has with respect to that account.

Exam Topic
Alert

> If you are only choosing the timing of the trade, or the price at which to buy or sell, that alone does not make it a discretionary trade. *If you are not picking the mutual fund, it's not a discretionary trade.*

**Limited Authorization.** Limited power of attorney allows the named person to execute buy and sell orders only.

**Full Authorization.** Full power of attorney allows the named person to execute buy and sell orders and also permits withdrawal of funds from the account.

**Discretionary Powers to Broker-Dealer.** The client must sign a document explicitly granting discretionary authorization, and this authorization must be received and approved by a principal before any discretionary trades can be made. Authorization can last a maximum of three years before it must be renewed.

All trades must be marked "discretionary," and a principal must sign off on all discretionary trades (at least the same day). Furthermore, all trades must stay within the investment objectives that the client has laid out for the account. Finally, all persons monitoring a discretionary account are sensitive for signs of **churning** the account (making excessive trades to generate commissions).

**Documentation of Trading Authority.** For new accounts other than personal accounts, there are extra documents required to establish who has the authority to make trades for the account. Here are a few of those accounts and the paperwork needed:

**Corporate Accounts.** A corporation is a separate legal entity organized under state law. As such, the broker-dealer requires the company's Articles of Incorporation and/or Corporate Charter stating that the corporation is authorized to buy and sell securities. The broker-dealer also needs a specific corporate resolution stating which person(s) are authorized to make trades on behalf of the corporation. The resolution may also state the objectives for the corporate account and detail specific investments in which the corporate account may or may not invest.

**Partnership Accounts.** Partnerships are a contract between two or more persons to pool money, resources, and talents in a business, project, or venture in exchange for a share of the profits (or losses) generated by their association. To open a securities account, the broker-dealer needs a copy of the partnership agreement, signatures of all general partners, and any other documentation that details who has the authority to open the account and make trades on behalf of the partnership.

**Trust Accounts.** Trust accounts are set up to benefit one party (beneficiary) but are controlled by a third party (fiduciary). A **fiduciary** is a person in a position of trust, held by law to high standards of good faith and loyalty. The fiduciary is authorized by court order or appointed by another official document to manage the account for the beneficiary. The broker-dealer will need a copy of either of these along with the new account form. By law, a fiduciary cannot delegate authority or responsibility for the account.

**Fiduciaries/Administrators.** Another common type of trust account where fiduciaries are used involve minors. Again, the appointed fiduciary or administrator has a fiduciary responsibility to the minor and control over the account's investments. The broker-dealer needs the appropriate documentation granting authority to the fiduciary or administrator in order to set up the account.

**Investment Advisor.** Investment advisers are persons registered to give investment advice for a fee. In addition to providing one-on-one advice to clients or issuing newsletters to dispense investing advice, some investment advisors actually invest money on behalf of clients. This can be done in a blind pool (called an omnibus account) where client identities are not disclosed, or in a fully disclosed account where the client identities are known. In the latter instance, the broker-dealer is responsible for obtaining new account forms and any necessary agreements or documents from each client, as well as maintaining current client data.

## 2.3.3

# Forms of Ownership of Mutual Fund Shares

Once the broker-dealer has received (and verified) the appropriate information, the account can be opened. The next issue becomes who actually owns the shares. As we saw in the last section, there are limited numbers of people authorized to trade for the account and withdraw funds. That does not mean that the person trading for the account is necessarily the person who owns the shares. Let's examine some different account types, along with ownership issues that must be considered.

## 2.3.3.1 Individual Registration

This is the least complicated account ownership situation. An individual account is setup with only one named person on the account, so that one person alone owns the shares. That individual, though, can grant power of attorney to another party, giving that party trading authority over the account, as we saw in the previous section, but that does not change ownership of the shares.

## 2.3.3.2 Joint Accounts: Joint Tenants with Right of Survivorship

A joint account is set up with two or more people named on the account. With any type of joint account, all parties own an undivided interest in the account. This means that everyone owns a part of each share; there is no way to discern who owns which shares. Because of this, any one of the joint owners can enter a buy or sell order on behalf of the account. This also means that whenever any security is sold, the check must be written to *all* parties jointly.

**Joint Tenants with Right of Survivorship (JTROS)** is a type of joint account where upon the death of one party, that party's interest in the account is passed to the other parties of the account. To have this arrangement, all parties must have an equal share in the account. This is a common arrangement between spouses.

## 2.3.3.3 Joint Accounts: Tenants in Common

This also is a joint account set up with two or more people named on the account. All parties own an undivided interest in the account, so any one of the joint owners can enter a buy or sell order on behalf of the account, and checks from sale of shares must be written to *all* parties jointly.

**Joint Tenants in Common (JTIC)** is a type of joint account where upon the death of one party, that party's interest in the account is passed to his or her estate. This means that each of the joint tenants can name their own beneficiary. With this arrangement, parties can have unequal shares.

## 2.3.3.4 Trust Accounts

As we saw in the last section, trust accounts are set up to benefit one party (beneficiary) but are controlled by a third party (fiduciary). A fiduciary is a person in a position of trust, held by law to high standards of good faith and loyalty. As such, the fiduciary must be prudent with the trust account and act solely in the best interests of the beneficiary. Furthermore, the fiduciary cannot delegate authority or responsibility for the account, nor share in the profits of the account. A fiduciary only receives compensation authorized by the trust documents. The actual shares are still owned by the beneficiary (or other designated party).

## 2.3.3.5 Custodial Accounts: UGMA/UTMA

The Uniform Gift to Minors Act (UGMA) and Uniform Transfer to Minors Act (UTMA) provide a simple way for property to be transferred to minors without a formal trust account. Instead, a custodian is appointed to administer the account of donated property. (Note that the donor can also be the custodian of the account, such as a parent.) The shares held in the account must be an **irrevocable gift** to the minor and follow certain other requirements. The size of the gift is unlimited, but gift tax is owed for amounts exceeding $11,000 per year.

**Custodians** have a fiduciary responsibility to the minor and full control over the account's investments. Custodians may not invest in any speculative or risky investments (e.g., options), nor use margin buying in the account. All warrants and rights must be sold or exercised—they can't be allowed to expire. Also, a custodian can't give discretionary power over the account to others and can't borrow from the account. There can only be one minor and one custodian per account, but the minor can have many accounts, and a custodian can be appointed to many different accounts.

UGMA and UTMA accounts use the minor's Social Security number. Account income over $1500 is taxed at the parents' rate until the minor pays tax at age 14. Later, the **shares are registered to the beneficiary upon attaining the age of majority** in that state. In other words, ownership of the shares are transferred from the trust account into the minor's name. (Note that if the minor dies beforehand, the securities go into the minor's estate and are *not* transferred to the parents or custodian.)

# 2.4 Contractual Plan, Periodic Payment Plan

Contractual plans and periodic payment plans are very similar in operation, but they are technically different. Both are plans for accumulating mutual fund shares by regular investments over a period of years. The main difference is that the **periodic payment plan** (also called a **voluntary accumulation plan**) is simply an investment contract between an investor and the mutual fund, whereas the **contractual plan** is a specific structured investment offered by a contractual plan company. The plan company does not have its own mutual fund, but instead it has a portfolio that contains mutual funds from other investment companies.

Think of it this way: contractual plans must always have periodic payment plans, but periodic payment plans do not have to be part of a contractual plan or through a contractual plan company. Another important point is that both of these are binding on the plan company or mutual fund that offers them, but they are *not* binding on the investor. The investor can quit making payments and terminate either plan at any time but may incur a penalty for doing so. That's because the investor is usually given certain advantages for signing up for these plans, such as reduced sales charges or the ability to start and maintain the investment for smaller payments than would typically be required for opening a mutual fund account. Let's look at some characteristics of these investments, then prospectus requirements, and finally operation of the contractual plan (with emphasis on points you may see asked on the Series 6 exam).

## 2.4.1

# Characteristics

First, let's discuss characteristics that these two share. In fact, on the Series 6 exam, it's unlikely you will be asked to distinguish between the two. Instead, think of these two as the same until we get to the requirements and operation sections. There we will mention some technical distinctions and point out some possible test questions. Here, consider how contractual plan and periodic payment plan characteristics differ from regular mutual funds. That's where questions are more likely to come from rather than having you pick the two apart. Shared characteristics include:

## 2.4.1.1 Fixed Total Investment

These plans call for investors to commit to a fixed investment amount that will be invested over the life of the plan. That amount is then divided by the time period chosen to come up with the scheduled payments.

## 2.4.1.2 Fixed Time Period

These plans also have investors choose a fixed time period over which payments will be made. Typical contractual plans call for payments to last for 10 to 15 years. Periodic payment plans can be more flexible since they are offered directly by the mutual fund, with payment plans running up to 20 years.

## 2.4.1.3 Fixed Payments at Regular Intervals

Both plans require payments to be made at regular intervals, usually monthly. The payment amount is fixed based on the total investment and time period chosen.

## 2.4.1.4 Fixed Sales Charges

Fixed sales charges are agreed upon when an investor gets into one of these plans. Two considerations with sales charges are breakpoints and load calculations. These will be discussed in upcoming sections.

### 2.4.1.5 Fixed Custodial Fees

Custodial fees are fixed at the time the plan is entered into. This is more applicable to contractual plans, which have custodians that administer the plan, act as transfer agent, and perform other duties. (Contractual plans do not have a mutual fund to trade, so they do not need portfolio managers.)

### 2.4.1.6 Automatic Reinvestment

Most plans offer investors the chance to have automatic reinvestment of dividend and capital gains distributions at the NAV price.

### 2.4.1.7 Partial Liquidation and Reinstatement Privileges

Some of the plans allow investors to liquidate a portion of their holdings to raise cash and then pay back the money at a future date with reinstatement of privileges in the plan to previous levels. Each plan will spell out the conditions under which this may be done.

### 2.4.1.8 Lump Sum Purchase

Most plans allow for a single lump sum payment to be made for an investor to get into the plan. This feature is more relevant for contractual plans, which must choose to allow the single-payment option. (Mutual funds already inherently have the lump sum purchase option available, with mutual funds offering periodic payment plans as an additional choice for customers.)

### 2.4.1.9 Breakpoints

Reduced sales charges are offered to investors for breakpoints based on the total amount of the investment commitment over the life of the plan. (This is why there may be a penalty for early termination, since the amount actually invested up to that earlier time would likely be less than the breakpoint amount.)

2.4.2

# Prospectus Requirements

This is where the similarities end between contractual plans and mutual funds that offer periodic payment plans. We have discussed mutual fund prospectuses at length. While the mutual fund only needs to send out one prospectus (its own), the contractual plan is required to send out **two prospectuses** (one for the contractual plan company itself, and one for the mutual fund it's reselling to investors).

The contractual plan is offered through a contractual plan company that is set up under the provisions of the Investment Company Act of 1940. As such, the contractual plan company has its own set of rules and regulations to follow. A contractual plan is actually set up like unit investment trusts (UITs) mentioned at the beginning of this chapter. (In fact, another name for a contractual plan is a **participating unit investment trust.**) Like UITs, the contractual plan's portfolio is not traded. Thus, there is no portfolio manager and no management fee. Instead, contractual plans have custodial fees paid to the plan's custodian who performs administrative functions and other duties, such as transfer agent. All of these points are detailed in the contractual plan prospectus. The other prospectus that the contractual plan company must give out is the prospectus from the underlying mutual fund in which the plan's clients are investing. Let's look at both of these.

## 2.4.2.1 Plan Prospectus

The Investment Company Act of 1940 requires that all contractual plan companies provide investors with a prospectus. It must give all details about the contract plan company, including history, management, plan objectives, plan investments, fees, and sale charges.

## 2.4.2.2 Prospectus of Underlying Fund

The contractual plan company is also required to give potential investors the prospectus from the underlying mutual fund the contractual plan is using. This is because every contractual plan investment actually consists of two investments. The investor puts money into the contractual plan company, which then buys shares in a mutual fund.

2.4.3

# Operation of Contractual Plan

You probably have some idea of how a contractual plan operates, but there are some important points that we'll emphasize in this section. Although there are few contractual plan companies in operation today (mostly because the voluntary periodic payment plans offered by mutual funds have filled this need), contractual plans represent a handful of potential questions on the Series 6 exam.

## 2.4.3.1 Mutual Fund Underlying Asset

A contractual plan needs a mutual fund as its underlying asset. Investors buy unit shares in the contractual plan company, which in turn buys mutual fund shares with that money. (Remember, this is why two prospectuses are needed.) The contractual plan company does not operate its own mutual fund. Instead, it offers services to investors, such as payment plans and term life insurance, to justify its role in the transaction.

## 2.4.3.2 Plan Sponsor/Company

A contractual plan company operates on behalf of the mutual fund, in effect acting as a sponsor or underwriter. Although the contractual plan company is sponsoring the mutual fund, the contractual plan company is independent and actually issues shares in itself—not the mutual fund—so it must be registered with the SEC. All mutual fund underwriters must be NASD members.

## 2.4.3.3 Act of 1940, Section 27

The Investment Company Act of 1940, Section 27, deals with the various rules and restrictions placed on contractual plan companies and the securities they sell. Among other things, this section specifically deals with the sales charges that these contractual plan companies may impose.

Here we'll look at the **front-end load** option. You should know that:

▷ 9% is the maximum sales load that may be charged on the total of all payments.

**Example:** A client agrees to invest $200 per month for 10 years. The total of all payments is $24,000 ($200 × 12 mos. × 10 yrs.), so the maximum sales load that may be charged on the account is $2160 ($24,000 × 9%).

▷ 50% is the maximum deduction from monthly payments for sales load in the first year.

**Example:** A client agrees to invest $200 per month for 10 years. In the first year, payments will total $2400 ($200 × 12 mos.), so the maximum amount of sales load that may be deducted in the first year is $1200 ($2400 × 50%).

▷ Proportionate deductions must be made for the balance of the sales load.

**Example:** A client agrees to invest $200 per month for 10 years. If the plan took the maximum amount of sales load in the first year ($1200—see above), then the $960 balance of the sales load ($2160 total at 9%, minus the $1200) must be evenly divided over the remaining 9 years of monthly payments.

Other points you should know about contractual plan companies:

▷ **minimum payments** can't be less than $20 to start, nor less than $10 monthly.

▷ **redeemable securities** must be issued so that investors can cash in any time.

▷ **proceeds of payments must be deposited with trustee or custodian.**

## 2.4.3.4 Right to Refund

If an investor in a contractual plan decides to cancel the plan within the first 45 days, the investor has the right to a refund. During this 45-day window, the refund equals the full sales charges paid to the plan, plus the NAV of the investment. The 45-day window begins when the investor receives the "Notice of Right to Refund" letter from the plan.

# 2.4.3.5 Notice of Right to Refund

The plan is required to send an investor within 60 days a "Notice of Right to Refund" letter. This letter must outline the investor's rights under the Investment Company Act and explain how a refund can be obtained.

# 2.4.3.6 Right of Withdrawal

There is an additional right that investors have when paying into a front-end load contractual payment plan. If the investor chooses to withdraw from the plan within the first 18 months, the investor receives back the sales charges paid plus the current NAV of the investment, minus a 15% fee that is kept by the fund. Beyond the 18-month window, if an investor terminates the plan then, he or she only receives back the investment's NAV and loses the sales charges.

# 2.4.3.7 Spread-Load Option

The Investment Company Act of 1940 was amended in 1970 to provide contractual plan companies with another sales load option. This new option is called the **spread-load option.** Here are the points to know:

> ▷ **9%** is the maximum sales load that may be charged on the total of all payments.
> ▷ **20%** is maximum deduction from monthly payments for sales load in first year
> ▷ **16%** is maximum average sales load per year that can be taken in first four years.
> ▷ **45-day right to refund** rules apply: the investor has 45 days to cancel after receiving "Notice of Right to Refund" letter and still receive refund of all sales charges and current NAV (plan has 60 days to send the letter).
> ▷ **After 45 days, the investor who cancels only receives current NAV.**

Let's go through a couple of sample questions you might see on the Series 6 exam, asking you to figure contractual plan refunds. (Questions requiring calculations are more likely to use the Act of 1940. Remember, with the Act of 1940, after 18 months only the NAV is refunded. Questions that mention the Act of 1970 may have the investor cancelling after 45 days—in which case only the NAV must be refunded.)

## EXAMPLE 1

An investor signed up for a contractual plan, and has agreed to pay $300 per month for 10 years. What's the total amount of sales charge that the investor will pay in years 2 through 10? (Assume plan takes max charges.)

a. $300

b. $3240

c. $1800

d. $1440

Step 1: The total of all payments is $36,000 ($300 x 12 mos. x 10 yrs.).

Step 2: The maximum sales load on the account is $3240 ($36,000 x 9%).

Step 3: The maximum sales load deducted in first year is $1,800 ($3,600 x 50%).

Step 4: $1440 is the balance of the sales load ($3240 total at 9%, minus $1,800), so the correct answer is d.

## EXAMPLE 2

An investor has a contractual plan of $100 per month for 20 years. After 10 months, the investor cancels the plan. Under Act of 1940 rules, how much will the customer get back? (Assume the plan takes max charges.)

a. $100 + NAV

b. $150 + NAV

c. $350 + NAV

d. $500 + NAV

Step 1: The total of all payments made is $1000 ($100 × 10 mos.).

Step 2: The maximum sales load deducted in first year is $500 ($1,000 × 50%).

Step 3: Plan company can keep 15%, which is $150 here ($1,000 × 15%).

Step 4: Customer refund is $350 ($500 sale load paid, minus $150 plan company fee) plus the NAV of the investment, so the correct answer is c.

# 2.x

# Summary

**2.1** Investment companies assemble a pool of funds from small investors, invest the funds for the group, and collect a management fee. Company sells shares; investors own part of the large, joint account.

**2.1.1** Three types of investment companies under the Investment Company Act of 1940: Unit investment trust (UIT)—fixed portfolio of securities, no portfolio manager so no management fees, no board of directors, no secondary market trading. Face amount certificate—only debt backs face certificate, pays preset interest. Management companys—can be open end or closed end. Closed end: fixed number of shares, buy and sell on exchange, only whole shares, price is supply and demand. Open end: no limit on number of shares, continuous primary offering (need prospectus), partial shares okay, buy/sell through issuer, POP = NAV + Sales Charge.

**2.1.2**  Mutual funds, three pluses: liquidity (seven days), diversification, pro management. Mutual fund is a packaged security, all fundholders have undivided interest. Full or fractional fund shares possible; when redeemed no one else gets them. Board of directors (must be 40% noninterested): chooses fund direction, hires Investment Advisor (IA); IA is portfolio manager: paid from fund assets, two-year contract—renewed annually, can't change fund direction or delegate job.

12b-1 fee paid to market/distribute fund, not investment advice. Must renew annually with majority vote of board, noninterested board, and shareholders. Shareholders also vote on board members, change in fund objective, and proxies. Shareholders get semiannual report—at least one must be audited.

Sales charge is cost of buying fund; expense ratio is cost of owning fund. Sales charge: noload, front load or back load. Max fee is 8.5% if fund offers breakpoints, auto reinvest of dividends/capital gains, and rights of accumulation.

Distribution fee max is 8.5% if breakpoints offered, auto reinvest, accumulated rights; if not, max is 6.25%. Only distribution fee paid to underwriter from sales charge. Underwriter: advertises/markets fund, sells to broker-dealer or public (same POP). Custodian: protects assets, collects money. Transfer agent: book entry, disburse.

**2.1.3**  Types of fund distributions: net income if fund collects interest or dividends, capital gains when fund sells assets (only realized gains are taxable event), return of capital when fund cashes out assets. If reinvested, still taxable.

**2.1.4**  Fund conveniences/services are day-to-day investing decisions by portfolio manager, safekeeping of securities, exchange privilege, can buy partial shares, diversification kept if partial sell-off, loan collateral (but can't borrow to buy), simple recordkeeping/tax info, easy diversification/inquiry/redemption, automatic reinvestment, systematic withdrawal, check writing, phone trades.

**2.1.5**  Fund objectives: growth (aggressive = small/mid cap, conservative=large cap), income (bonds, utilities, preferred stock), growth and income (stock, bonds, cash balanced—preset formula), specialized (sector, special situation—high risk), asset allocation (no preset formula), tax-exempt (still pay capital gains tax).

Fund types: money market (target NAV is $1), bond (munis, preferred stock), Ginnie Mae (preserve capital), index (match it, not beat it!), other (ADR, gold).

**2.1.6**  Mutual fund comparisons—Nonstatistical: objectives and policies versus actual portfolio investments, management team, risk factors. Statistical: total return (annual return includes reinvestment of dividends/capital gains, minus fees), standardized yield (SEC formula—*no* capital gains), expense ratio.

**2.1.7**  Mutual funds stats are in prospectus (1-, 5-, 10-year history), shareholder reports, information services, financial periodicals, ads and sales literature. NASD requires use of graphs (1, 5, 10 years), current yield numbers must be based on past 12 months, and must show highest sales charges, can't say "safe."

**2.1.8** Fund shares go from underwriter to dealer to investor, or underwriter to investor. (Investor pays same POP.) No-load funds can go fund to investor.

**2.1.9** All clients pay POP. POP = NAV + Sales Charge. (NASD members get discount.) POP = ask price; NAV= bid price; NAV = (Assets - Liabilities) ÷ # Shares. Forward pricing means orders are placed before price is known since NAV is calculated at end of day. NAV isn't affected by buying, selling shares; mostly NAV goes up and down because of stock/asset values in fund portfolio.

Sales charge (spread or load): no-load, load (front or back), 12b-1 market fee. Front end, customer buys fewer shares; back end, all money buys shares and fee is paid when sold (lower if fund held longer); 12b-1 max is .75% if load and .25% if no load.

**2.1.10** Client can save sales charges: (1) reinvesting dividends, capital gains (taxable!) (2) exchanging in same family of funds, (3) breakpoints, (4) letters of intent, (5) rights of accumulation. (Breakpoint selling is a violation of NASD rules.)

**2.1.11** Dollar cost averaging is investing same amount each time, but amount buys different number of shares. Result is lower cost/share, but it doesn't guarantee profit.

**2.1.12** Redemption of mutual fund shares: may be required in writing (over certain amounts, different address, etc.), telephone (but may have floor limit), check writing (but may not be able to close account this way), through dealer. Fund may require signature guarantee (by broker-dealer, bank, etc, but *not* notary public). Redemption price is NAV; fund must pay within seven days.

**2.1.13** Mutual fund is required to create a prospectus as part of its registration. Fund can't market itself during quiet period; effective date is when SEC clears. Prospectus must have SEC "no approval" clause, and contain information on fund objectives, fees, expense table, financial statement (past 10-year performance), rights, redemption, withdrawal plans, management team, other information.

Prospectus must be updated every 16 months; must be sent on request, with ad/sales literature or with confirmation if investor sent money based on profile statement. Statement of additional information (SAI) has technical explanations, fee calculations—legally considered part of prospectus (but only sent by request).

**2.2** Mutual funds have specific tax laws that apply to the fund and to fund investors.

**2.2.1** Conduit theory/Subchapter M theory/pipeline theory says mutual fund is only a conduit for passing through gains, losses, and income to shareholders. If fund passes through at least 90% of capital gains, dividends, etc., then fund qualifies under IRS rules (subchapter M) as a regulated investment company and pays no tax.

Portfolio turnover is a percentage that shows how often fund sells assets. Important—if fund holds asset for less than 12 months, it's a short-term gain.

Short-short rule says if more than 30% of assets are held for less than 3 months, then the mutual fund loses its special tax-exempt status.

**2.2.2**  Shareholder must report all gains to IRS. If no valid Social Security number given to broker-dealer, then broker must withhold 31% tax. Taxes are only affected for realized (actual) gains and losses, not paper gain and losses. Taxes on distributions depend on how long fund held the security, not the investor. Investor holding period only kicks in when fund shares are sold. Reinvested capital gains and dividends are taxable events—so are exchanges.

Tax basis of shares: purchase price, plus allowed expenses for original owner. For gifted securities, cost basis and holding period (short or long) same as donor. For inherited securities, cost basis is stepped up to value on date of death, and inherited securities are always considered long-term capital gains.

Wash sale is when substantially similar securities (or options on them) are bought, sold within 30 days before or after (61-day window). Losses can't be deducted. Bond swap: exception if bonds change two things (e.g., rate, date).

**2.3**  New customer accounts need new account form. Must be cash for mutual fund. Accounts other than personal accounts need authorizing documents.

**2.3.1**  Open accounts must follow broker-dealer guidelines, designed to comply with SEC and NASD rules. Accounts may have minimum investment requirement. Client chooses cash or automatic reinvestment for distributions.

**2.3.2**  Account documentation includes, name, address, legal age, Social Security or TIN number (if not, must withhold 31% tax), employer information (if client works for another NASD member, must inform them).

If client grants trading authority to others, need documentation. Discretionary trades: must be in writing and approved by principal (trade is only discretionary if you pick security + amount + buy or sell). Power of attorney can be limited (can only execute buy/sell orders) or full (can execute orders and take money out).

Corporations need Articles, corporate resolution. Partnerships need signatures of general partners, partnership agreement. Trust needs trust document or court order. Fiduciary needs official document. Investment advisor needs papers.

**2.3.3**  Mutual fund ownership can be individual, joint, trust account, or UGMA/UTMA.

Joint account can be joint tenants with right of survivorship (JTROS)—owners have equal shares, pass to the other upon death, used for married; or joint tenants in common (JTIC)—can be unequal shares, go into estate on death.

UGMA/UTMA gives simplified asset transfer to minors. Only one minor and one custodian per account. Use minor's Social Security number. Parents' tax rate until age 14, then minor's tax rate. Once asset goes in, can't take it back.

Custodian has fiduciary duty. Upon death of minor, account goes into minor's estate, not to custodian and not to parents.

**2.4** Contractual plan and periodic payment plan are similar. Both only bind fund, but allow client to agree to invest more with installment investments to get breakpoints or invest less. Contractual plan is separate investment company that resells other mutual funds; periodic payment plan is offered by regular fund.

**2.4.1** Both plans call for fixed total investment, fixed time period, fixed payments at regular intervals, fixed sales charges, automatic reinvestment, partial liquidation/reinstatement privileges, lump sum purchase option, and breakpoints.

Contractual plan has custodial fees instead of management fees because the plan has custodian administering the plan (no portfolio to manage, so no fee).

**2.4.2** Prospectus is required by the mutual fund offering a periodic payment plan, but *two* prospectuses are required for contractual plan companies—one from the contractual plan company itself and one from the mutual fund it's selling.

**2.4.3** A contractual plan company has another investment company's mutual fund as its underlying asset, so the contractual plan company is acting as a sponsor or distributor for that mutual fund.

Under the Investment Company Act of 1940, the maxium sales charge is 9% (front end), 50% from first year's payments, with rest averaged over balance of plan life. Minimum payments can't be less than $20 to start, nor less than $10 per month. Securities must be redeemable; payments deposited with trustee or custodian. Client can get refund within 45 days after "notice of refund" letter (plan must send out within 60 days). Withdrawal before 18 months entitles client to refund of fees, minus 15% to fund, plus current NAV of shares.

Under 1970 amendment, cancellation anytime after 45-day refund period only lets client get back NAV of the investment. Also uses spread-load option: 9% maxium sales charge, 20% maxium from first year's payments, and 16% average sales load taken in first 4 years. Fund must send refund letter within 60 days.

# Chapter 2 Review Quiz

1. When do open-end investment companies need to give out a prospectus?
   a. always, because the open-end offering is a continuous primary offering
   b. always, because exchange traded securities must give prospectuses
   c. SEC rules say each time old shares are redeemed
   d. open-end companies only need to give out prospectus during quiet period

2. An asset allocation mutual fund would have funds
   a. invested in open-end and closed-end investment companies.
   b. invested in stocks, bonds, and annuity contracts.
   c. invested in stocks, bonds, and cash.
   d. invested in REITs and UITs.

3. An index fund has the fund manager
   a. try to beat the index.
   b. try to match the index.
   c. lag behind the index.
   d. ignore the index.

4. The NAV of a mutual fund
   a. is made up of the fund's net assets divided by the number of shares outstanding.
   b. is an equivalent term to bid price used for other securities.
   c. is figured once at the end of each day, so orders use forward pricing.
   d. all of the above

5. Which of the following has the most impact on NAV?
   a. money going into the fund (new buyers)
   b. money going out of the fund (redemptions)
   c. dividend payments from companies the fund is holding
   d. the value of the stocks in the fund

6. When computing the sales charge
   a. POP is always greater than NAV.
   b. NAV is always greater than POP.
   c. POP and NAV are equal.
   d. the management fee must always be added to POP.

7. Which of the following is NOT an advantage of mutual funds?
   a. diversification
   b. professional management
   c. liquidity
   d. tax shelter

8. Which of the following is NOT a job of the board of directors of a mutual fund?
   a. establish investment policies and direction of the fund
   b. set the NAV and POP for the fund shares
   c. establish dividend and capital gains policy for the fund
   d. hire the investment advisor

9. Which of the following is paid from the mutual fund sales charges?
   a. financial advisor
   b. custodian
   c. underwriter
   d. board of directors

10. What is the maximum sales charge a mutual fund can have?
    a. 8.5%
    b. 9%
    c. it depends on the NAV
    d. there is no maximum

11. Who is responsible for safeguarding the assets of a mutual fund?
    a. investment advisor
    b. underwriter
    c. custodian
    d. transfer agent

12. Which of the following is NOT a taxable event?
    a. reinvestment of mutual fund dividends and capital gains
    b. exchanging a mutual fund within the same family of funds
    c. an increase in the NAV of the mutual fund
    d. all of the above are taxable events

13. With a mutual fund, what does the expense ratio measure?
    a. the ratio of sales charges to expenses
    b. the cost of owning the fund
    c. the cost of acquiring the fund
    d. the cost of management fees divided by the sales charge load

14. Portfolio turnover is
    a. the percentage of a mutual fund's portfolio sold during the past year.
    b. the number of fund shares your client has sold since opening the account.
    c. the number of people who have invested money in a mutual fund.
    d. the percentage of people buying a fund compared to the number selling.

15. What is the reason FIFO is used by the IRS when figuring tax liability?
    a. because the first shares purchased would have the highest cost basis, and thus maximize tax revenues
    b. because the first shares purchased would have the lowest cost basis, and thus maximize tax revenues
    c. because the investor is not permitted to choose an alternative method
    d. the IRS doesn't used FIFO, it uses LIFO

16. A novice investor could be put into all of the following mutual funds, EXCEPT
    a. a money market fund
    b. a growth fund
    c. a sector fund
    d. an income fund

17. What must a contractual plan send out?
    a. one prospectus
    b. two prospectuses
    c. three prospectuses
    d. a contractual plan is not required to send out anything

18. What happens to funds in a UGMA/UTMA account upon death of the minor?
    a. assets pass to the state
    b. assets pass to the minor's estate
    c. assets pass to the parents
    d. assets pass to the custodian

19. Which type of joint account allows an automatic transfer to a spouse at death?
    a. JTROS
    b. JTIC
    c. community property
    d. probated estate

20. Under what conditions may discretionary authority be given?
    a. if client gives written consent
    b. if principal signs off on all trades before they are made
    c. if registered sales representative signs a power of attorney
    d. all of the above

21. If a client refuses to give a Social Security number
    a. the account cannot be opened.
    b. the account can be opened, but tax must be withheld at client's tax bracket.
    c. the account cannot be opened without IRS approval.
    d. the account can be opened, but 31% tax must be withheld, regardless of the client's tax bracket.

22. An investor bought a mutual fund 3 months ago. The fund sold an asset it had held for the previous 18 months, and makes a capital gains distribution. The investor
    a. has a short-term capital gain.
    b. has a long-term capital gain.
    c. has no tax liability if reinvesting the capital gains.
    d. owes no tax now because the investor has not owned the fund long enough.

23. The wash sale rule as it applies to mutual funds, says that
    a. a client may never buy and sell securities within a 61-day window.
    b. a client can only sell securities within a 61-day window.
    c. if a client buys and sells the same securities within 61-day window, any loss may not be used to reduce tax liability.
    d. a client can only exchange a fund for one of the same type or not take a loss.

24. When can a mutual fund be purchased on margin (credit)?
    a. only if forward pricing is used
    b. only if it is a no-load mutual fund
    c. anytime, because there is no restriction
    d. never, because it is a primary offering

# 3

# Variable Contracts and Retirement Plans

*This chapter covers the balance of products that you will likely sell as a Limited Representative. Variable contracts are offered by life insurance companies but require a licensed Limited Representative to sell them. Retirement plans are offered by various companies, financial institutions, investment companies, and others. There are many nuances in the different rules for each type of investment, as well as qualifications and limitations that must be observed for each.*

*When you have finished studying this chapter, you will have a grasp on the wide range of retirement investment options available to your clients. You will know which clients are eligible for which plans, how they can get into them, and how they can get their money out of them.*

*Although this chapter is the shortest in the textbook, nevertheless, there are some important concepts introduced here—particularly the IRA contribution limits, which are popular test topics and the ERISA rules outlined on the last page of this chapter. This chapter ("Variable Contracts and Retirement Plans") represents about 16% of the total test: approximately 16 questions of the total 100 questions on the Series 6 exam.*

## This chapter will be broken up into two sections:

**3.1** **Variable Contracts.** This first section examines variable contracts, including who offers them and why. The insurance company structure is discussed briefly, including a description of what a separate account is and why it is necessary. Variable annuity contracts are also broken down by ways to get into them and ways to get money out of them. Finally, this section defines the different types of life insurance available, before focusing on the variable life insurance policies that also have an investment component. Payment plans, death benefits, and taxation are all discussed in this section.

**3.2** **Retirement Plans.** This section looks at many different types of retirement plans available. There is some analysis of the various types of individual retirement accounts (IRAs) that clients can qualify for, as well as a discussion of the contribution and distribution rules that must be adhered to in order for the investments to qualify for tax deferral. Keogh plans are discussed as an alternative retirement plan that can also act as a supplement to an IRA account. Finally, this section goes over the various corporate pension plans that are available, differentiating between qualified and unqualified plans, before discussing contributions and distributions. This section ends with an important discussion of the ERISA legislation rules that govern what companies can and cannot do with their corporate pension plans.

# key terms

**Annuities:** a series of equal payments, often set up as insurance contracts because they are for the life of the holder.

**Cash value:** money built up in a life insurance policy or other separate account, which may be borrowed against or used to figure the surrender value. Also see: **surrender value.**

**Death benefit:** the amount of money a beneficiary receives upon death of the contract holder.

**ERISA:** Employees Retirement Income Security Act of 1974, which established rules that corporate pension plans must follow in order to receive favorable tax treatment from the IRS for pension plan contributions.

**401(k) plan:** a qualified salary reduction plan used for retirement, whereby employees can contribute pretax dollars into a tax-deferred retirement account.

**403(b) plan:** a retirement plan for employees of nonprofit organizations, tax-exempt organizations, and schools allowing money to be invested tax-deferred. Also called a **tax sheltered annuity (TSA).**

**Individual retirement account (IRA):** personal, tax-deferred retirement account. There are several varieties of IRAs, such as education, Roth, and SEP-IRA.

**Keogh plan:** retirement plan for people who have self-employment income. Also referred to as an **HR 10 plan.**

**Premium:** the money an investor pays to buy an insurance contract. (Also, the money an investor pays to buy an option contract, and the amount above par that is paid for a bond or other security.)

**Rollover:** when an IRA account balance is transferred directly from one custodian to another, or when an investor takes possession of the IRA funds (permitted once a year) and redeposits them into another IRA account within 60 days.

**Separate account:** an account established and maintained by an insurance company under state law, where income, gains, and losses stay in that account, apart from income, gains, or losses generated by any other insurance company account.

**Surrender value:** the current value of the separate account units or the cash value of an insurance policy, minus any outstanding loans and interest, minus fees. Also see: **cash value.**

**Units:** piece of ownership with variable annuity contracts. (Same as "share" with mutual funds.)

**Vesting:** the right of ownership that an employee gains in retirement plans and other benefits from years of service at a company.

# 3.1

# Variable Contracts

**Variable contracts** are packaged securities, often put together by insurance companies, responsible for managing the funds in the investment portfolio. These can also be referred to as **variable annuities** or **variable annuity contracts.** Variable annuity contracts are set up to offer guaranteed payments to the investor for life, although the amount is not guaranteed. The amount that will be paid out to the variable annuity contract-holder depends on the value of the investments in the separate account maintained by the insurance company.

# 3.1.1

# Separate Accounts

The investment portfolio for variable annuity contracts is set up as a separate account from the insurance company's general account, because the variable annuity contract holder assumes some of the market risks of the insurance company's investments. In return, the investor shares some of the capital appreciation of the investments. The gains in the separate account directly benefit the contractholders who put money in, since the amount of annuity payments received is tied to account performance. When investors pay into an annuity account, they relinquish control of the funds to the insurance company. Because of this, variable annuity contracts are considered securities under the Investment Company Act of 1940.

# 3.1.1.1 Definition

Under the Investment Company Act of 1940, a **separate account** is defined as an account established and maintained by an insurance company under state law, where income, gains, and losses stay in that account, apart from income, gains, or losses generated by any other insurance company account. Thus, the separate account (which pays out on annuity contracts) is segregated from the insurance company's general account (which pays out on insurance claims).

**CHARACTERISTICS.** The insurance company can have their own investment advisor manage the funds that are in the separate accounts. If the insurance company employs the investment advisor, the separate account is said to be **directly managed,** and the insurance company is **regulated like a mutual fund.** The insurance company can also choose to delegate this responsibility to an outside investment advisor. If the insurance company contracts with an outside firm, then the separate account is said to be **indirectly managed,** and the insurance company is **regulated like a unit investment trust.**

**UNDERLYING INVESTMENTS.** The investment policies of the insurance companies with regard to these separate accounts are detailed in the prospectus for the variable annuity contract. Although they are generally more aggressive with separate account investments than they are with general account investments, one of the objectives for the separate account is still conservation of capital. Although the separate accounts invest in stocks, they are still likely buying more conservative stocks, such as blue chips, rather than speculative stocks, such as IPOs. Along with this conservatism, though, the separate accounts are also invested with an eye toward long-term growth and capital accumulation. Again, reading the prospectus for the variable annuity contract is the best way for the investor to understand these goals.

3.1.2

# Variable Annuity Contracts

**Annuities** are simply a series of equal payments, often set up as insurance contracts because they are for the life of the holder. These annuity contracts can be set up as either fixed or variable. Although the majority of the questions on the test will deal with variable annuity contracts, let's briefly compare fixed and variable contracts before we discuss other variable contract issues: types, feature, sales charges and expenses, valuation, and tax treatment.

## 3.1.2.1 Comparison

All annuity contracts have payments made for the life of the contractholder. With a fixed annuity contract, clients invest money, which goes into the insurance company's general account. In exchange for this investment, fixed annuity contractholders receive a fixed monthly payment for the rest of their life. With a variable annuity contract, clients invest money, which goes into a separate account at the insurance company. The policyholder can direct the investments and pick securities in which to invest (within limits, e.g., no options), or the policyholder can allow a professional fund manager working for the insurance company to direct the investments. In exchange for this investment, variable annuity contractholders receive a monthly payment for life, but the amount varies depending on the performance of the investments in the separate account.

**PAYMENTS, GUARANTEES, RISK.** As stated, the fixed contractholder receives fixed monthly payments guaranteed at that amount and guaranteed to continue for the rest of his or her life. This is good on the one hand because the insurance company is bearing the market risk for how well the underlying investments will perform. Even if the investments do poorly, the annuity amount is guaranteed. On the other hand, it can be bad because annuity contractholders bear the inflationary risks (a.k.a. purchasing power risks) so that in the future their payments may not buy as much.

The variable annuity contractholder receives monthly payments, guaranteed to continue for the rest of his or her life, but the amount is not guaranteed and will vary. Here the variable contractholder has traded in the inflationary risk for market risk. In exchange for the variable annuity contractholder taking on some of the market risk of the investments, the insurance company shares some of the capital appreciation of the investments to help offset the variable contractholder's inflationary risk.

There are other risks which must be analyzed by the investor before an informed decision can be made. Investors need to feel that the money they are investing with the insurance company will be invested wisely. They need to learn as much as possible about the safety, stability, and track record of the insurance company. Whether it is a fixed contract where all money is dumped into a general account, or a variable annuity where investor money is put into a separate account, the investor must still rely on the investment capabilities and management experience of the insurance company. A fixed annuity contract is worthless if the insurance company folds; a variable annuity contract can only keep pace with inflation through savvy investing. This is where risk assessment comes in.

**CONTRACTHOLDER OBJECTIVES.** The objective of any client who buys an annuity should be a desire for a guaranteed stream of income payments to start at some point in the future and continue for life. The client's objective may likely be for retirement purposes. If the client is looking for safe, steady, dependable income to serve as the main source of income, then a fixed annuity would be the better option. If the client is looking for a good return on investment and growth potential to supplement other retirement income, then variable annuity would be a better option.

## 3.1.2.2 Types of Variable Annuities

There are a few variations of variable annuity contracts offered by insurance companies. Annuity contracts can be immediate or deferred and purchased with a single payment or periodic payments.

**IMMEDIATE: SINGLE PAYMENT.** An **immediate annuity** is an annuity contract that is purchased with a lump sum payment, with the annuity payments scheduled to begin immediately (usually no longer than two months out). Annuity payouts may be set up so they are received for a set period of time, or for the life of the contractholder.

Note that an immediate annuity can only be purchased with a single, lump sum payment. (It would be a little silly to start making monthly periodic payments to the annuity and begin receiving immediate annuity payments at the same time.)

**DEFERRED: PERIODIC PAYMENTS OR SINGLE PAYMENT.** A **deferred annuity** is an annuity contract where the investor chooses to start receiving the annuity payments at a future date (chosen by the contractholder). Annuity payments may be received for a set period of time or for the life of the contractholder, depending on how it is set up. Deferred annuities can be purchased with a single, lump sum payment or with periodic payments spread out over time. Most investors buy annuity contracts by investing money with periodic payments (often monthly) because they do not have enough money to make a large lump sum payment.

# 3.1.2.3 Features

There are several features of variable annuity contracts that make them attractive investments for some clients.

**TAX DEFERRED ACCUMULATION.** One beneficial feature of annuity contracts is that the invested earnings are allowed to grow tax-deferred until payouts begin at retirement, or until withdrawal by contractholder. (Changing separate account investments within the same family of funds does not create a taxable event either.)

**VOTING RIGHTS.** Another feature to consider is the rights of the variable contract owners. We said earlier that the investor relinquishes control of the invested funds to the insurance company, but the investor does still retain some measure of control as outlined in the prospectus. The primary means for exercising this control is voting. The variable annuity contractowner can vote on such things as the selection of investment advisors and money managers, changes in investment policy or strategy, and other proxies. Annuity contractholders receive one vote per unit held. (Note that when discussing annuities, the term *units* is used. This is roughly equivalent to the term *shares* we use when discussing mutual funds.)

**SETTLEMENT OPTIONS.** Although investors could choose to withdraw their money in one lump sum or over a period of time—even before reaching retirement age—on the Series 6 exam always assume that the contractholder *annuitizes* the annuity. This means that the investor holds the contract until the agreed-upon date when reaching retirement age and collects regularly scheduled payments until death.

When the investor elects to annuitize, there are two things that are important (besides how many units the investor owns): the age and sex of the investor, and what type of payout settlement option the investor will elect. The age and sex of the investor are important for the insurance company's calculations because the annuity needs to pay out for the rest of the investor's life. Upon annuitization, the investor can choose a payout method by electing one of four settlement options: life annuity (also called straight life), life annuity with period certain, life annuity with amount certain, or life annuity with joint and last survivor. Let's explain each of these.

Option 1: **Life annuity.** The annuity will payout for as long as the contractholder lives, but payments end upon his or her death. This results in the **largest monthly payments** (still based on the value of the separate account) but is the biggest gamble because there is no guaranteed payout amount. The contractholder could die early, before the principle and interest have been returned on the annuity investment, and the beneficiaries receive nothing. This option is also called **straight life** or **life only.**

Option 2: **Life annuity with period certain.** The annuity will payout for as long as the contractholder lives, but upon his or her death if payments have not been made for a certain, predetermined amount of time, then the beneficiaries would continue to receive those payments until the time is over.

Option 3: **Life annuity with amount certain.** The annuity will payout for as long as the contractholder lives, but upon his or her death if a certain, predetermined amount of money has not been paid out (or a certain number of annuity units have not been cashed out), then the beneficiaries would continue to receive those payments until the agreed upon amount is reached. This option is also called **refund life annuity.**

Option 4: **Life annuity with joint and last survivor.** The annuity will payout for as long as the contractholder lives, and then upon his or her death payments will continue to the contractholder's spouse until the death of the spouse. Since payments are made until both parties die, these are the **smallest monthly payments.** Insurance company calculations are based on age and sex of both parties. Payments cease upon the death of both parties, and nothing is paid to beneficiaries regardless of how little has been paid out. This option is also called **joint and last survivor** or **survivor annuity.**

**OTHER CONTRACTUAL PROVISIONS.** Other clauses in annuity contracts may include:

**mortality guarantee:** the contract will pay out until the death of the investor;

**expense guarantee:** expenses over a certain level (as agreed upon up front in the contract) will be paid by the insurance company;

**death benefit:** this is the amount of money a beneficiary receives upon death of the contractholder; if he or she dies before annuitizing, then a beneficiary collects the amount paid in or the value of the units (whichever is greater);

**surrender value:** before annuitizing, an investor can cancel the annuity contract and receive the current value of the separate account units, minus fees;

**exchange privilege:** the investor may choose to trade the annuity contract for another insurance company investment, as detailed in the contract.

## 3.1.2.4 Sales Charges and Expenses

Variable annuity contracts can have front-end or back-end sales charges, very similar to those for mutual funds. These charges are incurred during the accumulation period (when the contractholder is investing money to buy units—or shares). There are other additional charges and expenses that are incurred after the investor annuitizes. All of these sales charges and expenses must be detailed in the investment contract. Let's examine each of them.

**LEVEL SALES CHARGE.** The level sales charge is taken out up front when the annuity contract is purchased. If a lump sum payment is made, then the sales charge is part of that single payment. If a periodic payment plan is used, then the sales charge is deducted from each monthly payment. Like mutual funds, the maximum sales charge permitted is 8.5%. Sales charges may be used to cover marketing expenses, administrative fees, or other costs detailed in the contract prospectus. Breakpoints, rights of accumulation, etc. may also be offered if detailed in the prospectus.

**DEFERRED SALES CHARGES.** Deferred sales charges are collected when an annuity contract is cashed in. Here, too, the maximum sales charge is 8.5%. The deferred sales charge (or back-end load) is often done on a decreasing scale such that the longer the investment is held, the lower the sales charge (decreasing to nothing at some point). These sales charges also cover the same items as the level sales charge and are detailed in the prospectus for the annuity contract.

**OTHER CHARGES AND EXPENSES.** In addition to those charges incurred when the investment is entered into and during the accumulation stage, there are other charges and expenses that must be paid. These include **investment management fee, mortality risk, expense risk, premium taxes,** and **administrative expenses.** These costs are deducted from the special account's income or assets. The prospectus contains information on how the mortality expenses, operating expenses, etc. are calculated and the maximum amounts that they will be for the contract.

# 3.1.2.5 Valuation of Variable Annuity Contract

There are several differences with how variable annuity contracts are valued compared with other managed investments. There are no "shares" to speak of, instead variable annuity contracts are sold in **units.** The value of a unit is calculated based on the value of the investments in the separate account. Like the NAV of a mutual fund, the value of a variable annuity contract share must be calculated at least once per day, usually at the close of trading. There are accumulation units and annuity units.

**ACCUMULATION UNITS. Accumulation units** are the measure of how much of an interest the investor owns in the separate account, based on the amount of payments the investor makes into the separate account during the accumulation stage. The **accumulation stage** is the time when the investor is making regular payments into the separate account as an investment. (Think: accumulation stage = pay in stage) After all sales charges and other fees are deducted from these payments, the investor has a net investment amount which is applied towards the purchase of more accumulation units. At the end of each trading day, the value of an individual unit is calculated. The value of the investor's units can then be calculated as the individual unit price times the number of units owned. This number, minus any fees and early withdrawal penalties, is the surrender value of the accumulation units.

**ANNUITY UNITS. Annuity units** are the measure of how much of an interest the investor owns in the separate account, based on the amount of payments the investor is entitled to receive during the annuity stage. The **annuity stage** is the time when the investor is receiving payments from the separate account. (Think: annuity stage = pay out stage) At the time that the variable annuity contract is converted from the accumulation stage to the annuity stage, a calculation is done. This calculation is based on the assumed interest rate (AIR) and also considers other factors, such as the projected mortality risk of the individual investor. The result is that a certain number of accumulation units converts into a certain number of annuity units.

The value of these annuity units is directly related to the value of the underlying portfolio. At the end of each trading day, the value of an individual unit is calculated. The investor redeems a set number of annuity units each month, but the value of the annuity units that are cashed in fluctuates with the value of the underlying separate account. So the investor is guaranteed to receive payments for life, but the amount of that payment is dependent on the value of the separate account portfolio.

**ASSUMED INTEREST RATE.** The **assumed interest rate (AIR)** is an estimated interest rate that the insurance company uses when calculating the projected payout on a variable annuity contract. This is not a guaranteed rate of return, but a means to calculate the conversion from accumulation units to annuity units. Once the conversion from accumulation units to annuity units has taken place, the annuity units become a set amount and no further calculations done. The AIR is then used as the benchmark for measuring performance of the separate account and thus determining payout amounts.

Each month, the AIR is compared to the actual rate of return on investment that the separate account achieves. If the actual rate of return is the same as the AIR, then the payment for that month is the same as the previous month. If the actual rate of return for the separate account is more than the AIR, then the monthly payment increases. If the actual rate of return for the separate account is less than the AIR, then the monthly payment decreases. It is important to note that the increase or decrease in the payment amount is not equal to the AIR or the actual rate of return. Instead, a separate formula is used as detailed in the prospectus. Just know that the payment moves up or down in tandem with the up and down movements of the actual rate of return relative to the AIR. Here is an example.

## EXAMPLE

The investor has entered the annuity stage. The AIR is 5%, and the first payment is $638. Here is a sample payout schedule:

| Month | Rate of Return for Prior Month | AIR (Assumed Interest Rate) | Payment |
|---|---|---|---|
| 1 | n/a | 5% | $638 |
| 2 | 6% | 5% | $642 |
| 3 | 24% | 5% | $670 |
| 4 | 5% | 5% | $670 |
| 5 | −3% | 5% | $656 |
| 6 | 2% | 5% | $648 |

Note that the AIR is always constant—it is set once the annuity stage begins. Also note in the fourth payment in our example that the high payment stayed the same, even though the rate of return dropped from 24% down to 5%, because the rate of return did not drop below the relative AIR. Even though the fifth month saw a dramatic drop in the rate of return, the decrease in payment was based on the prior month's payment only, so that payment was still higher than the first or second payments. Finally, the payment went down between the fifth and sixth month because, even though the rate of return for the separate account went up from the previous month, that rate was still below the AIR, so the payment declined.

# 3.1.2.6 Tax Treatment

Unlike mutual funds, variable annuities are a good way to defer taxes. Not only does the invested money grow tax-deferred until it is drawn out at retirement age, but all dividends, capital gains, and other distributions are also tax deferred. This is because these distributions are automatically reinvested into the separate account, rather than being paid directly to the investor (which is the case with mutual funds). In fact, this is a double bonus because in addition to the tax deferral, such reinvested distributions also increase the value of the investor's units.

One other distinction that we must make when considering taxes is the status of the annuity. When figuring tax liability, there are actually two kinds of variable annuity contracts: qualified and nonqualified. **Qualified** variable annuities have the invested amount paid for with pretax dollars. (An example would be an annuity in an IRA account or one that was paid for by an employer.) This means that although the money is allowed to grow tax-deferred, all money that is taken out is fully taxable as ordinary income. This makes sense, since pretax dollars have never paid taxes, so the investor has no cost basis. Furthermore, if an investor withdraws money before age 59½, then the entire amount is subject to a 10% tax penalty.

**Nonqualified** variable annuities have the invested amount paid with after-tax dollars. This allows them to have a cost basis so that only a portion of the withdrawal amount is subject to taxation.

For the Series 6 exam, you should always assume that a variable annuity contract is nonqualified for tax purposes, unless a question specifically tells you otherwise.

Exam Topic
Alert

Let's look at taxes with nonqualified annuities.

**ACCUMULATION PERIOD.** During the accumulation period, invested money is allowed to grow tax deferred. Dividends, capital gains, and other distributions also remain tax deferred until payouts begin on the contract, investor withdrawals are made, or the annuity contract is surrendered. If the investor takes money out with any of these scenarios before age 59½, the IRS charges a 10% tax penalty on the interest portion of the withdrawal. To maximize tax revenue, the IRS says that all withdrawals are taxed last in, first out (LIFO) so the amounts that accrued tax-deferred (e.g., interest) are all considered to be withdrawn first and taxed, before the investor can consider a withdrawal to be part of the cost basis. The investor must pay ordinary income tax for any amount above the cost basis.

*There are no capital gains taxes with annuities.*

**ANNUITY PERIOD.** During the annuity period, the cost basis is adjusted to take into account the investor's life expectancy. (The IRS has tables to help compute this.) This new cost basis is then spread over the investor's expected life, such that each year the payments received are allocated with a portion being considered a return of principal and a portion being considered interest on the investment. (This is referred to as the **exclusion allowance**.) The amount that is considered interest is taxable to the investor as ordinary income in that year.

**TAXATION AT SURRENDER.** If the investor chooses to surrender the variable annuity contract prior to annuitization, the value of the contract is treated as a withdrawal, and ordinary income tax is due on any amount the investor receives over the investment in the annuity. The investor may also be subject to the 10% penalty if he or she is not yet age 59½ at the time of surrender.

**DEATH BENEFITS.** During the accumulation period, if the contractholder dies, death benefits from the contract are transferred to a beneficiary. The beneficiary may take the amount as a withdrawal and pay ordinary income tax on any amount over the investment in the annuity, or the beneficiary may elect (within 60 days of owner's death) to take a payout option and pay tax the same as other annuity payouts.

Just a few variable annuity contract reminders. First, although regulations between mutual funds and variable annuity contracts are similar, an important difference is that variable annuity contract earnings grow tax-deferred. Furthermore, all payouts or withdrawals are always considered return of principal or ordinary income. There are no capital gains with variable annuity contracts. Also remember that the test assumes investors annuitize their variable annuity contracts. If a contract is annuitized, then the investor will have guaranteed income for life.

3.1.3

# Variable Life Insurance

**Variable life insurance** is a type of insurance offered whereby policyholders can invest the cash value of the policy in securities. The policyholder can direct the investments and pick securities in which to invest (within limits, e.g., no options), or the policyholder can allow a professional fund manager working for the insurance company to direct the investments. Either way, a separate account is used for these investments, and the increase or decrease in the value of the investment portfolio directly affects the life insurance policy's cash value (money built up in the policy) and death benefit (money paid to beneficiary upon death of contractholder).

# 3.1.3.1 Comparison

In order to better understand how variable life insurance works, it's best to compare variable life policies with the other types of available insurance policies that you will encounter. There actually are five main types of insurance: **term life, whole life, universal life, variable life,** and **variable universal life.** We'll define each of these, then compare variable, universal, and whole life insurance. On the Series 6 exam, many of the insurance questions will focus on variable life, because persons who sell variable life insurance must be registered with the SEC.

**Term life insurance** is insurance that only provides coverage for a certain period of time (term), with a renewable premium due at the end of each term (usually each year) to keep the death benefits active. The premium due on a term policy often rises as the insured gets older. There is no cash value built up in the policy, but term insurance is much cheaper than other types of insurance which have a cash value.

**Whole life insurance** is insurance that offers a death benefit for the entire (whole) life of the insured person, as long as the premiums are paid on time. The premium due on a whole life policy is usually level and does not rise as the insured person gets older (as is the case with term insurance). Whole life policies build up a cash value, which is invested by the insurance company (with no input from policyholders) in an effort to increase the cash value for policyholders. The earnings from whole life policies grow tax-deferred. Policyholders can borrow against the cash value of the policy by taking out a policy loan. The death benefits paid out are reduced by the amount of any loan balance that is still outstanding, plus interest.

**Universal life insurance** is insurance that combines the low cost of term life insurance with the benefits of whole life insurance because it allows cash value to build up tax-deferred. While premium payments on whole life policies are fixed, the premium payments for universal life are flexible. This is because the policyholder can pay in more than the minimum premium amount at any time to increase the cash value of the policy and thus increase the death benefit. The policyholder can also move money into a savings-type account to increase the amount of money available for a policy loan. The "universal" aspect to the policy comes from the wide range of choices the policy holder has with the amount of premium paid and the ability to shift the cash value between different tax-deferred vehicles offered by the insurance company (usually with no sales charges).

**Variable life insurance** is insurance where policyholders can invest the cash value of the policy in securities. The policyholder can direct the investments and pick securities in which to invest (within limits, e.g., no options), or the policyholder can allow a professional fund manager working for the insurance company to direct the investments. The cash value and death benefits of a variable life policy are directly related to the value of the investment portfolio in the separate account (although there is a guaranteed minimum death benefit, regardless of how poorly the separate account performs). The cash value of the policy can be borrowed against, and earnings grow tax-deferred until any income distributions are withdrawn by the policyholder. Like whole life policies, the premium payments are fixed. Variable life insurance is also called **variable whole life insurance.**

**Variable universal life insurance** is insurance that gives policyholders the flexibility of adjusting premium payments and death benefits as with universal life, but with the separate account and investment choices of variable life. The cash value grows tax-deferred until withdrawn, and the policy may also be borrowed against.

**VARIABLE, UNIVERSAL, AND WHOLE LIFE.** These are the three insurance types you need to know for the Series 6 exam, with the emphasis on variable life. Let's summarize the main differences between these three in the chart below before moving on to an in-depth discussion of the characteristics of variable life insurance.

## COMPARE AND CONTRAST: VARIABLE, UNIVERSAL, WHOLE LIFE INSURANCE

chart 3.1.3.1

| Compare: | Variable Life | Universal Life | Whole Life |
|---|---|---|---|
| Death Benefits | fluctuates with separate account, but has guaranteed minimum | fluctuates based on premiums paid; no guaranteed minimum | guaranteed minimum, as long as premiums are paid |
| Cash Value | no guarantee, because policyholder directs the investments | minimum guarantee, because money goes in general account | guaranteed, money goes into general account |
| Risk | policyholder assumes all risk of trying to grow cash value above death benefit minimum | policyholder can decide to put in more money to build cash value or put money elsewhere | risk is that insurance company will make poor investments, lowering policy's cash value |
| Premium Payments | payment amounts are fixed and paid on regular schedule | payment amounts are flexible, policyholder picks schedule | payment amounts are fixed and paid on regular schedule |
| Policyholder Objectives | policyholder wants to direct portfolio to maximize death benefits and cash value | policyholder wants maximum flexibility to change coverage amount and cash value | policyholder wants minimum death benefit guaranteed and cash value buildup in policy |

**OBJECTIVES OF VARIABLE LIFE INSURANCE POLICYHOLDER.** There are several reasons why a policyholder would choose a variable life policy. Beyond the guaranteed minimum death benefit, the policy's death benefit and cash value have potential to be worth significantly more if the separate account's investment portfolio does well. The policyholder can choose to have the insurance company's professional manager direct the policy's investments, or the policyholder can make investment decisions on his or her own. Finally, as the cash value of the policy grows, the policyholder is building wealth tax-deferred and can take out a policy loan against this value.

Exam Topic Alert

Remember a few key points about variable life insurance: premiums are fixed, they go into a separate account, and the cash value and death benefits are directly related to the value of the separate account (even if the policyholder chooses to let professional managers from the insurance company direct the investments).

# 3.1.3.2 Features

There are several features of universal life insurance that you need to know for the Series 6 exam. These include loans, voting rights, settlement options, other contractual provisions, and charges, fees, and expenses.

**LOANS.** With variable life insurance, the policyholder can borrow against the cash value that has built up in the insurance policy. Usually the loan amount is limited to a certain percentage of the cash value, as stated in the insurance contract. The insurance company does not have to allow 100% of the cash value to be borrowed, but the law does say that the minimum amount that must be available is 75% after the insurance policy has been in force for at least three years. When a policyholder takes out a policy loan, that money accrues interest. If the total loan amount plus interest exceed the cash value of the policy (because of a drop in the value of the separate account portfolio), then the policyholder is required to make a payment to bring the loan balance down within a month. If the loan is not repaid when the policyholder dies, then the loan amount, plus interest and fees, is deducted from the death benefit.

**VOTING RIGHTS OF POLICYHOLDERS.** A policyholder has some measure of control over the management of the separate account as outlined in the contract. The primary means for exercising this control is voting. The variable life policyholder can vote on such things as the selection of investment advisors and money managers, changes in investment policy or strategy, and other proxies. Policyholders receive one vote per $100 of cash value in the policy.

**SETTLEMENT OPTIONS.** When a life insurance policy becomes payable (usually at the death of the insured), the beneficiaries can choose to take the money owed as a single lump sum payment, or they can choose one of several other settlement options.

**Interest Option.** Here all of the proceeds due are left invested in the insurance company, which pays out a guaranteed interest rate (almost like a savings account). The insurance company also makes additional payments if the separate account investments do well. The beneficiary can change to a different settlement option any time—even change to a lump sum option and withdraw the remaining balance due.

**Fixed Amount Option.** Here the beneficiary receives a fixed amount in equal payments (usually monthly) until all the money due has been paid out. The payments consist of a guaranteed interest portion and a partial repayment of principal.

**Fixed Period Option.** Here the beneficiary receives equal payments over a fixed period of time. The time period could be as short as 5 years, but is often 10 to 20 years. Payments may be increased if the separate account investments do well.

**Life Income Option.** Here the beneficiary receives the money due, paid out over the rest of the beneficiary's life. In essence, the beneficiary is buying an annuity with the proceeds. The size of the payments depends on the age and sex of the beneficiary and which of four "life income" options is chosen.

Option 1: **Pure life income** provides income for as long as the beneficiary lives, but payments end upon death of the beneficiary.

Option 2: **Life income with period certain** pays income for as long as the beneficiary lives, but if he or she dies before a predetermined amount of time, then a second beneficiary would receive the payments until the time is over.

Option 3: **Refund life income option** has the beneficiary receive payments for life, but upon his or her death if a predetermined amount of money (usually the original proceeds due) has not been paid, then a second beneficiary would receive the payments until the agreed-upon amount is reached.

Option 4: **Joint and last survivor life income option** pays out for as long as two recipients live. Upon death of one, payments will continue to be paid to the other until that person's death. This is often done by husband and wife.

**OTHER CONTRACTUAL PROVISIONS.** Other clauses in variable life contracts include:

**expense limitation:** expenses over a certain level (as agreed upon up front in the contract) will be paid by the insurance company;

**termination:** if the policyholder stops making premium payments as agreed, then the policy is terminated, and the policyholder can collect the cash value;

**surrender value:** the value of the insurance policy is equal to the cash value, minus any outstanding loans, plus interest and fees, if the policy is turned in.

**EXCHANGE PRIVILEGES.** The policyholder may choose to exchange investments by transferring some or all of the money he or she has contributed to the separate account, and move it to another insurance company investment, as detailed in the contract. (Exchanging from one type of life insurance policy to another life insurance policy is considered a "conversion," and must follow the conversion guidelines in the next section. An exchange within the insurance company's offerings is not a taxable event and usually does not incur any fees payable to the insurance company.)

**CONVERSION PRIVILEGE.** The policyholder may choose to convert from one type of life insurance policy to another with the same insurance company, as detailed in the contract. The period during which this conversion is allowed may be limited by the insurance company's contract, but by law it must be available for at least 24 months. If conversion of the policy takes place within 24 months, there is no need for the insured to take another physical exam or provide other evidence of insurability. (This type of conversion within the insurance company's offerings is not a taxable event and usually does not incur any fees payable to the insurance company.)

**SALES CHARGES AND EXPENSES.** The maximum sales charge that may be charged for a variable life insurance policy is 9%. (This is because variable life is considered a contractual plan, like those we discussed at the end of Chapter 2.) The 9% sales charge is the maximum that can be charged over the contract's life of 20 years or less, or the life expectancy of the policyholder, whichever is less.

**Sales Charge Structure.** The sales charge amount is deducted from each premium payment. Also, with variable life insurance:

▷ **9%** is the maximum sales load that may be charged on the total of all payments;

▷ **50%** is maximum deduction from monthly payments for sales load in first year;

▷ **45-day right to full refund:** client has 45 days to cancel after the processed application (federal law), or 10 days after getting the policy (state law), whichever is longer, and policyholder gets full refund of *all* payments;

▷ **after 45 days, client has two years to cancel:** first year—client gets back cash value plus 30% of sales charges; second year—client gets back cash value plus 10% of sale charges; third year or later—client only gets back the policy's cash value.

**Other Charges and Expenses.** There are other charges and expenses beyond the sales charges that must be paid as part of a variable life insurance policy, such as **mortality costs, investment management fee, administrative expenses,** and **cost of insurance.** The prospectus contains information on how these expenses are calculated and the maximum amounts that they will be for the contract. For the Series 6 exam, it is important to note that some of these charges and expenses are deducted from the premiums paid by the policyholders, and some are paid out of the separate account assets. Charges that come out of the **gross premium** paid are **administrative expenses, sales charges,** and **state taxes.** Everything else is paid out of the separate account.

---

An easy way to remember this for the Series 6 exam is **GASS—G**ross premium: **A**dministrative expenses, **S**ales charges, **S**tate taxes. All other charges and expenses are paid from the separate account.

Exam Topic Alert

# 3.1.3.3 Valuation of a Variable Life Insurance Policy

When talking about the value of a variable life insurance policy, there are actually two values that need to be considered. There is the cash value of the policy used for figuring loan amount, investment monies, and surrender value; and there is the death benefit value used to determine how much is paid out upon death of the policyholder. Both of these depend on the value of the underlying investments in the separate account.

**SEPARATE ACCOUNTS.** The investment portfolio for variable life policies is set up as a separate account from the insurance company's general account (just like for variable annuities). This is done because the variable life policyholder assumes the market risks of the insurance company's investments. In return, the policyholder shares some of the capital appreciation of the investments in the form of a higher cash value for the policy.

**Cash Value.** Since the cash value of the variable life policy is directly related to the value of the investments in the separate account, there is no guaranteed minimum cash value amount for the variable life policy. If the separate account does well, then the cash value goes up. If the separate account does poorly, then the cash value goes down—and can drop below the initial policy value, even theoretically dropping down to no value. If the cash value of the policy drops below any policy loan amount that is outstanding, the policyholder is required to make a payment within a month.

Since the cash value is tied to performance of the separate account, variable life policies are considered securities under the Investment Company Act of 1940. This is true whether the policyholder directs the investments or relinquishes management control of the funds to professional managers at the insurance company.

The cash value of the variable life policy is usually calculated at the end of each trading day, but by law it must be calculated at least once per month.

**Death Benefit.** The death benefit is also tied to the value of the separate account with a variable life insurance policy. Although there is a guaranteed minimum death benefit (stated in the policy when issued), the value of the death benefit can fluctuate with the value of the separate account. The calculation for this uses an assumed interest rate (AIR), just like variable annuities. The AIR number or calculation is stated in the original policy contract when issued. If the separate account performs better than the AIR, the death benefit will be higher than the guaranteed minimum death benefit. If the separate account performs worse than the AIR, then the death benefit decreases (but is always at least the guaranteed minimum death benefit).

The insurance company must recalculate the death benefit at least once a year. If the separate account has performed poorly for an extended period of time, any negative recorded earnings must be overcome by higher separate account earnings before the death benefit will actually rise. This is something to keep in mind when answering questions on the Series 6 exam. Also note that the AIR has no effect on the cash value of a variable life policy.

# 3.1.3.4 Tax Treatment of Variable Life Insurance

There are several tax items that affect variable life insurance. Let's look at taxes during the life of the policy, upon death of the insured, and upon surrender of the policy.

**During the life of the policy,** no taxes are due as long as the policy stays in force. The policyholder pays no taxes on income or capital gains that accumulate in the separate account. Instead, these items build up the cash value of the policy, with taxes owed once the policy pays out a death benefit or the policyholder surrenders the policy and terminates the insurance contract. Also, there are no taxes due on money taken out as a policy loan.

If a question on the Series 6 exam asks you to calculate the taxes due on a variable life policy still in force, or the taxes due on the capital gains from the separate account, watch for a trick. Remember, there are no taxes on capital gains, interest, income, or policy loans with variable life insurance.

**Upon the death of the insured,** no income taxes are due from the beneficiary. Instead, the value of the death benefit is added into the deceased person's estate and taxed that way. Estates are given an exclusion of $700,000 upon which no tax is due. This amount is current for the 2002 and 2003 tax years and will gradually rise up to $1,000,000 by 2006. Estates that are transferred to spouses, however, are given a marital deduction that excludes the entire estate from paying tax during the life of the surviving spouse. Upon death of the second spouse, estate taxes are due.

**Upon full or partial surrender of the policy,** taxes are due on the money received over and above the premium payments that were put into the variable life policy. The payments are treated as the cost basis, and the rest is taxed as ordinary income (regardless of how long payments were made or the length of the contract). **1035 exchanges** are an exception, allowing the exchange of cash value from one life insurance policy to buy another (and avoid capital gains taxes due on the first policy) as long as the second policy costs the same or more.

Since this falls under the like-kind exchange qualifying rules, life insurance may be exchanged for an annuity but an annuity may *not* be exchanged for life insurance. Watch this on the Series 6 exam.

Exam Topic Alert

# Retirement Plans

Most investors have two goals: save money for retirement and avoid as much taxation as possible. Many retirement plans help achieve both of these goals. Proper estate planning is essential so that as much as possible of an investor's hard-earned money can be passed on to heirs instead of the government. This section will not turn you into an estate tax expert but will help you speak intelligently with clients about the subject—and know when to advise clients to seek professional advice. We will look at individual retirement accounts (IRAs), Keogh plans, and corporate pensions.

# Individual Retirement Account (IRA)

The **Individual Retirement Account (IRA)** is a personal, tax-deferred retirement account. There are actually several variations of the traditional IRA that are now available to investors. These include educational IRAs, Roth IRAs, and SEP-IRAs. We will go through an explanation of the rules for traditional IRAs, and then briefly mention some of the important differences inherent in Roth and SEP-IRAs.

# 3.2.1.1 Purpose

IRAs are a means for investors to build up money that will be available to them when they reach retirement age. The main incentive to open an IRA and contribute to it (aside from having income to spend during retirement) is that the money invested is permitted to grow tax-deferred until it is withdrawn from the account. Furthermore, there are provisions for some of the contributions to be tax deductible so this can also reduce an investor's immediate tax burden.

# 3.2.1.2 Funding

There is a limit on the amount of annual contributions that an investor may make to an IRA. The funding limit is $2000 for individuals, $4000 for married couples filing jointly. If these limits are exceeded, there is a 6% excess contribution penalty imposed by the IRS. (Rollovers are not subject to these limits, as we shall see.) Contributions can be invested in stocks, bonds, government securities, mutual funds, limited partnerships, annuities, CDs, standard bank accounts, and U.S. gold or silver bullion coins. IRA contributions may not be invested in antiques, paintings, collectibles, rare coins, gold bullion, or life insurance.

# 3.2.1.3 Eligibility/Contribution Limits

Anyone who earns income (from other than investments) is eligible to make tax-deferred contributions of up to $2000 per year to an individual retirement account (IRA). Nonworking spouses may also make a tax-deferred contribution of up to $2000 if they file a joint tax return. Persons with earned income (and nonworking spouses) may contribute to IRAs until age 70½. Contributions are fully deductible if the investor is not eligible to be in another retirement plan (e.g., a company-sponsored plan). In other situations, contributions may be fully, partially, or not deductible based on the individual's adjusted gross income and other factors. Contributions may be made until April 15 following the tax year of eligibility. Even if the investor is not eligible to make tax deductible contributions, he or she may still make nondeductible contributions with after-tax dollars that can grow tax-deferred until they are withdrawn at retirement age.

# 3.2.1.4 Rollover/Transfer Rules

Change of employment does not affect the plan, as long as the IRA is transferred directly from one custodian to another. Furthermore, the investor may take possession of the IRA funds once each year, as long as the funds are redeposited into another IRA account within 60 days. This is called a rollover. Lump sum distributions from a qualified retirement plan (e.g., when a person changes employers) may be rolled over into a new retirement plan without incurring tax consequences. There is no limit on the amount that an investor can rollover, but any amount not rolled over within that time frame is subject to ordinary income tax (and an added 10% penalty if the investor is not yet 59½ years of age).

# 3.2.1.5 Taxation

Funds invested in IRAs are permitted to grow tax-deferred until distribution at retirement. Dividends and capital gains from IRA investments are also tax-deferred as long as the money stays invested in the plan. Distribution options upon retirement (or disability) include receiving regularly scheduled payments (e.g., monthly), or receiving a lump sum payment. Distributions are taxed as ordinary income when received, unless they are rolled over into another qualifying plan within 60 days. Lump sum payments are immediately taxable and may not be averaged out to lower the tax burden.

# 3.2.1.6 Distribution Rules

The minimum age to begin receiving IRA distributions without incurring penalties is 59½. If IRA distributions are taken before age 59½, the funds are taxed as ordinary income with an added 10% tax penalty. Funds can be withdrawn before age 59½ without incurring penalties if the person becomes disabled or will use the money to pay medical expenses, to pay educational expenses, or as a down payment for the first-time purchase of an investor's principal residence.

The latest that a person can begin taking distributions without incurring penalties is age 70½. If IRA distributions have not begun by age 70½, the IRS estimates the amount of distribution that should have been made and taxes the funds at the person's ordinary income tax rate with an added 50% tax penalty.

# 3.2.1.7 Simplified Employee Pension (SEP) Plans

One special kind of IRA is the SEP. A **SEP-IRA** (Simplified Employee Pension-IRA) is a tax-deferred retirement plan that is often used by small businesses or sole proprietors who do not offer other retirement plans.

**Eligibility, Contribution.** Employers can make contributions equal to 15% of the employee's total compensation, up to a maximum of $25,500. Contributions and investment earnings grow tax-deferred until distributions begin at retirement (age 59½) or disability. All distributions are taxed as ordinary income. Except for higher contribution limits, all regular IRA rules apply, including early withdrawal penalties.

# 3.2.1.8 Roth IRAs

Another special kind of IRA available to investors is the Roth IRA. The **Roth IRA** is a retirement plan with contributions that are *not* tax deductible, but which permits qualified distributions to be taken tax-free upon retirement. Since the Roth IRA funds are taxed before they go into the plan, they come out tax-free.

**Eligibility, Contribution.** Like regular IRAs, the Roth IRA permits persons with earned income to invest up to $2000 individually or $4000 for married couples filing jointly. Roth IRA contributions must have been invested in the plan at least five years prior to distribution in order to qualify for tax-free distribution. Like a regular IRA, a

10% penalty is imposed on distributions that start before age 59½, except in the case of disability, medical expenses, education expenses, first-time home purchase, or death. Unlike regular IRAs, there is no mandatory distributions that must occur by age 70½ (because the IRS has already collected its taxes). Regular IRAs may be converted to Roth IRAs without incurring any early withdrawal penalties, but ordinary income tax must be paid on the fund amount.

# Keogh/HR 10 Plans

Keogh plans are available to self-employed people who want to save for retirement. There's only one Keogh plan, but a person can have both a Keogh and IRA. Some rules (e.g., distributions) are the same as IRAs, but we'll point out key differences.

## 3.2.2.1 Purpose

Keogh plans are a means for self-employed people to build up money that will be available to them when they reach retirement age. The main incentive to open and contribute to a Keogh plan (aside from having income to spend during retirement) is that the money invested is permitted to grow tax-deferred until it is withdrawn from the account. Furthermore, there are provisions for contributions to be tax deductible so this also can reduce the immediate tax burden.

## 3.2.2.2 Funding

Funding for a Keogh plan comes from the employer, following the eligibility rules and contribution limits noted below. Keogh plan contributions are tax deductible to the contributor. Employees may also make additional contributions to the Keogh plan with after-tax dollars following the contribution limits noted below.

## 3.2.2.3 Eligibility and Employee Coverage

To be eligible, a person must have self-employed income. This can be in addition to any regular job or regular wages earned. If the self-employed person has full-time (1000 hours) adult employees (21 years old) who have worked for the employer at least one year, they must be included in the plan as well and given the same percentage contribution as the employer.

## 3.2.2.4 Contribution Limits

Maximum contributions by the employer are 25% of net income earned or $30,000, whichever is *less*. The 25% of net income earned equals 20% of precontribution income. So if a person made $80,000 gross × 20% = $16,000. Or take $80,000 −

$16,000 = $64,000 × 25% = $16,000. (It is unlikely that you will be asked to do these calculations on the Series 6 exam, but either way, just remember these numbers: **20% gross, 25% net.**) Employees may also contribute 10% of their earned income or $2500, whichever is less, in after-tax contributions. These non-deductible contributions made by employees with after-tax dollars are allowed to grow tax-deferred until they are withdrawn at retirement age. Contributions above these maximums incur a 6% penalty and do not grow tax-deferred.

## 3.2.2.5 Taxation

Funds invested in Keogh plans grow tax deferred until distribution at retirement. Dividends and capital gains from Keogh plans are also tax-deferred as long as the money stays invested in the plan. Distribution options upon retirement (or disability) include regularly scheduled payments (e.g., monthly) or receiving a lump sum payment. Distributions are taxed as ordinary income when received, unless they are rolled over into another qualifying plan within 60 days. Lump sum payments are immediately taxable and can't be averaged out to lower the tax burden.

## 3.2.2.6 Distribution Rules

The minimum age to begin receiving Keogh distributions without incurring penalties is 59½. If distributions are taken before age 59½, the funds are taxed as ordinary income with an added 10% tax penalty. Funds can be withdrawn before age 59½ without incurring penalties if the person becomes disabled or will use the money to pay medical expenses, to pay educational expenses, or as a down payment for the first-time purchase of an investor's principal residence.

The latest that a person can begin taking distributions without incurring penalties is age 70½. If distributions have not begun by age 70½, the IRS estimates the amount of distribution that should have been made and taxes the funds at the person's ordinary income tax rate with an added 50% tax penalty.

## 3.2.3

# Corporate Pension Plans

Corporate pension plans come in many varieties. The retirement plans we will talk about in this section all allow tax-deferred growth of invested dollars, but the main difference is to the employer. Some employer-sponsored retirement plans allow the corporation to deduct contributions from their corporate tax burden **(qualified plans),** some don't **(unqualified plans).** We'll only discuss qualified plans.

**Qualified plans** have several characteristics that distinguish them from unqualified plans. In addition to providing companies with a tax deduction for contributions, qualified plans must be approved by the IRS. Qualified plans must also treat all employees equally. The plan is a trust with a document that specifies the rights of the employees. The plan is funded by the employer (except 401(k)s), with at least annual contributions being made on behalf of the employee.

It is important to note that all qualified corporate retirement pension plans must also follow ERISA guidelines and regulations to maintain their favorable tax status. We will examine some key points about the ERISA legislation in the last section of this chapter, but first let's look at the two main categories of corporate pension plans: defined contribution plans and defined benefit plans.

## 3.2.3.1 Comparison: Defined Contribution Versus Defined Benefit

These two types of qualified pension plans are different in some important ways (e.g., contributions and benefits), but they share some characteristics (e.g., tax treatment, participation and vesting rules). We'll discuss contributions, benefits, and taxation here, and outline participation and vesting rules when we go over ERISA guidelines.

**Defined contribution plans** are a type of retirement plan where contribution amounts are fixed at a certain level, but benefit payouts are adjusted based on the return on investment of the retirement account funds. In some plans, employees make voluntary contributions that may or may not be matched by the company. In other plans, money is contributed by the employer based on employee's salary and years of company service. Maximum combined annual contribution by employer and employee is 25% of employee's compensation or $30,000, whichever is *less*. The employee usually has options as to where the money will be invested. Employer contributions are tax deductible for the corporation and are not taxed to the employee as income until retirement. Benefits paid out during retirement are taxed as ordinary income to the recipient.

**Defined benefit plans** are a type of retirement plan where benefit amounts are fixed at a certain level based on the employee's years of service to the company. Contributions may come solely from the employer, or sometimes from employees as well. Contribution amounts can be much larger than with other types of plans, because more may need to be invested in the near term to pay the defined benefit amount to older employees who are closer to retirement age. Such plans pay no taxes on their investments. Employer contributions are tax deductible for the corporation and are not taxed to the employee as income until retirement. Benefits paid out during retirement are taxed as ordinary income to the recipient.

Exam Topic Alert

For the Series 6 exam, note the key differences between these two types of plans: defined contribution plans have fixed contribution with variable benefits, whereas defined benefit plans have fixed benefits with variable contributions. Because of this, with defined contribution plans, the employee has the investment risk because the benefits can fluctuate; with defined benefits plans, the employer has the investment risk because the company must guarantee a fixed benefit payout.

# 3.2.3.2 Types of Defined Contribution Plans

There are three main types of defined contribution plans: profit-sharing plans, 401(k) plans, and 403(b) plans. Note that if an employee leaves a firm or changes jobs, money that has vested in these plans may be transferred to another qualifying plan (rolled over) with rules similar to IRAs. However, if a corporate retirement plan is cashed out after age 55 but before age 59½ because the person leaves the company for any reason (early retirement, laid off, buy out, fired), then money taken out is exempt from the 10% early withdrawal penalty.

**Profit-Sharing Plans.** With this type of plan, funding is done by the employer, who agrees to make contributions to the retirement accounts of employees annually when the company makes profits above a certain level. The key advantage for employers is that the contributions may be skipped when profits do not reach a certain level, at the discretion of the employer. The maximum contribution permitted is 15% of the employee's compensation. When all employees are treated equally, this is a qualified plan. That means that employer contributions are tax deductible for the corporation and are not taxed to the employee as income until retirement. Benefits paid out during retirement are taxed as ordinary income to the recipient.

A variation on the profit-sharing plan is the employee stock ownership plan (ESOP). With this type of plan, the employer pays into the employees' retirement plan with stock rather than cash. This means that the employer can conserve cash reserves and is still permitted a tax deduction for the stock's fair market value.

**401(k)/Payroll Deduction Savings Plans.** The most common payroll deduction plan used for retirement is the **401(k) plan.** This is a qualified plan, whereby employees can elect to contribute pretax dollars to a retirement account where the money will grow tax-deferred. Although many of these are "employee-pays-all" plans, some employers also match employees' 401(k) contributions. Employees may contribute up to $10,500 or 25% of an employee's compensation, whichever is less.

> Note that most other "payroll deduction" plans are unqualified. In fact, the 401(k) plan is usually called a "salary reduction" to make that distinction clear.

Exam Topic Alert

Employees can usually choose from a number of investment options, although the employer-matching portion may be subject to restrictions. Employers receive a corporate tax deduction for contributions, and employee contributions are a **salary reduction** that is taken out before gross income is figured for tax purposes. Thus, the employee is able to avoid taxes on the contributions when made, allowing the money to grow tax-deferred until distributions begin at retirement. Distributions may begin at age 59½ and must start by age 70½. Early withdrawal penalty is 10%. Benefits paid out during retirement are taxed as ordinary income to the recipient.

**403(b)/Tax-Deferred Annuity Plans.** A **403(b) plan,** also called a **tax sheltered annuity (TSA),** is a retirement plan that allows employees of nonprofit organizations, tax-exempt organizations, and schools to invest money tax-deferred, using a salary reduction plan so that employees are able to avoid taxes on the contributions when made. Employees may contribute up to $10,500, and employers can match up to 25% of an employee's compensation or $30,000, whichever is less. Additional contributions may be made with after-tax dollars.

Distributions may begin at age 59½ and must start by age 70½. Early withdrawal penalty is 10%. Benefits paid out during retirement are taxed as ordinary income to the recipient.

Note that although *annuity* is part of the name, TSA funds can invest in CDs, mutual funds, etc. Also, on the Series 6 exam, assume *annuity* means nondeductible, unqualified retirement plan unless a question says it's a TSA. Finally, note that students are *not* eligible to participate in 403(b) plans or TSAs.

# Employees Retirement Income Security Act (ERISA)

Congress felt that employers were abusing company retirement plans, mostly favoring the owners and executives at the expense of the hourly workers. In an effort to protect them and ensure that they were treated fairly, ERISA was enacted in 1974.

ERISA only applies to corporate (and other private sector) retirement plans and excludes government (and other public sector) retirement plans. (Watch this on the Series 6 exam!)

In order to maintain their favorable tax treatment, all qualified plans must follow ERISA guidelines. ERISA defines certain rules and procedures that must be adhered to by employers in order to take tax deductions for contributions made to employees' retirement plans. Some of the key points of the ERISA legislation are noted in this section.

**Employee Participation.** All full-time, adult employees who have worked for the employer at least one year must be included in the plan. Full-time adult employees are defined as workers over the age of 21 who have worked at least 1000 hours in the preceding year.

**Funding.** Contributions must be invested separately from other corporate funds, and all IRS limits must be observed.

**Fiduciary Responsibility.** Plan administrators have a fiduciary responsibility to protect the assets of the fund for the beneficiaries. Risk must be a primary consideration when investing. Investments such as short sales, naked options, and buying securities on margin are not allowed.

**Vesting. Vesting** is the right of ownership that an employee gains in retirement plans and other benefits from years of service at a company. Once this right is gained, it cannot be taken away just because a person leaves the company. Instead, benefits accrue in the retirement pension plan, or the employee is given a chance to rollover the funds into another account. This stops companies from firing workers before they reach retirement age just to avoid paying retirement benefits. Under the Tax Reform Act of 1986, employers have two choices: employees must be 100% vested after their fifth year, or employees can be 20% vested after their third year with 20% more added each year until 100% in their seventh year.

**Nondiscrimination Tests.** The formula used to determine the percentage of contributions made by the employer must be the same for all employees in the plan. Treating workers differently is a sure way to have the plan disqualified.

**Communications.** All employees must receive a written description of the retirement plan, including their rights under the plan, contribution amounts, and distribution information. Qualified plans must also provide employees with a means to name a beneficiary for their contributions upon death. A vesting schedule must be provided as well. Employees must be told what options are available to them, including amounts, if any, they may invest, and matching funds available from the company. They must be given an annual statement that shows the status of their account. Any updates to the plan must also be provided in writing to employees as soon as the changes are made or scheduled for implementation.

# 3.X Summary

**3.1** Variable contracts are packaged securities, often from insurance companies, who are responsible for managing the funds. Also called variable annuities.

**3.1.1** Insurance company can have the separate account directly managed (in which case it's regulated like a mutual fund), or indirectly managed using an investment advisor or outside contractor (in which case it's regulated like a UIT).

**3.1.2** Annuities are payments for life. Fixed guarantees amount, Variable doesn't. Premiums paid for a fixed annuity go into the insurance company general account, premiums paid for a variable annuity go into insurance company separate account.

Premium can be single lump sum or periodic payments, but only lump sum for immediate payout. Payouts can be immediate or deferred; lump sum or systematic withdrawal (Life Annuity, Life + Period Certain, Life + Amount Certain, Life + Joint Survivor). Life only is highest payment; survivor is lowest.

Annuities can have front-end loads or back-end loads-maximum sales charge is 8.5%.

Variable annuity has accumulation units, annuity units. Conversion done at retirement and assumed interest rate (AIR) is chosen. If separate account rate of return is higher than AIR, payment goes up; if lower than AIR payment falls. AIR is constant, number of annuity units is constant, value of units and payment can change.

Qualified annuity is paid with pretax dollars, so it is taxed as income when taken out at age 59½. Money grows tax-deferred but 10% penalty if withdrawn early. Surrendered contract, treated as withdrawal. Annuities have no capital gains.

### 3.1.3

Variable life insurance has cash value to invest. Cash value and death benefit vary with value of separate account investments. Has minimum guaranteed death benefit but no guaranteed cash value-policyholder assumes market risk. Value grows tax-deferred, contractholder can borrow against cash value. Law says contractholder must be able to borrow at least 75% of value after third year.

Policyholder has one vote per $100 of cash value. Settlement options are interest, fixed amount, fixed period, and life income (usually to beneficiary).

Contractholder may have exchange privilege, conversion privilege (law says open for at least 24 months), refund option 45 days, cancel within 2 years (first year refund = cash value + 30% sales charge, second year = cash value + 10%, third year = cash value only). Maximum sales charge is 9% (50% in first year).

Death benefit varies with AIR (can't rise with negative earnings carryover). AIR has no effect on cash value. Death benefit must be calculated at least once per year. Death benefit taxed in estate. A 1035 exchange allows an insurance policy to be traded for another investment, like an annuity. Review the life insurance comparison chart on page 129.

### 3.2

Retirement and tax avoidance are two investment goals of many investors.

### 3.2.1

Individual retirement plans are open to anyone who makes earned income (not investment income). IRA $2000 contribution limit plus $2000 for spouse. Amount is tax deductible if person isn't eligible for another plan. Money grows tax-deferred. Withdrawals at age 59½ to 70½ with no penalties. If not, 10% tax penalty early, 50% tax penalty if late. Can invest in stocks, bonds, mutual funds, U.S. gold coins, etc., but not antiques, collectibles, rare coins, etc.

Rollover is when an IRA account balance is transferred directly from one custodian to another or when an investor takes possession of the IRA funds (only once a year) and redeposits them in another IRA account within 60 days.

Roth IRA is not tax-deductible, but using after-tax money means tax free later. SEP-IRA has higher limits (15% of payment, maximum is $25,500). Other rules are the same.

3.2.2 Keogh plans are for the self-employed or employees of noncorporate entity. All full-time (1000 hours) adult (over age 21) employees must participate. Maximum contribution is the lesser of 25% net earnings (20% gross) or $30,000. Distributions start at 59½ with no penalty; if not by age 70 then 10% penalty.

3.2.3 Employee-sponsored plans are qualified or unqualified. Qualified is tax deductible if all employees are treated the same, have trust account, and follow rules. Defined contribution plan has fixed amount put in by employer-limited to lesser of $30,000 or 25% of employee's compensation. A corporation can deduct contribution. Benefits are taxed as ordinary income to recipient at retirement. Defined benefit plan has employer agree to pay employee a fixed amount at retirement-no limit to contributions, need to invest more for older workers. Corporation can deduct contribution. Benefits are taxed as ordinary income.

Profit-sharing is qualified if all participate; company can deduct contribution. 401(k) is salary reduction, with employee putting pretax money into account; employer may match funds. Distributions between 59½-70, follow same rules. 403(b) is for nonprofits, tax-exempt, and schools (*not* students). Employees can contribute up to $10,500, employers can match up to the lesser of $30,000 or 25% of employee's compensation. Distributions from age 59½ to 70, follow same rules. (403(b) also called tax sheltered annuity (TSA)).

3.2.4 Tax favorable plans must follow ERISA guidelines. All full-time (1000 hours) adult (age 21) employees must be included. Funds must be kept separate from company accounts. Fiduciary duty means no risky investments. Vesting must be 100% in the fifth year, or 20% each year beginning in third year so that 100% vesting occurs by the seventh year. The company must treat all employees in plan equally (nondiscrimination). Everyone must get written description of plan, annual report of contributions, means to name beneficiary, vesting schedule, and details of available options.

# Chapter 3 Review Quiz

1. All of the following are characteristics of variable annuity contracts, EXCEPT
   a. funds are deposited into a separate account.
   b. insurance companies bear the entire market risk.
   c. payments are guaranteed for the life of the contractholder.
   d. payments are based on comparison of actual return to assumed interest rate.

2. The table is a variable annuity payout schedule. What is the third month's payment?

   | Month | Prior Mo. Return | AIR | Payment |
   |-------|--------|-----|---------|
   | 1 | n/a | 6% | $537 |
   | 2 | 9% | 6% | $565 |
   | 3 | 7% | 6% | $ ? |

   a. $537
   b. $556
   c. $565
   d. $573

3. Which type of annuity payout would pay a client the highest monthly payment?
   a. life annuity
   b. life annuity with period certain
   c. life annuity with amount certain
   d. life annuity with joint and last survivor

4. Which of these is NOT paid from the gross premium of variable life insurance?
   a. sales charges
   b. administrative expenses
   c. management fee
   d. taxes to the state

5. What is the maximum a person can contribute to a Roth IRA with no penalties?
   a. $2000
   b. $4000
   c. $10,500
   d. 25% of net income earned

6. What is the capital gains owed on a variable annuity contract held for 18 months?
   a. this is taxed at the long-term capital gains rate
   b. there are no capital gains with annuities
   c. it depends on the length of time the asset was held in the separate account
   d. need more information to answer the question

7. Which of the following actions would NOT incur a tax penalty?
   a. withdrawing funds for personal use from an IRA before age 59½
   b. not withdrawing funds from a standard IRA by age 70
   c. rolling over IRA contributions with a direct custodian to custodian transfer
   d. withdrawing funds from IRA and putting them in another IRA after 90 days

8. Which of the following must occur under ERISA?
   a. all employees must be treated equally
   b. employees must be 100% vested by the fifth year (or seventh year if gradual)
   c. employees must receive a written description of the plan and benefits
   d. all of the above

# 4

# Securities Industry Regulations

*This final chapter is one of the most important. It covers the laws and regulations that you must observe when you work within the securities industry. You must have at least a basic understanding of what is expected of you and what you are prohibited from doing, if you want to have a long and successful career.*

*When you have finished studying this chapter, you will know all of the major legislation that governs the securities industry, as well as which agencies have oversight and jurisdiction. You will also understand the policies and procedures that the various institutions and organizations use to ensure compliance with the law.*

*Some of the material in this chapter may seem technical and complicated, but it really isn't. To help you absorb the material, many of the important laws and concepts are repeated in several places to illustrate for you how the same law is applied in different situations. Also pay special attention in studying the last two sections: NASD prohibited practices (4.5.3) and review of NASD (4.5.4). Do your best to read through everything one time thoroughly, then go back and review the "test keys" where we've highlighted topics that could potentially appear as test questions on the exam. This chapter ("Securities Industry Regulations") represents about 25% of the total test: approximately 25 questions of the total 100 questions on the Series 6 exam.*

## This chapter will be broken up into five sections:

**4.1 General Industry Regulations.** This first section introduces some of the key legislation that forms the foundation for all securities laws. In addition, there is a thorough discussion of the role of the NASD and many of the membership, conduct, and procedural rules that the NASD has put in place.

**4.2 Regulations Related to Marketing/ Prospecting.** This section examines each of the major laws and rules of the first section, and shows how they apply to marketing and prospecting. The focus is not only on the personnel aspects, but also on the various means of communication used when dealing with the public.

**4.3 Rules Related to Sales Presentation Materials.** This section looks at the major laws and rules of the first section as they relate to sales presentation materials. Several rules and standards are noted, as there are specific additional requirements when showing facts and figures to the public.

**4.4 Rules Related to Transactions.** This section deals with the important aspects of client transactions. Applicable federal laws are discussed, including Federal Reserve Regulation T, settlement procedures, and NASD conduct rules.

**4.5 Subsequent and Ongoing Communication and Service.** This section discusses NASD rules on recordkeeping, dispute resolution, conduct and procedures. The end of this section also has a synopsis of activities prohibited by NASD.

## key terms

**Advertising:** any kind of public communication that comes from the brokerage firm, but is not specifically distributed by the firm, and as such the brokerage firm has no control over who receives the material. (e.g., TV, magazine, website)

**Arbitration:** an alternative means of dispute resolution whereby an impartial third party or panel of people listen to evidence presented by both sides and render a decision, thus avoiding the expensive and time-consuming court system.

**Churning:** excessive trading to generate commissions (significant increase in trades after account became discretionary). **This is a violation of NASD rules.**

**Free-riding:** when part of a new stock issue is held back by the firm so that it can be resold later at a better profit. **This is a violation of NASD rules.**

**Front running:** when a broker-dealer executes a trade for the firm or an "insider" based on nonpublic information (e.g., a large block trade that will affect the price of the trade) to the firm or "insider's" advantage. In other words, the firm makes their own trade first to gain an advantage. **This is a violation of NASD rules.**

**Insider trading:** the illegal practice of trading securities on the basis of material information that has not been made public yet or providing nonpublic material information to others who trade on the information.

**Sales literature:** any written, electronic, or oral material distributed by a brokerage firm upon the request of a client, sent by the firm to a selected group of people, or disseminated in any other way such that the brokerage firm has control over who receives the material. (e.g., brochure, research report, e-mail newsletter)

**Securities Act of 1933:** requires all securities to be registered before they can be sold to the public, requires use of a prospectus with full disclosure of all pertinent information, and prohibits false and misleading information with several anti-fraud provisions. (Focus is on the primary market.) Also called the **Paper Act.**

**Securities Exchange Act of 1934:** regulates secondary market activity, outlaws fraud and market manipulation, regulates sales and activity by company insiders, requires broker-dealer firms and sales representatives to be registered, and created the Securities and Exchange Commission (SEC). Also referred to as the **People Act.**

**Self-Regulatory Organizations (SRO):** created by federal securities laws to help maintain a fair and orderly trading environment, to help oversee various aspects of securities industries, and to aid in enforcement of securities rules and regulations. (e.g., NASD) Each SRO also adopts and enforces its own "industry rules."

**Selling away:** doing a trade or collecting a commission that does not go through the broker-dealer firm. **This is a violation of NASD rules.**

**Tombstone ads:** special ads placed by broker-dealer firms to draw attention to a prospectus or announce some other major business event without the ad being a specific offer to sell or buy securities.

**Withholding:** when part of new stock issue is held back in the firm's account or sold to family members, employees, or insiders. **This is a violation of NASD rules.**

# 4.1

# General Industry Regulations

There are several laws that govern the securities industry and the conduct of those who sell, buy, or broker securities. In addition to these federal laws, there are numerous conduct rules put forth by various regulatory and oversight agencies.

## 4.1.1

# Securities Act of 1933

The Securities Act of 1933 requires that all securities must first be registered before they can be sold to the public. The Act of 1933 regulates new issues in the primary market. The act requires the use of a prospectus to provide full disclosure of all pertinent information relative to a company's business and finances so that investors can make informed investment decisions. The act also prohibits false and misleading information from being disseminated with several antifraud provisions.

The Securities Act of 1933 is sometimes referred to as the **Paper Act** because of all the paperwork and filings that it requires. The focus of the act is on the primary market for new issues. Much of the language of the law focuses on the duties and responsibilities of the issuer and the underwriter. The act does *not* approve securities, nor does it ascertain the value of an issue or a company. The act only ensures that investors are provided with full and fair disclosure about the issue and the issuer. The act clears a registration and allows a public offering to take place.

# 4.1.1.1 Definitions

There are several terms defined by the Act of 1933, but there are two in particular that you can expect to be tested on: issuer and underwriter.

An **issuer** is any entity that can legally sell and distribute new securities. Issuers have a responsibility under the law to make accurate and timely reportings of their finances to investors and to follow all laws and procedures proscribed by the Act of 1933. Note that the act mostly covers corporations as issuers, because municipalities, U.S. government, and nonprofit groups are exempt from registration.

An **underwriter** is a broker-dealer firm acting in the capacity of an investment banker that buys a new issue of securities and resells them to the public. Underwriters take on the risk of raising the money, and make a profit on the spread between what they pay the company for the securities and what they resell them for.

Note that the Act of 1933 is not enforceable at the state level. Instead, states have **Blue Sky laws** that cover many of these same disclosure and registration issues.

Exam Topic Alert

# Securities Exchange Act of 1934

The Securities Exchange Act of 1934 regulates secondary market activity by outlawing fraud and market manipulation, regulating sales and activities by company insiders, and requiring broker-dealer firms and securities sales representatives to be registered. The Act of 1934 is focused on the secondary marketplace. This act created the Securities and Exchange Commission (SEC) to oversee the securities markets and enforce the regulations of this act and the Securities Act of 1933.

The Securities Exchange Act of 1934 is sometimes referred to as the **People Act** because of all the various people required to be registered under the act or whose activities the act regulates. The focus of the Act is on the secondary markets where outstanding stock issues are traded on exchanges or OTC. The purpose of the act is to protect investors and investments from fraud and manipulation. In fact, even securities or transactions that are exempt from registration under the act of 1933 are not exempt from the antifraud provisions of the Securities Exchange Act of 1934.

You may be asked some questions about the Securities Exchange Act of 1934 (also called the **Exchange Act** or People Act). Before we cover some important topics in detail, here's a synopsis of what the Act of 1934 covers. Remember: **SIMMERS PAN,** or: **SIMMER + PAN.**

> ▷ **S**EC was created,
> ▷ **I**nsider activities regulated,
> ▷ **M**argin rules were created,

▷ **M**anipulation of the markets was prohibited,

▷ **E**xchanges and all people who trade on them must be registered with the SEC,

▷ **R**egistration and filings must be done regularly by listed companies,

▷ **+S**hort sales were regulated,

▷ **P**roxies were required to include specific information so voters are informed,

▷ **A**nnual statements from broker-dealers were required to be given to clients,

▷ **N**et capitalization rules applied to broker-dealers to limit their indebtedness.

# 4.1.2.1 Definitions

You will likely be tested on several terms defined in the Act of 1934: broker, dealer, security, investment contract, and statutory disqualification.

A **broker** is one who acts as an agent, arranging securities trades for a commission.

A **dealer** is one who acts as a principal, buying and selling securities from their own inventory for a markup or markdown.

A **broker-dealer** is a securities brokerage firm and/or investment banking house that is in the business of securities buying, selling, and advising. (Note that a firm cannot act as a broker *and* dealer in the same transaction, so a firm cannot both make a commission and charge a markup for the same sale. We'll explain more later.)

A **security** is any investment relationship with a company (and the instrument that represents that investment). This can be equity ownership in a company (stock), debt with a company (bond), a pooling of investment instruments (mutual fund), or any instrument transferring a future right (option). (Municipal and U.S. government bonds are also securities, but they are exempt securities not covered by the act.)

An **investment contract** is an agreement whereby one or more persons contribute money and expect to make a profit from the entrepreneurial and managerial efforts of others. In essence, an investment contract is a security when the persons contributing money do not participate in management duties. The decision in *Howie v SEC* (1948) sets forth three requirements that make something a security:

▷ an investment with "consideration" (money changes hands);

▷ the money is part of a "common enterprise" (money from many people goes into the same investment); and

▷ any income is "derived solely from the efforts of others."

**Statutory disqualification** says that a candidate for a securities license may be disqualified if he or she is, or has been, subject to disciplinary action by the SEC, a Self-Regulatory Organization (SRO, such as the NYSE or NASD), or a securities governing body of a foreign country. Automatic, statutory disqualification is in effect if the person:

▷ has ever been expelled or suspended by a securities industry governing body (SEC, SRO, or foreign equivalent),

▷ caused another person or firm to be expelled or suspended by a securities industry governing body (SEC, SRO, or foreign equivalent),

▷ has a felony conviction,

▷ has a misdemeanor conviction related to money or securities in past ten years,

▷ is under an SEC order (or foreign equivalent) barring participation in the securities industry, or

▷ is under a court order barring participation in the securities industry.

# 4.1.2.2 Securities and Exchange Commission (SEC)

The SEC is a federal government agency created by the **Securities Exchange Act of 1934** to oversee the securities industry, establish regulations governing the issuance and sale of securities, and enforce the securities laws enacted by Congress. As we saw in the previous section, **securities** are defined very broadly as any investment relationship with a company. In order for the SEC to perform its oversight functions, all securities industry participants must register with the SEC. Industry participants include:

▷ **exchanges** where securities are bought and sold,

▷ **companies** wishing to issue or sell securities, and

▷ **broker-dealers** in the business of securities buying, selling, and advising.

# 4.1.2.3 Registered Securities Associations

The **Maloney Act of 1938** was an amendment to the Act of 1934, allowing broker-dealers to form or join associations to help enforce the securities laws. These registered securities associations came to be known as SROs. **Self-Regulatory Organizations (SRO)** were created by federal securities laws to help maintain a fair and orderly trading environment, to help oversee various aspects of the securities industries, and to aid in the enforcement of securities rules and regulations. SROs fall under the jurisdiction of the SEC and are responsible for the conduct of their own members. As such, each have adopted and enforce their own set of "industry rules," which members agree to abide by as a condition of participation in the market or exchange. This is in addition to those rules and regulations set out by the SEC and various state regulatory bodies.

Each major exchange has its own SRO charged with oversight of activity within that marketplace. The three largest SROs are the New York Stock Exchange (NYSE), the National Association of Securities Dealers (NASD), and the Municipal Securities Rulemaking Board (MSRB). We will briefly mention some points about the NYSE and MSRB, but we will spend considerable time focusing on the rules and procedures of the NASD. These rules form the basis for much of what you will encounter in your career—and on the Series 6 exam.

Note that both the NYSE and the NASD have the power to enforce their regulations on registered member firms and registered persons who work for those firms. Also note that the NYSE and the NASD do not have the power to enforce each other's rules and regulations; they may only discipline their own members. Finally, the MSRB does *not* have the power to enforce the rules it makes, but instead relies on the NASD, other SROs, and the SEC for enforcement.

**NYSE.** The **New York Stock Exchange (NYSE)** is an SRO responsible for all activities related to securities listed and traded on the New York Stock Exchange. To become a member firm, one of the 1366 individual "seats" must be purchased. Member firms and salesperson employees of member firms must register with the NYSE and agree to abide by its rules and regulations. The NYSE also has responsibility for some of the regional stock exchanges in the United States. (e.g., Philadelphia Stock Exchange).

**MSRB.** The **Municipal Securities Rulemaking Board (MSRB)** is an SRO responsible for all activities related to municipal bonds and other intrastate government securities that are issued, sold, or traded. Firms and employees associated with those firms must be qualified in accordance with MSRB rules and agree to abide by its regulations.

### 4.1.2.3.1. THE NATIONAL ASSOCIATION OF SECURITIES DEALERS (NASD).
The NASD is an SRO responsible for all activities related to securities that are sold in the over-the-counter (OTC) market. The NASD also has regulatory authority over investment banking, investment companies, and limited partnerships.

#### 4.1.2.3.1.1. Certificate of Incorporation.
According to the NASD Certificate of Incorporation, its stated objectives and purposes are:

▷ to promote the investment banking and securities business through cooperative effort;
▷ to provide a medium through which its membership may confer, consult, and cooperate;
▷ to promote self-discipline and self-regulation among members; and
▷ to investigate and adjust grievances of members and the public.

#### 4.1.2.3.1.2. By-Laws.
The NASD by-laws define the purpose, structure, rules and procedures of operations. Power emanates from the board of governors to district offices, with a command structure designed primarily to enforce rules and handle complaints.

NASD has a national board of governors and 13 district offices run by district committees. The board supervises all national NASD activities, including membership activities and approvals, handles complaint appeals, and sets NASD rules and policies. District Offices handle complaints via District Business Conduct Committees (DBCC) and also take care of nonpayment and nondelivery issues.

**Definitions.** The NASD by-laws define the **investment banking or securities business** as a broker, dealer, municipal securities dealer, or government securities dealer that underwrites, distributes, sells, or buys securities for the account of another. The

NASD by-laws also expand on the Act of 1933 definitions of **broker** and **dealer** to include not only persons, but also partnerships, corporations, and other organizations who engage in the role of broker or dealer, with the exception of banks, which are excluded from the NASD definitions.

**Qualifications.** Any registered broker-dealer in good standing with the SEC may apply to become an NASD member. Salesperson employees of member firms must also be registered with NASD and agree to abide by its rules and regulations.

**Membership.** A signed membership application and the appropriate fee must be sent to the NASD. The applicant agrees to comply with federal securities laws, follow the rules of NASD, and abide by its rulings, sanctions, and arbitration decisions. Applicant's also agree to keep their information current at all times, notifying NASD within 30 days of any changes or updates.

**Registered Representatives and Associated Persons.** Registration is required for all employees of a member stock exchange broker-dealer, if those employees will be involved with the sale or promotion of securities. Series 7 registration allows an individual to sell all types of securities offered by the member broker-dealer (except commodities futures). Series 6 registration allows an individual to sell investment company products (e.g., unit investment trusts, closed-end and open-end investment company products, mutual funds) and variable contract products (e.g., variable annuity contracts, retirement plans, IRAs).

Note that a Series 6 limited representative is specifically prohibited from selling Real Estate Investment Trusts (REITs), Direct Participation Programs (DPPs), limited partnerships, and all securities that trade on the secondary market.

Exam Topic Alert

**Qualifications** include the requirement that a salesperson be sponsored by a member broker-dealer firm, submit fingerprints, pass a background check, pass the required examination, and follow all securities laws and rules. The person must also not be subject to any of the statutory disqualifications noted in the previous section.

**Applications** must be on the form prescribed by the NASD, containing an agreement to comply with federal securities laws and SRO rules, and an agreement to file changes and amendments with the NASD within 30 days (or within 10 days for statutory disqualification items). Applications must also be signed.

**Notification** must be given to the NASD by a member firm within 30 days after termination, but firms may not terminate an employee during an investigation for securities violations or other pending SRO actions. The licensed sales representative must also be given a copy of the notice. Furthermore, the NASD does not permit a transfer of registration. Instead, the person must resign from one firm (using form U-5) and reapply for registration with the new firm (using form U-4). The U-4 form must be filed within two years, or the person must requalify for license registration.

**Retention of jurisdiction** is two years. This means that whether a person is terminated or chooses to resign voluntarily, the NASD still retains jurisdictional authority over that person for an additional two-year period. Thus a person must still provide information requested by the NASD and be bound by its disciplinary actions.

**Disciplinary Proceedings.** The NASD board has the authority to establish procedures for disciplinary proceedings involving members. Members are entitled to a disciplinary hearing where specific charges are brought, and members are given a chance to defend against such charges. A record is kept of the proceedings, with findings detailing the specific act that constituted the violation, the rule that was violated, the basis upon which any findings are made, and the sanction(s) imposed.

**Powers of Board to Prescribe Sanctions.** The NASD board is authorized to impose appropriate sanctions on members who violate NASD rules, violate rules of the Treasury Department, refuse to submit disputes to arbitration or comply with hearing requests, or refuse to abide by official board rulings or pay fines as directed. Penalties for violations may include censure, fines, suspension, termination of membership, prohibition against association with other members or member firms, and other sanctions as deemed appropriate by NASD.

**4.1.2.3.1.3. Membership and Registration Rules.** The Series 1000 Rules cover membership and registration issues. You will probably not need to know any specific numbers here, but you should know a few specific concepts that we will highlight. Under NASD rules, filing incomplete, inaccurate, misleading, or false information that's not amended or corrected is considered conduct inconsistent with just and equitable principles of NASD and may be cause for disciplinary action.

**Failure to register personnel** who engage in activities that require registration is a violation of NASD rules that may be cause for disciplinary action.

**Registration of principals** is required for all persons who actively perform duties as a principal. A person may not be registered as a principal if there is no intent to employ the person in that capacity or the person is no longer active in the firm. Under these rules, a **principal** is defined as a sole proprietor, officer, partner, manager, supervisor, or corporate director who is actively engaged in managing, supervising, or training in an investment banking or securities firm.

**Registration of representatives** is required for all persons who actively perform duties as a representative. A person may not be registered as a representative if there is no intent to employ the person in that capacity or the person is no longer active in the firm. Under these rules, a **representative** is defined as an employee involved with the sale or promotion of securities. There are two main categories of registered sales representatives you must be familiar with:

> ▷ **General Securities Representatives** take the Series 7 exam and may sell all types of securities (except commodities futures).
> ▷ **Limited Representatives** take the Series 6 exam and may sell investment company products (e.g., mutual funds) and variable contract products (e.g., IRAs). (They can't sell REITs, DPPs, limited partnerships, or secondary market securities.)

**Registration of assistant representatives** is required for all persons who perform order processing functions in a broker-dealer firm. Registration consists of passing a special exam and meeting NASD requirements (including fingerprinting). Assistant representatives can interact with the public, but only to receive unsolicited orders. They are *not* permitted to actively solicit transactions, nor give investment advice, nor make recommendations. They must be paid an hourly wage or salary that is not a commission-based compensation. Assistant representatives may not act in any other capacity and must be directly supervised on-site by a registered principal.

**Persons exempt from registration** under NASD rules include those whose functions are solely clerical or administrative, persons not actively engaged in the investment banking or securities business, persons acting as corporate officers for the firm in name only, floor brokers registered with the exchange, and those dealing exclusively with municipal or commodities transactions. Those exempt from registration may collect commissions if they are foreign people or firms not required to register under U.S. securities laws, are transacting business for foreign nationals, or have a written compensation agreement in place (and approved by the NASD) that provides for full disclosure of the compensation paid as a result of the transaction.

**Confidentiality of exams** is of utmost importance to the NASD. It is a serious violation for anyone to attempt to remove portions of the exam from the official testing center or to try in any other way to pass questions from the exam to others.

**4.1.2.3.1.4. Conduct Rules.** The Series 2000 Rules cover business conduct. Again, you will probably not need to know specific numbers, but you are likely to see a question on one or more of several key concepts covered in this area of NASD rules. The overriding concept is that NASD members should observe high standards in the conduct of their business, and uphold just and equitable principles of trade.

**General standards** state that member firms should make a bona fide distribution of securities to the public at the public offering price, even if the securities have become a **"hot issue"** (trading above the issue price in the secondary market).

There are three violations of NASD rules that you need to know the definitions of:

▷ **Free-riding** is when part of a new stock issue is held back by the firm so that it can be resold later at a better profit than the original public offering price.

▷ **Withholding** is when part of a new stock issue is held back by the firm in its own account, or sold to family members, employees, or other insiders.

▷ **Front running** is when a broker-dealer executes a trade for the firm or an "insider" based on nonpublic information (such as an imminent block trade that will affect the price of the trade) to the firm or "insider's" advantage. In other words, the firm makes their own trade first to gain an advantage.

Exam Topic Alert

**RESPONSIBILITIES RELATED TO EMPLOYEES.** The Series 3000 Rules cover several areas that deal with employees, associates, and supervisory procedures. Some of these procedures may be test questions. Another important area for you to know is the restrictions on outside business activities. Let's look at these.

**Supervision** of employees at a broker-dealer firm must be done by a Registered Principal who has passed the Series 24 exam and obtained a Principal License. Registered Principals of member firms are ultimately responsible for all office activities. In addition to supervising registered sales representatives, a Registered Principal must also approve all new accounts, client trades, sales literature, and ads.

A **supervisory system** must be established that is reasonably designed to achieve compliance with all securities laws, regulations, and NASD rules. This includes designation of a registered principal responsible for each office location, assignment of registered sales representatives to a particular principal, a process to monitor and review activities, and a meeting at least once annually with all registered sales representatives.

**Written procedures** must be in place to implement the supervisory system, along with written procedures put in place to maintain and enforce compliance with securities laws and regulations.

**Internal inspections** are required to detect and prevent violations of securities laws and NASD rules. These inspections must at a minimum consist of an annual review of office procedures, customer accounts, and the supervisory jurisdiction of each office location.

**Written approval** must be given by a registered principal for all correspondence (written or electronic) that takes place with the public relating to securities, the securities business, or the investment banking activities of the member firm.

**Qualifications investigated** by member firms include background checks of all prospective registered sales representative candidates. The broker-dealer firm is responsible for conducting this investigation into the character, business reputation, experience, and qualifications of the individual before certifying the person to the NASD on his or her application form. This background check includes inquiries to securities firms that the applicant may have worked for in the past.

**Important definitions** from this section include OSJ and branch office. An **Office of Supervisory Jurisdiction (OSJ)** is any office of an NASD member where one or more of the following take place: new accounts are approved; customer orders are reviewed, endorsed, or executed; customers' funds or securities are held; public offerings, private placements, or market making occurs; advertising or sales literature is approved; or activities of persons at other branch offices are supervised. A **branch office** is any location identified to the public or customers (by a sign, advertising, letterhead, or otherwise) as a location at which an NASD member conducts investment banking or securities business.

**Outside business activities of associated persons** must be disclosed to the member firm in writing, so that the firm has knowledge of the activity and can then decide whether or not to consent to the activity. This must be done for all business activities from which the person would receive compensation (other than from a passive investment). Special care is taken by the NASD because seemingly unrelated activities, such as giving a speech, could be misconstrued as a solicitation of business or misinterpreted as promoting a specific security, and thus subject to the public communication rules and other regulations.

**4.1.2.3.1.5. Procedural Rules.** The Series 8000 Rules cover complaints, investigations, and sanctions. NASD investigates all complaints. Disputes involving rules violations or misconduct go through NASD's Code of Procedure (COP). Disputes involving money go to arbitration using NASD's Code of Arbitration Procedure (CAP). Arbitration is mandatory for monetary complaints among NASD members. Client complaints against members filed with NASD fall under NASD's Code of Procedure.

The NASD manual showing all rules, regulations and By-Laws must be made **available to customers** at all times, in a readily accessible place, and shown to clients or customers upon request.

**Complaints by the public** against NASD members are investigated by the NASD. Clients can force member firms to arbitrate disputes, but member firms can only compel clients to submit to arbitration if the customer has signed a consent form. Clients who choose arbitration waive their right to pursue the matter in court.

**Complaints by the District Business Conduct Committee (DBCC)** are brought against members who are accused in disciplinary matters. Each of the 13 district offices of the NASD use the DBCC to handle conduct complaints and also to take care of any nonpayment or nondelivery issues. Decisions of the DBCC may be appealed to the NASD national board of governors.

**Complaints by the board of governors** are reserved for serious breaches of fiduciary duty or misconduct, and for appeals of decisions by other enforcement bodies. The board supervises all national NASD activities (including membership activities and approvals), handles appeals, and sets NASD rules and policies.

**Investigations** of complaints fall under the NASD Code of Procedure, which gives the NASD the right to **inspect the books and records** of the member firm, the right to request statements from the parties involved, and the right to require an appearance before the hearing board. Refusal to comply with requests from the investigative body is a violation that can result in disciplinary action.

**Sanctions for violations of NASD rules** can include censure, fines, suspension, termination of membership, prohibition against association with other members or member firms, and other sanctions as deemed appropriate by the NASD.

The **effect of suspension** is that a person is no longer permitted to be associated with a member firm in any way—not even in a clerical or ministerial capacity. A member firm may not pay a suspended person commissions or other remuneration (directly or indirectly) for securities transactions that occur during a suspension.

**Release of disciplinary information** is made by the NASD upon request and may include employment history of a member, disciplinary history of a member (by the NASD or federal, state, or foreign securities agencies), all pending disciplinary actions, any criminal indictments or convictions, any civil judgments, arbitration decisions, civil litigation, pending investigations, or other information the NASD deems appropriate.

**Payment of fines or sanctions** must be made to the NASD in a timely fashion. After seven days written notice, the NASD may suspend, expel, or revoke registration of a member for failure to pay any imposed fine, sanction, cost, etc.

**Cost of proceedings** is borne by the member whose conduct caused the disciplinary proceedings to take place. The adjudicator of the disciplinary matter has the authority to deem what cost is fair and appropriate under the circumstances.

**Code of Procedure.** The Series 9000 Rules cover the NASD Code of Procedure. Remember, all NASD disputes involving rules violations or misconduct go through the Code of Procedure (COP), and NASD disputes among members involving money go to arbitration following the NASD Code of Arbitration Procedure (CAP).

Note that the COP (for misconduct) *is **not** the same as* CAP (for money disputes)!

**Disciplinary actions by the DBCC** are the result of hearings that follow rules outlined in the COP. NASD has 13 district offices run by district committees that handle complaints via District Business Conduct Committees (DBCC). DBCC also takes care of nonpayment and nondelivery issues. If a hearing goes against a member, sanctions begin 30 days after the final written report is complete. Decisions and sanctions may be appealed to the NASD board, to the SEC, or to federal court.

**Review of disciplinary actions by the board of governors** occurs by an appeal of a member within 25 days after a decision has been issued. Any issues not raised or objected to in the appeal are considered waived and consented to.

**Application to the SEC for review** can be made by a member within 25 days after a decision has been issued. Any SEC decision is appealable to federal court.

**Imposition of sanctions and costs** are enforced by the Membership Department of the NASD. Decisions of the board or other disciplinary body are effective when the member is served with the decision. Within seven days after a hearing, the Membership Department shall issue a written report, instructing the member of the sanctions to be imposed and the costs that the member must pay.

**Summary suspension, expedited procedures,** and other special courses of action are available to the NASD board to use as they see fit. **Summary suspension** is typically invoked when a member has already been suspended or expelled from another self-regulatory organization (i.e., NYSE) or when the member is in such dire financial trouble as to pose a safety threat to clients, investors, or other members. **Expedited procedures** are typically used when a delay in reviewing a decision would unduly harm a member (e.g., suspension of principal closes an entire office).

# 4.1.2.4 Fingerprinting of Securities Industry Personnel

The SEC requires fingerprinting of all employees of broker-dealer firms who:

> ▷ handle cash or securities,
> ▷ supervise people who handle cash or securities,

▷ are involved with the sale of securities to the public, or

▷ supervise people who are involved with the sale of securities to the public.

4.1.3

# Securities Investor Protection Act of 1970

The **Securities Investor Protection Act of 1970** was passed by Congress to protect investors from broker-dealer insolvency. The main mechanism by which this objective was achieved was through the creation of the Securities Investor Protection Corporation (SIPC).

## 4.1.3.1 Purpose

The **Securities Investor Protection Corporation (SIPC)** was set up as a nonprofit corporation by Congress. Its purpose is to protect investors from broker-dealer insolvency by providing a fund that insures the cash and securities in an investor's account up to $500,000 total, with a limit of $100,000 paid in cash. These limits are for each separate customer account, so a husband and wife with separate accounts would count as two customer accounts. If the husband and wife had a third joint account, then that would count as a third separate customer account.

Remember, these limits are per customer, not per account, but also watch questions where separate *and* joint accounts are discussed—you need to know the *total* limit.

Exam Topic Alert

## 4.1.3.2 Membership

All broker-dealers registered with the SEC or one of the national stock exchanges are required to be members of the SIPC.

If a brokerage firm fails, the SIPC first tries to merge it with another member firm. If that is not possible, then SIPC liquidates the firm's assets and pays off customer accounts up to the stated limits. All debit balances owed by the customer are subtracted from the market value of the securities when determining the payout amounts due. If the amount due a customer exceeds the maximum SIPC payout limit, then the investor becomes a general creditor of the bankrupt broker-dealer firm.

Note for the Series 6 exam that *the SIPC does not protect investors against market risks or bad investments, and SIPC is **not** an agency of the U.S. government.*

Exam Topic Alert

# Investment Advisors Act of 1940

The Investment Advisors Act of 1940 was passed by Congress to protect the public from fraud and misrepresentation. The main mechanism used to achieve this objective was the requirement that all investment advisors (IAs) be registered.

## 4.1.4.1 Purpose

The **Investment Advisors Act** was passed by Congress to require registration as a means to combat fraud, misrepresentation, and deceit by investment professionals. Among the provisions of the act, for example, is a requirement that IAs disclose all potential conflicts of interest, such as the IA owning a particular stock about which he or she is making a recommendation. The act provides conduct regulations, as well as disciplinary sanctions for noncompliance.

## 4.1.4.2 Definitions

An **Investment Adviser (IA)** is anyone who gives investment advice for a fee. The compensation can be a flat fee or it can be a percentage of the assets managed. An IA can be part of an investment advisory service working with many companies; a consultant working one-on-one with a particular company, perhaps as the portfolio manager of an investment company; or an IA may produce a newsletter offering the same investment advice to all subscribers. In all these cases, investment advisors must register with the SEC and are subject to the Investment Advisors Act of 1940.

Persons associated with an investment advisor must also be registered if they interact with the public, with certain exceptions noted in the next section.

## 4.1.4.3 Registration

Investment advisors who comply with federal registration guidelines are often referred to as Registered Investment Advisors (RIA).

**Requirements.** Requirements for federal registration includes registering with the SEC after having passed the appropriate examination. Persons who currently hold a Series 6 license would be required to pass the Series 65 exam to become an RIA; persons who have a Series 7 license would be required to pass the Series 66 exam to become an RIA. The various state securities regulatory bodies often have their own additional registration requirements for conducting business or offering investment advice as an IA within their state. This can range from simple notification and registration with the state authority, to the requirement of additional testing and other compliance measures.

**Exemptions.** The main exemption from registration that you should be aware of is for regular salaried employees, working exclusively for a particular company, and who only give advice to that company. An example would be an economic advisor, hired as a regular salaried employee by a bank, who only gives advice and analysis to the bank for internal purposes and does not share that information with the public.

Note that the Investment Advisors Act of 1940 applies to those who receive compensation solely for their investment advice, not to those who give investment advice incidental to their primary function, such as a stockbroker. To make this distinction clear, think about how a stockbroker is compensated. A stockbroker is receiving compensation primarily from the commission that the buying or selling of the stock generates, not from the investment advice itself. Likewise, anyone who sells mutual funds is not required to be a registered advisor. On the other hand, the investment advisor of a mutual fund *must* be registered under the act, since he or she is paid a fee by the fund for investing advice and guidance.

Exam Topic Alert

4.1.5

# Insider Trading and Securities Fraud Enforcement Act of 1988

The Insider Trading and Securities Fraud Act of 1988 **(ITSFEA)** was passed by Congress in an effort to discourage and punish insider trading. Section 10(b) of the Securities Exchange Act of 1934 already prohibited "insiders" from trading on the basis of material, nonpublic information, and Congress passed another law in 1984 to expand the definition of *insider* to just about anyone with nonpublic information. The ITSFEA of 1988 went much further in its effort to curb insider trading activity by (1) expanding those liable for damages from insider trading to include persons in a control relationship (e.g., employer, supervisor, etc.), (2) increasing civil penalties, (3) increasing criminal penalties, (4) giving the SEC more power and resources to combat insider trading, (5) creating a bounty system for the SEC to pay informers, and (6) requiring employers to establish written policies and enforce procedures designed to prevent misuse of nonpublic information and insider trading activities.

## 4.1.5.1 Prohibition on Misuse of Material, Nonpublic Information

It is illegal for persons to trade securities on the basis of material information that has not been made public yet. Material information is any important fact that would influence a person's decision. The SEC has issued Rule 10b5-1 to clarify the rules on what constitutes insider trading. Rule 10b5-1 says that insider trading liability arises when an insider is aware of material nonpublic information when making a trade, regardless of whether that information motivated the trade. The rule counteracts the position taken by some courts that the SEC must prove that a defendant actually "used" the nonpublic information in making the trade. Rule 10b5-1 also establishes an affirmative defense to insider trading liability for trades made based on "a pre-existing plan, contract or instructions that were entered into in good faith at a time when the insider was not aware of any material nonpublic information." In other words, if the person placed a trade order, then later learns of nonpublic information, the person is not guilty of insider trading if the person legitimately entered into the arrangement beforehand, with no prior knowledge, and executed the trade order at that time without any subsequent ability or attempt to influence the trade after learning the nonpublic information.

# 4.1.5.2 Civil Penalities

The 1988 Act (ITSFEA) allows the SEC to assess civil penalties against individuals who trade securities based on inside information, or tip-off others to any inside information. Civil penalties may also be imposed against a company (or the controlling persons of a company) for failure to take appropriate steps to prevent the trading on or tipping of inside information. Civil penalties can be equal to **the greater of $1,000,000 or three times the profit made or the losses avoided** by the person who traded based on the inside information. The person may also be required via court order obtained by the SEC to disgorge any profits to the SEC. The act also instituted a bounty program giving the SEC discretion to reward informants with up to 10% of any monetary penalty collected.

# 4.1.5.3 Criminal Penalties

The 1988 Act (ITSFEA) increased criminal penalties for trading on inside information, tipping off others to any inside information, or being criminally negligent in not stopping the trading on or tipping of inside information. Criminal penalties were increased, making the maximum jail term ten years for criminal securities law violations, with maximum criminal fines of $1,000,000 for individuals and $2,500,000 for nonnatural persons (e.g., corporations).

# 4.1.5.4 Liability to Contemporaneous Traders

Private parties who lost money on contemporaneous trades because of the actions of a person trading on inside information are permitted under the 1988 act (ITSFEA) to bring private court actions to sue for damages. Damages awards are limited to the amount of profits or losses actually involved. The trader, tipper, tippee, or controlling person or entity that failed to act can all be held jointly and severally liable. Claims under this provision of the law are actually rather rare. The statute of limitations is five years.

## 4.1.5.5 Policies and Procedures to Be Developed by Broker-Dealers

One of the purposes of the ITSFEA of 1988 was to provide greater incentives for employers to monitor employee activities in a control relationship. The act requires brokers-dealer firms and investment advisor firms to establish written policies, implement internal controls, and enforce procedures that monitor employees and associates in an effort to prevent insider trading and other misuse of material, non-public information. The act expanded the civil penalties to include liability for control persons (employers, supervisors, etc.) who neglect to take adequate steps to prevent insider trading. Note, though, that no person is liable under this section solely by employing another person, but liability of a controlling person under the act can occur if there is no policy in place or if there is gross negligence in enforcement of a policy.

# 4.2 Regulations Related to Marketing, Prospecting

Communication with the public for marketing or prospecting is one area that is highly regulated by the SEC and the various SROs. This is because the potential for false or misleading statements can have a seriously adverse impact on an unsophisticated investing public. In fact, securities rules and regulations define public communications very broadly, covering everything from advertising and sales literature to seminars and lectures. Marketing materials, research reports, educational materials, telephone solicitations, correspondence, press releases, and all electronic communications also fall under these rules.

Sales literature and advertising rules are an important area of regulation in the securities industry. Before we discuss some important rules, let's distinguish between the two terms because these may appear in a question on the Series 6 exam. **Sales literature** is distributed by a member firm in a way such that the brokerage firm has control over who receives the material (e.g., brochure, research report). **Advertising,** on the other hand, is not specifically distributed by the firm, and as such, the firm has no control over who receives the material (e.g., TV ad, phone book).

4.2.1

# Securities Act of 1933

The purpose of the Securities Act of 1933 is to ensure that investors are provided with full and fair disclosure about a new security issue and the issuer. To that end, the act requires, among other things, the use of a prospectus to provide full disclosure of all pertinent information. The act regulates when and how information about the offering can be disseminated, and it also prohibits false and misleading information from being disseminated with several antifraud provisions. There are several specific rules (and rule numbers!) that you should know for the Series 6 exam.

## 4.2.1.1 Rule 134—Communications Not Deemed a Prospectus

Rule 134 is sometimes referred to as the **Tombstone Ad Rule. Tombstone ads** are special ads placed by broker-dealer firms to draw attention to a prospectus or announce some other major business event, without the ad being a specific offer to sell or buy securities. A tombstone ad, though, is a communication with the public that is not considered a prospectus; thus, it does not violate the SEC's prohibition against advertising during the **cooling off period** for a new offering. The tombstone ad may contain limited, generic information about a specific security, but it directs the client on how to obtain more information (i.e., gives contact information stating where an investor can obtain the complete prospectus). Tombstone ads that advertise mutual funds may also indicate the type of fund and the fund's objectives. Since the tombstone ad is still a communication from the firm, it must be true, accurate, and not misleading.

## 4.2.1.2 Rule 135a—Generic Advertising

Rule 135a allows broker-dealer firms to promote the firm and the idea of investing in a specific type of investment vehicle (e.g., mutual funds), but without the ad mentioning any specific securities product by name. The generic ad may contain limited company information that instructs the client how to obtain more information. Of course, the generic ad is still a communication from the firm so it must be true, accurate, and free from misleading statements.

# 4.2.1.3 Rule 156—Investment Company Sales Literature

Rule 156 is also referred to as the **Antifraud Rule.** As we pointed out, the Antifraud Provision of the Act of 1933 says that all public communications, sales literature, and advertising must be true, accurate, and free from misleading statements. Rule 156 says that determination of whether an ad or sales literature is misleading depends on the context of its contents. For example, performance numbers of a mutual fund can be misleading if they are not presented properly and completely in their historical context. To avoid misinterpretations, fund advertising generally includes language to the effect that "past performance does not guarantee future results." This rule also identifies specific fund advertising practices that may be misleading, such as using an implied promise of future performance. Let's look at the definition of "sales literature" under this rule, then discuss some of the factors that should be considered when examining sales literature and advertising in light of Rule 156.

**Sales literature** is defined as any communication (whether in writing, by radio, or by television) used by any person to offer to sell or induce the sale of securities. Rule 156 also includes communications between issuers, underwriters, and broker-dealer firms if such communications (or information therein) may also be communicated to prospective investors in the offer or sale of investment company securities.

Under Rule 156 and the corresponding paragraphs of the Securities Act of 1933, it is unlawful for any person, directly or indirectly, to use sales literature that is materially misleading in connection with the offer or sale of securities issued by an investment company. Sales literature is considered materially misleading if it:

▷ contains an untrue statement of a material fact or
▷ omits a material fact necessary to make a statement not misleading.

Whether or not a particular description, representation, illustration, or other statement involving a material fact is misleading depends on evaluation of the context in which it is made. In considering whether a particular statement involving a material fact is (or might be) misleading, weight must be given to all pertinent facts.

A statement could be misleading because of:

▷ other statements made that give the wrong impression;
▷ the absence of explanations, qualifications, limitations, or other statements necessary or appropriate to make such statement not misleading; and
▷ general economic or financial conditions not being explained.

Representations about past or future investment performance could be misleading because of statements or omissions made involving a material fact, such as:

▷ portraying past income, gain, or growth of assets in such a way as to give the impression of investment results that are not justified by the facts;
▷ representations, express or implied, about future investment performance, security of capital, or possible future gains or income.

A statement involving a material fact about the characteristics or attributes of an investment company could be misleading because of:

▷ statements about possible benefits connected with or resulting from services to be provided without a balanced discussion of any risks or limitations;

▷ exaggerated or unsubstantiated claims about management skill or techniques, inflated or bogus credentials;

▷ unwarranted or incompletely explained comparisons to other investment vehicles or to indexes;

▷ statements that give a false impression about the safety of an investment company, security of investment funds, or the effects of government supervision.

**RULE 482—ADVERTISING BY AN INVESTMENT COMPANY.** Rule 482 is also referred to as the **Omitting Prospectus Rule.** In order to satisfy the requirements of the law, the advertising for an investment company is limited in what it can say (like the Rule 134 ads for new offerings). The ad must clearly state the source of the ad, may give general information about the securities, and tell the client how to obtain more information (i.e., the complete prospectus). Rule 482 is different, however, because even without a prospectus, the investment company is allowed to advertise certain performance data about the fund with three stipulations:

▷ the information in the ad must also appear in the prospectus;

▷ the ad must present the fund's total return for the past one, five, and ten years, calculated using a specific SEC formula; and

▷ the ad must state that the performance figures represent past performance, and that the investment return and principal value will fluctuate, and its value may be less than the original investment when redeemed.

# Investment Company Act of 1940

The Investment Company Act of 1940 also has requirements on sales literature to keep it from being misleading. **Rule 34b-1** deals with any sales material or related communications for mutual funds and variable annuities, used before (or at the same time) a client sees a fund's prospectus. Essentially, Rule 34b-1 says that if performance data are used in communications or ads, then to keep an ad from being misleading it must contain the same three stipulations as in Rule 482 above:

▷ the information in the ad must also appear in the prospectus;

▷ the ad must present the fund's total return for the past one, five, and ten years, calculated using a specific SEC formula; and

▷ the ad must state that the performance figures represent past performance, and that the investment return and principal value will fluctuate, and its value may be less than the original investment when redeemed.

# Securities Exchange Act of 1934

The Securities Exchange Act of 1934 has two specific antifraud provisions that you should know. **Section 10** prohibits the use of manipulative and deceptive practices in connection with any securities transaction. **Rule 10b-3** under this section specifically prohibits brokers or dealers from using any such deceptive practices. In both cases, the laws refer to any action considered fraudulent or deceptive under the law or by the rules of the SEC, whether committed directly or indirectly. This includes use of any means of communication (e.g., advertising) across state lines (interstate commerce) or through the mail. The clear language in the law that it is illegal to commit securities fraud or deception through public communications (such as ads or the mail) is the reason for inclusion of this rule here. We will go into more detail about how this law applies to insider trading and other specific prohibited actions in upcoming sections of this chapter.

# NASD Conduct Rules

NASD conduct rules also prohibit deceptive, false, and misleading information from being disseminated in communications with the public. Here we will discuss two rules as they relate to advertising and sales literature, but later we will see how these and other rules apply to sales presentation materials and transactions.

**USE OF MANIPULATIVE, DECEPTIVE, OR OTHER FRAUDULENT DEVICES.** This rule simply states that no member shall effect any security transaction, or induce the purchase or sale of any security, by means of any manipulative, deceptive, or other fraudulent device or contrivance. This rule encompasses everything from trades and market orders (which we will discuss in a future section) to specifically covering public communications and the mail.

**COMMUNICATIONS WITH THE PUBLIC.** This specific rule covering communications with the public has much more detail about what is permitted or prohibited in advertising and sales literature. First, let's review how NASD defines advertisements and sales literature.

**Advertisement** is defined as material published, or designed for use in, newspaper, magazine or other periodical, radio, television, telephone or recording, videotape, display, sign, billboard, telephone directory, electronic or public media.

**Sales Literature** is defined as any written or electronic communication distributed or made generally available to customers or the public, which does not fall under the definition of advertisement. Sales literature includes, but is not limited to, circulars, research reports, market letters, performance reports or summaries, form letters, telemarketing scripts, seminar texts, and reprints or excerpts of any other advertisement, sales literature, or published article.

**Approval and Recordkeeping.** Each item of advertising and sales literature must be approved with the signature or initial of a registered principal of the member firm prior to use or filing with the NASD. A separate file of all advertisements and sales literature, including name(s) of the person(s) who prepared them and/or approved their use, must be maintained for a period of three years from the date of use.

**Filing Requirements and Review Procedures.** Advertisements and sales literature from member firms selling securities or government securities, and registered investment companies (selling mutual funds, etc.), must be filed with the NASD's Advertising/Investment Companies Regulation Department. All firms must file *within* ten days of first use or publication by any member. New members must file ten days *prior to* first use and continue to file ten days prior to use for a period of one year. As part of their filing, members must state the actual or anticipated date of first use. Filing in advance of use is recommended. Members are not required to file advertising and sales literature that have previously been filed and are used without any changes.

In addition, every member's advertising and sales literature are subject to routine spot-checks. Upon written request from the NASD, each member must promptly submit the material requested. If the NASD or any District Business Conduct Committee (DBCC) determines that a member has departed from the standards of this rule and is likely to do so again, the member may be required to file all advertising and/or sales literature at least ten days prior to use, along with the anticipated date of first use. The member will be notified in writing of the types of material to be filed and the length of time the requirement will be in effect. The requirement may not exceed one year and can be appealed by a member.

**Standards Applicable to Public Communications.** All public communications must clearly state the name of the firm that is the source of the advertising and sales literature. The **only exception to this is recruitment advertising,** which may be done blind to protect the identity of the firm seeking to hire new representatives. Fictitious names and dba's ("Doing Business As") are permitted if they are registered with the SEC and the NASD or other appropriate SRO. Parent company names and/or divisional names are permitted if they actually exist and the ad or sales material clearly states the relationship between the company and divisions.

Also, public communications (including business cards) must, in addition to the member's name, mention the member's affiliation with the NASD. The NASD name or logo must be the same size or smaller than the member's name and cannot be in a more prominent position. The purpose here is not to mislead the public into thinking that the NASD somehow endorses the activities of that member. Finally, all ads and sales literature must be honest, free from misleading statements, and adhere to the principles of full and fair disclosure in order to fulfill the letter and spirit of NASD rules and regulations. Let's look at a few general and specific standards for public communications.

**General Standards.** All member communications with the public must be based on principles of fair dealing and good faith and should provide a sound basis for evaluating the facts discussed or services offered. No material fact or qualification may be omitted if the omission would cause the advertising or sales literature to be misleading. Exaggerated, unwarranted or misleading statements or claims are prohibited in all public communications of members.

In judging whether a communication (or a particular element of a communication) may be misleading, several factors should be considered, including but not limited to:

▷ the overall balance and treatment of risks and potential benefits and
▷ the sophistication of the audience to which the communication is directed.

**Specific Standards.** In addition to those general standards, the following specific standards apply to public communications (advertising and sales literature):

▷ Claims and Opinions: must not contain promises of specific results, exaggerated or unwarranted claims or opinions for which there is no reasonable basis.
▷ Testimonials: must state that it may not represent the experience of other clients; it is not indicative of future performance; and if it is a paid testimonial.
▷ Offers of Free Service: statements that a report, analysis, or other service will be furnished free or without any condition or obligation must be accurate.
▷ Claims of Research Facilities: may not be made for research or other facilities beyond those which the member actually possesses or can provide.
▷ Hedge Clauses: may not be used if they are misleading or inconsistent with the content of the material.
▷ Recruiting Advertising: must not contain exaggerated or unwarranted claims and cannot refer to specific earnings figures or ranges that are unreasonable.
▷ References to Regulatory Organizations: may not imply endorsement or approval by the NASD or any federal or state regulatory body.
▷ Claims of Tax-Free/Tax-Exempt Returns: if tax liability is only postponed or deferred, that fact must be disclosed and state which taxes are avoided.
▷ Comparisons must be clear and provide a fair and balanced presentation, including any differences between the subjects.
▷ Predictions and Projections: investment performance may not imply that gain or income realized in the past will be repeated in the future.

# 4.3 Rules Related to Sales Presentations and Materials

Rules relating to sales presentations and materials are also heavily regulated by the SEC and the various SROs. This section will cover the creation and use of prospectuses (Securities Act of 1933), public versus nonpublic information (Securities Exchange Act of 1934) and NASD Conduct Rules in this area.

## 4.3.1 Securities Act of 1933

Remember that the purpose of the Securities Act of 1933 is to ensure that investors are provided with full and fair disclosure about a new security issue and the issuer. Whenever there is an offer to sell a new security issue, the issuer of the securities must prepare and disseminate a prospectus to provide full disclosure of all pertinent information.

**DEFINITIONS.** Under the Act of 1933, whether the initial contact with the public for a new security issue is a simple ad or a full-blown sales presentation, certain procedures must be followed or conditions met to satisfy the law's requirement that all initial offers to sell be accompanied by a prospectus. As used in the act:

**Offer to sell** includes every attempt or offer to dispose of, or an offer to buy, a security or interest in a security, for value. (Preliminary negotiations or agreements between the issuer and underwriter are specifically excluded from this definition.)

Exam Topic Alert

Remember, generic and tombstone ads are exempted if they meet certain guidelines, such as stating where interested parties can obtain a complete prospectus. Once a prospectus has been sent, all subsequent communications regarding the same security cease to automatically be considered a prospectus. You can see the importance of complying with the advertising laws and using the exemptions provided. Otherwise, the broker-dealer firm would have to turn a simple ad into a complete prospectus to avoid violating the securities laws.

**Prospectus** is a formal written document detailing the financial information, business plan, and operating history of a company that is selling securities. As defined in the act, though, any initial communication (any notice, circular, advertisement, letter, or communication, written or by radio or television, that offers any security for sale or confirms the sale of any security) is considered a prospectus and must include certain legal requirements (e.g., detailed financial information), or the communication is in violation of securities laws. That's true unless it's exempted.

## PROHIBITIONS RELATING TO INTERSTATE COMMERCE AND THE MAIL.
Under the Act of 1933, it is unlawful for a person to offer to sell securities by delivering a prospectus to anyone by any means of transportation or communication across state lines (interstate commerce) or through the mails unless a registration statement has first been filed with, and passed by, the SEC. Except for the exceptions noted above, all communication, ads, sales literature, sales presentation materials, etc. are considered a prospectus if they are the first substantive contact with the client.

**Requirement to Deliver Prospectus.** The securities laws are designed to make sure that the potential investor receives the complete picture of a new investment and as soon as possible. Since the best means of telling the whole story is the prospectus, the law requires delivery of the prospectus to the investor as early as possible. The best way to do that is to consider everything under the law a prospectus until a client receives a prospectus. Sales presentation materials are not granted the same exemptions as advertising materials. If a client has not yet received a prospectus, any sales presentation materials shown to the client must fulfill the legal requirements of a prospectus and cover all of the same facts so as not to violate securities laws. Otherwise, the sales presentation materials may not be used unless accompanied or preceded by delivery of an actual prospectus document.

## CIVIL LIABILITIES ARISING IN CONNECTION WITH PROSPECTUSES. The
Act of 1933 states that any person who offers or sells a security that includes an untrue statement of a material fact, or omits a material fact necessary to make the statements not misleading, shall be liable to the person purchasing such security. The person may sue in court to recover the consideration paid for such security (plus interest, minus any money received for surrendering or selling the security), or for damages if the person no longer owns the security.

**Inclusion of untrue statements of material fact or exclusion of material facts required to be stated** in a prospectus shall make a person liable for civil damages, unless the person who offered or sold the security can prove that all or part of the amount lost or recoverable is not a result from the part of the prospectus or other communication that included the untrue statement or excluded the material fact. In other words, for civil liability cases to be successful, the investor must show that the untrue material fact or excluded material fact contributed to an actual loss.

**FRAUDULENT INTERSTATE TRANSACTIONS.** The Act of 1933 makes it unlawful for any person to offer or sell securities across state lines (interstate commerce) or through the mails using public communications (e.g., sales presentation material) in an attempt to obtain money or property by means of any fraud, untrue statement of a material fact, or any omission of a material fact.

**UNLAWFUL REPRESENTATION.** The Act of 1933 does *not* approve securities, nor does it ascertain the value of an issue or the worth of a company. Just because securities are registered and comply with all of the filing laws and regulations we have discussed, this does not mean that the statements contained therein are accurate. The act only clears a registration, allowing a public offering to take place. In fact, it is unlawful to state, imply, or represent that any sales presentation materials, prospectuses, etc. are somehow approved by the government, the SEC, or any other official government or oversight body.

**Exam Topic Alert**

**SEC "No Approval" Clause.** To avoid any potential confusion by investors, the law states that a prospectus used for the sale of securities must contain a disclaimer on its cover that says "These securities have not been approved by the SEC."

**4.3.2**

# Securities Exchange Act of 1934

The Securities Exchange Act of 1934 has specific antifraud provisions that we have mentioned. As the act relates to securities sales and sales materials, there are some additional rules that you should know for the Series 6 exam. These cover fraud and deceit with material information, nonpublic information, and insider trading.

## 4.3.2.1 Manipulative and Deceptive Devices

Section 10(b) of the Act of 1934 is a general antifraud provision. In fact, when a person commits an insider trading violation, Rule 10b-5 is often cited as one of the laws violated. Simply put, **Rule 10b-5** states that a person commits fraud by employing any manipulative or deceptive device or scheme. This can be through use of a materially false statement or omission, or by misuse of nonpublic material information. This has become known as the "misappropriation theory." Although it is useful in criminal cases brought by the government, it can be tough for civil liability cases. That's because in order to collect damages, a plaintiff must prove that there was a "scheme to defraud" that was relied upon in connection with the purchase or sale of securities and that this intent to defraud caused damage. Some courts, though, have used a liberal interpretation of the law by characterizing insiders who trade on nonpublic information as having committed "fraud and deceit" by disregarding their fiduciary responsibility to the corporate shareholders they're supposed to be serving.

**Insider Trading.** Remember, we said that it is illegal for persons to trade securities on the basis of material information that has not been made public yet. This is the classic definition of **insider trading. Material information** is any important fact that would influence a person's decision and would include such things as a pending merger that has not been announced or a new patent that is about to be issued. If it has not been announced, it is considered **nonpublic information.** Announcing it to a few persons does not make it "public information." In fact, the SEC has adopted guidelines for when and how information is considered "public." **Insiders** are any persons who have access to confidential or sensitive information about a company before it is released to the public. "Insiders" become **tippees** if they give nonpublic information to others. Tippees can be held criminally and civilly liable for any insider trading that occurs, along with the person who does the trade.

Remember, we said the SEC has issued Rule 10b5-1 to clarify that insider trading liability arises when an insider is aware of material nonpublic information when making a trade, regardless of whether that information motivated the trade. So any "insider" must be careful not to reveal nonpublic information to anyone else so they are not considered a tippee for the insider trading actions of another.

## 4.3.2.2 Registration and Regulation of Brokers, Dealers

One of the ways that the Act of 1934 combats fraud and deceptive practices is by requiring registration of brokers, dealers, broker-dealer firms, and securities sales representatives. Even if securities or transactions are exempt from registration, there is *never* an exemption for any security or any person from the antifraud provisions of the Securities Exchange Act of 1934.

**Fraud and Misrepresentations.** For misrepresentations to rise to the level of fraud, Rule 15c1-2 requires that a statement or omission must be made with knowledge or reasonable grounds to believe that it is untrue and misleading.

**Misrepresentations as to Registration.** Under Rule 15c1-3, the definition of "manipulative, deceptive, or other fraudulent device or contrivance" includes any misrepresentation by a broker, dealer, registered sales representative, etc. to imply that "registration" means that the SEC has in any way approved of the person, the broker-dealer firm, a security investment, or any securities transaction.

4.3.3

# Securities Investor Protection Act of 1970

The **Securities Investor Protection Act of 1970** was *not* empowered by Congress to protect investors from broker-dealer fraud. In cases of fraud, the SIPC may join in an effort to recover funds through the courts, acting as a trustee or using a court-appointed trustee. There is no investment fraud "insurance" offered by any agency in the United States. Remember, the SIPC is only authorized to step in when a broker-dealer firm goes bankrupt. At that time, customers may file claims for losses.

Exam Topic Alert

For the Series 6 exam, it is important for you to remember that the SIPC fund **maximum limit on claims** is up to $500,000 total, with a limit of $100,000 paid in cash for each separate customer account. A person with an individual account and a joint account could collect twice—once for each account—but not if the person had two separate accounts both solely in that person's name.

4.3.4

# NASD Conduct Rules

NASD conduct rules also prohibits deceptive, false, and misleading information from being used in sales presentation materials. We will review the two rules we discussed earlier and show how they apply here and also add another important rule you need to know that deals with customers' funds, securities accounts, and things a broker-dealer or registered sales representative may or may not do with them.

## 4.3.4.1 Use of Manipulative, Deceptive, or Fraudulent Devices

The rule states that no member shall effect any security transaction, or induce the purchase or sale of any security, by means of any manipulative, deceptive, or other fraudulent device or contrivance. This rule encompasses everything from trades and market orders (which we will discuss in a future section) to specifically covering advertising, sales literature, and sales presentation materials.

## 4.3.4.2 Communications with the Public

This specific rule covers communications with the public in detail. Let's review how the NASD defines advertisements and sales literature, since these will likely appear in some form on the Series 6 exam.

**Advertisement** is defined as material published, or designed for use in, newspaper, magazine, or other periodical, radio, television, telephone, or recording, videotape, display, sign, billboard, telephone directory, electronic, or other public media. Remember, the broker-dealer firm has no control over who views them once they have been produced and disseminated.

**Sales Literature** is defined as any circulars, research reports, market letters, performance reports or summaries, form letters, telemarketing scripts, seminar texts, and reprints or excerpts of any other advertisement, sales literature, or published article. Remember, these are items that the broker-dealer firm has control over who receives the information. Sales presentation materials fall under the broad definition of "sales literature." Let's look at some additional points you need to know.

**Approval and Recordkeeping.** Just like advertising and sales literature, all sales presentation materials must also be approved by signature or initial of a registered principal of the member firm, prior to use or filing with the NASD. A separate file of all materials, including name(s) of the person(s) who prepared them and/or approved their use, must be maintained for a period of three years from the date of use.

**Filing Requirements and Review Procedures.** As a form of sales literature, sales presentation materials must be filed with the NASD within ten days of first use by any member (ten days prior for new members). Additional rules apply for sales presentation materials that use rankings or comparisons of the investment company with other investment companies. All such materials must include a copy of the ranking or comparison used. If the ranking or comparison category is not generally published or was created, directly or indirectly, by the investment company, it must be filed with the NASD for review at least ten days *prior to* use. If changes are requested by the NASD, the materials may not be published or circulated until the changes specified by the NASD have been made, or until the materials have been reapproved.

**Standards Applicable to Public Communications.** All sales presentation materials must clearly state the name of the firm that is the source of the materials. Fictitious names and dba's ("Doing Business As . . .") are permitted if they are registered with the SEC and the NASD, or other appropriate SRO. Parent company names and/or divisional names are permitted if they actually exist and the sales material clearly states the relationship between the company and divisions.

Also, sales presentation materials must mention the member's affiliation with the NASD, but the NASD name or logo must be the same size or smaller than the member's name—and not in a more prominent position—so as not to mislead the public into thinking the NASD endorses the sales presentation materials or the member.

**General Standards.** All sales presentation materials must be based on principles of fair dealing and good faith and should provide investors with a sound basis for evaluating the facts discussed, services offered, or securities investment. In preparing sales presentation materials, members must bear in mind that inherent in investment are the risks of fluctuating prices and the uncertainty of dividends, rates of return, and yield. Exaggerated, unwarranted, or misleading statements or claims are prohibited. No untrue statements may be made, and no material fact or qualification may be omitted if it would cause the materials to be misleading.

In judging whether a particular element of sales presentation materials may be misleading, several factors should be considered, including a new third factor:

▷ the overall balance and treatment of risks and potential benefits;
▷ the sophistication of the audience to which the communication is directed;
▷ the overall clarity of the communication, keeping in mind that complex or overly technical explanations may be worse than too little information.

**Specific Standards.** Beyond those general standards, some specific standards apply to sales presentation materials (note some repeats from the ads section):

▷ Necessary Data: especially the name of the member that is the source of the communication and the date when the materials were first published.

▷ Recommendations: must be made with some basis in fact, with documentation provided to the client upon request, and disclosure of any interest or relationship the broker-dealer firm has with the company represented by the security.

▷ Claims and Opinions: must not contain promises of specific results, exaggerated or unwarranted claims or opinions for which there is no reasonable basis.

▷ Testimonials: must state that it may not represent the experience of other clients; it is not indicative of future performance; and if it is a paid testimonial.

▷ Claims of Research Facilities: may not be made for research or other facilities beyond those which the member actually possesses or can provide.

▷ Hedge Clauses: may not be used if they are misleading or inconsistent with the content of the material.

▷ Periodic Investment Plans: must state the plan (e.g., dollar cost averaging) does not assure a profit and does not protect against loss in declining markets.

▷ Identification of Sources: tables, charts, graphs, or other illustrations used by members in advertising or sales literature should disclose the source.

▷ Claims of Tax-Free/Tax-Exempt Returns: if tax liability is only postponed or deferred, that fact must be disclosed, and state which taxes are avoided.

▷ Comparisons: the purpose of the comparison must be clear and provide a fair and balanced presentation, including any differences between the subjects.

▷ Predictions and Projections: investment performance illustrations may not imply that gain or income realized in the past will be repeated in the future.

# 4.3.4.3 Customers' Securities or Funds

The NASD **prohibits** several practices:

▷ **guaranteeing profits** (or promising future buybacks at set prices)

▷ **sharing client profits** (only permitted in proportion to money actually invested in account by a member—firm and client can't have joint account)

▷ **borrowing money** from clients or **lending money** to clients (unless client is a bank)

▷ **unauthorized use of client's money**

# 4.4 Rules Related to Transactions

Rules relating to transactions are the next area of SEC and SRO regulations we will examine. In addition to transaction laws in the Act of 1934 and NASD rules, the Federal Reserve has several regulations that must be observed.

## 4.4.1

# Securities Exchange Act of 1934

The Securities Exchange Act of 1934 antifraud provisions also cover fraud and deceit with transaction confirmations and account recordkeeping. Let's briefly look at these areas.

## 4.4.1.1 Manipulative and Deceptive Devices

Remember, we mentioned that Section 10(b) of the Act of 1934 is a general antifraud provision. Specific language of **Rule 10b-10** requires broker-dealer firms to deliver written confirmation of transactions to customers no later than completion of the transaction (i.e., the settlement date). This is in addition to the other disclosures required under the law. The confirmation may not contain any false or misleading statements and must include:

▷ date and time of the transaction;

▷ identity, price, and number of shares bought or sold;

▷ yield and maturity information for bond trades;

▷ any fees associated with the trade; and

▷ if the firm acted as a broker or dealer (and/or market maker) in a transaction.

If the firm acted as a broker (arranging the trade with another broker-dealer firm), then the confirmation must disclose details about the other party involved in the transaction, as well as the source and amount of commission charged by the firm. If the firm acted as a dealer (trading with its own inventory), then that fact must be disclosed along with the markup or markdown amount charged. Alternatively, the confirmation may state that the firm's compensation information is available upon request. In addition, some investment company products that are no-load funds may report fee and compensation information to customers in a quarterly or monthly written report instead of with each transaction that takes place.

## 4.4.1.2 Accounts and Records

Member firms and registered sales representatives must retain all records of correspondence with customers regarding trades and must maintain records about the securities that the client owns and all transactions that have been made with the firm. These detailed records are sometimes referred to as the **customer book.** Keeping these account records is important in case a dispute arises in the future. Furthermore, it is the registered sales representative's responsibility to check the accuracy of all data entered and all trades made. After making a successful trade, he or she compares the report of the trade execution against the order ticket and then reports the trade execution to the customer along with the other required confirmation information.

Exam Topic Alert

All client account records, statements, and confirmations must be kept for six years (the past two years must be accessible). **Rule 17a-8** extends these responsibilities to include recordkeeping and reporting of currency and foreign transactions. (The rule allows the Treasury Secretary to monitor for money laundering activities.)

4.4.2

# Federal Reserve Board, Regulation T

The **Federal Reserve Board** (also referred to as **the Fed**) is responsible for U.S. monetary policy, maintaining economic stability, regulating commercial banks, and regulating the extension of credit from broker-dealer firms to their clients via the establishment of margin requirements.

A margin account is one basic type of securities account that a client can open. Opening a margin account means that the customer is going to buy securities on credit.

Exam Topic Alert

Remember, new issues and mutual funds may *not* be purchased on credit.

**Margin** is the amount that a customer must have on deposit with a broker-dealer to buy securities on credit. The customer is only permitted to borrow a portion of the securities price and must cover the balance with cash or by depositing other securities the customer owns. Federal Reserve Board **Regulation T (Reg T)** states that a person must have on deposit the higher of $2000 or 50% of the purchase price of the eligible securities bought on margin. Broker-dealer firms can establish their own margin rules requiring more to be deposited.

## 4.4.2.1 Cash Accounts

A cash account (sometimes called a **special cash account**) is the other of the two basic types of accounts that a client can open. With a cash account, all securities are paid for in cash, either from funds already on deposit with the broker, or by the customer delivering cash or check within the settlement rules established by the broker-dealer firm (within Federal Reserve limits) for the type of trade involved. Some accounts, such as IRAs, can only be opened with a cash account.

**Prompt payment** for securities purchased is required under the law. Reg. T requirements call for settlement (payment) to take place within 5 business days (although most SROs, such as the NASD, require payment within 3 business days). **Extensions of time** may be negotiated and agreed upon beforehand, but cash accounts may be restricted if any balance owed for a cash transaction is still outstanding after 20 business days. Restrictions may be removed from the account upon payment of amount owed, or transferring the account to a margin account. **Frozen accounts** can result if a client doesn't settle a cash account as agreed, or the client doesn't answer a Reg T call by depositing cash or securities within 5 days. In this case, the broker must sell out the position and freeze the account for 90 days. **Arranging for loans** by others is prohibited, since the Federal Reserve regulates the extension of credit from broker-dealer firms to clients. Broker-dealers may not loan money to clients (except in a margin account), borrow money from clients (unless the client is a bank), and cannot hypothecate customer securities in a cash account.

# 4.4.3

# NASD Conduct Rules

There are numerous NASD conduct rules related to securities transactions. Much of our discussion of the rules will focus on definitions and terminology you may encounter in your securities career and on the Series 6 exam.

## 4.4.3.1 Use of Manipulative, Deceptive, or Fraudulent Devices

This rule is the recurring prohibition against fraud, deceit, and misrepresentation. It is the cornerstone upon which all other NASD rules are built. The code of conduct that NASD members agree to follow acknowledges that this is grounds for suspension and/or other disciplinary action. Some of the toughest penalties and sanctions under the law are for fraud and manipulation involving securities transactions.

# 4.4.3.2 Recommendations to Customers

This rule covers suitability issues when making recommendations to clients. In order to protect the interests of the investing public, the NASD requires that the broker-dealer firm and the registered sales representative determine whether or not the stock or security being recommended is an appropriate investment for the client given the client's financial status, tax status, investment objectives, and investment experience. The following must be considered:

**Fair dealing with customers** is a fundamental responsibility that the NASD requires to be at the heart of all sales efforts. Some of the practices that are unethical and **violations of NASD rules** that have resulted in disciplinary action include:

> **Recommending speculative securities** to customers without determining whether or not the securities were suitable for the client.
>
> **Excessive trading activity** in a customer's account to generate commissions. This is called **churning** and is usually determined by a significant increase in trades after an account becomes discretionary.
>
> **Trading in mutual fund shares** as short-term trades because of the excessive sales charges that customers incur.
>
> **Fraudulent activity** that consists of discretionary account transactions beyond what the customer has authorized, or other types of unauthorized transactions, for which a customer is later sent a confirmation order, or misuse by borrowing customers' funds or hypothecating customers' securities without the required executed agreements.
>
> **Recommending purchases beyond customer capability** to pay for them or getting a customer into a scheduled investment contract they can't afford.
>
> **New or derivative financial products** trading encouraged for customers who do not have sufficient experience or knowledge with such investments. Clients must be made aware of the risks involved in trading options, warrants, etc.

Note that institutional customers and clients with at least $10 million under management in a securities portfolio are exempt from these suitability concerns.

# 4.4.3.3 Customers' Securities or Funds

The NASD has strict guidelines with regard to handling of customers' securities or funds. The basic rule simply states that "no member or person associated with a member shall make improper use of a customer's securities or funds." This covers specific **NASD prohibitions** we mentioned before as possible test questions on the Series 6 exam:

> ▷ **guaranteeing profits** (or promising future buybacks at set prices)
> ▷ **sharing client profits** (only permitted in proportion to money actually invested in account by a member—firm and client can't have joint account)
> ▷ **borrowing money** from clients or **lending money** to clients (except banks)
> ▷ **unauthorized use of client's money** (this includes hypothecating customer securities that are fully paid for and in a cash account)

**Segregation and identification of securities** is also required under this rule. This means that the customer's fully paid (cash) securities must be kept separate from any margin securities the customer has on account. Furthermore, margin securities must have physical segregation with a separate list, tab, envelope, or folder that clearly identifies the customer's name and be entered on the books of the member firm as belonging to that customer.

## 4.4.3.4 Dealing with Nonmembers

This rule requires all NASD member firms to buy and sell securities with nonmember firms at the same prices and on the same conditions as they are traded to the general public. An interpretation of this rule allows banks to be treated as (and receive the same pricing as) member firms.

**Sharing Commissions.** NASD rules prohibit sharing, directly or indirectly, of any commissions or other compensation from securities transaction with individuals or entities that are not properly registered with the appropriate securities license.

Nonmembers of the NASD who were formerly licensed and have since retired in good standing (or members transferring to a new firm) may continue to collect commissions previously earned, so long as a valid written contract was entered into prior to retirement or transfer between the individual and the member firm, providing for the continued payment of such compensation.

Exam Topic Alert

## 4.4.3.5 Variable Contracts of an Insurance Company

Variable life insurance and variable annuity contracts (variable contracts) are considered securities because the policyholders assume investment risk. Thus, variable contracts are "securities" under federal law and subject to NASD rules. In addition to prohibitions against false and misleading statements and the other general NASD rules that members agree to follow, there are two specific areas that you need to know.

The first area deals with compensation. With limited exceptions, persons who sell variable contracts may only accept compensation from their employing member firm. In other words, the insurance company or an investment company or another entity may *not* pay a registered sales representative a commission. Furthermore, the person may not receive securities nor another item of value as compensation from the insurance company, etc. NASD rules also limit gifts, stating that gifts to employees of a member firm must be approved by the firm and can't be conditioned on sales or performance.

The annual gift limit set by the NASD is $100 ($50 limit for mutual fund distributors). Although occasional gifts may exceed this limit (e.g., meal, single-game tickets), lavish gifts are always unacceptable (e.g., vacation, season tickets).

Exam Topic Alert

The other area you may see on the test concerns the NASD limits on sales charges with variable contracts. NASD rules limit variable contract sales loads to 8.5% of premiums paid under the contract. The NASD has proposed a rule change that would eliminate any limits on sales loads and instead use a standard whereby sales charges must be a "reasonable" component of the aggregate sales charges.

## 4.4.3.6 Investment Company Securities

Investment company products, such as mutual funds, may be sold by NASD members, as long as the product or fund makes the appropriate disclosures in its prospectus. The NASD rules, however, state that broker-dealer firms may not recommend one fund over another on the basis of the commission level that the member or firm will receive from the sale. In turn, fund managers are not permitted to pay members or firms higher commission levels for increased sales. This is to take away any conflict of interest and have the member or firm recommend a fund based on a client's needs—not the commission levels.

NASD rules also prohibit demanding additional commissions as a condition of selling the fund, allocating brokerage commissions in such a way that firms with higher sales receive higher percentages, creating or sponsoring an incentive program in violation of NASD rules, providing extra bonuses based on sales of a particular fund, creating a "recommended" fund list, and revealing commission levels to anyone other than management personnel. Other prohibited acts include using funds sales levels with the fund distributor to negotiate larger commissions, conditioning sales agreements on sales levels, and allocating brokerage funds or resources to favor one fund over another.

## 4.4.3.7 Private Securities Transactions

NASD conduct rules prohibit any person associated with a member firm from participating in a private securities transaction, unless prior written approval is obtained from the member firm. The NASD wants all transactions to go through the broker-dealer firm so that the firm can monitor compliance with the law. The rules also require that all commissions and compensation for securities transactions go through the member firm.

**Written notice** must be obtained from the member firm prior to participation in any private securities transaction. The associated person must describe in detail the proposed transaction, the person's proposed role, and whether he or she has received or may receive selling compensation from the transaction.

**Transactions for compensation** require the member firm to respond in writing, either approving or disapproving of the person's participation. If the transaction is approved, it must be recorded on the firm's books and records, and supervised by the firm. If the transaction is not approved, the person may not participate.

**Definitions** under this rule are as follows:

**Private securities transaction** means any securities transaction outside the regular course or scope of an associated person's employment with a member. Transactions involving immediate family members are exempt from the private securities transaction rules only if no commission is involved, and the representative's own investments in investment company or variable annuity securities are also excluded. Private transactions done without the broker-dealer's permission are referred to as **selling away** and are prohibited by NASD rules.

**Selling compensation** means any compensation paid to a person, directly or indirectly, from any source, in connection with the purchase or sale of a security.

## 4.4.3.8 Transactions for or by Associated Persons

NASD conduct rules require that broker-dealer firms be given written notice before one of their associated persons or employees can open an account with another broker-dealer. All new account forms have a box that clients check indicating whether or not they are employed with another broker-dealer firm. If checked, the firm must notify the person's employer. The NASD firm has the option of requesting duplicate trade confirmations from all trading activity with the firm. This rule also applies to accounts with other financial institutions, where the associated person or employee is required to provide disclosure and/or notification to the employing member firm.

**Obligations.** Associated persons or employees of a member firm must notify his or her employer, in writing, of the intention to open an account or place an order with an investment adviser, bank, or other financial institution prior to the execution of any initial transactions. The employing firm, upon written request, has the right to receive duplicate copies of trade confirmations, statements, or other information concerning the account or order.

**Exemptions.** Personal transactions involving Investment Company Shares, Unit Investment Trusts, and Variable Contracts are exempt from these notification rules.

## 4.4.3.9 Books and Records

Registered sales representatives and member firms must maintain records about the securities that the client owns and all transactions that have been made with the firm. These detailed records are sometimes referred to as the **customer book.** All of the information in the customer book, along with correspondence, order tickets, execution reports, trade confirmations, client statements, and account records must be kept for six years (past two years must be accessible).

**Customer Account Information.** Members must keep current information on:

> ▷ customer's name and residence;
> ▷ whether customer is of legal age;

> ▷ signature of the registered sales representative who introduced the account and signature of the supervisor or manager who accepted the account; and

> ▷ if the customer is a corporation, partnership, or other legal entity, the names of any persons authorized to transact business on behalf of the entity.

Prior to the first transaction in an account, a member shall make an effort to obtain:

> ▷ customer's tax identification or Social Security number;

> ▷ occupation of customer and name and address of employer; and

> ▷ whether customer is an associated person of another member.

Other items of note:

> ▷ for new accounts, each member shall obtain from the customer, within 15 days of account approval, a signed, written agreement to follow NASD rules;

> ▷ for equity securities trading under $5 per share **(penny stocks),** an executed customer suitability agreement, if required; and

> ▷ for discretionary accounts, a member shall also:
>   1. obtain signature of persons authorized to exercise account discretion;
>   2. record the date such discretion is granted; and
>   3. record the customer's age or estimated age (except for municipals).

# 4.4.3.10 Prompt Receipt and Delivery of Securities

The SEC requires that all orders to sell be marked as long or short. Sales that are marked long indicate that the securities are in the customer's account or that they can be delivered by the settlement date. If an order execution is marked sell (sell long), *you must know the location of the securities.* Often they are held by the broker-dealer firm in street name for ease of transfer, but this is not always the case. If the securities are being held by a client, you must be reasonably sure that they can be delivered on time. For orders marked short, the firm must believe that it can borrow and deliver the securities.

# 4.5 Subsequent and Ongoing Communication and Service

Rules regarding subsequent and ongoing communication and service comprise a number of important NASD rules that we need to discuss. We will briefly touch on keeping a written record of complaints, then go into some detail about NASD procedural rules for its Code of Arbitration.

## 4.5.1 NASD Conduct Rules

The NASD conduct rules we will mention here have to do with complaint procedures. You may see a question or two on the Series 6 exam that asks about complaints in this section or the Code of Procedure in the next section.

### 4.5.1.1 Standards of Commercial Honor and Principles of Trade

All members must observe high standards of commercial honor, and just and equitable principles of trade in the conduct of business activities and services. This is the best way to stay within the law and reduce the incidents of customer complaints.

### 4.5.1.2 Books and Records

Registered sales representatives and member firms must keep and preserve in each office of supervisory jurisdiction, either a separate file of all written complaints of customers and action taken by the member, or a separate record of such complaints and a clear reference to the files containing the correspondence connected with such complaint.

**Complaint** is defined as any written statement of a customer (or any person acting on behalf of a customer) alleging a grievance involving the activities of any persons under the control of the member in connection with the solicitation or execution of any transaction, the sale of securities, or a dispute involving funds of that customer.

# NASD Procedural Rules—Code of Arbitration Procedure

The NASD conduct rules we will mention here have to do with complaint procedures. Member firms and employees agree to submit disputes to arbitration as a condition of becoming registered members. Often customers sign arbitration agreements when opening new accounts. You may see a few questions on the Series 6 exam about complaints in this section or the Code of Procedure in the next section.

## 4.5.2.1 Administrative Provisions

NASD members who have disputes with other NASD members are required to submit the matter to arbitration. The arbitration ruling is final and binding.

**Failure to act** under provisions of the Code of Procedure is considered a violation. This includes failing to submit to arbitration for matters in dispute, failing to abide by an arbitration ruling, refusing to comply with requests from the investigative body, or failing to pay any award or fine that is imposed.

**Matters eligible for arbitration** include disputes among members, disputes between members and licensees or associated persons, and disputes with customers.

**Composition and appointment of panels** depends on the amount of money involved in the dispute, according to rules laid out in the Uniform Code of Arbitration.

## 4.5.2.2 Uniform Code of Procedure

There is a uniform procedure used to resolve disputes under NASD rules. Once the claimant files the arbitration paperwork and pays the required fee, the respondent has 45 days to answer the complaint, with an additional 10 days for the claimant to reply. After this initial written discovery phase, hearings are held. During this time, the matter may be resolved prior to the final ruling. The arbitration ruling is final and binding.

**Required Submission.** Arbitration is mandatory for NASD members with a monetary dispute or who have a dispute with another member. Customers can also choose arbitration in disputes with members, but members can only compel customers to use arbitration if the customer has signed an arbitration consent form.

**Simplified Arbitration.** For NASD claims involving $25,000 or less, simplified arbitration is an option. The advantage to simplified arbitration is that the parties do not have to appear in person at a hearing, which could make it a less costly choice. With simplified arbitration, the arbitrator renders a decision by reviewing documents and written accounts of the facts from the parties involved.

**Awards.** Awards are made by the arbitrator or arbitration panel. All awards must be paid in cash to the prevailing party. Awards may not be credited to an account, unless authorized by terms of the award, or agreed to in writing by the parties. Awards must be honored upon receipt or within a specified time period. Failure to pay an award is a violation of NASD rules and can subject the nonpaying member to additional fines, suspension, other sanctions, or disciplinary actions.

4.5.3

# Summary of NASD Prohibited Activities

Here is a review of prohibited activities you may see on the Series 6 exam:

- ▷ **selling away** (doing a trade or collecting a commission that does not go through the broker-dealer firm)
- ▷ **making unsuitable trade recommendations** (too speculative for client's investment objectives, beyond customer's purchasing capabilities, or not right for client's tax situation—MSRB only)
- ▷ **making unauthorized trades** (without discretionary authority or properly executed power of attorney)
- ▷ **churning** (excessive trading to generate commissions, usually determined by significant increase in trades after account became discretionary)
- ▷ **short-term mutual fund trades** (because of excessive sales charges)
- ▷ **breakpoint selling** (keeping client trades just below breakpoints where they would save on mutual fund sales charges)
- ▷ **selling dividends** (telling clients to buy stocks right before ex-date just to capture a dividend is considered unethical since stock price will drop the dividend amount after ex-date, but client has immediate tax event.
  *Note:* Some firms/funds do this, but for the Series 6 it's a bad idea.)
- ▷ **unauthorized use of client's money** (this includes hypothecating customer securities that are fully paid for and in a cash account)
- ▷ **sharing client profits** (except in proportion to money RR actually invested)
- ▷ **borrowing money** from clients or **lending money** to clients
- ▷ **guaranteeing profits** (or promising future buybacks at set prices)

4.5.4

# Review of the NASD

- ▷ Registered Principals of member firms are ultimately responsible for all office activities, supervision of Registered Representatives (RR), and must approve all new accounts, client trades, sales literature, ads.

▷ Registered Principals must have a Principal License (Series 24) and register with the NASD; Registered Options Principal needs a ROP License (Series 4).

▷ RR must be registered with the NASD through employing member firm after passing exam, then they can collect commissions, interact with the public, and sell. Series 7 = most securities, but not commodity futures; Series 6 = investment company products (mutual funds), and variable products (annuities, life insurance).

▷ NASD member RR can take **outside job with knowledge and consent of firm.**

▷ RR **must resign and reapply** (not transfer) to join another member firm.

▷ RR may voluntarily leave a member firm; no retest if they rejoin within two years.

▷ Continuing education: Firm Element (annual training given by firms); and Regulatory Element (within 120 days of second year, then every three years; the NASD varies content of this computer-based regulatory training).

▷ **NASD name or logo can't be bigger** or more prominent than member name.

▷ All compensation must be paid through the broker-dealer firm.

▷ Code of Arbitration Procedure (CAP) for monetary disputes; Code of Procedure (COP) for discipline.

▷ Disciplinary matters heard by DBCC; appealed to Board of Governors.

▷ Penalties can include fine, censure, suspension, or expulsion.

# 4.X Summary

**4.1** Several federal laws and numerous conduct rules govern the securities industry.

**4.1.1** Securities Act of 1933 (Paper Act): regulates new issues, primary markets, investment banking, promotes full and fair disclosure. Registration procedures in place; prospectus required. Need complete company information history, financials, market, management, use of proceeds.

**4.1.2** Securities Exchange Act of 1934 (People Act): regulates outstanding issues, secondary market, fair and orderly markets, antifraud provisions (*no one* is exempt), proxies required, registration of firms and people, created SEC.

Registration is required for all member stock exchange broker-dealer employees involved with the sale or promotion of securities. Registration consists of passing the appropriate exam and complying with SEC and SRO rules. A person is disqualified from becoming registered if he or she has been disciplined by SEC, SRO, foreign; expelled, suspended before; felony conviction; misdemeanor for money/securities in the last 10 years; barred by SEC, foreign, court order.

SEC is federal government agency that oversees all industry participants: exchanges, companies, broker-dealers, employees. Fingerprinting required for all who handle cash, sell stocks to public, and supervisors of either group.

The SRO was created to help keep market fair and orderly, help enforce securities rules. NYSE: oversees activities of New York Stock Exchange and regional exchanges. NASD: responsible for over-the-counter, investment banking, limited partnership. MSRB: oversees activities related to municipal bonds, other intrastate government. NASD and NYSE can't enforce each other's rules; MSRB needs NASD to enforce.

Transfer of registration not permitted. Must resign, reapply within two years. Registration ceases 30 days after termination but can't terminate if under investigation. NASD keeps jurisdiction for two years. The NASD requires arbitration for disputes between members. Rule violation sanctions may include censure, fine, suspension, termination. Penalties can be cumulative.

The NASD requires written notice of outside business (duplicate trades on request). All transactions, commissions, and compensation must go through the firm. Prohibited practices include free-riding (holding back part of a new stock issue to resell it later at higher price), withholding (holding back part of a new stock issue for family, friends, or insiders), front running (doing firm trade first).

**4.1.3** The SIPC protects investors from broker insolvency (not bad investment). Each account is insured to $500,000 total, limit of $100,000 in cash. If firm fails, SIPC tries to merge, then liquidates and pays. Debit balances subtracted. If not enough, investor becomes general creditor of firm. SIPC is *not* an agency of the U.S. government.

**4.1.4** Investment Advisor's Act of 1940 requires registration of investment advisors, (except salaried employees). Must disclose if advisor has interest in the stock.

**4.1.5** Insider trading is trading on nonpublic information or giving nonpublic information to others (tipping). Act of 1934 prohibits, Act of 1984 expanded "insiders" to anyone with non-public info, ITSFEA (Act of 1988) expanded liability to bosses. ITSFEA civil penalty for traders, tippers, bosses: $1,000,000 or 3 times the profit; criminal penalty for traders, tippers, criminally negligent boss: ten years in jail, $1,000,000 (person), $2,500,000 (corporation). The ITSFEA also has a bounty for informers, liability to contemporaneous traders, written policy required by brokers.

**4.2** All public communications must comply with SEC and SRO rules. Advertising is not specifically distributed by firm, and firm has no control over who sees it. Sales literature is distributed by firm, so firm can control who sees it.

**4.2.1** Distinction between advertising and sales literature is important. Tombstone ads and prospectuses are exempt, but they have their own rules. Tombstone ads may not mention specific securities for sale and must state how to obtain a prospectus. Mutual fund tombstones can state type of fund or objectives. All ads and sales literature must be true, accurate, and free from misleading statements; approved by a registered principal of the firm; and kept on file for three years.

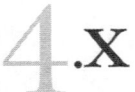

**4.2.2** Investment company ads, sales literature, etc. must follow three rules if it shows performance data: information must also be shown in prospectus, total return must be shown for past 1, 5, 10 years using SEC formula, must state that figures are past performance and that value will fluctuate (even below original value).

**4.2.3** Rule 10b-3 of Act of 1933 says it's illegal to commit securities fraud via the mail. Act of 1934 also says it is deceptive to imply SEC registration is a government endorsement.

**4.2.4** The NASD doesn't approve ads, sales literature, or sales presentation materials, but they must be sent to the NASD within ten days of first use; new firms must file all ads and sales literature at least ten days before first use during the firm's first year.

**4.3** The Act of 1933 requires prospectus. The Act of 1934 addresses use of non-public information for insider trading. Other laws and rules (NASD) cover presentation materials.

**4.3.1** Prospectus required to provide full disclosure. It needs complete company information, history, financials, market, management, and use of proceeds. Prospectus also needs risk assessment, legal opinion, and legal action. Final prospectus includes price and fees, and states "These securities have not been approved by the SEC." Must deliver prospectus to client on request or at first substantive contact.

**4.3.2** For insider trading laws, "material information" is defined as any important fact that would influence a person's decision; "nonpublic information" is defined as information not announced to the public. Rule 10b5-1 says you don't need to "use" information to trade in order to be liable, you only need to "know" information at the time of the trade to be liable.

**4.3.3** The SIPC does not pay out in cases of fraud, but it does help investors with court. Again, each separate account is insured to $500,000 total, limit of $100,000 in cash, but one person with two accounts can only collect once; however, if the person has one separate account and one joint account, then that counts twice.

**4.3.4** All public communications must state name of firm, except for recruiting. Fictitious names or dba's must be filed with SEC and SRO. The NASD logo may not be bigger or more prominent than member name.

**4.4** The SEC, Federal Reserve, and SROs (e.g., NASD) have transaction rules to follow.

**4.4.1** The Act of 1934 requires broker-dealers to give client written confirmation of trades (date, time, price, number of shares, fees, broker's function). All correspondence, confirmations, records, etc. are the "customer book"—must keep six years (two years accessible).

**4.4.2** The Federal Reserve regulates credit from broker-dealers to clients with Reg. T. Margin is the amount that must be on deposit with broker to buy stock on credit. Reg. T: client must have on deposit the higher of $2000 or 50% value of stocks. Reg. T settlement rules for cash account are T+5 (SRO is T+3). Can negotiate more time but if don't settle as agreed then account is frozen for 90 days. Arranging other loans from or to clients is also prohibited (except banks).

**4.4.3** Some NASD violations: recommending securities beyond client capabilities (too expensive, speculative, unfamiliar), excessive trading, mutual fund trading, fraudulent activity, guaranteeing profits (promising buybacks), sharing client profits (unless put money in—but firm and client can't have joint account).

Can't share commissions with unregistered people, can't accept gifts over $100 ($50 for mutual funds). Private securities transactions are prohibited without prior written notice. Employee transactions with other firms must also have written notice; employer firm can request duplicate trade orders.

**4.5** Other ongoing communications and interactions with clients deal with more laws, rules and regulations for complaints, procedures, and prohibited acts.

**4.5.1** NASD rules call for all customer complaints to be kept on file.

**4.5.2** Arbitration can solve disputes faster and cheaper than court. The NASD Code of Procedure (COP) for discipline, Code of Arbitration Procedure (CAP) for fines. Simple arbitration (no personal appearance) for the NASD if less than $25,000.

**4.5.3** More prohibited practices: review the list of NASD prohibitions on page 211.

**4.6** Review of NASD structure and rules: review the bullet points on pages 211–212.

# Chapter 4 Review Quiz

1. Which of these people would NOT need to be fingerprinted under SEC rules?
   a. registered representative
   b. broker-dealer principal
   c. clerical person who opens the mail
   d. receptionist who answers phones

2. Which of the following self-regulatory organizations does NOT have the power to enforce its own rules?
   a. New York Stock Exchange
   b. National Association of Securities Dealers
   c. Municipal Securities Rulemaking Board
   d. all of the above can enforce their own rules

3. To transfer membership status in a SRO, a registered sales representative must:
   a. notify the NASD of the intent to transfer.
   b. notify the SEC of the intent to transfer.
   c. resign from one firm and reapply with another.
   d. apply with a new firm then resign from the first if the new firm accepts him or her.

4. Which of the following is NOT a characteristic of sales literature?
   a. it is distributed in such a way the firm has control over who receives it
   b. it is distributed in such a way the firm has no control over who receives it
   c. it is sent out upon request of a client
   d. it is sent by the firm to a select group of people

5. All of the following rules apply to advertising EXCEPT:
   a. it must be approved by a principal of the firm.
   b. it must be approved by the NASD.
   c. it must clearly state the name of the firm (except recruitment ads).
   d. if mutual fund returns are used, they must be calculated using the SEC method.

6. Which of the following must submit advertising to the SEC before it is used?
   a. broker-dealers in their first year
   b. issuers of municipal securities
   c. all NYSE, NASD, and MSRB members
   d. investment companies

7. All of the following are prohibited activities EXCEPT:
   a. selling away.
   b. discretionary trading.
   c. churning.
   d. selling dividends.

8. The NASD's simplified arbitration:
   a. allows for more discovery than regular arbitration.
   b. is a good first step in seeking redress through the court system.
   c. does not require the parties to make a personal appearance.
   d. all of the above

9. All of the following are associated with the Securities Act of 1933 EXCEPT:
   a. registration of new issues.
   b. prohibits dissemination of false, misleading or fraudulent materials.
   c. registration of broker-dealer firms.
   d. the Paper Act.

10. All of the following are associated with Securities Exchange Act of 1934 EXCEPT:
    a. registration statement must be filed.
    b. prohibits fraud and market manipulation.
    c. registration of sales representatives.
    d. People Act.

11. Which of the following Acts created the SEC?
    a. Paper Act
    b. People Act
    c. Trust Indenture Act
    d. Insider Trading Act

12. According to the ITSFEA Act of 1988, who is defined as an insider?
    a. only officers and directors of a company
    b. anyone who has confidential information
    c. only investors who own at least 5% of the company stock
    d. any person who trades in the stock

13. Which of the following are true about the SIPC?
    a. it is a government agency
    b. it guarantees investors' accounts against market risk
    c. it insures investors' money against broker-dealer insolvency
    d. all of the above

14. Which of the following is the best SEC "no approval" clause?
    a. "This is not an offer to sell securities nor solicit orders."
    b. "This is an offer to sell securities and solicit orders."
    c. "These securities have been approved by the SEC."
    d. "These securities have not been approved by the SEC."

15. An investor has two individual accounts and one joint account with a spouse at a brokerage firm that goes bankrupt. How much cash can he collect from SIPC?
    a. $100,000 cash
    b. $200,000 cash
    c. $300,000 cash
    d. $500,000 cash

16. For how long must the "customer book" be kept?
    a. six years
    b. two years
    c. three years
    d. only as long as the customer is a client

# Exam Manual Extras

# Series 6
# Securities
# Practice Exam #1

1. On what basis are the gains on a variable annuity taxed ?
   A. Long-term capital gains
   B. Short-term capital gains
   C. Ordinary income
   D. Tax exempt

2. The investment adviser for a mutual fund:
   I. Usually makes trades within the portfolio to meet the investment objective
   II. Always makes trades to meet the investment objective
   III. Is paid an adviser's fee
   IV. Must inform investors of tax status for fund distributions

   A. I, III
   B. III, IV
   C. II, IV
   D. II, III, IV

3. The yield to maturity for a bond purchased at a premium will be:
   A. Lower than the coupon
   B. Higher than the nominal rate
   C. Cannot be calculated
   D. Is always the same as the coupon

4. Member firms must file advertising and sales literature with the NASD within:
   A. 30 days of use
   B. 10 days of use
   C. No filing requirement if firm is over 5 years old
   D. 15 days before use

5. Under the rules for UGMA:
   A. The donor may not be the custodian
   B. The donor may be the custodian
   C. The custodian must be the Registered Representative
   D. The minor may not be the beneficiary of more than one account

6. A corporate bond selling on the resale market has a price of 95 per bond with a coupon rate of 5%. What is the current yield for this bond?
   A. 5%
   B. 5.76%
   C. 4.76%
   D. 5.26%

7. What happens if a company wants to sell more shares of common stock than has been authorized?
   A. Any future new issue is reduced in price
   B. It must amend its charter or Articles of Incorporation
   C. It cannot satisfy outstanding warrants
   D. Book value will decrease

8. An investment allocation made by a client is a part of these products:
   I. Universal life policies
   II. Variable annuities
   III. Variable universal life insurance
   IV. Indexed annuities

   A. II, III
   B. I, IV
   C. III, IV
   D. II

9. What securities act created the prospectus ?
   A. The Securities Act of 1933
   B. The Securities Act of 1934
   C. The Securities Exchange Act of 1934
   D. The Insider Trading Act of 1988

10. An open-end mutual fund:
    A. Authorizes a certain number of preferred shares
    B. Authorizes an infinite number of shares
    C. Authorizes a certain number of common shares
    D. Publicly trades on the NYSE

11. A client indicates they would like to buy outstanding shares of XYZ corporation. Where would the client buy these shares ?
    A. The primary market
    B. The secondary market
    C. The contingent market
    D. None of the above

12. A prospectus may be provided:
    I. In advance of the sales presentation
    II. After the sales presentation
    III. Only after settlement
    IV. With an IPO the client has purchased

    A. I, IV
    B. II
    C. II, III, IV
    D. I

13. Calculate the percentage of sales charge for a fund with a NAV of $16.63 and a POP of $17.51.
    A. 5.0 %
    B. 5.3%
    C. 6.25%
    D. 4.26%

14. A bond issue with a sinking fund will:
    A. Be more stable in price
    B. Have a trustee
    C. Both A and B
    D. Neither A nor B

15. A UIT contains all of the following:
    A. Board of directors
    B. Investment adviser
    C. Active portfolio manager
    D. None of the above

16. An example of a publicly traded fund is:
    A. Open-end fund
    B. Closed-end fund
    C. Common stock IPO
    D. Variable annuity

17. In a mutual fund, which of the following requires majority vote of shareholders:
    A. Changing investment strategy or policy
    B. Changing sales load
    C. Changing from closed end to open end
    D. All of the above require the majority vote of shareholders

18. A client owns a variable annuity with a company you represent. Who is responsible for making the investment choices, and who assumes the risk for those choices?
    I. The insurance company
    II. The client
    III. The client is responsible for the choices made, and the company is responsible for the risk of those choices
    IV. The Registered Representative

    A. I, IV
    B. II, IV
    C. II
    D. II, IV

19. What activities may be done by a Registered Representative during the cooling off period ?
    A. Obtain indications of interest
    B. Distribute a preliminary prospectus
    C. Both A and B
    D. Neither A nor B

20. Under what circumstance may a Registered Representative accept a postdated check for a new issue ?
    A. Only on IPOs
    B. Never
    C. Only on open-end mutual funds
    D. Only on bond funds

21. A client is in the 37% tax rate, when federal, state, and local taxes are considered. The client tells you some moderate risk is acceptable, but the primary concern for an investment she is considering is avoidance of tax. Your recommendation could include:
    I. A state specific municipal bond fund
    II. An aggressive growth fund
    III. A government bond fund
    IV. A corporate bond fund

    A. I, II, III
    B. III, IV
    C. I
    D. III

22. SIPC may include coverage for:
    A. Market risk
    B. Commodities
    C. Futures
    D. None of the above

23. SIPC provides up to $500,000 in coverage. How much of this amount may be in cash?
    A. The entire amount
    B. The entire amount for mutual funds only
    C. $50,000
    D. $100,000

24. When a request for cash distribution is made by a client to an open-end mutual fund, the shares are said to be canceled. What does this mean?
    A. Shares are resold to the highest bidder
    B. Shares are destroyed
    C. Shares are placed on the resale market
    D. Shares become closed end

25. For a person in the 37% tax rate, calculate the tax equivalent yield for a municipal bond with a YTM of 4.8% and a coupon rate of 5%.
    A. 7.62%
    B. 7.94%
    C. 5%
    D. 4.8%

26. An exchange differs from OTC in what way ?
    A. An exchange has a definite location to buy and sell securities
    B. An exchange does not have a central location to buy and sell securities
    C. The exchange is used for after hours trading only
    D. NASDAQ stocks only trade on an exchange

27. A variable annuity contains the following:
    I. Investment risk for the investor
    II. Principal is guaranteed
    III. Market risk for the insurer
    IV. Rate of return depends upon the performance of the investments placed within the separate account

    A. I, II, III
    B. I, IV
    C. II, IV
    D. II, III

28. If a corporation buys the stock of another corporation, the dividends paid are:
    A. Fully taxable
    B. 50% excluded from federal taxation
    C. 70% excluded from federal taxation
    D. None of the above

29. If you recommend a client buy a mutual fund immediately before the ex-date for dividends, you would be:
    A. Within compliance guidelines
    B. Accused of not selling dividends
    C. Accused of selling dividends and cause an increased tax liability for the client
    D. Doing the client a favor, since the price is lower for the fund immediately before the dividend ex-date

30. Your discussion with a client reveals they have a moderate tolerance for risk, but need an investment with growth potential. The client is 56 years old, debt is low, and children are all adults. What investment would be most suitable?
    A. Blue-chip stock fund
    B. Balanced fund
    C. Aggressive growth fund
    D. Bond fund

31. Under securities laws, private transactions:
    I. Are allowable without disclosure
    II. Cannot be done under any circumstance
    III. Require broker-dealer approval
    IV. Require disclosure of compensation

    A. I, IV
    B. III, IV
    C. II
    D. I

32. During your conversation with a client, you learn that $14,000 of the $55,000 he wants to invest must be available during the next seven months. The client has a high tolerance for risk.

    Your recommendation is:
    A. Invest the $55,000 in money market
    B. Invest $55,000 in an aggressive growth fund, withdrawing cash as needed
    C. Place $14,000 in money market and divide the rest between an aggressive growth fund and a sector fund
    D. Place all of the money in a government bond fund and reinvest after seven months

33. As a Registered Representative, what is the maximum value of gifts you may receive, over a 12-month period, from a mutual fund distributor?
    A. $500
    B. $50
    C. $100
    D. $0

34. What are some advantages of a Roth IRA?
    I. Contributions are pretax dollars
    II. Contributions are aftertax dollars
    III. Distributions are tax free
    IV. Accumulations within the account grow tax deferred

    A. I, III, IV
    B. I, IV
    C. III
    D. II, III, IV

35. A corporation has issued 5,400,000 shares out of 6,000,000 with 200,000 shares held in their treasury. How many shares are outstanding ?
    A. 5,400,000
    B. 6,000,000
    C. 5,200,000
    D. 600,000

36. A mutual fund may offer a reduced sales charge for a larger amount of money placed into the fund. This is known as:
    A. CDSL
    B. Back-end load
    C. Front-end load
    D. Breakpoint

37. Describe the term *Registered Principal:*
    I. Supervises Registered Representatives
    II. Approves all new accounts
    III. Approves all trades
    IV. Is always a member of NYSE

    A. I, II
    B. I, II, III
    C. I, II, III, IV
    D. II, III

38. Individuals who own a variable life policy have voting rights as follows:
    A. One share - one vote
    B. One vote per $1000 in cash value
    C. One vote per $100 in cash value
    D. Statutory voting rights

39. A nonqualified plan:
    A. May discriminate
    B. May not discriminate
    C. Must be approved by SIPC
    D. Must have 100% participation

40. Based upon the S&P ratings, which of these is considered to be investment grade ?
    I. BB
    II. BBB
    III. A
    IV. AAA

    A. II, III, IV
    B. I, II, III, IV
    C. III, IV
    D. IV

41. The advantages of a JTROS account include:
    I. Equal ownership
    II. No probate upon death
    III. A Registered Representative may accept orders from either person listed on the account
    IV. Unequal ownership

    A. II, III, IV
    B. I, II, III
    C. II, III
    D. III, IV

42. A client has expressed the desire to invest in the stock market and receive income plus growth potential in the share price. Which of these investments would be an acceptable choice?
    A. Blue-chip stocks
    B. Small cap stocks
    C. Utility company stocks
    D. Both A and C

43. A client owns a number of bonds which have the possibility of being called. What does this mean to your client?
    A. The bonds must be given up if called, since the client has sold calls on these bonds
    B. A bond may not be called without a 12-month notice
    C. The issuer may purchase any bond held by the client after the call date
    D. The insurer may purchase any bond held by the client after the call date

44. Subchapter M requires an investment company to distribute at least _____% of net investment income to shareholders.
    A. 100%
    B. 85%
    C. 90%
    D. 30%

45. A fixed annuity has:
    I. Fixed interest rate
    II. No market risk
    III. Purchasing power risk
    IV. Guarantee of principal

    A. I, II, III
    B. I, III, IV
    C. III, IV
    D. I, II, III, IV

46. The NASD is the self-regulatory organization for the over-the-counter market because of:
    A. The Maloney Act of 1938
    B. Creation of the MSRB
    C. Insider Trading Act of 1988
    D. The Securities Act of 1933

47. How often must an investment company produce reports for clients each year?
    A. Quarterly
    B. Semiannually
    C. Annually
    D. No requirement

48. An example of a defensive stock is:
    A. Automotive
    B. Heavy equipment
    C. Utilities
    D. Durable goods

49. An investment banker:
    A. Loans money to companies for IPOs
    B. May be known as an underwriter
    C. May buy securities from a company and resell those securities to the public
    D. Both B and C

50. Under what circumstances will an underwriter commit to a standby underwriting?
    A. When existing stockholders do not exercise their preemptive right to buy additional stock
    B. When a company's credit rating is bad
    C. A standby underwriting doesn't exist
    D. None of the above

51. What type of security normally uses a competitive bid to obtain an underwriter?
    A. IPO for stock
    B. Corporate bond
    C. Municipal bond
    D. GNMA

52. If you, as a Registered Representative, resign from your present broker-dealer, when must continuing commissions be discussed?
   A. After you have transferred to the new broker-dealer
   B. Before you leave your present firm
   C. Cannot receive continuing commissions
   D. None of the above apply

53. As a stockholder of ABC Tech Group, you own 2000 shares and receive notice of the next annual meeting. There are four issues to be voted upon at the annual meeting and you particularly like one issue, which is identified as INFO. As a stockholder of ABC Tech Group, you may vote on a cumulative basis. How many votes may you cast for INFO ?
   A. 2000
   B. 6000
   C. 1000
   D. 8000

54. How does the accumulation phase of a variable annuity differ from the annuity phase?
   A. There is no difference
   B. An investor makes deposits to the annuity during the accumulation phase
   C. An investor receives money from the annuity during the annuity phase
   D. Both B and C

55. Withdrawal plans for mutual funds could include which of the following choices?
   I. Life with ten years certain
   II. Fixed dollar
   III. Fixed time
   IV. Life only

   A. I, IV
   B. II, IV
   C. II, III
   D. II, III, IV

56. What do Ginnie Maes and Treasuries have in common?
   A. Both are backed by FDIC
   B. Both are backed by the taxing authority of the U.S. Government
   C. Both are mortgage backed securities
   D. None of the above apply

57. A Registered Representative must register as an investment adviser if:
   A. Conducting a group of seminars
   B. Discretionary authority is granted
   C. Charging a fee for investment advice
   D. Limited POA is granted over an account

58. If you, as a Registered Representative, resign from your broker-dealer, what form must be prepared on your behalf?
   A. U-5
   B. U-4
   C. Reg U
   D. Reg T

59. If a mutual fund is being held in a regular investment account, which is not tax sheltered, which method of taxation would be chosen?
   A. The IRS would choose identified shares and the client would choose FIFO
   B. Client would choose identified shares and the IRS would choose FIFO
   C. Both would choose identified shares
   D. Both would choose FIFO

60. A variable life insurance policy has which fees deducted from the gross premium?
   A. Sales load, state premium taxes
   B. State premium taxes, administrative fees
   C. Administration fees, state premium taxes, and sales load
   D. Sales load, administrative fees

61. The transfer agent for an open-end mutual fund may do any of these activities:
   I. Issue new shares to a client
   II. Redeem shares for a client
   III. Send customer confirmations
   IV. Provide safekeeping of a fund's assets

   A. I, IV
   B. I, II, III
   C. III, IV
   D. II, IV

62. A Keogh plan (HR-10) is a:
   A. Qualified retirement for incorporated business
   B. Qualified retirement plan for unincorporated business
   C. Nonqualified retirement plan
   D. Key person plan

63. Define an insider.
   A. Any person having access to public information
   B. Any person having access to nonpublic information
   C. A common stockholder
   D. A holder of debt securities

64. You are planning to discuss dollar cost averaging with a client. What are the main items you will discuss?
   I. A constant amount in dollars would be placed into the fund
   II. A constant number of shares would always be purchased
   III. A lower average cost per share may be realized by dollar cost averaging
   IV. You can guarantee a profit by dollar cost averaging

   A. II, IV
   B. I, III
   C. II, III
   D. III

65. Profit sharing plans are chosen by many companies. What are the main advantages to the company?
   A. A definite annual contribution is not required
   B. A very small annual contribution is required to keep the plan in force
   C. Profit sharing plans are qualified plans
   D. Both A and C

66. A brand-new issue is about to come to market and is now in the cooling off period. What type of advertising may be done by the broker-dealer during this period of time?
   A. No advertising may be done until the issue is released for sale
   B. A tombstone ad may be run
   C. A red herring ad may be run
   D. A blind ad may be run

67. Municipal bonds will often use the term *ex-legal*. What does this term mean?
    A. The issue may have a low credit rating
    B. The issue will not conform to blue sky regulations
    C. No legal opinion will be issued for the bond
    D. A legal opinion will be issued for the bond

68. You have a client who has a particular interest in southwest U.S. company stock funds. In the course of your conversation, you advise the client of the following:
    I. Since this type of fund concentrates in a particular area, or particular type of security, it is called a sector fund
    II. Risks may be higher for a sector fund
    III. Risks are generally lower for a sector fund
    IV. This is also called a specialized fund

    A. I, II, IV
    B. I, III, IV
    C. III, IV
    D. I, II

69. A 1035 exchange may be used for policies and contracts without creating a tax liability for the client. What type of exchanges may be made?
    A. Life to annuity contract
    B. IRA to life
    C. Annuity to life
    D. 401(k) to annuity

70. The three main areas covered by the Securities Exchange Act of 1934 are:
    I. The secondary market
    II. The resale market
    III. Trading activities
    IV. Outstanding securities

    A. I, II, IV
    B. I, II, III, IV
    C. III, IV
    D. II, IV

71. Excessive trading in a client's account is called:
    A. Accumulation
    B. Fraud
    C. Churning
    D. Pegging

72. In variable products the separate account is referred to as where the investments are located. What's the significance of the separate account?
    A. An investment allocation may be made to balance risk
    B. Investments held in a separate account almost always contain market risk
    C. Investments held in a separate account usually do not contain market risk
    D. Both A and B

73. Market risk may be defined as:
    A. Assets minus liabilities of a company
    B. A perception of what a company will do in the future
    C. The risk of default
    D. The assurance a company will gain value in the future

74. You have a prospect stating an intense interest in foreign stock funds. What are a few of the areas you would discuss with this prospect?
    I. Overall tolerance for risk
    II. Importance of knowing the fund objectives
    III. Good performance may be eliminated by currency risk
    IV. Fund performance in the past is no indicator for the future

    A. I, II, IV
    B. I, IV
    C. I, II, III, IV
    D. II, III

75. A client wants the bond certificate for a book entry bond. You tell them:
    A. A book entry bond does not have a certificate
    B. A book entry bond must be held fully paid in the account for 30 days before it may be delivered
    C. A book entry bond is held by the custodian
    D. A "book entry" bond does not exist

76. As a Registered Representative holding a series 6 license, you may sell all of the following products EXCEPT:
    A. Open-end mutual funds
    B. Individual stock issues
    C. Unit Investment Trusts
    D. Closed-end funds in their primary offering

77. The prospectus for a mutual fund must include a history of performance. This history must include all of the following EXCEPT:
    A. One year
    B. Five year
    C. Ten year
    D. All of the above must be included, if applicable

78. Does a mutual fund distributor maintain an inventory of mutual fund shares?
    A. Yes
    B. No
    C. Only during periods of high volume
    D. Only if 12b-1 charges are excessive

79. At what age must a mandatory distribution begin for a traditional IRA?
    A. 59½
    B. 70½
    C. Does not apply
    D. 90

80. An advantage of cumulative preferred stock is:
    A. If a dividend is missed, it must be made up before a new dividend may be declared
    B. Cumulative preferred stock has a par value of $1000
    C. Cumulative preferred stock is considered to be a senior security
    D. High growth potential is a major goal

81. Blue sky laws require state registration of all those listed below EXCEPT:
    A. Broker-dealers
    B. Registered Representatives
    C. Nonprofit organizations
    D. Securities to be sold within the state

82. Which of the following securities has no reinvestment risk ?
    I. Coupon bonds
    II. Zero coupon bonds
    III. GNMA
    IV. CMOs

    A. II
    B. II, III, IV
    C. I, IV
    D. III

83. A STRIP contains the following features:
    I. Backed in full by the U.S. Government
    II. Always sold at a deep discount
    III. Always sold at par
    IV. Produces a monthly income

    A. I, II
    B. II, IV
    C. I, IV
    D. III, IV

84. A prospect you are working with wants an investment to provide both growth and income. Assuming the risk profile is suitable, what investment choices could you recommend ?
    I. Preferred stocks
    II. Utility company stocks
    III. Aggressive growth stocks
    IV. Cyclical stocks

    A. I, II, III
    B. II, III
    C. I, II
    D. III, IV

85. If a variable annuity is annuitized, monthly income can vary in hopes of keeping up with inflation. Monthly income is calculated based on:
    A. AIR
    B. CPI
    C. Bond index
    D. OEX

86. You have a client who wants you to explain a municipal bond fund. List a few of the key features you would discuss:
    I. Tax-exempt income
    II. Tax-deferred income
    III. Higher income tax rates mean a higher tax equivalent yield
    IV. Moderate to lower income tax rates make a municipal bond a more suitable investment

    A. I, IV
    B. I, III
    C. II, IV
    D. IV

87. Open-end mutual funds can use dollar cost averaging because:
    A. Fractional shares may be purchased
    B. Odd lots may be purchased
    C. Round lots may be purchased
    D. CDSL applies

88. A client thinks the price of JKL stock is going to go up in price in a few months but does not want to buy the stock at this time. What strategy could be used to accomplish this goal?
    A. Buy a put
    B. Buy a call
    C. Sell short
    D. Sell a call

89. A prospect is in need of increased income for $20,000 she has to invest and is in the 15% tax bracket. You're discussing the bond funds she could choose. Rank the following bond funds in order of highest to lowest income potential.
    I.   Government bond fund
    II.  Corporate bond fund
    III. High-yield corporate bond fund
    IV.  Municipal bond fund

    A. I, III, II, IV
    B. IV, III, II, I
    C. III, I, IV, II
    D. III, II, I, IV

90. A debenture held by a client is considered to be:
    A. Secured debt
    B. Unsecured debt
    C. A general creditor position
    D. Both B and C

91. Describe a money market fund.
    I.   No-load mutual fund
    II.  Target NAV is set at one dollar
    III. Used for liquidity and safety
    IV.  An open-end fund

    A. I, II, III
    B. I, II, IV
    C. II, III
    D. I, II, III, IV

92. In option contracts, the price at which the stock may be purchased or sold is called:
    A. The put price
    B. The call price
    C. The exercise price
    D. The premium price

93. A client wants to receive a monthly income with a high level of safety. From the following investment options, what would be the most secure choice for this client?
    A. Government bond fund
    B. Blue-chip stock fund
    C. Corporate bond fund
    D. High-yield corporate bond fund

94. A mutual fund must always redeem shares at:
    A. The fund's POP
    B. The fund's NAV
    C. The secondary market price
    D. A premium, as compared to par

95. Which of the following investments is appropriate for an IRA?
    A. Collectibles (art, rare coins, etc.)
    B. Common stock
    C. Life insurance
    D. Municipal bonds

96. Mutual funds operate with a continuous public offering. This means:
    A. A prospectus must always be provided to the client
    B. The fund is always in its IPO
    C. Shares may not be purchased on margin
    D. All of the above are correct

97. A client tells you their investments need to keep pace with inflation. Assuming they have a tolerance for risk, what investments are suitable:
    I.   Common stock funds
    II.  Aggressive growth funds
    III. Bond funds
    IV.  Balanced funds

    A. I, II
    B. I, III
    C. II, IV
    D. III, IV

98. When must trade confirmation be sent to client?
    A. No later than the settlement date
    B. Five days after the settlement date
    C. Three days before the settlement date
    D. On a monthly basis

99. The Investment Company Act of 1940 requires ___ % of an investment company's Board of Directors to be noninterested persons.
    A. 25
    B. 40
    C. 60
    D. 75

100. How often is a mutual fund NAV calculated?
    A. Monthly
    B. Weekly
    C. Daily
    D. As required

**End of Final Exam # 1**

# Series 6
# Securities
# Practice Exam #2

1. UITs have the following characteristics:
   I. Do not have a board of directors
   II. Have a board of directors
   III. Manage their portfolios
   IV. Do not manage their portfolios

   A. II, III
   B. I, IV
   C. I, III
   D. II, IV

2. Investors always buy open-end funds at the:
   I. NAV
   II. POP
   III. CY
   IV. YTM

   A. I, IV
   B. III
   C. IV
   D. II

3. A red herring refers to:
   I. The summary prospectus
   II. The indication of interest
   III. A period of time for accepting orders
   IV. The preliminary prospectus

   A. IV
   B. III, IV
   C. I
   D. None of the above

4. Full and fair disclosure to the client is best described by the:
   I. Investment Act of 1952
   II. Insider Trading Act of 1988
   III. Securities Act of 1933
   IV. Blue Sky laws

   A. IV
   B. II
   C. III
   D. I, III

5. Common stock is often referred to as:
   I. A secondary means of raising capital
   II. A debt position
   III. An equity position
   IV. A primary means of raising business capital.

   A. I, IV
   B. II
   C. IV
   D. III, IV

6. A variable product has which characteristics?
   I. A separate account
   II. Investment choices
   III. Is considered a registered product
   IV. Market risk

   A. I, II, III, IV
   B. II
   C. III
   D. IV

7. Purchasing power risk is associated with:
     I.   Variable annuities
     II.  Common stock
     III. Mutual funds
     IV.  Fixed annuities

   A. II
   B. I, III
   C. IV
   D. None of the above

8. A zero coupon bond:
     I.   Is bought with income as a primary goal
     II.  Does not produce income
     III. Accretes in value
     IV.  Matures at par

   A. I, III
   B. I, III, IV
   C. II
   D. II, III, IV

9. You have a 42-year-old client, married with no children. Your review indicates both the husband and wife file a joint tax return and are in the 37% tax bracket. They'll take limited risk but want their money in a high-quality investment. Which of the following investments may be appropriate?
     I.   High-yield bond fund
     II.  Aggressive growth fund
     III. Precious metal fund
     IV.  Municipal bond fund

   A. None of the choices are appropriate
   B. IV
   C. II, III
   D. I

10. Many investments are liquid. However, for a person who needs a portion of their money available to meet current expenses, your recommendation should be:
     I.   Money market fund
     II.  Government bond fund
     III. Corporate bond fund
     IV.  GNMA fund

   A. II, IV
   B. I, IV
   C. III
   D. I

11. The NASD is the SRO for:
     I.   NYSE
     II.  AMEX
     III. MSRB
     IV.  OTC

   A. I, II
   B. IV
   C. III
   D. I, II, III

12. A closed-end fund may do the following:
     I.   Trade at a premium or a discount
     II.  Redeem shares directly from the fund
     III. Trade on the NYSE
     IV.  Be purchased in a round lot

   A. I, III, IV
   B. I, II, IV
   C. II
   D. II, III, IV

13. How is the growth of a variable annuity taxed?
    I. Long-term capital gains
    II. Not taxed—similar to death benefit of life insurance
    III. Ordinary income
    IV. Ordinary income, if before age 59½

    A. I
    B. I, IV
    C. II
    D. III

14. Statutory voting is described as:
    I. Allocation of votes
    II. Antidilution
    III. One share—one vote
    IV. A preemptive right

    A. III, IV
    B. III
    C. IV
    D. I, IV

15. State securities laws are called:
    A. Insurance laws
    B. Blue Sky laws
    C. Commission laws
    D. Firm element laws

16. If a variable annuity is annuitized:
    I. Month to month income may vary
    II. Month to month income may not vary
    III. An interest rate is assumed to calculate the payment, which is called the AIR
    IV. The monthly payment will always increase over time

    A. I, IV
    B. II, III
    C. III, IV
    D. I, III

17. If a mutual fund is diversified, which is/are true?
    I. It doesn't own more than 10% of any company's outstanding voting stock
    II. 50% of assets are invested
    III. It is called a "sector" fund
    IV. No more than 5% of assets are invested in any one company

    A. II
    B. III
    C. I, IV
    D. I, II

18. Bonds are selling at a premium when their price on the secondary market is:
    A. Below par
    B. At par
    C. Above par
    D. Bonds never sell at a premium on the secondary market

19. An investor has indicated to you she needs income with safety of principal. Your recommendation should be:
    I. An individual stock
    II. A government bond fund
    III. A high-yield bond fund
    IV. An index fund

    A. I, IV
    B. II
    C. III
    D. II, IV

20. An investor has indicated growth in his portfolio is needed to meet some long-range goals. The investor is 45 years old, an active common stock purchaser, and is aware of the risks involved in the stock market. Your recommendation could include:
    I. Blue-chip stock funds
    II. Aggressive growth funds
    III. Utility stock funds
    IV. Hedge funds

    A. I, II, III, IV
    B. I, II, III
    C. III, IV
    D. I, IV

21. Discussions about common stock often center around *limited liability*. What does this mean?
    I. The investor cannot lose more than they have invested
    II. The investor is always guaranteed a minimum return of 3%
    III. Limited liability does not apply to common stock
    IV. Limited recourse applies to common stock

    A. I
    B. III
    C. IV
    D. I, IV

22. In the organization of a mutual fund, what area is responsible for redeeming shares and keeping track of customers' names and addresses?
    I. Custodian
    II. Wholesaler
    III. Transfer Agent
    IV. Investment Advisor

    A. I, IV
    B. I, III
    C. III
    D. I

23. Your recommendation to a client is to buy an index fund. A few of the reasons you believe this recommendation is suitable for the client are
    I. Active portfolio management
    II. Lower internal fund costs
    III. Fewer trades, lower taxes each year
    IV. Index will tend to follow market performance

    A. I, II, III, IV
    B. II, IV
    C. IV
    D. I, II, IV

24. You have a client who has a special need for growth, since retirement is within the next five years and a moderate amount of risk is acceptable. In view of this situation, all of the following are acceptable EXCEPT:
    A. Government bond fund
    B. Blue-chip stock fund
    C. Utility stock fund
    D. Special situation funds

25. Variable life insurance policies have a variable death benefit. Is it possible for the variable death benefit to decrease from year to year ?
    A. No, since there is no market risk
    B. Yes, since there is market risk
    C. Does not apply, since the death benefit is guaranteed
    D. None of the above are correct

26. The maximum fine a broker-dealer may receive for criminal penalties from insider trading is:
    A. $1,000,000
    B. $2,500,000
    C. $500,000
    D. $7,500,000

27. A Registered Representative changing broker-dealers must:
    I.   Transfer to the new broker-dealer
    II.  Resign from the old broker-dealer
    III. Reapply to the new broker-dealer
    IV.  Must discuss continuing commissions before resigning from the old firm

    A. I, IV
    B. II, IV
    C. II, III, IV
    D. IV

28. A JTIC account is opened with unequal interest between the two account owners.
    A. Unequal interest is allowed in this type of account
    B. Unequal interest is not allowed in this type of account
    C. Each account owner has a right of survivorship
    D. Upon death of one account owner, the account reverts 100% to the other remaining owner

29. A basic definition for a security is:
    A. A debt stake in a company
    B. An ownership stake in a company
    C. Both of the above
    D. Neither of the above

30. The formula for net worth is:
    A. Assets minus liabilities
    B. Liabilities plus assets
    C. Equity plus liabilities
    D. None of the above

31. May mutual funds be purchased on margin ?
    A. Yes
    B. No
    C. Yes, if held for 30 or more days
    D. No, unless it is part of a fund family

32. The separate account for variable products is:
    I.   Where the investments are located
    II.  An account usually subject to market risk
    III. Always protected by state guaranty fund
    IV.  Commingled with the general account

    A. I, II, IV
    B. II, III
    C. III
    D. I, II

33. The Insider Trading and Securities Fraud Enforcement Act of 1988 refers to:
    A. Tippers
    B. Tippees
    C. Control personnel
    D. All of the above

34. A call option gives the right to:
    I. The call owner to sell a stock at a preset price
    II. The call owner to buy a stock at a preset price
    III. The owner of the call to exercise the call at any time before expiration
    IV. The seller of the call to exercise the call at any time before expiration

    A. I, IV
    B. II, III
    C. IV
    D. I, III

35. An underwriter for a mutual fund is also known as a distributor.
    A. True
    B. False
    C. Neither apply to mutual funds
    D. Used for new common stock issues only

36. All of the following are investment grade EXCEPT:
    A. BBB
    B. A
    C. BB
    D. AA

37. A client, in her early 30s, indicates an interest in long-term growth investing. She understands risk versus reward and has an amount of money she wants to invest for a higher return. Which of the following could be suitable for her?
    I. Government bond fund
    II. GNMA fund
    III. Aggressive growth fund
    IV. An equity fund

    A. I, II
    B. III
    C. I
    D. III, IV

38. 12b-1 sales charges are:
    A. Front-end loads
    B. Asset based
    C. Back-end loads
    D. None of the above

39. You have a chart that shows exactly what the client needs to know. This chart has been a favorite of yours for a while but is not approved for use by your broker-dealer. You should:
    A. Use the chart
    B. Do not use the chart
    C. Use the chart, since it is easier to understand, as compared to those approved by your broker-dealer
    D. None of the above

40. Deductions from the gross premium of variable universal life insurance include all of the following EXCEPT:
    A. CDSL
    B. Premium taxes by the state
    C. Administrative fee
    D. Sales load

41. The Investment Company Act of 1940 regulates all of the following EXCEPT:
    A. Face-Amount Certificate Companies
    B. Unit Investment Trusts
    C. Closed-end funds
    D. Corporate bonds

42. Place the business cycles in order of occurrence
    I. Expansion
    II. Contraction
    III. Peak
    IV. Trough

    A. I, II, III, IV
    B. I, III, II, IV
    C. IV, II, III, I
    D. II, I, III, IV

43. A variable universal life policy separate account provides investment choices for the client. These investment choices will determine to a substantial degree the:
    I. Increase in death benefit, if any, over time
    II. Increase in cash value over time
    III. Value of the separate account, and a decrease in the separate account values may result due to poor investment performance
    IV. Taxes paid by the beneficiary

    A. I, II, III
    B. I, IV
    C. III, IV
    D. II, III

44. An investor has indicated a need to maximize current income. What would you suggest?
    I. Aggressive growth funds
    II. Utility funds
    III. GNMA funds
    IV. Corporate bond funds

    A. I, III
    B. I, II
    C. IV
    D. I

45. During the cooling off period of an IPO, which of the following may be done?
    A. Take orders
    B. Take an indication of interest
    C. Distribute the red herring
    D. Both B and C

46. What type of advertising may be done during the cooling off period?
    A. Normal advertising about the product
    B. Tombstone ads
    C. Red herring ads
    D. Co-op ads

47. Bonds usually have a face, or par, value of:
    A. $100
    B. $10,000
    C. $5000
    D. $1000

48. The Securities Exchange Act of 1934:
    A. Created the SEC
    B. Regulates trading activities
    C. Both A and B
    D. Neither A or B

49. When dividends from mutual funds, or stock, are paid out to an investor:
    A. An exclusion of 70% for taxes is granted
    B. Dividends are fully taxable
    C. Dividends are tax exempt
    D. Dividends are tax deferred

50. The formula for current yield is:
    A. Interest rate divided by market price
    B. Annual interest divided by par value
    C. Semiannual interest divided by par
    D. Semiannual interest divided by market price

51. Municipal bonds are generally suitable for:
    A. Individuals in a low tax bracket
    B. Individuals in a high tax bracket
    C. Individuals paying no tax
    D. IRA and 401(k) plans

52. A nondiversified mutual fund:
    I.   May specialize in one industry
    II.  May be known as a sector fund
    III. May be known as a specialized fund
    IV.  Contains a higher level of risk when compared to a diversified fund

    A. I, II
    B. II
    C. I, II, III, IV
    D. III

53. Blue Sky laws require state registration of:
    A. Securities
    B. Broker-Dealers
    C. Registered Representatives
    D. All of the above

54. The dollar value of an insurance company's separate account:
    A. Has a guaranteed minimum amount
    B. May be subject to market risk
    C. Is not guaranteed
    D. Both B and C

55. When buying bonds, the maturity date is an important consideration, since:
    A. The longer the term, the greater the risk
    B. The longer the term, the lower the risk
    C. Usually a longer term bond will offer a lower interest rate
    D. Long-term bonds are always used for growth

56. A growth fund could be suitable for:
    I.   An individual with a tolerance for risk
    II.  Increased value over time
    III. High monthly income
    IV.  Younger investors

    A. I, II, IV
    B. I, III
    C. II, IV
    D. III

57. The Securities Exchange Act of 1934
    I.   Regulates the secondary market
    II.  Regulates trading activities
    III. Regulates outstanding securities
    IV.  Created the prospectus

    A. I, III, IV
    B. I, II, III
    C. IV
    D. II, IV

58. A pool of securities in which an investor owns an amount in proportion to the investment made describes:
    A. UIT
    B. Individual common stock
    C. Mutual fund
    D. Both A and C

59. A nonqualified variable annuity uses funds as part of its separate account. If a switch is made by a client to a different fund within the family of funds:
    A. A taxable event occurs
    B. No taxable event occurs
    C. Taxation occurs for the realized gain on a long-term gain basis
    D. None of the above is correct

60. A hot issue is:
    I. An issue that immediately sells much above the IPO on the secondary market
    II. An issue that immediately sells much above the IPO on the resale market
    III. May be purchased by immediate family members supported by the Registered Representative
    IV. May not be purchased by immediate family members supported by the Registered Representative

    A. I, II, IV
    B. II, III
    C. I
    D. III

61. Owning common stock gives an investor an ownership position in a company. This ownership position for this type security is known as:
    A. A senior security
    B. A junior security
    C. A debenture
    D. A bond

62. Taxation of mutual funds held in a cash account is treated differently compared to taxation within a variable annuity. A few of these differences include:
    A. Mutual funds are taxed at ordinary income rates
    B. For long-term gains, mutual funds are taxed at the lower long-term gains rate
    C. A 1099 is generated for gains within a mutual fund, even though no withdrawal of funds has been made over the prior year
    D. Both B and C

63. Regular way settlement in securities transaction refers to:
    A. T + 3 days
    B. T + 5 days
    C. Same day settlement
    D. DDT

64. A broker-dealer may act as either a broker or dealer.
    A. This statement is not true.
    B. A broker-dealer may act on both sides of a transaction, as broker and/or dealer without disclosure to the client.
    C. A broker-dealer must disclose in what capacity they acted in regard to a client's transaction.
    D. A broker-dealer always acts as a broker for client transactions.

65. A risk unique to a foreign stock fund is:
    A. Full recourse
    B. Currency risk
    C. Limited letter of credit recourse
    D. Default

66. Yield to maturity for a discount bond will be:
    A. Higher than its coupon
    B. Higher than its nominal rate
    C. Lower than its nominal rate
    D. Both A and B

67. A client has a certain amount of money for which they would like to receive an income for life. They need the highest income possible and they do not have any concern for retention of principal for a beneficiary. You recommend:
    A. Immediate annuity - Life only
    B. Immediate annuity - Life, 20-year certain
    C. High-yield bond fund
    D. GNMA

68. The Maloney Act of 1938
    A. Set up the NASD as SRO for the OTC
    B. Set up the MSRB as oversight for OTC
    C. Both A and B
    D. None of the above is correct

69. Regulation T:
    A. Regulates the extension of credit to clients from broker-dealers
    B. Regulates settlement of securities
    C. Prevents credit from being used to buy IPO, mutual funds and other new issues
    D. All of the above

70. SIPC collects annual assessments from broker-dealers. What does it do?
    I. Protects customer accounts in excess of $1,000,000
    II. Protects customers against the default of their broker-dealer
    III. Protects clients against market risk
    IV. Protects customer accounts up to $200,000 in cash

    A. I, II, IV
    B. II, IV
    C. II
    D. III

71. A zero coupon bond may be used for a variety of purposes. One of its main features is:
    A. Very stable price in the resale market
    B. No reinvestment risk
    C. Does not have an active secondary market
    D. Initial purchase price is always at par

72. The continuing education requirement for Registered Representatives includes:
    A. A firm element
    B. A regulatory element
    C. Both A and B
    D. Neither A nor B

73. A variable annuity is said to have two distinct phases. These are:
    A. Accumulation
    B. Annuity
    C. Deferral and withdrawal
    D. Both A and B

74. Common stock actually distributed to investors is known as:
    A. Issued stock
    B. Authorized stock
    C. Treasury stock
    D. Convertible stock

75. Par value of common stock is:
    I. Not of importance to investors
    II. Has a value for accounting purposes
    III. May be known as paid in capital
    IV. May be described as surplus capital

    A. I, II
    B. IV
    C. I, II, III, IV
    D. II, III, IV

76. The shares an open-end investment company offers for sale are:
    A. Not redeemable
    B. Redeemable
    C. Reissued upon surrender
    D. Sold in the secondary market

77. You have a client in their early 50s who has indicated they understand reasonable risk of an investment. They want an investment to provide a good dividend, plus reasonable growth. Your recommendations could include:
    A. Growth funds
    B. Income funds
    C. Growth and income funds
    D. Bond funds

78. Roth IRA contributions are:
    A. Pretax dollars
    B. Aftertax dollars
    C. Tax exempt upon distribution
    D. Both B and C

79. A SEP plan is:
    A. A qualified retirement plan for small business
    B. A nonqualified plan for large corporations
    C. A qualified retirement plan for large corporations
    D. A deferred compensation plan for selected individuals

80. Continuing education for the series 6 license has a regulatory element. This means you will take a test at a designated testing center:
    A. on your first anniversary as a Registered Representative
    B. within 120 days of your second anniversary as a Registered Representative and every three years thereafter
    C. within 120 days of your third anniversary as a Registered Representative and every two years thereafter
    D. Your attendance at a firm element meeting each year is required, but no other testing is required

81. ERISA guidelines for retirement plans refer to:
    A. Beneficiaries
    B. Vesting
    C. Participation
    D. All of the above

82. A mutual fund which contains a declining sales charge, such as 5%, 4%, 3%, 2%, 1%, is called:
    A. A front-end load fund
    B. A back-end load fund
    C. A 12b-1 fund
    D. A no-load fund

83. SIPC is in place to protect:
    A. Banks
    B. Broker-dealers
    C. Employees
    D. Clients

84. Antidilution provision for stockholders provides:
    A. Protection against market loss
    B. A preemptive right
    C. Protection of the proportionate share of the company owned by the stockholder
    D. Both B and C

85. The safekeeper of a mutual fund's securities is known as:
    I. Investment advisor
    II. Transfer Agent
    III. Underwriter
    IV. Custodian

    A. II, III
    B. IV
    C. I, III
    D. III

86. A mid cap mutual fund would contain stocks of companies with a capitalization of:
    A. 5 to 10 billion dollars
    B. Over 15 million dollars
    C. From 1 to 5 billion dollars
    D. From 1 to 5 million dollars

87. A client, age 58, wants an investment with the highest possible monthly income. You discuss risk versus reward and the possibility of losing principal. The client agrees that loss of principal would be acceptable. You recommend:
    A. High-grade corporate bond fund
    B. Low-grade corporate bond fund
    C. GNMA fund
    D. Municipal bond fund

88. A GNMA is often referred to as an extremely safe investment. Why is this true ?
    A. GNMA is backed by FDIC
    B. GNMA is backed by mortgages
    C. GNMA is backed by the full faith of the U.S. Government
    D. GNMA is backed by FSLIC

89. Your client wants an investment that would limit the amount of realized gains but have good growth potential. You recommend:
    I. Aggressive growth funds
    II. GNMA
    III. Index funds
    IV. Corporate bond funds

    A. I, II
    B. II, III
    C. II, IV
    D. III

90. When a new issue comes to market, the SEC:
    A. Approves a company and recommends the new issue for purchase
    B. Approves the company, but does not recommend the issue for purchase
    C. Clears the issue for distribution
    D. Clears the issue and recommends it for retail purchase

91. A Registered Representative may have outside employment, other than their member firm:
    A. Never
    B. With prior approval
    C. Only on a part-time basis
    D. None of the above

92. How often must the death benefit for a variable life policy be calculated?
    A. Annually
    B. Monthly
    C. Daily
    D. As required

93. Simplified arbitration is a method to speed up the handling of complaints. It is used for:
    A. Complaints over $25,000
    B. Complaints over $100,000
    C. Complaints $25,000 and under
    D. Not used to resolve complaints

94. Financial reports for mutual funds must be released to clients at least:
    A. Semiannually
    B. Quarterly
    C. Annually
    D. As deemed necessary

95. The maximum front end load charge for a mutual fund is:
    A. 8½% in the first year
    B. 5% in the first year
    C. 9% in the first year
    D. .25% in the first year

96. Portfolio turnover rate for a mutual fund reflects upon a fund's:
    A. Expense ratio
    B. Commission charge
    C. Negative return
    D. CDSL

97. Issuers exempt from Securities Act
    of 1933 are:
    I.   U.S. Government
    II.  Nonprofit organizations
    III. U.S. Territories
    IV.  Municipalities

    A. I, II
    B. II, III, IV
    C. I, II, III, IV
    D. I

98. The default option for taxation on
    the gains of mutual funds held in a
    cash account is:
    A. FIFO
    B. LIFO
    C. Indexing
    D. MEWA

99. Preferred stock:
    A. Appreciates more rapidly than
       common stock
    B. Appreciates less rapidly than
       common stock
    C. Has features of both debt and
       equity securities
    D. Both B and C

100. What is the only type of advertising
     which may be done without
     disclosing the name of the broker-
     dealer ?
     A. Product advertising
     B. Recruitment advertising
     C. Tombstone advertising
     D. SIPC advertising

**End of Final Exam # 2**

# Glossary

*The definitions given here explain how the listed terms are used in the securities markets. Some of the terms have additional meanings, which can be found in a standard dictionary.*

**Accrued Interest**—interest that has accumulated because it has not yet been collected.

**Accumulation, Rights of**—SEE: **Rights of Accumulation.**

**Accumulation Stage**—the time when the investor is making regular payments into the separate account as an investment and determines the amount of accumulation units. ALSO SEE: **Accumulation Units.** COMPARE: **Annuity Stage.**

**Accumulation Units**—the measure of how much of an interest the investor owns in the separate account, based on the amount of payments the investor makes into the separate account during the accumulation stage. ALSO SEE: **Accumulation Stage.** COMPARE: **Annuity Units.**

**Active Income**—SEE: **Earned Income.**

**Adjusted Cost Basis**—the original price, plus any commissions, adjustments or allowable expenses. (Used for computing tax liability.) Also referred to simply as **Basis** or **Cost Basis,** although these latter two terms should technically refer to the original price only.

**ADR**—SEE: **American Depository Receipts.**

**Advance Refunding**—a method of primary financing that lowers the interest rate of a municipality's debt obligation by selling more bonds when rates are lower, to replace bonds that are at a higher rate.

**Advantages, Tax**—SEE: **Tax Advantages.**

**Advertising**—any kind of public communication that comes from the brokerage firm but is not specifically distributed by the firm, and as such, the brokerage firm has no control over who receives the material. (e.g., TV, magazine, website). COMPARE: **Sales Literature.**

**Aggressive Investments**—stocks of rapidly growing companies that have prospects for above-average growth but with prices that are highly volatile over time when compared to the broader market. (Some stocks in an aggressive portfolio would be high-techs and start-ups. An aggressive portfolio would use margin.) COMPARE: **Defensive Investments.**

**Agreement, Indenture**—SEE: **Indenture Agreement.**

**Agreement, Repurchase**—SEE: **Repurchase Agreement.**

**AIR**—SEE: **Assumed Interest Rate.**

**AMBAC Indemnity**—municipal bond credit insurance company. SEE: **Credit Enhancement.**

**American Depository Receipts (ADR)**—a U.S. substitute for foreign common stock. ADRs allow U.S. investors to collect dividends and enjoy the capital gains of the foreign stock but do not have voting rights or preemptive rights. (No SEC registration is required for company.)

**Amortization**—the process of reducing an amount by dividing it into smaller equal payments over a period of time.

**Amortize**—act of amortization. SEE: **Amortization.**

**And Interest**—when the buyer of a security must pay the quoted price of the bond or note plus accrued interest since last interest payment was made. COMPARE: **Traded Flat.**

**Annuities**—a series of equal payments, often set up as insurance contracts because they are for the life of the holder. ALSO SEE: **Variable Annuities, Fixed Annuities.**

**Annuitize**—to convert an annuity contract from accumulation stage to annuity stage so that the investor can begin to collect payments from the value that has built up in the annuity.

**Annuity, Deferred**—SEE: **Deferred Annuity.**

**Annuity, Immediate**—SEE: **Immediate Annuity.**

**Annuity Stage**—the time when the investor is receiving payments from the separate account. At the time that the variable annuity contract is converted from the accumulation stage to the annuity stage, a calculation is done to determine the basis for future payments. ALSO SEE: **Annuity Units.** COMPARE: **Accumulation Stage.**

**Annuity Units**—the measure of how much of an interest the investor owns in the separate account, based on the amount of payments the investor is entitled to receive during the annuity stage. ALSO SEE: **Annuity Stage.** COMPARE: **Accumulation Units.**

**Antidilution Provision**—SEE: **Preemptive Rights.**

**Arbitrage**—profiting from price difference between two like securities, commodities, etc., trading simultaneously in two different markets.

**Arbitration**—an alternative means of dispute resolution whereby an impartial third party or panel of people listen to evidence presented by both sides and render a decision, thus avoiding the court system. (Often final and binding.)

**Ask**—offer to sell at quoted price. COMPARE: **Bid.**

**Asset Allocation Fund**—a balanced mutual fund that has multiple asset classes and which tilts its asset balance between stocks, bonds, and cash depending on market conditions.

**Assets**—things of value that are owned or in one's possession. (e.g., cash, stock, land). ALSO SEE: **Liabilities, Net Worth.**

**Assumed Interest Rate (AIR)**—an estimated interest rate that the insurance company uses when calculating the projected payout on a variable annuity contract. (This is not a guaranteed rate of return, but a means to calculate the conversion from accumulation units to annuity units. The AIR is a set figure, used as a benchmark to measure performance of the separate account, and thus determine payout amounts.)

**Authorization, Limited**—SEE: **Limited Authorization.**

**Authorization, Full** — SEE: **Full Authorization.**

**Authorized Stock**—the stock originally approved by a corporation in its Articles of Incorporation. (This is the maximum number of shares that the company may create.)

**Authorizing Resolution**—the issuer's authority to sell the bond issue, authorizing the action, describing the size of the issue, the interest rate on the bonds, and cover other legal issues. (As part of the authorizing resolution, or as a separate action, the municipality will also have an award resolution, awarding the securities underwriting contract to the chosen underwriter.)

**Averaging, Dollar Cost**—SEE: **Dollar Cost Averaging.**

**BA**—SEE: **Banker's Acceptance.**

**Back End Load**—when a sales charge is added to an investment when it is sold (e.g., with a mutual fund, the length of time the investment is held often determines the sales charge that is added at time of sale—and often can drop to 0% by about the fifth year). If the load declines over time, it is often referred to as a **contingent deferred sales load (CDSL)** or **contingent deferred sales charge (CDSC)**. Back-end load funds are referred to as **Class B shares**. SEE: **No-Load, Front-End Load.**

**Balance of Payments**—measures the difference between all goods and services purchased between two countries. This includes all transactions made over a certain time period, comparing the amount of foreign currency taken in with the amount of domestic currency paid out. COMPARE: **Balance of Trade.**

**Balance of Trade**—one component of the balance of payments that only counts goods and ignores the services and investment components. This is also referred to as the **current account**. COMPARE: **Balance of Payments.**

**Balance Sheet**—a financial report that shows the financial status of an entity with regard to assets, liabilities, and net worth as of a particular date. COMPARE: **Income Statement.**

**Bank Grade Bonds**—SEE: **Investment Grade Bonds.**

**Bankers' Acceptance (BA)**—a time draft drawn on a particular bank, whereby the bank accepts responsibility for payment. Essentially BAs work like a letter of credit and are money market instruments.

**Basis**—the original price. ALSO SEE: **Adjusted Cost Basis.**

**Basis Point**—1/100%, or .01 of yield. A basis point is the smallest unit of measure used to quote yields. It takes 100 basis points to equal 1%. (For example, if we say that the yield on a bond is 1/4 point higher, we are saying that it rose 0.25%, or 25 basis points.)

**Bear**—one who has a negative view of the market, and thinks that the market will fall. COMPARE: **Bull.**

**Bearer Bonds**—bonds where the person holding the bond is the owner.

Coupons are detached from the bond and submitted to collect interest payments. COMPARE: **Registered Bonds.**

**Bearish**—negative outlook, thinking that the markets will fall. COMPARE: **Bullish.**

**Best Efforts**—an agreement with the investment banking firm acting as agent and broker in selling the securities, buying only what it needs to fills orders, and without any obligation to purchase unsold securities from the issuer. COMPARE: **Firm Commitment.**

**Bid**—offer to buy at a quoted price. COMPARE: **Ask.**

**Bid Wanted**—bid request by a broker-dealer when there is no activity in the stock, but the dealer wants sell some and wants traders to submit a bid. COMPARE: **Offer Wanted.**

**Blue Chip**—common stocks from well-known companies who have a long history of growth and a reputation for good management. Dividends are usually paid out on a fairly consistent basis. Blue chips are usually nationally known corporations, and their products or services are familiar to many people. The common stock of these companies is considered relatively safe and stable.

**Blue Sky laws**—name given to various state laws requiring issuers to register their new issues and provide financial information for securities sold in their state. Compliance can be achieved by: filing notice, coordinated registration, or qualifying independently.

**Bond**—security that pays interest, and returns the principal investment amount upon maturity. Also called a fixed-income security.

**Bond Ratings**—SEE: **Ratings.**

**Bonds, Bank Grade**—SEE: **Investment Grade Bonds.**

**Bonds, Bearer**—SEE: **Bearer Bonds.**

**Bonds, General Obligation (GO)**—SEE: **General Obligation Bonds.**

**Bonds, Investment Grade**—SEE: **Investment Grade Bonds.**

**Bonds, Zero Coupon**—SEE: **Zero Coupon Bonds.**

**Book Entry Bonds**—registered bonds that do not have a certificate given with them.

**Book Value**—net worth figure for a company divided by the number of shares outstanding.

**Bottom Line**—company's operating income (EBIT), minus debt service, minus taxes. Also referred to as **net income** or **net income after tax (NIAT).**

**Breakpoint**—the investment dollar level at which investors are eligible for a reduced sales charge. COMPARE: **Letters of Intent, Rights of Accumulation.**

**Breakpoint Selling**—keeping a client's trades just below breakpoints where the investor would save on sales charges. (This is a **violation** of NASD rules.)

**Broker**—one who arranges trades for a commission as an agent.

**Broker-Dealer**—securities brokerage house and/or investment banking firm.

**Broker-Dealer's Concession**—part of the sales charge paid to compensate the broker-dealer.

**Bull**—one who has positive view of the market and thinks the market will rise. COMPARE: **Bear.**

**Bullish**—positive outlook, thinking that the markets will rise. COMPARE: **Bearish.**

**Business Cycles**—general swings in business activity, resulting in expanding activity and contracting activity during different phases of the cycle. The phases in the cycle are expansion, peak, contraction, and trough. (Remember: EPCoT. See each entry separately.)

**Buyer**—one who buys something. Also called long. SEE: **Long.**

**Call**—1. redeeming a bond or preferred stock before maturity by paying principal and interest owed and often a call premium, as per terms stated in the security; 2. option that gives an investor the right to buy a certain number of shares of a security at a preset price before a certain date. COMPARE: **Put.**

**Call Premium**—additional money paid to a bond holder when a bond is called and paid off early.

**Call Protection**—period of time during which a bond may not be called early.

**Call Risk**—the chance that a bond issuer or preferred stock issuer may call (redeem) the security before the actual maturity date. ALSO SEE: **Reinvestment Risk.**

**Capital, Preservation of**—SEE: **Preservation of Capital.**

**Capital Gain**—the increase in value above the adjusted cost basis that is realized by an investor when an asset is sold. COMPARE: **Capital Loss.**

**Capital Growth**—an investment objective that tries to make the original amount of invested money appreciate over the long term.

**Capital Loss**—the decrease in value below the adjusted cost basis that is realized by an investor when an asset is sold. COMPARE: **Capital Gain.**

**Capital Risk**—the chance that an investment will lose value without something bad having happened to the underlying issuer (company).

**Cash Settlement**—money built up in a life insurance policy or other separate account, which may be borrowed against or used to figure surrender value. COMPARE: **Surrender Value.**

**Cash Value**—settlement occurs the same day when paying cash. (COMPARE: regular way settlements, which settle T + 3 or T + 1.)

**CD**—SEE: **Certificate of Deposit.**

**CDSC**—Contingent Deferred Sales Charge. SEE: **Back-End Load.**

**CDSL**—Contingent Deferred Sales Load. SEE: **Back-End Load.**

**Certificate**—SEE: **Stock Certificate.**

**Certificates of Deposit (CD)**—debt securities, issued by financial institutions. ("Standard" CD sold by neighborhood banks to depositors are non-negotiable. "Jumbo" CD (minimum face value $100,000) sold by commercial banks to investors as a time deposit are negotiable and thus are money market instruments.)

**Churning**—excessive trading to generate commissions, usually determined by significant increase in trades after account became discretionary. (**Prohibited** by NASD rules.)

**Class A Shares**—Mutual fund with a front-end load. SEE: **Front-End Load.**

**Class B Shares**—Mutual fund with a back-end load. SEE: **Back-End Load.**

**Class C Shares**—Mutual fund with a level load. SEE: **Level Load.**

**Class D Shares**—Mutual fund with a hybrid load (starts as front end, changes to back end).

**Closed-End Management Company**—investment company that offers a fixed number of shares to investors and use the funds raised to operate a packaged security. The company is closed end because after the initial offering of shares to the public, the fund is closed out and no further investments are accepted. Closed-end fund shares trade on an exchange, where investors buy and sell shares after the initial offering. COMPARE: **Open-End Management Company.**

**CMO**—SEE: **Collateralized Mortgage Obligation.**

**CMV**—Current Market Value. SEE: **Long Market Value.**

**Cold Calling**—any telephone solicitation made when the caller does not have a prior relationship with the party being called. (Defined by Telephone Consumer Protection Act of 1991.)

**Collateralized Mortgage Obligations (CMOs)**—vehicle for issuing mortgage-backed securities, separated into different groups based on maturity dates, which pass-through principal and interest payments to investors. CMOs are private sector issues backed by a pool of Fannie Mae, Freddie Mac, or other mortgages.

**Combined Offering**—sale of stock in the primary market with some of the sale proceeds going to the company treasury and some going to present shareholders. ALSO SEE: **Primary Offering, Secondary Offering.**

**Commercial Paper**—short-term debt issued by corporations to finance inventories, accounts receivable, and other obligations. (not issued by commercial banks.)

**Commission**—small percentage of transaction price collected by a broker-dealer when they act in a brokerage capacity to arrange a trade. COMPARE: **Markup, Markdown.**

**Common Stock**—an ownership interest in a corporation that conveys to the holder certain rights, including the right to vote for the board of directors and certain other issues and the right to receive a proportionate share of any declared dividend. COMPARE: **Preferred Stock.**

**Community Property**—a type of joint account that is not recognized in all states.

**Companies, Investment**—SEE: **Investment Companies.**

**Companies, Management** — SEE: **Management Companies.**

**Companies, Nonmanagement** — SEE: **Nonmanagement Companies.**

**Company** — a business entity. SEE: **Corporation.** COMPARE: **Partnership.**

**Conduit Theory**—theory that says if the investment company passes through at least 90% of its dividends and net income from capital gains and meets other IRS guidelines, then the fund is merely a conduit for passing through capital gains, thus allowing those monies to be taxed only once at the personal level. Also referred to as Subchapter M theory or pipeline theory.

**Consumer Price Index (CPI)**—measures the fixed cost of a market basket of goods and services. CPI includes components from food, transportation, energy, housing, clothing, etc. (Often used as an inflation adjuster for cost-of-living increases.)

**Consumption**—buying a product or service and using it until it has no remaining value.

**Contingent Deferred Sales Charge (CDSC)**—SEE: **Back-End Load.**

**Contingent Deferred Sales Load (CDSL)**—SEE: **Back-End Load.**

**Contraction**—falling demand and business activity, generally accompanied by decreases in industrial production, falling consumer demand, heavy debt loads for consumer and businesses, increases in bankruptcies (personal and corporate), rising unemployment, and a falling stock market. COMPARE: **Expansion.** ALSO SEE: **Business Cycles.**

**Control Persons**—people who own 10% or more of a company. (The stock they own is considered control stock.)

**Conversion**—exchanging one security for another (usually convertible bonds or convertible preferred stock are exchanged for a fixed number of shares of common stock).

**Conversion, Forced** — SEE: **Forced Conversion.**

**Conversion Price**—the price at which a stock should trade before a bondholder considers conversion.

**Conversion Privilege**—1. the right of a bond holder to exchange (convert-

ible) bonds for a fixed number of shares of common stock. 2. the redemption of shares from one family and using the proceeds to buy another mutual fund within the same families of funds. (Often there's a time limit to complete the conversion to qualify for reduced or waived sales charges.)

**Conversion Ratio**—number of shares of stock an investor would receive for converting bonds.

**Convertible Preferred Stock**—preferred stock that can be traded in for common stock in the company at a preset price. (Because of this feature, the price of convertible preferred stock may fluctuate in line with the common stock, and the dividend paid on convertible preferred stock is usually lower.)

**Cooling Off Period**—the time after the registration statement is filed, but before the securities can be offered for sale to the public. During this period, the SEC reviews the registration statement and preliminary prospectus. The investment banking firm continues its due diligence and may place tombstone ads or distribute a preliminary prospectus to potential investors to gauge interest. No securities may be sold during this time. (Supposed to last 20 days but is often longer.)

**Corporates**—another term for corporate bonds.

**Corporation**—a separate legal entity organized under state law. COMPARE: **Partnership, Sole Proprietorship.**

**Correction**—a price decline in the overall market resulting from an overbought situation. Theory: since there are few buyers left, a price drop is imminent. SEE: **Overbought.**

**Cost Basis**—SEE: **Adjusted Cost Basis.**

**Cost Inflation**—An increase in the cost of goods or services. COMPARE: **Demand Inflation.**

**Coterminous**—debt situation where multiple taxing authorities have jurisdiction over the same group of people, and both issue debt that taps the same taxpayer. (An example is a county and city that share boundaries and both issue bonds.) Also called **overlapping debt.**

**Countercyclical Stocks**—common stocks that generally rise when economic conditions worsen. The best example of a countercyclical stock is the food sector (because demand is constant regardless of economic conditions). COMPARE: **Cyclical Stocks.**

**Coupon**—nominal interest rate the issuer will pay on a security, expressed as a percentage. (Term comes from old bearer bonds which had physical coupons that were detached and submitted to collect interest payments.)

**Covered Call**—when the writer of the call option actually owns the stock to back up the contract. COMPARE: **Uncovered Call.**

**Covered Option**—when the writer of the option actually owns the stock to back up the contract. COMPARE: **Uncovered Option.**

**CPI**—SEE: **Consumer Price Index.**

**Credit Enhancements**—insurance offered by private companies that guarantees principal and interest payments on municipal bonds, allowing the issuer to offer a lower rate. Two large municipal bond insurers are **Municipal Bond Investors Assurance (MBIA)** and **AMBAC Indemnity.** If they insure an issue against default, bonds become AAA rated.

**Credit Risk**—risk that an investment will lose money because it is not repaid. This is also called **repayment risk** or **financial risk.**

**CROP**—Compliance Registered Options Principal.

**Cumulative (Voting)**—a type of voting whereby stockholders receive a total number of votes equal to their total number of shares of stock, then the stockholder may place all of those votes for a single board member, or divide the vote anyway he or she wants. (This gives minority shareholders more influence when voting.) COMPARE: **Statutory (Voting).**

**Cumulative Preferred Stock**—preferred stock allows dividends to accrue so that in the event that dividends cannot be paid, the unpaid dividends become a liability that must be paid in full before any regular dividends can be paid to common stockholders.

**Currency Risk**—the chance of foreign exchange loss because of fluctuations in the value of foreign money vis-à-vis the dollar. Also referred to as exchange risk.

**Current Account**—SEE: **Balance of Trade.**

**Current Income**—an investment objective that tries to generate an immediate cash flow from a portfolio of investments.

**Current Market Value (CMV)**—SEE: **Long Market Value.**

**Current Yield**—1. the coupon rate of the bond divided by the purchase price paid. 2. the actual rate of return a stock pays in dividends based on its current market price. This gives investors a gauge of the actual rate of return on their stock investment, just like CY calculations do for bond yields. Current yield for stocks is figured as dividends per share divided by market value per share.

**CUSIP Number**—Committee on Uniform Securities Identification Procedures (CUSIP) number used to identify all listed stocks and registered bonds. CUSIP number makes tracking securities and settling transactions easier.

**Custodian**—person who watches over something and has a fiduciary responsibility. With a UGMA/UTMA account, the custodian is a fiduciary to the minor, since the custodian has full control over the account's investments.

**Customer Book**—detailed records kept about the securities a client owns and all transactions that have been made with the firm. (Kept for six years, with past two years readily accessible.)

**Cyclical Stocks**—common stocks that generally rise and fall quickly in response to economic conditions. Examples of cyclical stocks are automobile stocks and housing-related stocks. COMPARE: **Countercyclical Stocks.**

**Date, Expiration**—SEE: **Expiration Date.**

**Date of Record**—cut-off date for an investor to be considered the owner of record and eligible to receive rights, dividends, etc. SEE: **Ex-Date.**

**Dated Date**—date a bond was issued and from which date accrued interest is calculated.

**DCA**—SEE: **Dollar Cost Averaging.**

**Dealer**—one who buys and sells from their inventory as a principal for a markup or markdown.

**Death Benefit**—amount of money a beneficiary receives upon death of the contractholder.

**Debenture**—an unsecured bond.

**Deduction**—reduction in the amount of income taxes are figured on. COMPARE: **Tax Credit.**

**Defensive Investments**—stocks with prices that are more stable over time than the broad market and high grade bonds. (Some stocks in a defensive portfolio include utilities, blue-chip stocks, and high-grade preferred stock.) COMPARE: **Aggressive Investments.**

**Deferred Annuity**—an annuity contract that has an accumulation period for a certain amount of time, followed by an annuity stage scheduled to begin at a future date chosen by the contractholder. COMPARE: **Immediate Annuity.**

**Deferred Compensation Plan**—an unqualified retirement plan where employees agree to receive less money now in exchange for retirement benefits. (This is only a contract, not a guarantee, so employees can lose out if company can't pay in the future or employee leaves the company. Benefits are taxed as income to recipient when paid at retirement, and deductible by the corporation when paid.)

**Demand Inflation**—Too much money chasing too few goods. COMPARE: **Cost Inflation.**

**Depreciate**—to decline in value.

**Depreciation**—amortization of a man-made asset so as to allocate the loss in value of the asset over its expected useful life. (e.g., buildings, vehicles, and equipment)

**Depression**—a severe economic downturn caused by excess supply and rising unemployment that leads to falling demand, reduced purchasing power, and deflation of prices. Depressions see dramatic rises in unemployment, acute public caution, and fear.

**Derivative Security**—an instrument whose value is dependent on the value of another underlying security. For example, SEE: **Option.**

**Detachable**—when warrants (or other paired security) may be sold separately to anyone. COMPARE: **Nondetachable.**

**Direct Participation Program (DPP)**—a type of limited partnership investment that allows investors to receive the cash flow, capital gains, losses and tax benefits of the underlying partnership business activity, without the liability incurred with a general partnership.

**Discount**—the amount below par that an investor pays for a bond, preferred stock, or other security. ALSO SEE: **OID.**

**Discount Rate**—interest rate charged by Federal Reserves banks on loans to member commercial banks. Also called **federal discount rate.**

**Discount Yield**—a way to figure yield on T-bills, whereby you divide the discount by the face amount of the bond and multiply that by 360 divided by the days to maturity.

**Disintermediation**—when funds flow out of banks and institutions and into other short-term investments seeking higher yields.

**Distribution Fees**—compensation paid to a distributor (wholesaler, sponsor, underwriter) from sales charges. Also called underwriter's concession. ALSO SEE: **12b-1 Fees.**

**Diversification, Portfolio**—SEE: **Portfolio Diversification.**

**Dividend Exclusion**—rule whereby U.S. corporations do not have to pay corporate income tax on 70% of the dividend income they receive from other U.S. corporations.

**Dividends**—a distribution of company earnings to stockholders as voted on by the board of directors. Dividends are paid out to shareholders on a pro rata basis, based on the percentage of stock ownership in the company. The dividends are usually paid in cash, but they can also be paid out in stock or even sometimes with company products (this is rare, but actually anything of value can be distributed as a dividend).

**DJIA**—SEE: **Dow Jones Industrial Average.**

**Dollar Cost Averaging (DCA)**—an investment method whereby a set dollar amount is invested at regular intervals. (Investor buys fewer shares when the price is high, but more when the price is low, so the average price per share and total investment cost are both lower because the average price per share is lower than the average share price.)

**Double Auction**—pricing mechanism that constantly gets pricing information from buyers and sellers. The instant reporting of trades provides for a true free market, where supply and demand dictate the price of a particular stock issue. COMPARE: **Firm Quote.**

**Double Barreled Bond**—revenue bonds which are guaranteed by an additional (usually larger) entity than just the issuer, giving the investor two sources (revenue and taxes) from which to collect the interest and principal.

**Dow Jones Composite Index**—combines the DJIA, Dow Jones Transportation Average (DJTA), and Dow Jones Utility Average (DJUA) into a single number. ALSO SEE: **DJIA.**

**Dow Jones Industrial Average (DJIA)**—a price-based average of 30 industrial stocks that trade on the NYSE. (Dow Jones also has a number of other averages that track the transportation sector, utility concerns, and others.)

**Downtick**—SEE: **Minus Tick.**

**Due Diligence**—process of researching information, gathering data, and verifying what is learned about the company.

**Due Diligence Meeting**—meeting that serves as the final analysis and verification of the company's financial information and use of proceeds. (Once all questions are answered to everyone's satisfaction, the details of the registration statement, final prospectus, and underwriting agreement are finalized. The price of the issue is also set.)

**Earned Income**—money generated from providing labor, goods, or services. Also called **Active Income.** (e.g., salary, wages, tips, bonuses, employee compensation, pensions, Social Security payments, annuity payments)

COMPARE: **Investment Income, Unearned Income.** ALSO SEE: **Passive Income.**

**Earnings After Taxes (EAT)**—this is figured by subtracting out the taxes that are owed by the company. EAT is also referred to as **net income** or **net income after tax (NIAT)** and is the figure people commonly call **the bottom line.** It is a true indication of the money that was actually made by the company.

**Earnings Before Interest and Taxes (EBIT)**—a company's gross sales, minus returns, minus cost of goods sold, minus selling expenses, minus depreciation. EBIT is also referred to as **operating income.**

**Earnings Per Share (EPS)**—straight division of profit by the number of common, outstanding shares. Also called **Earnings per Common Share.** Earning per share is the value of a company's profit, figured as if it were distributed to all stockholders. The calculation is common earnings divided by outstanding common shares. ALSO SEE: **Fully Diluted Earnings Per Share, Price-Earnings Ratio, Dividend Payout Ratio, Current Yield.**

**EAT**—SEE: **Earnings After Taxes.**

**EBIT**—SEE: **Earnings Before Interest and Taxes.**

**Effective Date of Registration**—the date when final clearance of the prospectus is received from the SEC. (From this point, the underwriters may solicit orders to sell securities.)

**Employees Retirement Income Security Act (ERISA)**—a 1974 law designed to protect workers and ensure that they were treated fairly in their retirement plans. ERISA only applies to corporate (and other private sector) retirement plans, but it excludes government (and other public sector) retirement plans. In order to maintain their favorable tax treatment, all qualified plans must follow ERISA guidelines, including participation by all eligible full-time employees, funding segregated from other corporate accounts, vesting of 100% in fifth year or 20% in third year plus 20% more each year to 100%, all employees in the plan must be treated equally, and employees must receive written description of the plan and the options available to them.

**Equity**—1. an ownership interest in a company. 2. the difference between what has been paid on an obligation and the value of the asset.

**Equity Securities**—instruments that signify an ownership interest in a company. (i.e., stocks)

**ERISA**—SEE: **Employees Retirement Income Security Act.**

**Exchange Privileges**—a privilege offered by some mutual funds whereby an investor can change funds within the same families of funds without sales charges (but this still is a taxable event).

**Exchange Rate**—the price that one country's currency can be converted into another country's currency.

**Exchange Risk**—SEE: **Currency Risk.**

**Exchanges**—place where securities are bought and sold.

**Ex-Date**—the last date that a person can buy a stock and still have time to settle the transaction and be the owner of record to receive rights or dividends. ALSO SEE: **Date of Record, Ex-Dividend, Ex-Rights.**

**Ex-Dividend**—stock that no longer gives the holder the right to collect the upcoming dividend that was announced. ALSO SEE: **Date of Record, Ex-Date.**

**Execution**—to fulfill or perform an order as directed. (Also: the act of signing.)

**Exempt Securities**—securities that do not fall under the rules or jurisdiction of a particular oversight body. (e.g., U.S. government Treasuries) COMPARE: **Nonexempt Securities.**

**Exercise**—the contractholder will make use of his or her rights to buy or sell securities under the contract.

**Exercise Price**—the price at which the contractholder can exercise the option. Also called **strike price.**

**Ex-Legal**—"without a legal opinion;" stamped onto bond documents when a bond issuer does not want to go to the trouble or expense of obtaining a legal opinion on the bond issue.

**Expansion**—growing demand and business activity, generally accompanied by increases in industrial production, consumers who are eager to buy more goods and services, increased demand for housing (especially more new home permits), and a rising stock market. COMPARE: **Contraction.** ALSO SEE: **Business Cycles.**

**Expense Ratio**—the amount of expenses that a mutual fund charges its shareholders each year for running the fund. Formula is expenses divided by fund's net assets. This is the cost of owning a fund. COMPARE: **Load.**

**Expiration Date**—the date before which an option must be exercised.

**Ex-Rights**—stock that no longer gives the holder the right to buy shares from the new rights offering at a discounted rate. ALSO SEE: **Date of Record, Ex-Date.**

**Extension Risk**—the chance that homeowners will be late making payments on their mortgage, which could in turn affect payouts to investors.

**Fair Market Value (FMV)**—the present worth of an asset, based on the price that a reasonably informed buyer would pay and a reasonably informed seller would accept, with no duress or coersion.

**Feasibility Study**—an evaluation or study done to demonstrate to investors the economic soundness of a proposed project and revenue bond issue. (Term used with **revenue bonds.**)

**Fed Funds Rate**—target rate established by the Fed as a way to influence other interest rates.

**Federal Discount Rate**—interest rate charged by Federal Reserve banks on loans to member commercial banks. Also called **discount rate.**

**Federal Funds**—the monies used by commercial banks to cover reserve requirements with the Federal Reserve Banks. Most loans are overnight and are made at the Fed Funds rate.

**Federal Home Loan Mortgage Corporation (FHLMC)**—Nonprofit, federally chartered institution that functions as a buyer and seller of savings and loan residential mortgages.

**Federal Housing Administration (FHA)**—Government agency that insures mortgage loans.

**Federal National Mortgage Association (FNMA)**—The nation's largest, and privately owned, investor in residential mortgages.

**Federal Open Market Committee (FOMC)**—a body that controls the Fed's sale and purchase of government securities. The body is made up of the seven members of the Federal Reserve Board plus the President of the Federal Reserve Bank of New York and four other Federal Reserve Bank Presidents.

**Federal Reserve Banks**—banks that provide services to financial institutions, e.g. check clearing. (One main office in each Federal Reserve district.) All nationally chartered commercial banks must join Federal Reserve and buy stock in its district reserve bank.

**Federal Reserve Board (the Fed)**—Body responsible for U.S. monetary policy, maintaining economic stability and regulating commercial banks.

**Federally Related Institutions**—arms of the U.S. government that have the authority to issue securities for the needs of their agency. Most federally related securities are backed by the full faith and credit of the U.S. government. These include the Government National Mortgage Association (GNMA or Ginnie Mae), Small Business Administration, General Services Administration, and many others.

**Fees**—SEE: **12b-1 Fees, Distribution Fees, Management Fees.**

**Fiduciary**—a person in a position of trust, held by law to high standards of good faith and loyalty.

**Filing Date**—when the registration statement is received by the SEC. (This begins the cooling off period.) ALSO SEE: **Cooling Off Period.**

**Final Prospectus**—a formal written document detailing the financial information, business plan, and operating history of a company that is selling securities, but with changes requested by the SEC, as well as additions of the final offering price, the sales spread that the investment banking firm will make for selling the issue, and a disclaimer that "the securities have not been approved by the SEC" must be printed on the front of every prospectus. (The final prospectus is distributed on the effective date of the offering period, which begins once the SEC has cleared the prospectus for distribution. A copy of the final prospectus must be sent to investors no later than with the sales confirmation.) COMPARE: **Preliminary Prospectus.**

**Financial Risk**—SEE: **Credit Risk.**

**Firm Commitment**—a guarantee by the investment banking firm that the entire issue will be sold. Issuer is guaranteed the money since the investment banker will buy all unsold shares or bonds. COMPARE: **Best Efforts.**

**Firm Quotes**—the price at which the broker-dealer must be willing to sell or buy at least one round lot (100 shares of stock or 5 bonds). (Firm quote is only good for the number of shares quoted.) Backing away from a firm quote is a violation of NASD rules. COMPARE: **Subject Quotes, Workout Quotes.**

**First In, First Out (FIFO)**—inventory method considers the first goods produced or acquired to be the first items sold. (This can make gross sales appear lower, but profit margins higher, because older goods would have been made less expensively before inflation raised the cost of raw materials.) COMPARE: **Last In, First Out.**

**Fiscal Policy**—the federal government's plan for spending, taxation, and debt management. COMPARE: **Monetary Policy.**

**Fixed Annuity Contract**—an annuity where the payments are a fixed monthly amount. COMPARE: **Variable Annuity Contract.**

**Fixed-Income Security**—SEE: **Bonds.**

**Flat, Traded**—SEE: **Traded Flat.**

**Flow of Funds**—statement (often as part of the Indenture Agreement) that details the order in which revenues will be used. (Term used with revenue bond.) ALSO SEE: **Net Revenue Pledge, Gross Revenue Pledge.**

**FMV**—SEE: **Fair Market Value.**

**Forced Conversion**—when a company calls its bonds; therefore, it is more advantageous for the bondholder to convert to common stock than surrender the bond.

**Forward Pricing**—when buy and sell orders for something (such as mutual fund shares) are placed before the final price is known, but the purchase or sale price is based on the next value (NAV) calculation.

**401(k) Plan**—qualified salary reduction plan used for retirement, where employees can elect to contribute pre-tax dollars to a retirement account where money grows tax-deferred. Many employers also match employees' 401(k) contributions. Employees may contribute up to $10,000 (subject to constant revisions). Distributions may begin at age 59½ and must start by age 70½. Early withdrawal penalty is

10%. Benefits paid out during retirement are taxed as ordinary income to the recipient.

**403(b) Plan**—SEE: **Tax-Deferred Annuity Plan.**

**Fourth Market**—the direct trading of large blocks of securities between institutional investors to avoid brokerage commissions. Quotes can be obtained through an electronic communications network service called **Instinet.**

**Free Riding**—when a broker-dealer holds back part of a new issue of stock so that it can be resold later at a better profit than the original public offering price. (This practice is prohibited by NASD rule.) ALSO SEE: **Withholding**

**Front-End Load**—when a sales charge is added to the sales price of an investment when it is purchased (e.g., with a mutual fund, invested amount buys a reduced number of shares because of the load). Front-end load funds are often referred to as **Class A shares.** COMPARE: **No-Load, Back-End Load.**

**Front Running**—when a broker-dealer executes a trade for the firm or an insider based on nonpublic information (e.g., a large block trade that will affect the price of the trade) to the firm's or insider's advantage. In other words, the firm makes their own trade first to gain an advantage. (Prohibited by NASD rule.)

**Full Authorization**—authority granted to another person, permitting buy-sell orders to be executed by that person and allowing the person to withdraw funds from the account. COMPARE: **Limited Authorization.**

**Gain**—SEE: **Capital Gain.**

**GDP**—SEE: **Gross Domestic Product.**

**General Obligation (GO) Bonds**—bonds paid for out of the general revenue of the municipality, which may also use additional tax revenues or borrow funds to cover any shortfall. GO bonds are backed by the full faith and credit of the issuer, however, most require voter approval (especially if the bond issue will raise taxes). COMPARE: **Revenue Bonds.**

**GO Bonds**—SEE: **General Obligation Bonds.**

**Ginnie Mae**—mortgage-backed pass-through certificate, backed by the full faith and credit of the U.S. government. (Named for the GNMA government agency. SEE: **Government National Mortgage Association.**)

**GNMA**—SEE: **Government National Mortgage Association.**

**GNP**—SEE: **Gross National Product.**

**Government National Mortgage Association (GNMA)**—Government owned corporation that guarantees payment of principal and interest to investors that buy its mortgage-backed securities on the secondary markets.

**Government Sponsored Entities (GSE)**—privately owned but publicly chartered entities created by the government to help out farmers, students, homeowners, and others by lowering borrowing costs. Most GSE securities are backed by the agency issuing them and are *not* backed by the full faith and credit of the U.S. government. Some GSEs include Federal Farm Credit Consolidated Bank, Federal Home Loan Bank, Student Loan Marketing

Association (Sallie Mae), Federal National Mortgage Association (FNMA or Fannie Mae), and Federal Home Loan Mortgage Corporation (FHLMC, Freddie Mac).

**Gross Domestic Product (GDP)**—measures the value of all goods and services produced in the United States. Includes consumer spending, government spending, and net value of exports. (Does *not* include net foreign investment.) COMPARE: **Gross National Product.**

**Gross National Product (GNP)**—measures the value of all goods and services produced in the United States, as well as all net foreign investment. GNP includes consumer spending, government spending, and net value of exports. COMPARE: **Gross Domestic Product.**

**Growth, Capital**—SEE: **Capital Growth.**

**Growth Stocks**—common stocks from companies that have shown faster than average increases in earnings over past several years, but they're likely not paying dividends. (Usually have higher price-earnings ratios.)

**GSE**—SEE: **Government Sponsored Entities.**

**High-Yield Bonds**—corporate bonds with a credit rating of BB or lower. Also referred to as **junk bonds** because the companies issuing them may have a poor credit rating or short operating history with little sales or earnings on which to base the price of the bond.

**Hold in Street Name**—securities left in broker-dealer's name and held by the broker-dealer to facilitate future sales.

COMPARE: **Transfer and Ship, Transfer and Hold.**

**Hot Issue**—issue where the market price moves above the public offering price almost immediately after the stock begins trading in the open market (after-market). ALSO SEE: **Free Riding, Withholding.**

**Hypothecation**—using something as collateral.

**Hypothecation Agreement**—allows the broker-dealer to use the securities as collateral. Also referred to as a **margin agreement.**

**IA**—SEE: **Investment Advisor.**

**IDB**—SEE: **Industrial Development Bond.**

**Immediate Annuity**—an annuity contract purchased with a lump sum payment, with the annuity stage scheduled to begin immediately (usually no longer than two months out). COMPARE: **Deferred Annuity.**

**Imputed Interest**—equivalent to interest earned on a zero coupon bond due to its appreciation over time (used by IRS in tax calculations).

**Income**—money generated from any source. ALSO SEE: **Earned Income, Investment Income, Passive Income, Unearned Income.**

**Income, Active**—SEE: **Earned Income.**

**Income, Current**—SEE: **Current Income.**

**Income, Earned**—SEE: **Earned Income.**

**Income, Investment**—SEE: **Investment Income.**

**Income, Passive**—SEE: **Passive Income.**

**Income, Unearned**—SEE: **Investment Income.**

**Income Statement**—a financial report that summarizes an entity's income and expenses over a given period of time. Also called a profit and loss statement. COMPARE: **Balance Sheet.**

**Income Stocks**—common stocks that regularly pay good dividends to stockholders and are in industries where companies are expected to continue doing so. Utilities, banks, and insurance company stocks are good examples.

**Indenture Agreement**—an agreement that must be part of a corporate bond issue under the Trust Indenture Act of 1939. Also called **trust indenture** or **bond indenture agreement,** the agreement is between the issuer and a qualified, independent trustee overseeing protective clauses and promises to bondholders.

**Index**—a statistical composite that measures up and down price movements of a representative sample from a group, as a way to track the overall health and direction of the markets, an industry, a sector, etc. (e.g., S&P 500).

**Index Fund**—a type of mutual fund designed to track a particular recognized index and match its portfolio composition and movements.

**Individual Retirement Account (IRA)**—a personal, tax-deferred retirement account. There are several varieties of IRAs, but most allow contributions of up to $2000 per person per year, with married spouses also able to put in $2000 if filing jointly. (Some IRA plans have immediately tax deductible contributions. All contributions and investment earnings grow tax-deferred until distributions begin at retirement.) ALSO SEE: **Roth IRA, SEP-IRA.**

**Industrial Development Bond (IDB)**—bonds used to finance fixed assets, which are then leased to private corporations. These are a type of revenue bond, but they are usually *not* tax exempt because they are designed to help private parties. Repayment of the debt relies on lease payments from corporate tenants.

**Industrial Revenue Bond**—SEE: **Industrial Development Bond.**

**Inflation**—increase in cost of goods or services; or too much money chasing too few goods.

**Inflation, Cost**—an increase in the cost of goods or services.

**Inflation, Demand**—too much money chasing too few goods.

**Inflationary Risk**—chance that the value of assets or income will decline relative to the prices of other goods and services. Also called **purchasing power risk.**

**Initial Public Offering (IPO)**—when a company that is going public for the first time sells new shares in a new issue stock offering.

**Inside Quote**—highest bid and lowest ask price.

**Insider Trading**—the illegal practice of trading securities on the basis of material information that has not been made public yet, or providing non-public material information to others who trade on the information.

**Insiders**—any persons who have access to confidential or sensitive information about a company before it is released to the public. This definition includes officers, directors, key employees of a company, and stockholders owning over 10% of a publicly traded company.

**Instinet**—allows direct, computer-based trading between institutional investors. (Acronym for Institutional Networks Corporation, owned by Reuters, and is an SEC registered exchange.)

**Instruments, Money Market**—SEE: **Money Market Instruments.**

**Intent, Letters of**—SEE: **Letters of Intent.**

**Interest**—1. A right or share in something (such as a joint account). 2. A charge a borrower pays to a lender for the use of lender's money.

**Interest, Accrued**—SEE: **Accrued Interest.**

**Interest, And**—SEE: **And Interest.**

**Interest, Imputed**—SEE: **Imputed Interest.**

**Interest Rate Risk**—risk that changes in interest rates will adversely affect investment value.

**Investment**—when capital is used to create money via income-producing instruments, or to create capital appreciation from a risk-oriented venture.

**Investment Advisor (IA)**—anyone who gives investment advice for a fee. The compensation can be a flat fee, or it can be a percentage of the assets managed.

**Investment Company**—a firm that assembles a pool of funds from small investors, invests those funds for the group, and collects a management fee for services. (Regulated under the Investment Company Act of 1940.)

**Investment Grade Bonds**—bonds that have one of the top four ratings from Moody's (Aaa, Aa, A, Baa) or S&P (AAA, AA, A, BBB). Also called **bank grade bonds.**

**Investment Income**—money generated from securities or other assets. This could mean interest from bonds, dividends from stocks, or capital gains from the sale of securities. Also referred to as **unearned income.**

**Investment Risk**—chance that adverse conditions will cause an investment's value to drop.

**Investment, Trust**—SEE: **Unit Investment Trust.**

**Investments, Aggressive**—SEE: **Aggressive Investments.**

**Investments, Defensive**—SEE: **Defensive Investments.**

**IPO**—SEE: **Initial Public Offering.**

**IRA**—SEE: **Individual Retirement Account.**

**Issued Stock**—stock that has been distributed by the corporation. (Held by founders, sold to investors, given to employees, etc.)

**Joint Tenants In Common (JTIC)**—a type of joint account where upon the death of one party, that party's interest in the account is passed to his or her estate. This means that each of the joint tenants can name their own beneficiary. With this arrangement, parties can have unequal shares. COMPARE: **Joint Tenants with Right of Survivorship.**

**Joint Tenants with Right of Survivorship (JTROS)**—a type of joint account where upon the death of one party, that party's interest in the account is passed to the other parties of the account. To have this arrangement, all parties must have an equal share in the account. This is a common arrangement between spouses. COMPARE: **Joint Tenants In Common.**

**JTIC**—SEE: **Joint Tenants In Common.**

**JTROS**—SEE: **Joint Tenants with Right of Survivorship.**

**Junk Bonds**—SEE: **High-Yield Bonds.**

**Keogh Plan**—H.R.-10 (Keogh) plans are retirement account plans for people who have self-employed income. Keogh plans are tax deductible to the contributor, and the funds accumulate tax free until distribution at retirement at age 59½. Distributions are taxed as ordinary income. There is a 10% penalty for withdrawals before age 59½, and withdrawals must start no later than age 70½. Maximum contributions by the employer are 25% of net (20% of gross) earned income or $30,000, whichever is *less*. (This plan may be contributed to in addition to an IRA plan.)

**Know Your Customer**—concept that says it's responsibility of broker-dealer and RR to have a complete and accurate understanding of a client's financial situation so as to give appropriate advice and suitable recommendations.

**Last In, First Out (LIFO)**—inventory method considers the last goods produced or acquired to be the first items sold. (This can make gross sales appear higher, and profit margins lower, because the most recent goods made would have higher raw material costs compared to raw materials bought awhile ago.) COMPARE: **First In, First Out.**

**Legal Opinion**—when a bond attorney examines a bond issue to determine its legality, and whether or not it qualifies for tax exempt status. ALSO SEE: **Unqualified Legal Opinion, Qualified Legal Opinion, Ex-Legal.**

**Legislative Risk**—the risk of a change in the law that adversely affects an investment. This usually refers to domestic policies, such as new clean air requirements or tax law changes. COMPARE: **Political Risk.**

**Letters of Intent (LOI)**—a commitment by an investor to invest a certain amount of money within 13 months in exchange for being entitled to receive breakpoint sales charge rates now. (Letter may be back-dated up to 90 days to encompass previous investments.) ALSO SEE: **Breakpoint Sales.** COMPARE: **Rights of Accumulation.**

**Level 1**—access level on NASDAQ system. SEE: **NASDAQ.**

**Level 2**—access level on NASDAQ system. SEE: **NASDAQ.**

**Level 3**—access level on NASDAQ system. SEE: **NASDAQ.**

**Level Load**—a small sales charge paid annually for the life of a mutual fund. (The amount does not change, thus the word *level*.) Level load funds are often referred to as **Class C shares.**

**Liabilities**—any debt, financial obligation, or claim that another has on the ownership of an asset. (e.g., credit card bill, car installment loan, home mortgage). SEE: **Assets, Net Worth.**

**LIFO**—SEE: **Last In, First Out.**

**Limited Authorization**—authority granted to another person, only permitting buy-sell orders to be executed by that person and not allowing the person to withdraw funds from the account. COMPARE: **Full Authorization.**

**Limited Partnership**—an investment structure that allows investors to receive the cash flow, capital gains, losses, and tax benefits of the underlying partnership business activity without incurring the liability of a general partner.

**Liquid Net Worth**—SEE: **Net Spendable Income.**

**Liquidation**— the selling off of securities or other assets to raise cash for withdrawal, to pay an amount owed, or as the result of a bankruptcy.

**Liquidity**—ease with which assets can be converted into cash (at or near full market value).

**Liquidity Risk**—the chance that an investor may not be able to convert an investment, security, or asset into cash when needed.

**LMV**—SEE: **Long Market Value.**

**Load**—sales charge added to the price of an investment (e.g., a spread is added to NAV for a mutual fund to get the POP). This is also referred to as a **sales charge.** This is the cost of buying a mutual fund. COMPARE: **Expense Ratio.** ALSO SEE: **No-Load, Front-End Load, Back-End Load.**

**LOI**—SEE: **Letters of Intent.**

**Long**—a position in a stock, option, etc. when an investor **buys** it. You can also say that the investor is the **owner** or **holder** of the option, or is **long** the option. (These terms are synonymous: **buyer = owner = holder = long.**) COMPARE: **Short.**

**Long Call**—buy a call option (a bullish strategy). COMPARE: **Short Call, Long Put.** ALSO SEE: **Short Put.**

**Long Market Value (LMV)**—the present worth of a client's portfolio at the end of the valuation period. Also referred to as **current market value.** COMPARE: **Short Market Value.**

**Long Put**—buy a put option (a bearish strategy). COMPARE: **Short Put, Long Call.** ALSO SEE: **Short Call.**

**Loss**—SEE: **Capital Loss.**

**Management Companies**—companies that are in the business of managing money for other people and as such have a manager responsible for actively managing the company's investment portfolio. (e.g., mutual fund; Management companies can be either open-end or closed-end.) ALSO SEE: **Open-End Management Company, Closed-End Management Company.** COMPARE: **Nonmanagement Companies.**

**Management Fees**—compensation paid to the Financial Advisor and others responsible for managing the mutual fund portfolio, paid as a percentage of the fund's net asset value.

**Margin**—amount customer must have on deposit with broker-dealer to buy securities on credit.

**Margin Account**—one of the two basic types of accounts that can be opened with a broker-dealer (the other being a cash account).

**Marginable Securities**—securities eligible for a client to buy and sell in a margin account. (Mutual funds and other new issues are *not* marginable securities.)

**Marginal**—meaning that only the portion of income that falls above each bracket is taxed at that higher level. ALSO SEE: **Tax Bracket, Progressive Tax.**

**Markdown**—money subtracted from the price of securities when a broker-dealer buys securities for customers. (A **markup** is money added to the price of securities when a customer buys securities from a broker-dealer.) COMPARE: **Commission.**

**Market Maker**—brokerage firm that has taken a position (built up an inventory) in a certain stock, and stands ready to honor quoted bid and ask prices for round lots. (Market makers help maintain OTC market stability, allowing OTC to function.) COMPARE: **Specialist.**

**Market Risk**—risk common to all investments of the same type or classification, owing more to broad market conditions or investor sentiment toward a particular sector of stocks or bonds. Also called **systematic risk.**

**Market Value**—stock price that investors will pay in marketplace, driven by supply and demand.

**Markup**—money added to the price of securities when customer buys securities from a broker-dealer. (A markdown is money subtracted from the price of securities when a broker-dealer buys securities for customers.) COMPARE: **Commission.**

**Maturity**—the date when a bond becomes due and payable. ALSO SEE: **Term Maturity, Series Maturity, Serial Maturity.**

**Maturity, Serial**—SEE: **Serial Maturity.**

**Maturity, Series**—SEE: **Series Maturity.**

**Maturity, Term**—SEE: **Term Maturity.**

**MBIA**—Municipal Bond Investors Assurance, a credit insurance company. SEE: **Credit Enhancement.**

**Minus Tick**—term for when the previous trade occurred at a lower price than the one before it, so the price of a security is going down. Also called **downtick.** COMPARE: **Plus Tick.**

**Monetary Policy**—the government's mechanism through which it can exert control over the supply and cost of money. Monetary policy also has the goals of economic growth, full employment, and international balance of payments, plus monetary policy tries to maintain stability in prices, interest rates, and financial markets. COMPARE: **Fiscal Policy.**

**Money Market Instruments**—short-term debt obligations that are due and payable in 12 months or less. Examples of money market instruments are **repurchase agreements, commercial paper,** and **negotiable CDs.**

**Money Supply**—the total amount of money in circulation in a country's economy at a given time, including not only cash, but also deposits in savings and checking accounts. Too much money in circulation leads to inflation.

**Moody's**—Moody's Investors Service is a rating service, providing information on bond issues, commercial paper, preferred stock, and municipal short-term notes. It publishes several bond and stock books providing analysis of issuers. (For bond rating service, SEE: **Investment Grade Bonds**) Moody's also publishes facts, information and research on bonds.

**MSRB**—SEE: **Municipal Securities Rulemaking Board.**

**Multiplier Effect**—1. the effect that investment has in creating additional income and other benefits to all those who participate in a project, through ownership, providing labor, or being a supplier to that business. 2. In monetary theory, this refers to the expansion of money supply resulting from banks' ability to lend money in excess of its reserves.

**Municipal Bond**—debt obligations of state and local governments. ALSO SEE: **General Obligation Bonds, Revenue Bonds.**

**Municipal Bond Investors Assurance (MBIA)**—a credit insurance company. SEE: **Credit Enhancement.**

**Municipal Securities**—SEE: **Municipal Bonds.**

**Municipal Securities Rulemaking Board (MSRB)**—self-regulatory organization responsible for all activities related to municipal bonds and other intrastate government securities that are issued, sold, or traded.

**Municipals**—another term for municipal bonds.

**Munis**—another term for municipal bonds.

**Mutual Fund**—a pooled investment, managed by an investment company, offering an undivided interest in the portfolio to holders of shares in the fund. Three advantages of mutual funds are liquidity, diversification, and professional management.

**Naked Call**—SEE: **Uncovered Call.**

**Naked Option**—SEE: **Uncovered Option.**

**NASD**—SEE: **National Association of Securities Dealers.**

**NASDAQ**—National Association of Securities Dealers Automated Quotation (NASDAQ) system that links broker-dealers by telephone and computer to facilitate trades. The service has three levels:

**Level 1:** This shows *only* the highest price and lowest ask price (the **inside quote**) for any NASDAQ stock that has at least two active market makers. These quotes, though, aren't firm until confirmed by another broker-dealer. RR have access to this level but cannot use it to guarantee any prices.

**Level 2:** This provides quotes from *multiple market makers,* showing the current firm quote (good for a minimum of 100 shares) and the quote size available. This level of access is primarily for institutional investors.

**Level 3:** This has the same info as levels 1 and 2, but also lets market makers *update or change their stock quotes.* This level is for market makers only.

**National Association of Securities Dealers (NASD)**—self-regulatory organization responsible for all activities related to securities sold in the over-the-counter market. Also has regulatory authority over investment banking, investment companies, and limited partnerships.

**NAV**—SEE: **Net Asset Value.**

**Net Asset Value (NAV)**—the value of a mutual fund and its shares, derived by taking the fund's assets minus liabilities, then dividing that result by the number of outstanding shares. NAV is the bid price at which fund shares are redeemed. COMPARE: **Public Offering Price.**

**Net Income**—SEE: **Earnings After Taxes.**

**Net Spendable Income**—figure arrived at by subtracting expenses from income (usually calculated for individuals, not companies).

**Net Worth**—the value that is left over after adding up all assets and subtracting all liabilities from that total. (Also referred to as **shareholder's equity** when talking about a company's net worth.) ALSO SEE: **Assets, Liabilities.**

**New York Stock Exchange (NYSE)**—self-regulatory organization responsible for all activities related to securities listed and traded on New York Stock Exchange and some regional exchanges (e.g., Philadelphia Stock Exchange).

**No Load**—when no sales charge is added to the price of an investment (e.g., no spread is added to a mutual fund so NAV equals POP). COMPARE: **Front-End Load, Back-End Load.**

**Nominal Quotes**—pricing quote for informational purposes only, if given with a qualified statement. COMPARE: **Firm Quotes.**

**Nondetachable**—when warrants (or other paired security) can only be transferred with the bond, preferred stock, or security they were sold with. COMPARE: **Detachable.**

**Nonexempt Securities**—securities under the jurisdiction of a particular oversight body and thus must comply with their rules. (e.g., SEC) COMPARE: **Exempt Securities.**

**Nonmanagement Companies**—investment companies with a fixed portfolio of investments that investors put their money into, so there is no need for a portfolio manager. (e.g., unit investment trust) COMPARE: **Management Companies.**

**Nonqualified Annuity**—variable annuity that had the investment amount paid for with after-tax dollars. This allows it to have a cost basis so that only a portion of the withdrawal amount (interest portion) is subject to taxation. COMPARE: **Qualified Annuity.**

**Nonqualified Retirement Plan**—SEE: **Unqualified Retirement Plan.**

**Nonvoting Stock**—subclasses of common stock (e.g., Class A, Class B) that do not carry voting rights.

**NYSE**—SEE: **New York Stock Exchange.**

**NYSE Composite**—measures all common stocks listed on the New York Stock Exchange, including four subindexes (Industrials, Transportation, Utilities, Finance). The index tracks the change in market value of NYSE stocks, adjusted to reduce effects of market capitalization changes, new listings, and delistings.

**Offer, Tender**—SEE: **Tender Offer.**

**Offer Wanted**—ask request by broker-dealer when there is no activity in the stock, but the dealer wants to buy some and wants traders to submit a bid. COMPARE: **Bid Wanted.**

**Offering, Rights**—SEE: **Rights Offering.**

**OID**—SEE: **Original Issue Discount.**

**Open-End Management Company—** investment company that continually offers shares to investors, and uses the funds raised to operate a packaged security, such as a mutual fund. The company is open end because it does a continuous offering, with the fund continuing to grow over time. Shares of the open-end fund can only be sold and redeemed by the fund that issued them. COMPARE: **Closed-End Management Company.**

**Open Market Operations—**when the Fed sells or buys government securities as a means of controlling supply of, and demand for, money. Interest rates are affected because as the Fed buys and sells securities, it makes more or less money available for banks to lend.

**Option—**the right, but not obligation, to buy or sell something at a predetermined price and under predetermined conditions (time limit and/or other conditions).

**Option, Covered—**SEE: **Covered Option.**

**Option, Naked—**SEE: **Uncovered Option.**

**Option, Uncovered—**SEE: **Uncovered Option.**

**Original Issue Discount—**bonds that are sold at a discount from par value when they are first issued.

**Outstanding Stock—**stock presently held by shareholders. (e.g., investors, founders, employees)

**Overbought—**a market condition whereby prices have risen so sharply that some are predicting a price decline (correction) in the overall market: because there are few buyers left, a price drop is imminent. COMPARE: **Oversold.** ALSO SEE: **Correction.**

**Overlapping Debt—**SEE: **Coterminous.**

**Oversold—**a market condition whereby prices have fallen so sharply that some are predicting a price rise in the overall market: because there are few sellers left, a price rise is imminent. COMPARE: **Overbought.**

**Owner—**one who possesses (or has the right to possess) a thing. Also called **long.** SEE: **Long.**

**Packaged Securities—**investments created by combining several other investments. (e.g., **Mutual Funds, REITs**)

**Paper, Commercial—**SEE: **Commercial Paper.**

**Paper Act—**SEE: **Securities Act of 1933.**

**Par Value—**1. the face value of a security. (e.g., $1000 is typical for a bond); 2. arbitrary value assigned by a company to authorized stock.

**Parity—**when the value of convertible bonds and the common stock price intersect, such that the conversion would be an even exchange.

**Partnership—**a contract between two or more persons to pool money, resources, and talents in a business, project, or venture in exchange for a share of the profits (or losses) generated by their association. COMPARE: **Corporation, Sole Proprietorship.**

**Passive Income—**income derived from any business activity in which the person is not an active participant. (e.g., limited partnerships or real estate). Tax law changes in 1986: passive losses are only deductible against passive income. COMPARE: **Earned Income.**

**Payroll Deduction Savings Plan**—SEE: **401(k) Plan.**

**PE Ratio**—SEE: **Price-Earnings Ratio.**

**Peak**—the top of a business cycle, where expansion begins to level off as demand catches up with supply. From this point, production and prices will begin to fall. COMPARE: **Trough.** ALSO SEE: **Business Cycles.**

**Penny Stock**—over-the-counter (OTC, i.e., non-listed) equity securities that trade for less than $1 per share (although they may trade up to $5 to $10 per share) but are highly volatile because companies who issue the stock usually have short and erratic operating histories.

**People Act**—SEE: **Securities Exchange Act of 1934.**

**Pink Sheets**—name of the daily publication of the National Quotation Bureau showing wholesale interdealer listing bid and ask prices of OTC **stocks** not listed on NASDAQ. (Pink sheets get their name from the color of paper they're printed on.) COMPARE: **Yellow Sheets.**

**Pipeline Theory**—SEE: **Conduit Theory.**

**Plus Tick**—term for when the previous trade occurred at a higher price than the one before it. In essence, the price of the security is heading up. Also called an **uptick.** COMPARE: **Minus Tick.**

**Plus Tick Rule**—rule that says a short sale can only occur on a plus tick or zero-plus tick. COMPARE: **Minus Tick.**

**Point**—equal to 1% change in the value of a bond. (Fractions of a point are called **Basis Points,** where 1 basis = 1/100 a point).

**Point, Basis**—SEE: **Basis Point.**

**Political Risk**—the risk of a change in government policy that adversely affects an investment. This usually refers to a foreign country, such as when an industry is nationalized or protectionist measures are adopted that affect specific import or export products. COMPARE: **Legislative risk.**

**POP**—SEE: **Public Offering Price.**

**Portfolio Diversification**—spreading out risk by holding investments in varying types, amounts, and asset classes.

**Portfolio Management**—a means of bringing a portfolio in line with customer investment objectives, tilting the balance from extremely aggressive to very conservative.

**Portfolio Turnover**—the percentage of a fund's portfolio that's sold during the year, expressed as a percentage to show how often mutual funds buy and sell their holdings. Portfolio turnover is calculated as gross proceeds from sales divided by total assets.

**Preemptive Rights**—the right of existing stockholders to buy, in proportion to their current holdings, additional shares of a new issue by the company before the stock is offered to the public. Also called **antidilution provision.**

**Preferred Stock**—an ownership interest in a corporation that pays a specified dividend rate. Owners of preferred stock have limited liability, get paid dividends before common stockholders, and can recoup assets in a liquidation before common stockholders. Preferred stockholders usually do not receive voting rights or preemptive rights and do not get to share in the capital appreciation of the company. COMPARE: **Common Stock.**

**Preliminary Prospectus**—gives some details about the offering to gauge investor interest, but must clearly state that it is "not an offer to sell securities nor solicit orders." (Because this warning is printed in red, a preliminary prospectus is sometimes referred to as a **red herring.**) The preliminary prospectus gives financial details about the issue and about the company, including a detailed use of proceeds statement, history of the company, management team, and risks to investors. (The preliminary prospectus is distributed during the cooling off period. There's no final public offering price, and all information is subject to change before the final prospectus is issued.) COMPARE: **Final Prospectus.**

**Premium**—1. the amount above par that an investor pays for a bond, preferred stock, or other security; 2. the price an investor pays to buy an insurance policy or option contract.

**Premium, Call**—SEE: **Call Premium.**

**Premium, Waiver of**—SEE: **Waiver of Premium.**

**Preservation of Capital**—an investment objective that ensures that the original amount of money invested is as safe as possible.

**Price, Exercise**—SEE: **Exercise Price.**

**Price, Strike**—SEE: **Strike Price.**

**Price-Earnings Ratio**—an indication of how much an investor is paying for a company's earning power. Company with high growth potential can command higher PE multiple. PE is derived by taking market price per share of stock and dividing that by earnings per share.

**Pricing, Forward**—SEE: **Forward Pricing.**

**Primary Market**—sale of new securities issues directly by the issuer to investors. COMPARE: **Secondary Market.**

**Primary Marketplace**—where new securities issues are sold. COMPARE: **Secondary Marketplace.**

**Primary Offering**—sale of stock in the primary market, with the proceeds from the sale of stock going into the company treasury. COMPARE: **Secondary Offering.** ALSO SEE: **Combined Offering.**

**Principal**—1. With regard to a loan, the amount originally borrowed. COMPARE: **Interest.** 2. With regard to an investment, the face amount. 3. With regard to a transaction, a person who grants another person (an agent) authority to represent him or her in dealings with third parties. 4. In general, one of the parties to a transaction (such as a dealer), as opposed to those who are involved as agents or employees (such as a Registered Representative).

**Principal, Risk of**—SEE: **Risk of Principal.**

**Privilege, Conversion**—SEE: **Conversion Privilege**

*Pro Rata*—a method of proportionate allocation, meaning that each gets a percentage share based on the percentage of stock owned.

**Profit and Loss Statement**—SEE: **Income Statement.**

**Profit Sharing Plan**—plan where the employer agrees to make contributions to the retirement accounts of employees annually when the company makes profits above a certain level. Benefits paid out during retirement are taxed as ordinary income to the recipient. (When all employees are treated equally, this is a qualified, tax deductible plan.)

**Program Trading**—automated, computerized trading.

**Progressive Tax**—a system of taxation whereby people with higher incomes pay a higher percentage of their income in taxes. This is accomplished by the use of tax brackets. COMPARE: **Regressive Tax.**

**Prospectus**—a formal written document detailing the financial information, business plan, and operating history of a company that is selling securities. ALSO SEE: **Preliminary Prospectus, Final Prospectus.**

**Proxy**—a kind of absentee ballot, whereby the stockholder can vote on matters without having to attend an annual stockholder's meeting.

**Prudent Man Rule**—rule says that fiduciaries must act as any prudent man or woman would do when making investment decisions, with care and skill, to preserve capital, seek reasonable income, and avoid unreasonable risk and speculative investments. This rule serves as a guideline for those who have the duty and responsibility of investing money on behalf of beneficiaries. COMPARE: **Legal List.**

**Public Offering Price (POP)**—the price of buying a mutual fund share, derived by taking the NAV and adding the sales charges. POP is the ask price at which fund shares are purchased. COMPARE: **Net Asset Value.**

**Public Offering Prospectus**—document that explains the limited partnership investment, business plan, financial information, and information on the general partners. The prospectus must be filed with the SEC.

**Purchasing Power Risk**—SEE: **Inflationary Risk.**

**Put**—option that gives an investor the right to sell a certain number of shares of a security, at a pre-determined price, before a certain date. COMPARE: **Call.**

**Qualified Annuity**—variable annuity has the invested amount paid for with pretax dollars (e.g., an annuity in an IRA account, or a retirement account paid for by an employer). This means that although the money is allowed to grow tax deferred, all money taken out is fully taxable as ordinary income. COMPARE: **Nonqualified Annuity.**

**Qualified Legal Opinion**—a legal opinion issued by a bond attorney which says that the bond issue is only valid with certain qualifications (perhaps because of the inability to confirm some essential fact, or because of pending litigation). COMPARE: **Unqualified Legal Opinion, Ex-Legal.**

**Qualified Retirement Plan**—an employer-sponsored retirement account paid for with pretax dollars. This means that although the money is allowed to grow tax deferred, all money taken out is fully taxable as ordinary income. (Plan must treat all employees equally, must be IRS approved to qualify for tax deductible contributions, and must comply with ERISA.) COMPARE: **Unqualified Retirement Plan.**

**Quotes, Firm**—SEE: **Firm Quotes.**

**Quotes, Nominal**—SEE: **Nominal Quotes.**

**Quotes, Subject**—SEE: **Subject Quotes.**

**Quotes, Workout**—SEE: **Workout Quotes.**

**Rating Agencies**—entities that research corporate and municipal bond issues, and assign them a rating. Two notable agencies are Moody's and Standard & Poor's (S&P). Also referred to as **rating services.**

**Ratings**—values on a point scale that represent the likelihood that the issuer will default on a debt obligation. ALSO SEE: **Rating Agencies, Investment Grade Bonds.**

**Real Estate Investment Trust (REIT)**—separate trusts which specialize in real estate investment, collect funds to control real estate, and manage the portfolio.

**Real Estate Mortgage Investment Conduit (REMIC)**—a vehicle for issuing mortgage-backed securities, with the flexibility to issue the securities into different groups based on the maturity and the risk level of the pool of mortgages that back the securities.

**Recession**—a less severe economic downturn, characterized by two consecutive quarters of decline in the country's level of business activity as defined by the gross domestic product (GDP).

**Record, Date of**—SEE: **Date of Record.**

**Recovery**—a period of business activity marked by increasing production as supply is trying to catch back up to increasing demand. This is the precursor to an expansion phase of the business cycle and growth for the economy. ALSO SEE: **Business Cycles.**

**Red Herring**—term used to describe the preliminary prospectus because the disclaimer ("This is not an offer to sell securities nor solicit orders.") is often printed on the cover in red ink. SEE: **Preliminary Prospectus.**

**Redemption**—repayment of a debt obligation at maturity, or earlier.

**Redemption, Sinking Fund**—SEE: **Sinking Fund Redemption.**

**Redemption Price**—NAV price for mutual funds.

**Refunding**—replacing a debt obligation with another debt security that has different terms, such as a lower interest rate. ALSO SEE: **Advance Refunding.**

**Reg. T**—Federal Reserve Board Regulation T states that a person must have on deposit the higher of $2000 or 50% of the purchase price of the eligible securities bought on margin. (Reg. T also says that settlement must occur within five business days.)

**Registered Bonds**—bonds where the owner's name is recorded with the registrar, and interest payments are sent automatically or paid electronically. COMPARE: **Bearer Bonds.**

**Registered Representative (RR)**—an employee of a stock exchange member firm who acts as an account executive for clients, giving advice on which securities to buy and sell, and collecting a commission through the firm for services rendered. RRs must be licensed by the Securities and Exchange Commission (SEC), by one or more self-regulatory organizations (SRO), and by the state(s) in which he or she engages in securities activities.

Glossary

**Registrar**—appointed by the corporation to oversee the issuance of stock certificates, to make sure that no more than the total number of authorized shares of stock are in circulation, and to certify the authenticity of corporate bonds. (By law, the registrar must be an entity separate from the company, and the same entity cannot act as both registrar and transfer agent for the same corporation.) COMPARE: **Transfer Agent.**

**Registration, Effective Date of**—SEE: **Effective Date of Registration.**

**Registration Statement**—statement filed with the SEC that must disclose the purpose of the offering, how much money the company is going to raise, how the money will be spent, information on the company and its business, information on the company's principals (especially any prior securities trouble), any legal proceedings the company is involved in, and any other pertinent facts that investors would need to know to make an informed decision about buying the company's stocks or bonds. Also called a **registration letter.**

**Regressive Tax**—a system of taxation whereby all people pay the same tax rate, regardless of income (e.g., a sales tax). COMPARE: **Progressive Tax.**

**Regular Way**—settlement designation of T + 3 for corporate and municipal securities, and T + 1 for U.S. government securities. (COMPARE: cash settlements, which settle same day.)

**Regulation T**—SEE: **Reg. T.**

**Reinvestment Risk**—risk that the investor cannot replace a paid off investment with one of a similar yield. ALSO SEE: **Call Risk.**

**REIT**—SEE: **Real Estate Investment Trust.**

**REMIC**—SEE: **Real Estate Mortgage Investment Conduit.**

**Repayment Risk**—the chance that homeowners will default on the mortgage loan. ALSO SEE: **Credit Risk.**

**Repurchase Agreement**—an arrangement between buyer and seller to sell an asset now and then buy it back for a fixed price, and usually within a stated time frame. Also called **repo.** (This is a money market instrument.)

**Reserve Requirements**—percentage of deposits that commercial banks are required to keep on deposit, either on hand at the bank or in the bank's own accounts—in other words, money the bank can't lend to customers. By raising or lowering reserve requirements, the Fed controls the supply and cost of money, and the quality of credit. (The original purpose of reserve requirements was to help avert financial panic by giving depositors confidence that their deposits were safe and accessible, but they have also become a policy tool.)

**Reserve Split**—an attempt to adjust the price of a stock upward by decreasing the number of outstanding shares without changing the percentage of company ownership or total market value of shares held by each stockholder. ALSO SEE: **Stock Split.**

**Residual Claim (on Assets)**—In a bankruptcy, common stockholders are last in line to recoup any money. After all creditors and lien holders have been paid, common stockholders have a claim on any assets that are left.

**Return on Investment**—amount of money earned from invested capital.

**Revenue Bonds**—bonds paid for from the income (revenue) generated by a specific project. These are usually used for public works projects (e.g., roads or water treatment plants). Revenue bonds are backed by tolls or user fees from a project. Revenue bondholders usually cannot claim other revenue sources or general tax collections to pay the debt. COMPARE: **General Obligation Bonds.**

**Rights, Preemptive**—SEE: **Preemptive Rights.**

**Rights of Accumulation (ROA)**—breakpoint sales at a future time once the total amount of money invested has reached the breakpoint. (From that point forward, all newly invested money qualifies for the reduced sales charges.) ALSO SEE: **Breakpoint Sales.** COMPARE: **Rights of Accumulation.**

**Rights Offering**—an offer to existing common stockholders that allows them to buy additional shares of newly issued stock before it is offered for sale to the public. This is done to honor the preemptive rights of existing common stockholders. (Term used with **standby underwriting.**)

**Risk, Call**—SEE: **Call Risk.**

**Risk, Capital**—SEE: **Capital Risk.**

**Risk, Credit**—SEE: **Credit Risk.**

**Risk, Currency**—SEE: **Currency Risk.**

**Risk, Exchange**—SEE: **Currency Risk.**

**Risk, Extension**—SEE: **Extension Risk.**

**Risk, Financial**—SEE: **Credit Risk.**

**Risk, Inflationary**—SEE: **Inflationary Risk.**

**Risk, Interest Rate**—SEE: **Interest Rate Risk.**

**Risk, Investment**—SEE: **Investment Risk.**

**Risk, Legislative**—SEE: **Legislative Risk.**

**Risk, Liquidity**—SEE: **Liquidity Risk.**

**Risk, Market**—SEE: **Market Risk.**

**Risk, Political**—SEE: **Political Risk.**

**Risk, Purchasing Power**—SEE: **Inflationary Risk.**

**Risk, Reinvestment**—SEE: **Reinvestment Risk.**

**Risk, Repayment**—SEE: **Repayment Risk.**

**Risk, Systematic**—SEE: **Market Risk.**

**Risk, Timing**—SEE: **Timing Risk.**

**Risk of Bankruptcy**—the danger that a company will not be able to meet its debt service obligations. This is an important indication of a company's financial strength and credit risk. A company that is leveraged too much may not be able to pay off its debts if rates rise or the economy declines.

**Risk of Principal**—the chance that invested capital will decrease in value. Here one thinks of the investor who buys a stock that becomes worthless.

**ROA**—SEE: **Rights of Accumulation.**

**Rollover**—when an IRA account balance is transferred directly from one custodian to another, or when the investor takes possession of the IRA funds (permitted once each year) and redeposits the funds into another IRA account within 60 days. (Lump sum distributions from a qualified retirement plan, such as when a person changes employers, may be rolled over into a new retirement plan without incurring tax consequences. There's no limit on the amount investors can rollover, but any amount not rolled over within that time frame is subject to ordinary income tax and an added 10% penalty if they're not yet 59½ years of age.)

**ROP**—Registered Options Principal.

**Roth IRA**—an Individual Retirement Account (IRA) with contributions that are *not* tax deductible, but which permits qualified distributions to be taken tax-free upon retirement. Since the Roth IRA funds are taxed before they go into the plan, they are allowed to come out tax free. Like regular IRAs, the Roth IRA permits persons with earned income to invest up to $2000 individually or $4000 for married couples filing jointly. A 10% penalty is imposed on distributions that start before age 59½, except in the case of disability, medical expenses, education expenses, first-time home purchase, or death.

**RR**—SEE: **Registered Representative.**

**S&P 500**—index of stocks chosen to achieve distribution by broad industry groups, roughly relative to composition of the NYSE market. Each stock is representative of its industry group, so price movements are responsive to changes in that sector. Total market capitalization of a stock and its trading volume are important considerations, as stocks in the index are weighted. COMPARE: **DJIA.**

**Salary Reduction Savings Plan**—SEE: **401(k) Plan.**

**Sale, Wash**—SEE: **Wash Sale.**

**Sales Literature**—any written, electronic, or oral material distributed by a brokerage firm upon the request of a client, sent by the firm to a selected group of people, or disseminated in any other way such that the brokerage firm has control over who receives the material. (e.g., brochure, research report, e-mail newsletter). COMPARE: **Advertising.**

**Savings**—when a portion of income or other money is not spent immediately.

**SEC**—SEE: **Securities and Exchange Commission.**

**Secondary Market**—place where securities are bought and sold after original issue, with proceeds going to the investor selling the security. COMPARE: **Primary Market.**

**Secondary Marketplace**—where securities are bought and sold after their original issue. COMPARE: **Primary Marketplace.**

**Secondary Offering**—sale of stock in the primary market, with the proceeds from sale of stock going to present shareholders. COMPARE: **Primary Offering.** ALSO SEE: **Combined Offering.**

**Securities**—any investment relationship with a company (and the instrument that represents that investment). This can be equity in a company (stock), debt with a company (bond), a pooling of investment instruments (mutual fund), or any instrument transferring a future right (option).

**Securities Act of 1933**—requires all securities to be registered before they can be sold to the public, requires use of a prospectus with full disclosure of all pertinent information, and prohibits false and misleading information with several antifraud provisions. (Focus is on primary market.) Also called **Paper Act.**

**Securities and Exchange Commission (SEC)**—a federal government agency created by the Securities Exchange Act of 1934 to oversee the securities industry, establish regulations governing the issuance and sale of securities, and enforce the securities laws enacted by Congress.

**Securities Exchange Act of 1934**—regulates secondary market activity, outlaws fraud and market manipulation, regulates sales and activity by company insiders, requires broker-dealer firms and sales reps to be registered, and created the Securities and Exchange Commission (SEC). (There is never an exemption from the antifraud provisions of this act.) Also called the **People Act.**

**Securities Investor Protection Corporation (SIPC)**—established as a nonprofit corporation by an act of Congress in 1970 to protect investors from broker-dealer insolvency. SIPC provides a fund that insures the cash and securities in an investor's account up to $500,000 total, with a limit of $100,000 paid in cash for each separate customer account.

**Security, Derivative**—SEE: **Derivative Security.**

**Security, Fixed-Income**—SEE: **Bonds.**

**Self-Regulatory Organization (SRO)**—created by federal securities laws to help maintain a fair and orderly trading environment, to help oversee various aspects of the securities industries, and to aid in enforcement of securities rules and regulations. Each SRO also adopts and enforces its own industry rules.

**Seller**—one who sells something. Also called short. SEE: **Short.**

**Seller's Concession**—the amount of commission that will be paid to the selling group for issues that they actually sell.

**Seller's Option**—SEE: **Delayed Delivery.**

**Selling, Breakpoint**—SEE: **Breakpoint Selling.**

**Selling Away**—doing a trade or collecting a commission that does not go through the broker-dealer firm. (Prohibited by NASD rules.)

**Selling Dividends**—telling clients to buy stocks right before ex-date just to capture a dividend is considered unethical since stock price will drop equal to the dividend amount right after the ex-date, but client has an immediate taxable event. (Prohibited by NASD rules.)

**Selling Group**—a group formed to help distribute and sell an issue to the public. (Selling group members do not invest money to buy part of an offering like a syndicate [purchase group] does.) COMPARE: **Syndicate.**

**SEP-IRA**—a Simplified Employee Pension-Individual Retirement Account with contributions that are tax-deferred, often used by small businesses or sole proprietors without other retirement plans. Employers can make contributions equal to 15% of employee's total compensation, up to maximum $25,500. Contributions and investment earnings grow tax-deferred until distributions begin at retirement (age 59½) or disability. All distributions are taxed as ordinary income. Except for higher contribution limits, all rules for regular IRAs apply, including early withdrawal penalties. (10% penalty imposed if distributions start before age 59½, except in cases of disability, medical costs, education expenses, first-time home purchase, death. 50% penalty imposed if distributions don't start by age 70½.)

**Separate Account**—an account established and maintained by an insurance company under state law, where income, gains, and losses stay in that account, apart from income, gains, or losses generated by any other insurance company account. A separate account maintained by an insurance company has variable annuity contract payments put into it.

**Serial Maturity**—when bonds are all issued at the same time but come due on different staggered redemption dates.

**Series Maturity**—when bonds come due on different dates staggered apart because they were issued at different times.

**Shareholder's Equity**—SEE: **Net Worth.**

**Short**—a position in a stock, option, etc. when an investor **sells** it. You can also say that the investor is the **writer** of the option, or is **short** the option. (These terms are synonymous: *seller = writer = short.*) COMPARE: **Long.**

**Short Against the Box**—SEE: **Shorting Against the Box.**

**Short Call**—sell a call option (a bearish or neutral strategy). COMPARE: **Long Call, Short Put.** ALSO SEE: **Long Put.**

**Short Market Value (SMV)**—the present worth of the client's short stock position at the end of the valuation period. COMPARE: **Long Market Value.**

**Short Put**—sell a put option (a bullish or neutral strategy). COMPARE: **Long Put, Short Call.** ALSO SEE: **Long Call.**

**Short Sale**—when an investor sells a security that he or she doesn't own. (The investor *borrows the security* from a broker-dealer firm to sell it now and hopes to repay the security later by buying it at a reduced price at some point in the future.)

**Shorting Against the Box**—a technique where an investor does a short sale with the same security in which the investor also owns a long position. The short sale locks in a gain against drops in price, and the long stock the investor owns can be delivered later to cover the short sale. Tax law changes have curtailed the use of this technique. COMPARE: **Wash Sale.**

**Sinking Fund Redemption**—when a municipality calls bonds as soon as it has accumulated enough in a sinking fund to pay off the issue.

**SIPC**—SEE: **Securities Investor Protection Corporation.**

**SMV**—SEE: **Short Market Value.**

**Sole Proprietorship**—business enterprise set up by a single individual. COMPARE: **Corporation, Partnership.**

**Special Cash Account**—alternate name for a cash account; one of the two basic types of accounts that can be opened with a broker-dealer (the other being a margin account).

**Special Situation Stocks**—common stocks that are undervalued for a short period of time but are about to rise significantly because of an upcoming event. This could be a pending merger or acquisition, a new management team, or new product introduction.

**Specialist**—member of stock exchange given authority to act as broker and dealer (agent and principal) for other brokers and given responsibility of maintaining a fair and orderly market. (Specialist must be ready to buy and sell from the firm's own account to stabilize the market when there are supply and demand imbalances.) COMPARE: **Market Maker.**

**Speculation**—assuming higher risk in anticipation of higher returns.

**Speculative Stocks**—common stocks of rapidly growing companies that have prospects for above-average growth but with very volatile prices. Examples of speculative stocks would be high-tech companies and other start-ups. These stocks are more aggressive and are generally relied upon solely for capital appreciation since they usually offer no dividends.

**Spendable Income**—SEE: **Net Spendable Income.**

**Split**—SEE: **Stock Split; Reverse Split.**

**Spread**—the difference between what the underwriters pay to buy an issue and what public offering price they're able to sell the securities.

**SRO**—SEE: **Self-Regulatory Organization.**

**Standard & Poor's (S&P)**—provides numerous investment-related services including credit ratings, debt ratings, indexes, and research information. (For bond rating service, SEE: **Investment Grade Bond**) ALSO SEE: **S&P 500.**

**Standby Underwriting**—when an investment banking firm guarantees the issuing company that the firm will buy all shares that are not bought as part of the new issue offering. (Term used with **rights offering.**)

**Statutory (Voting)**—type of voting that follows the one share, one vote rule, where stockholders get a single vote on each issue or board member. COMPARE: **Cumulative (Voting).**

**Stock, Authorized**—SEE: **Authorized Stock.**

**Stock, Common**—SEE: **Common Stock.**

**Stock, Issued**—SEE: **Issued Stock.**

**Stock, Nonvoting**—SEE: **Nonvoting Stock.**

**Stock, Outstanding**—SEE: **Outstanding Stock.**

**Stock, Penny**—SEE: **Penny Stock.**

**Stock, Preferred**—SEE: **Preferred Stock.**

**Stock, Treasury**—SEE: **Treasury Stock.**

**Stock Certificates**—instruments that represent equity ownership in the company.

**Stock Power**—a document, separate from the stock certificate, granting another party power of attorney to transfer the stock.

**Stock Split**—an attempt to adjust the price of a stock downward by increasing the number of outstanding shares without changing the percentage of company ownership held by each stockholder, and without changing the total market value of all outstanding shares. In other words, as of the date of the stock split the stockholders all own the same proportionate share of the company as they did before, and the total value of their stock holdings is also the same. ALSO SEE: **Reverse Split.**

**Strike Price**—the price at which the contractholder can exercise the option. Also called **exercise price.**

**STRIPS**—zero coupon bonds backed by the U.S. government.

**Strong Dollar**—when the dollar can be exchanged for more of a foreign currency. This makes foreign imports cheaper, but it makes it more expensive for other countries to buy U.S. goods. Also, a strong dollar attracts deposits and foreign investment money into the United States. COMPARE: **Weak Dollar.**

**Subchapter M Theory**—SEE: **Conduit Theory.**

**Subject Quotes**—price is still negotiable or subject to final confirmation; not firm. ALSO SEE: **Workout Quote.** COMPARE: **Firm Quotes.**

**Subscription Price**—price at which a new offering is purchased, specifically the price of a rights offering. (Usually must be lower than the market price to absorb the new shares into the marketplace.)

**Surrender Value**—current value of the separate account units or cash value of an insurance policy, minus any outstanding loans and interest, minus fees. ALSO SEE: **Cash Value.**

**Sweetener**—SEE: **Warrants.**

**Syndicate**—group of investment banking firms working together to purchase all of the securities from an issuer, and resell them to the public. A syndicate is also called a purchase group. COMPARE: **Selling Group.**

**Systematic Risk**—SEE: **Market Risk.**

**T + 1**—Trade plus one business day. Settlement time for U.S. government securities.

**T + 3**—Trade plus three business days. Settlement time for corporate, municipal securities.

**T + 5**—Trade plus five business days. Settlement time as required by Regulation T.

**T-Bills**—SEE: **Treasury Bills.**

**T-Bonds**—SEE: **Treasury Bonds.**

**T-Notes**—SEE: **Treasury Notes.**

**T-Receipts**—SEE: **Treasury Receipts.**

**Tax, Progressive**—SEE: **Progressive Tax.**

**Tax, Regressive**—SEE: **Regressive Tax.**

**Tax Advantages**—investment objective whereby money is invested in structured ways or in particular kinds of investments to minimize taxes, defer taxes, or avoid taxes altogether.

**Tax Bracket**—section on the tax schedule that shows what percentage of income is owed in taxes based on the income being reported. (Tax brackets are marginal, meaning that only the portion of income that falls above each bracket is taxed at that higher level.)

**Tax Credit**—an actual dollar-for-dollar reduction in the amount of taxes owed. COMPARE: **Deduction.**

**Tax-Deferred Annuity Plan**—retirement plan that allows employees of nonprofit organizations, tax-exempt organizations and schools to invest money tax-deferred, usually through a payroll deduction plan. Employees may contribute up to $10,500, and employers can match up to 25% of employee's compensation or $30,000, whichever is less. Distributions may begin at age 59½ and must start by age 70½. Early withdrawal penalty is 10%. Benefits paid out during retirement are taxed as ordinary income. Also called a **Tax Sheltered Annuity (TSA)** or **403(b) Plan.**

**Tax Sheltered Annuity (TSA)**—SEE: **Tax-Deferred Annuity Plan.**

**Taxable Bonds**—long-term bonds issued by a municipality for private purpose projects (e.g., bond issued to build a sports team stadium). Because of the private purpose rules, the interest income on this type of bond is not exempt from federal taxation.

**Taxable Equivalent Yield**—the yield that would have to be paid out on a taxable bond in order for it to equal the yield paid out on a tax-free bond. (In other words, what yield on a corporate bond would give an investor the same yield as a tax-free municipal bond.)

**Taxation**—The process of a government levying a charge upon people or things.

**Telephone Solicitation**—any telephone call initiated to encourage a person to buy a good or service or make an investment. (Defined by Telephone Consumer Protection Act of 1991.)

**Tender Offer**—an offer to buy bonds (or other securities), often at a premium over current trading levels.

**Tendering**—when an issuer goes into the secondary market to buy back its own securities.

**Term Maturity**—when all bonds issued come due at the same time.

**Third Market**—the buying and selling of exchange listed stocks in the over-the-counter market by nonexchange member brokers and institutional investors.

**Time Draft**—a document that designates the date on which payment will be made. (Term used with **Banker's Acceptances.**)

**Timing Risk**—the danger that an investor will not pick the best time to buy or sell an investment and thus not maximize his or her gain. (Timing risk actually involves four risks rolled into one: getting in, getting out, transaction costs, and tax consequences.)

**Tombstone Ads**—special ads placed by investment companies, underwriters, or broker-dealer firms to draw attention to a prospectus (or other major business event) without the ad being a specific offer to sell or buy securities. (These can run during the cooling off period.)

**Total Return**—an investment objective that seeks capital growth with asset appreciation and interest or dividends.

**Traded Flat**—when bonds trade at the quoted price without accrued interest. (e.g., zero coupon bonds or when issuer is in default.) COMPARE: **And Interest.**

**Trading Profits**—profits earned from short term trades.

**Tranches**—separate maturity groups. (Term used with **CMOs.**)

**Transfer Agent**—appointed by the corporation to maintain ownership records, to issue and cancel certificates, and to resolve problems of lost, stolen, or destroyed stock certificates. (The transfer agent is the final arbiter in disputes of stock certificate authenticity.) COMPARE: **Registrar.**

**Transfer and Hold**—securities transferred into customer's name but held by the broker-dealer. COMPARE: **Transfer and Ship, Hold in Street Name.**

**Transfer and Ship**—securities transferred into customer's name and shipped to customer. COMPARE: **Transfer and Hold, Hold in Street Name.**

**Treasuries**—securities that are debt obligations of the U.S. government, backed by the full faith and credit of the U.S. government. (Considered the most risk-free investment money can buy.) U.S. Treasury securities can be U.S. Treasury bills (T-bills), U.S. Treasury notes (T-notes), and U.S. Treasury bonds (T-bonds).

**Treasury bills**—U.S. government bonds that mature in one year or less. (Face value is $10,000, price is quoted at discount from par.)

**Treasury bonds**—U.S. government bonds that mature in ten years or more. (Face value is $1000, prices are quoted as a percentage of par in 1/32 increments.)

**Treasury notes**—U.S. government bonds that mature in 1-10 years. (Face value is $1000, prices are quoted as percentage of par in 1/32 increments.)

**Treasury receipts**—zero coupon bonds based on Treasuries, but not backed by U.S. government.

**Treasury stock**—stock reacquired by the corporation. (It's issued, but not outstanding. Treasury stock may be held to resell at a future date, or reissued for incentives, bonuses, retirement plans, etc.)

**Trough**—bottom of a business cycle, where contraction begins to turn upward. Supply no longer exceeds demand, so production and prices begin to rise. COMPARE: **Peak.**

**Trust, Real Estate Investment**—SEE: **Real Estate Investment Trust.**

**Trust Account**—an account set up to benefit one party (beneficiary) but controlled by a third party (fiduciary).

**Trust Indenture** — SEE: **Indenture Agreement.**

**Trust Indenture Act of 1939**—act passed by Congress to give corporate bond investors the same kinds of protection that corporate stock investors have under the law. If a company is selling bonds within a 12-month period that are valued at more than $5 million and with maturities of longer than 270 days (9 months), the act requires corporate bonds to have a bond indenture agreement. SEE: **Indenture Agreement.**

**TSA**—Tax Sheltered Annuity. SEE: **Tax-Deferred Annuity Plan.**

**Turnover**—SEE: **Portfolio Turnover.**

**12b-1 Fees**—special assessments that allow mutual funds to collect money to reimburse marketing and distribution expenses. Also referred to as **distribution fees.**

**UGMA**—SEE: **Uniform Gift to Minors Act.**

**UIT**—SEE: **Unit Investment Trust.**

**UTMA**—SEE: **Uniform Transfer to Minors Act.**

**Uncovered Call**—when the writer of the call option does not own the stock to back up the contract. (This is a position of unlimited risk.)

**Uncovered Option**—when the writer of the option does not own the stock to back up the contract. COMPARE: **Covered Option.**

**Underwriter's Concession** — SEE: **Distribution Fee.**

**Underwriter's Spread**—compensation made up of the managing underwriter's fee, underwriting fee, and seller's concession. SEE: **Seller's Concession.**

**Underwriting, Standby**—SEE: **Standby Underwriting.**

**Unearned Income**—SEE: **Investment Income.** COMPARE: **Earned Income.**

**Uniform Gift to Minors Act (UGMA)**—act provides a simple way for property to be transferred to minors without a formal trust account and without an official guardianship having to be established. Instead, a single custodian is appointed, who acts as trustee of the account in charge of affairs for the minor. ALSO SEE: **Uniform Transfer to Minors Act.**

**Uniform Practice Code**—a set of rules set up by the NASD to establish standard methods and procedures for transactions between members. These rules have to do with how trades are executed and settled, such as establishment of regular way transaction settlement as T+3 for corporate and municipal securities, good delivery rules, confirmation procedures, and ex-date assignment, among other things.

**Uniform Transfer to Minors Act (UTMA)**—act adopted by all 50 states, mirroring the UGMA with two exceptions: the kind of gifts that may be given to a minor's account are expanded beyond cash and securities to include real estate, and other assets, and the age at which minors can take control of the account was raised to 21 or 25, depending on the state. ALSO SEE: **Uniform Gift to Minors Act.**

**Unissued Stock**—stock that has been authorized but not yet issued.

**Unit Investment Trust (UIT)**—a non-management investment company that invests in a fixed portfolio of securities. (The UIT will dissolve when the bonds mature, or on a specified date if the UIT is holding other securities.)

**Units**—piece of ownership with variable annuity contracts. (Same as shares with mutual funds.) SEE: **Accumulation Units, Annuity Units.**

**Unqualified Legal Opinion**—a legal opinion issued by a bond attorney which says that after thoroughly researching the bond issue, the municipality has the legal authority to issue the bonds. If the bonds qualify for tax exempt status, that will also be stated in the legal opinion. COMPARE: **Qualified Legal Opinion, Ex-Legal.**

**Unqualified Retirement Plan**—an employer-sponsored retirement account paid for with after-tax dollars. This allows it to have a cost basis so that only a portion of the withdrawal amount (interest portion) is subject to taxation. (Plan can treat employees differently, does not need IRS approval since contributions are not tax deductible, and no need to comply with ERISA.) COMPARE: **Qualified Retirement Plan.**

**Uptick**—SEE: **Plus Tick.**

**Value, Current Market**—SEE: **Long Market Value and Fair Market Value.**

**Value, Par**—SEE: **Par Value.**

**Value Line (VL)**—Value Line Investment Survey (VL) is a weekly subscription advisory service that ranks hundreds of investment debt securities for safety of principal and timeliness of repayment. It estimates which will have the best or worst price performance in the coming year and assigns each corporate debt issuer a risk rating based on stock price movements compared to market averages. (Other information on companies is also available through its various research reports and analyses.)

**Variable Annuities**—packaged securities, often put together by insurance companies, who are responsible for managing the funds in the investment portfolio. Variable annuity contract makes payments to the holder that vary based on value of underlying investments. COMPARE: **Fixed Annuity Contract.**

**Vesting**—the right of ownership that an employee gains in retirement plans and other benefits from years of service at a company.

**Voting, Cumulative**—SEE: **Cumulative Voting.**

**Voting, Statutory**—SEE: **Statutory Voting.**

**Waiver of Premium**—annuity clause that states if the investor becomes disabled and unable to make required payments, payments will be suspended but benefits will remain in force.

**Warrants**—an additional security offered along with the sale of another security, which allows the warrant holder to buy shares of common stock at some point in the future at a predetermined price. (These are a **sweetener.**)

**Wash Sale**—1. when the same securities (or substantially similar securities) are bought and sold simultaneously or within a short period of time. (Wash sales that occur 30 days before or 30 days after a transaction are not capital losses per IRS rules.). 2. buying and selling the same stock to show trading activity. (NASD rules prohibit this.)

**Weak Dollar**—when the dollar can be exchanged for less of a foreign currency. This makes foreign imports expensive but encourages other countries to buy more U.S. goods. COMPARE: **Strong Dollar.**

**When Issued**—a security that has been authorized but not officially issued yet. The shares are still tradeable, although the official settlement date may not be known (NASD's Uniform Practices Committee decides the final settlement date, settlement is Issue plus three days.)

**Wilshire 5000**— index measures the performance of all U.S.-based exchange-traded stock companies. Bulletin board traded companies are excluded because there is no readily available price data. The index is adjusted on a regular basis, with over 6500 capitalization-weighted stock returns.

**Withdrawal Plans**—a means of mutual fund redemption where the investor can receive fixed payments on a regular basis. Also referred to as **payout.** (Not designed to guarantee lifetime income like an annuity.)

**Withholding**—when a broker-dealer holds back part of a new issue so that it can be kept in the broker-dealers own account, or sold to family members, employees, or other insiders. (This practice is prohibited by NASD rules.) ALSO SEE: **Free Riding.**

**Workout Quote**—a price that is approximate because it depends on size of the order or market activity; not firm. ALSO SEE: **Subject Quotes.** COMPARE: **Firm Quotes.**

**Writer**—one who opens a position in a stock, option, etc., when an investor sells it. You can also say that the investor is the **seller** of the option, or is **short** the option. (These terms are synonymous: *seller = writer = short.*) COMPARE: **Long.**

**Yellow Sheets**—the name of the daily publication of the National Quotation Bureau showing wholesale interdealer listing bid and ask prices of OTC **bonds** not listed on the NASDAQ. (Yellow sheets get their name from the color of paper they are printed on.) COMPARE: **Pink Sheets.**

**Yield**—the rate of return earned on an investment.

**Yield, Current**—SEE: **Current Yield.**

**Yield, Discount**—SEE: **Discount Yield.**

**Yield, Equivalent**—SEE: **Taxable Equivalent Yield.**

**Yield, Taxable Equivalent**—SEE: **Taxable Equivalent Yield.**

**Yield-to-Call (YTC)**—the total rate of return that an investor will receive by holding a bond until it is called by the issuer, assuming the call is made at the first opportunity.

**Yield to Maturity (YTM)**—the total rate of return that an investor will receive by holding a bond to maturity.

**Zero Coupon Bonds**—bonds that are sold at a deep discount from par because they do not make periodic interest payments, but instead pay the full face amount at maturity.

**Zero Downtick**—SEE: **Zero-Minus Tick.**

**Zero-Minus Tick**—term for when the previous trade occurred at the same price as the one before it, but at a price lower than the last different price. The price of the security is stable, but it is still showing a downward trend. This is also referred to as a zero downtick. ALSO SEE: **Minus Tick, Short Sale.** COMPARE: **Zero-Plus Tick.**

**Zero-Plus Tick**—term for when the previous trade occurred at the same price as the one before it and at a higher than the last different price. The price of the security is stable but still in an upward trend. This is also referred to as a zero uptick. ALSO SEE: **Plus Tick, Short Sale.** COMPARE: **Zero-Minus Tick.**

**Zero Uptick**—SEE: **Zero-Plus Tick.**

# Index

Page numbers in *italics* indicate charts.

# Appendix 1: Answer Keys

## Answers to Chapter Quizzes

**Chapter 1** Securities and Markets; Investment Risks and Policies

| | |
|---|---|
| 1. C | 16. A |
| 2. B | 17. D |
| 3. D | 18. D |
| 4. B | 19. A |
| 5. B | 20. D |
| 6. D | 21. D |
| 7. A | 22. B |
| 8. D | 23. A |
| 9. C | 24. D |
| 10. D | 25. B |
| 11. B | 26. D |
| 12. C | 27. C |
| 13. A | 28. D |
| 14. B | 29. B |
| 15. C | 30. C |

**Chapter 3** Variable Contracts and Retirement Plans

| | |
|---|---|
| 1. B | 5. A |
| 2. D | 6. B |
| 3. A | 7. C |
| 4. C | 8. D |

**Chapter 2** Investment Companies, Taxation, and Customer Accounts

| | |
|---|---|
| 1. A | 13. B |
| 2. C | 14. A |
| 3. B | 15. B |
| 4. D | 16. C |
| 5. D | 17. B |
| 6. A | 18. B |
| 7. D | 19. A |
| 8. B | 20. A |
| 9. C | 21. D |
| 10. A | 22. B |
| 11. C | 23. C |
| 12. C | 24. D |

**Chapter 4** Securities Industry Regulations

| | |
|---|---|
| 1. D | 9. C |
| 2. C | 10. A |
| 3. C | 11. B |
| 4. B | 12. B |
| 5. B | 13. C |
| 6. A | 14. D |
| 7. B | 15. B |
| 8. C | 16. A |

# Answers to Practice Exam #1

1. **C** Variable annuities don't have capital gains. All invested money and other gains grow tax-deferred and are taxed as ordinary income when withdrawn. (Page 149)

2. **D** The investment adviser of a mutual fund must *always* adhere to a fund's objectives when making trades—not "usually" in "I." An adviser's fee is paid to the Investment Adviser and this fee is the largest single management fee associated with the fund. For taxes, the investment adviser/ fund manager advises all shareholders of the tax status for fund distributions, giving them a 1099. (Page 84, 2.1.2.2 and Page 90, 2.1.4.7)

3. **A** The yield-to-maturity (YTM) is always lower than the coupon (nominal) rate for a *premium bond*. (Page 40, Diagram is Key!)

4. **B** Member firms must file advertising and sales literature with the NASD advertising department within ten days of use—no matter how old the firm is. (Page 191, 198)

5. **B** UGMA (Uniform Gift to Minors Act) accounts allow the Donor to also be the Custodian for the account. For example, the mother of a child could be both donor and custodian for the child's account. (Page 125, 2.3.3.5)

6. **D** The correct answer is 5.26%. Remember, our formula: **Current Yield (CY) = Coupon ÷ Price**, so 5 ÷ 95 = 5.26%. Remember to put in the coupon rate (or interest rate) first, and also make sure that your calculator has the ability to carry out the answer to enough decimal places. Some of the business calculators are nice, but they only give you two places. (Page 39)

7. **B** A company would have to amend its charter or Articles of Incorporation by a shareholder vote to authorize more shares. (Page 5)

8. **A** Of the products mentioned, only the variable products use a separate account that gives the client investment choices. (Page 143, 3.1.1.1 and Page 150, 3.1.3)

9. **A** The Securities Act of 1933 (referred to as the Paper Act) created the prospectus to provide full and fair disclosure to potential investors. (Page 172, 4.1.1)

10. **B** Open-end mutual fund is from an open-end investment company, which is authorized to do a continuous offering of shares. (They're always considered new shares and require a prospectus.) (Page 80, 2.1.1.4)

11. **B** Outstanding shares are currently held by shareholders (Page 5, 1.1.1.1), so the client must buy them from another investor who is willing to sell them. This occurs in the secondary (resale) Market. (Page 31)

12. **D** Only in advance of sales presentation is correct, because the prospectus must be provided *no later than* the time of the sales presentation. Watch for this kind of wording on the test! Sales presentation materials aren't granted any exemptions, so under rules for requirement to deliver prospectus, sales presentation materials can't be used unless they are accompanied or preceded by a prospectus. (Page 195)

13. **A** This is one of the more involved calculations you may have to do. The formula is **$ Sales Charge ÷ POP = Sales Charge %.** To calculate, subtract the POP ($17.51) from NAV ($16.63) to get the sales charge $ ($.88). Take this ($.88) divided by POP ($17.51) to get 5.03%—*not* 5.3%! (Page 102, Formulas)

14. **C** The sinking fund provides funds to assist with the retirement of the bond issue, so it can offer a lower rate and has a more stable price. Corporate bonds have trustees per

the Indenture Act of 1939. (Page 17, Page 14)

15. **D** A UIT (unit investment trust) does not use any of the three choices listed, since the portfolio is fixed and is not managed. (Page 79, 2.1.1.1)

16. **B** A closed-end fund is the example of a publicly traded fund. This type of fund authorizes a specific number of shares, which are sold by an initial public offering. After the initial public offering is completed, the fund closes and future purchases, or liquidations, are made in the secondary market. (Page 79, 2.1.1.3)

17. **D** All three choices in this question would be viewed as a major change in mutual fund operation. Therefore, each requires shareholder approval. (Page 87, 2.1.2.7)

18. **C** The client is responsible for investment choices and market risk for choices made. A Registered Representative makes recommendations and is not involved in making investment decisions for a client, unless a limited power of attorney or discretionary authority are granted—and this question mentions neither. (Page 143, 3.1.2.1)

19. **C** A cooling off period refers to the period of time right before a new issue comes to market. Since an actual product does not exist during this time, a Registered Representative may gather indications of interest in the proposed new security. Registered Representatives must send a preliminary prospectus (red herring) to clients who indicate an interest. (Page 110, 2.1.13.1)

20. **B** A Registered Representative can't accept a postdated check for a new issue. Mutual funds and other new issues (such as an initial public offering—IPO) can't be bought on credit, so think of a postdated check as extending credit until the check date. (Page 202, 4.4.2)

21. **C** A state specific bond fund is correct, since that type of fund is usually free from federal, state and local taxes if issued by the client's state of residence. Thus, the higher the client's tax rate, the better the performance. The aggressive growth fund could possibly provide better total return, but risk is higher compared to a municipal bond fund. Government bond funds and corporate bond funds are both fully taxable. (Page 28)

22. **D** None of the choices are valid for SIPC. SIPC is consumer protection against broker-dealer default, not against market risk. Futures and commodities are distracters for this question, and are not even securities. (Page 183, 4.1.3)

23. **D** Up to $100,000 can be a cash claim. The total coverage is up to $500,000, including any claim made for cash. (Page 197, 4.3.3)

24. **B** Since there's no resale market for open-end mutual fund shares, a request for cash distribution is accomplished by redeeming (canceling) the number of shares required to meet the distribution. Canceled shares are never resold and are considered "destroyed." (Page 83 and Page 106, 2.1.12)

25. **B** To calculate tax equivalent rate, remember our formula: **Taxable Equivalent Yield = Muni Bond Yield ÷ (1 − Investor Tax Rate)**, so subtract $1 - .37 = .63$. Then, divide the coupon rate for the bond (5%) or .05, by that answer (.63), to get 0.07936 or 7.94%. (Page 29)

26. **A** Exchange refers to a central marketplace, such as the NYSE located on Wall Street. Securities sold OTC use a computer system to provide quotes and conduct business. No central marketplace exists for OTC. After-hours trading may occur in some OTC markets, and NASDAQ stocks trade OTC. (Pages 31–34)

27. **B** The investor chooses the investments for the separate account, and the rate of return does depend on performance of the investments in the separate account (I, IV). The payments are guaranteed to continue for life, but the amount and principal aren't guaranteed so II. is

wrong. The investor bears the market risk, so III is wrong. (Page 143, 3.1.2.1)

28. **C** Corporations receive a 70% exclusion for dividends received from stock owned in other U.S. companies. Individuals do not receive this same exclusion. (Page 8)

29. **C** The price of a mutual fund share is higher right before the ex-date, so a client who buys before the ex-date is getting fewer shares and gets the dividend distribution, which is an immediate taxable event. This practice is called selling dividends and is not in the client's best interest. (Page 38, Page 211, 4.5.3)

30. **A** From the choices listed, acceptable investments for moderate risk include the blue-chip stock fund, the balanced fund, and the bond fund. However, the question asks for the investment with growth potential, so the best answer is blue-chip stock fund. (Stocks = Growth, Bonds = Income) (Page 55)

31. **B** A private transaction is defined as a Licensed Representative selling a product their broker-dealer does not offer. If this is done without the broker-dealer's permission, it is referred to as selling away and is prohibited by NASD. (Page 206, 4.4.3.7)

32. **C** The need for the $14,000 within seven months is of concern, and those funds should be in a money market. Since the client's tolerance for risk is high, possible investments for the balance of the funds could be the aggressive growth fund and a sector fund. (Page 52 and Page 61, 1.5.3)

33. **B** Gifts received from a mutual fund distributor can't exceed $50 over a one-year period. Also, for the test, keep in mind a mutual fund distributor can also be called a mutual fund underwriter. (Page 203, 4.4.3.5)

34. **D** Contributions made to a traditional IRA are pretax dollars, but distributions are fully taxable. A Roth IRA does not allow pretax contributions, but does offer advantages of tax-deferred growth in the account and tax-free distributions. (Page 159, 3.2.1.8)

35. **C** Number of outstanding shares is number of shares issued minus treasury shares. (5,400,000 − 200,000 = 5,200,000) Remember, treasury shares are shares once issued and repurchased from shareholders. (Page 5)

36. **D** Reduced sales charges are available for front-end load funds, but the reduced sales charge is called a breakpoint. A breakpoint is a price reduction for buying a large volume of shares. (Page 104, 2.1.10.1)

37. **B** Registered Principal duties include supervising Registered Representatives, approving new accounts, and approving all trades. They're not always members of NYSE. (Could be NASD or other SRO.) (Page 178, Page 211)

38. **C** Variable life policies are unique in that a policyholder gets one vote for each $100 of cash value in the policy. (This is different than the one share – one vote that applies to stocks and mutual funds.) (Page 153)

39. **A** Since we mention in the text that qualified plans must treat all employees equally under ERISA guidelines, then we can deduce that nonqualified plans may discriminate. Don't be afraid of questions where you don't have direct knowledge—use what you know to answer. (Page 161, 3.2.3)

40. **A** S&P ratings of BBB or better are called investment grade. Those ratings are BBB, A, AA, and AAA. (Page 15, Chart)

41. **B** Don't be thrown by the word *probate* in "II"—it means that assets go into an estate and court upon death. Even if you don't know the meaning of that term, you should still be able to get this question right. If you know JTROS accounts have equal ownership, you can throw out IV and in turn answers A and D, leaving B as the only choice that includes I— equal ownership. (Test may also use JTWROS—joint account with right of survivorship.) (Page 125, 2.3.3.2)

42. **D** Blue-chip stocks are more stable, larger capitalization stocks that quite often pay a dividend. Small caps (capitalization) are usually newer, smaller companies who may reinvest their earnings in R and D instead of paying a dividend. Utility stocks are generally known for their income and are often a good choice for growth and income. (Page 57)

43. **C** A bond being called refers to the *issuer* (issuing company or government) having the right to repurchase bonds after the call date, if they choose to do so. The first choice is trying to confuse you—since it refers to your client selling calls it is referring to options (which also use the term *call*). Read all choices carefully, because D is a trick. (Page 19)

44. **C** Subchapter M of the IRS code refers to the conduit theory. It states that 90% or more of the net investment income earned by the fund must be distributed to shareholders, or else the investment company (fund) must pay tax on the full amount. (Page 114, 2.2.1.1)

45. **D** The fixed annuity contains all of the choices listed in the question. Fixed tells you that the interest rate is fixed, and there is no market risk for the investor because the principal is guaranteed. The only risk the investor has is purchasing power risk, meaning the possibility that the fixed annuity rate of return will not keep up with inflation. (Page 143, 3.1.2.1)

46. **A** The Maloney Act of 1938 set up the NASD (National Association of Securities Dealers) as the SRO (self-regulatory organization) for the over-the-counter (OTC) market. (Page 175, 4.1.2.3)

47. **B** Two reports (semiannual) are required each year. One of these reports must be an audited report. (Page 98)

48. **C** Utilities are the only example listed in this question that's a defensive stock, defined as stocks of companies likely to perform consistently through all economic cycles. (Page 55)

49. **D** Investment bankers do not loan money, but assist in bringing new issues to market. An investment banker (underwriter) may buy securities from a company and resell those securities to the public—especially if the underwriter made a firm commitment or does a standby underwriting. (Page 35)

50. **A** Existing stockholders may want to buy additional stock from a new issue being offered to protect their present level of ownership—called a pre-emptive right. If existing stockholders do not buy all of the new issue, an underwriter is normally standing-by to buy the remaining shares and market them to the public (standby underwriting). (Page 21)

51. **C** Municipal bond issues usually use a competitive bid process to get an underwriter (investment banker) to ensure that taxpayers who must repay the bonds get the best deal. (Page 35)

52. **B** Continuing commissions must be discussed prior to resignation from your present firm. If it's not discussed and there's no contract in advance, you won't receive commissions after you leave. (Page 198, 4.4.3.4)

53. **D** Cumulative voting means all the shareholder's votes could be placed on one issue if desired. Four issues will be voted on at the meeting, and the shareholder has 2000 shares of stock (4 Issues × 2000 Shares = 8000 Votes). 8000 votes could be cast for INFO. (Page 9)

54. **D** While many variable annuities are not annuitized (receiving a guaranteed lifetime income), they are still viewed as having two distinct periods—a pay-in stage and a pay-out stage. (Page 147, 3.1.2.5).

55. **C** Do not confuse mutual funds with annuities! Mutual funds cannot offer lifetime income. (Page 91, 2.1.4.12)

56. **B** Ginnie Maes (pass-through certificates offered by GNMA—Government National Mortgage Assn.) and Treasuries (T-bills, T-

notes, and T-Bonds) are all direct obligations of the U.S. Government (backed by full faith and credit—and taxing authority). As such, they are considered extremely safe issues. (Page 24 and Page 25, 1.1.2)

57. **C** If a fee for advice is charged, a Registered Representative must also register as an investment adviser. Power of attorney (POA), or limited power of attorney, would be an issue for discretion over an account and would concern who has trading authority. (Page 184, 4.1.4.2 and 4.1.4.3)

58. **A** A U-5 form is needed to relocate to a new broker-dealer. You will also complete a new U-4 and related forms before actually being employed as a Registered Representative for a different broker-dealer. (Page 177)

59. **B** FIFO (first in-first out) is the default method chosen by the IRS if the client does not make a choice for taxation, because this approach would normally be the highest exposure to taxation (oldest shares usually have the lowest cost basis). With identified shares, clients can keep good records and use the most favorable holding period and cost basis for their situation. (Page 118, 2.2.2.4)

60. **C** All three fees are deducted from the *gross premium*. (Page 155)

61. **B** The transfer agent for a mutual fund does issue and redeem shares for client's account. In addition, the transfer agent will provide a trade confirmation for each transaction and keep track of client names and addresses. The transfer agent is *not* responsible for the safekeeping of a fund's assets. (Page 87, 2.1.2.6)

62. **B** Keogh plans are unique because they are *not* available for incorporated businesses. Remember, the text said it is for people with self-employed income. (Page 160, 3.2.2)

63. **B** An insider is defined as any person who has access to nonpublic information. Simply having the information is not of concern. Acting on the information, or giving inside infor-

mation to others who may profit or avoid a loss, is of major concern. (Page 197)

64. **B** Dollar cost averaging is a method of lowering the average cost per share of a mutual fund by always buying the same dollar amount of the fund. This means the number of shares purchased will vary, depending upon the price, but it by no means infers that a profit may be guaranteed. (Page 105, 2.1.11)

65. **D** Profit sharing plans may be very effective for business, since they reward employees for a good year, but in a bad year, no definite contribution is required. (Page 163)

66. **B** A tombstone ad is the only ad that may be run prior to a security being released for sale to the public. One purpose of the ad is to help determine the overall interest in the proposed issue. (Page 188, 4.2.1.1)

67. **C** The term *ex-legal* means no opinion will be rendered by a bond counsel. This approach can be used for municipal bonds if there's little need to prove the bond is tax exempt, such as a public school issue. (Page 29)

68. **A** Risk for a sector (specialized) fund is generally higher compared to a diversified fund approach. Risk versus reward has to be a main discussion point, as well as the client's tolerance for risk. (Page 65 and Page 93)

69. **A** While the 1035 exchange is very flexible, the only allowable choice in this question is life to annuity. To help you here, think of the 1035 exchange as always coming from life insurance (or going only annuity to annuity). This cancels a few choices. (Page 156, 3.1.3.4)

70. **B** All of these are covered by the Exchange Act. In addition, note that secondary market and resale market have the same meaning. (Pages 173–174)

71. **C** Excessive trading in a client's account for the purpose of generating commissions is illegal and is

known as churning the account. (Page 123 and Page 204, 4.4.3.2)

72. **D** The overall purpose of a variable product is to expose the contract to market risk and to the rewards of investing in the market over a long period of time. This goal is assisted by having a number of investment choices available to the client in the separate account. (Page 142, 3.1.1)

73. **B** The overall risk of whether or not a stock will gain, or lose, value is a judgment call based upon factors, such as the company's competitive position with the products or services they provide. Thus, since market risk contains no guarantees of performance ("past performance does not guarantee future results"), choice B is best. (Page 52)

74. **C** All of the choices listed in the question are important discussion points. Risk for foreign companies is often even more pronounced, due to the currency risk mentioned. (Page 51, Page 53, Page 61)

75. **A** A book entry bond may not be delivered to a client, since a bond certificate does not exist. The proof of ownership for the client is the trade confirmation. (Page 13)

76. **B** Individual issues are not part of the series 6. View the products included in the series 6 license as always being sold in their initial offering (but no IPOs!); thus, they always require a prospectus. (Page 211, 4.5.4)

77. **D** Depending upon how old the fund is, the 1-year, 5-year and 10-year performance history must be included in the prospectus. (Page 98)

78. **B** Mutual fund distributors do not keep an inventory of mutual fund shares. Shares are sold to the distributor as needed to fill an order. The distributor receives the shares at NAV, adds the sales charge, and resells to the public at the POP. (Page 99, 2.1.8)

79. **B** Mandatory distribution for traditional IRAs must begin by April 1 in the year after the client turns 70½. If

at least a minimum distribution is not started, a 50% tax penalty applies to the amount that should have been taken. (Page 159, 3.2.1.6)

80. **A** Cumulative preferred stock provides for a missed dividend to be made up. Thus, before any new dividend is paid out, all unpaid dividends must be paid first. (Page 11)

81. **C** Nonprofit organizations are not required to register under the Securities Act of 1933 (they are exempt issuers); thus, they are also not required to register under the Blue Sky laws of the state. (Page 172, 4.1.1)

82. **A** Only the zero coupon bond does not have reinvestment risk. This is because the zero coupon bond is purchased at a deep discount from par (face) and builds (accretes) in value over time by compounding at a known percentage. Since they pay face value at maturity, there's no incentive for a company to call them early. (Page 16)

83. **A** A STRIP is a zero coupon bond issued by the Treasury Department. It is backed in full by the U.S. Government, and since it is a zero coupon bond, it is always purchased at a deep discount to par. (Page 26)

84. **C** Both preferred stocks and utility company stocks can provide reasonable growth and income. Aggressive growth stocks usually pay either a very small dividend or no dividend at all. Cyclical stocks, such as auto stocks, are unpredictable in providing either growth or income. (Page 43 and Page 55)

85. **A** AIR (assumed interest rate) is used as the basis for determining the monthly payout. If the separate account performance is above the AIR, the monthly payment increases; if performance is below the AIR, the monthly payment decreases. (Page 148)

86. **B** Municipal bond funds are exempt from federal tax. Municipal bond funds consisting of bonds from a client's state of residence may also be free of state and local taxes. Tax rates are of concern for the client,

since usually the higher the tax rate, the more suitable a municipal bond fund will be. (Page 27–28)

87. **A** Dollar cost averaging (DCA) lets a client invest the same amount of money each time, but that may not always buy a full share. For example, the client invests $850 each month. If the current share price is $12.62, the client buys 67.353 shares. Only mutual funds allow fractional share purchases. (Page 105)

88. **B** Since the client is bullish on the stock (market up), buying a call will accomplish the goal. Buying a call locks in a purchase price for the stock, no matter how high it rises before the call option contract expires. (Page 22)

89. **D** Since the client is in the 15% tax bracket, the equivalent tax rate for municipal bonds is not important to this client. Thus, the muni bond fund must be ranked last (two choices eliminated!). Proper order here: high-yield corporate bond, corporate bond fund, government bond fund, and muni bond fund. (Page 93–94)

90. **D** Debentures are considered to be unsecured debt, and upon default of the company, the client becomes a general creditor. (Page 16)

91. **D** All of the choices are correct. Money market funds are required by SEC to be no load, and they have a target NAV price of $1 to minimize taxes. Money market funds are usually a parking place for money that may be needed in the short term. (Page 94, 2.1.5.2)

92. **C** Exercise price, or strike price, is the price at which an option contract is completed. For a call, this is the price at which the stock can be purchased. For a put, this is the price at which the stock can be sold. (Page 22)

93. **A** The government bond fund is the best choice, since the underlying securities that make up the fund are government bonds. Remember, safety of principal is not a guarantee

of principal, but government issues are always the safest. (Page 65, 1.6.6)

94. **B** A mutual fund always redeems shares at the fund's NAV (net asset value). (Page 39)

95. **B** Common stock is the best choice, as it may be appropriate, assuming a client has the risk tolerance for it. Collectibles and life insurance are not allowed in an IRA. Municipal bonds are not suitable in an IRA (which is a tax-deferred account) since munis are already tax exempt. (Page 158, 3.2.1.2.)

96. **D** All choices are correct. Of particular importance to the Registered Representative is giving a current prospectus to the client no later than the sales presentation. (Page 195)

97. **A** Under the assumption that the client is okay with risk, common stock funds and aggressive growth funds provide the potential to keep up with, or exceed, inflation. Bond funds and balanced funds contain too many fixed income securities to offer a high growth potential. (Page 95)

98. **A** Trade confirmation must be sent no later than the settlement date. As a licensed Representative, you'll always receive a copy of the trade confirmation. (Page 202)

99. **B** The Investment Company Act of 1940 requires that at least 40% of an investment company's board of directors be independent, or noninterested, parties to the fund. Defined further, noninterested means no connection to the fund, other than being on the board of directors. (Page 83)

100. **C** NAV (net asset value) of a mutual fund is determined at the close of business every day. This is called forward pricing. Requests to buy or redeem shares are held until the end of the day. This ensures that both buyers and sellers receive the same share price. (Page 100, 2.1.9.1)

**End of Final Exam # 1**

# Answers to Practice Exam #2

1. **B** Unit investment trusts do not change their investments once the investments are chosen. Therefore, no management of the portfolio is needed and there is no board of directors. (Page 79, 2.1.1.1)

2. **D** Open-end investment company shares are always purchased at the POP (public offering price). (Page 39)

3. **A** A preliminary prospectus is known as the red herring and must be given to those people expressing an interest in the new issue. (Page 110, 2.1.13.1)

4. **C** Full and fair disclosure is best described by the Securities Act of 1933. Investment Act of 1952 does not exist. (Page 173)

5. **D** Purchasing common stock gives an investor ownership (equity) position in a company. It is also one of the primary means of obtaining business capital. (Page 4, 1.1.1.1 and Page 6)

6. **A** All choices are correct. Because a variable product has a separate account with investment choices and market risk, it must be sold by a registered representative (series 6 or series 7 license). (Page 142, 3.1.1)

7. **C** Purchasing power risk is associated with fixed interest rates, therefore, it is the risk normally attributed to fixed annuities. This type of risk is also sometimes referred to as the inability for an investment to keep up with inflation. (Page 143, 3.1.2.1)

8. **D** Zero coupon bonds are purchased at a discount and have a zero coupon that means pay no interest and do not produce income. The deep discount relates to a low purchase price, which grows in value (accretes) until bond matures at par. (Page 16)

9. **B** The factors relating to the municipal bond fund as the investment of choice for this example are the need for a high-quality investment and the high (37%) tax bracket. (Page 94, 2.1.5.2)

10. **D** The true definition of liquidity is immediate access of the funds at full price. Money market is the only choice that meets that definition. (Page 94, 2.1.5.2)

11. **B** The NASD (National Association of Securities Dealers) is the SRO (self-regulatory organization) for the over-the-counter (OTC). Remember this test uses a lot of abbreviations! (Page 176, 4.1.2.3.1)

12. **A** A closed-end fund can be called a publicly traded fund because it acts like a common stock. It is purchased on the secondary market after its initial offering, so it can trade at a premium or discount (like all stocks), can trade on NYSE, and is purchased in round lots. The only thing it can't do is be redeemed by the fund (that's only for open-end funds, like mutual funds). (Page 79, 2.1.1.3)

13. **D** Variable annuities do not have capital gains. All invested money and other gains grow tax-deferred and are taxed as ordinary income in the contract or when withdrawn. (Page 149)

14. **B** Statutory voting is one share per vote. Only cumulative voting is considered an allocation of votes. (Page 9)

15. **B** The state securities laws are called Blue Sky laws. (Page 145, 4.1.1) Note that the *firm element* refers to broker-dealer compliance issues and continuing education. (Page 211)

16. **D** A possible advantage of annuitizing a variable annuity is the varying monthly income. The result is good investment performance may increase monthly income. Conversely, a down market may decrease monthly income. (Page 145, 3.1.2.3 and Page 148)

17. **C** A diversified fund must pass the 5-10-75 test, which means at least 75% of assets must be invested, no more than 5% of its assets may be invested in any one company and the fund may not have a controlling interest (10% or more) in any company. (Page 81, 2.1.1.5)

18. **C** Bonds selling above par (above 100) are said to be selling at a premium. The secondary (resale) market is normally where a premium bond may be purchased. (Page 39)

19. **B** A government bond fund is the best choice since safety of principal is needed. Remember, a bond fund cannot guarantee principal, since there's no "maturity" date. (Pages 94–95)

20. **B** All of the choices except hedge funds are possibilities. The hedge funds are not mutual funds, and you will not have them as a part of your product offerings. (Page 95–96)

21. **A** Limited liability refers to a an investor being in a position to limit losses to the purchase price of the stock. Limited recourse is only for limited partnerships (e.g., DPPs). (Page 8)

22. **C** The transfer agent, sometimes referred to as the customer services agent, is the entity responsible for tracking requests to buy and sell, as well as keeping track of customer names and addresses. (Page 86, 2.1.2.6)

23. **A** All choices are correct. Index funds do offer lower realized gains each year compared to most common stock funds. (Page 94, 97, 115)

24. **D** All are acceptable except special situation funds. Special situation funds concentrate on turnaround and takeover candidates— they are high risk, high reward! (Page 93)

25. **B** Yes, depending upon performance of the underlying securities (separate account), the death benefit could decrease due to adverse market conditions, but will not decrease below the guaranteed minimum. (Page 156)

26. **B** Maximum broker-dealer fine is $2,500,000. (Individual is $1,000,000.) (Page 186, 4.1.5.3)

27. **C** The Registered Representative must resign from old firm and reapply with the new firm, since a license *may not be transferred*. Also, continuing commissions must be addressed before resignation. (Page 177, 203, 211)

28. **A** JTIC (Joint Tenants in Common) does allow for unequal ownership within the account. A major difference in this account is that upon death, the funds held by the decedent go to the decedent's estate, not to the remaining account owner. (Page 124, 2.3.3.3)

29. **C** A security is an investment relationship, either ownership (stock) or debt (bond). (Page 4, 1.1)

30. **A** Formula for this is Assets – Liabilities = Net Worth. (Page 59)

31. **B** Mutual funds may never be purchased on margin, which is true for any new issue. If the fund is held, fully paid, for 30 days or longer, the fund may be used as collateral for other loans or margin. (Page 89, 2.1.4.6)

32. **D** The separate account for variable annuities or variable universal life is subject to market risk, since the client must make investment choices. These investment choice are held in the separate account. (Page 142, 3.1.1)

33. **D** The scope of the act is intended to address the usage of inside (non-public) information for profit, or to avoid a loss. (Page 186)

34. **B** A call option owner controls the contract and has the choices. A call gives the owner the right to exercise the call and buy the stock at the exercise price. (Page 22)

35. **A** An underwriter is also referred to as the distributor, sponsor, or wholesaler for a fund. The fund distributes shares at the fund's NAV to the underwriter, who in turn wholesales

them to members of the selling group, or adds a sales charge and offers the shares to the public at the POP (public offering price). (Page 86, 2.1.2.4)

36. **C** BB, and below, are considered speculative or noninvestment grade, according to Standard & Poor ratings—think the more letters, the higher the rating. (Page 15, See Chart)

37. **D** As indicated in the question, the need is for growth. Since she understands risk, the stock funds would offer the best choices. (Stocks = Growth, Bonds = Income) (Page 55)

38. **B** 12b-1 charges are asset based fees for mutual funds, determined on an annual basis. These fees are reviewed quarterly by the fund's board of directors. (Page 103, 2.1.9.3)

39. **B** *Do not use the chart* since it has not been approved by your broker-dealer ! (Page 198)

40. **A** CDSL (contingent deferred sales load) is not deducted from the gross premium. CDSL are back-end load charges deducted for early surrender of the policy. Note: CDSL may also show up on the test as CDSC-contingent deferred sales charge. (Page 155)

41. **D** Corporate bonds, as listed in the question, are individual bonds—not bond funds—and are not covered under the Act of 1940, which only covers packaged securities. (Page 79)

42. **B** Expansion, peak, contraction, and trough is the correct order. (Remember: EPCoT) (Page 40)

43. **A** Since variable policies contain market risk, the death benefit and cash value of the policy are directly affected by investment choices made within the separate account. Taxes paid by a beneficiary is a distracter and does not apply. (Page 155, 3.1.3.3)

44. **C** Corporate bond funds would offer the highest income because different yields can be sought out based on bond quality. Utility funds is a tempting choice because they offer income, but that choice is paired with aggressive growth funds that pay no dividends. GNMA offers income with more safety, but income wouldn't be as high. (Page 94, 2.1.5.2)

45. **D** An indication of interest may be taken from a prospect, but not an actual order. Also, if an interest is indicated in the security, the preliminary prospectus (red herring) must be sent to the prospect. (Page 110)

46. **B** The tombstone ad is the only type of ad which may be run before the security is available for sale. (Page 188)

47. **D** The usual face amount par value for bonds is $1000. Once issued, bonds may sell on the resale (secondary) market at par, above par (premium), or below par (discount). (Note: preferred stock par value is $100.) (Page 15)

48. **C** Regulation of people and their activities, is a good way to remember the Securities Exchange Act of 1934. (Page 173, 4.1.2)

49. **B** Dividends are fully taxable to an individual investor. The 70% exclusion only applies to U.S. corporation buying other U.S. corporate securities. (Page 8 and Page 118)

50. **A** The correct formula for current yield is: **Current Yield (CY) = Coupon ÷ Price** Remember to put in the coupon rate (or interest rate) first. (Page 39)

51. **B** Since tax equivalent yield is a major factor in determining suitability for municipal bonds, higher tax brackets are more suitable for municipal bonds and bond funds. (Page 29)

52. **C** All choices are correct. Of course, some of these options are also true for diversified funds, but the key one is the higher risk level of a nondiversified fund. (Page 81, 2.1.2.1)

53. **D** Blue Sky laws refer to state registration of all three choices. (Page 172, 4.1.1)

54. **D** Only funds in an insurance company general account are guaranteed by the state. The separate account is subject to market risk and not guaranteed. (Page 142, 3.1.1)

55. **A** The more time until maturity, the greater the risk to the investor (because more time for negative events to occur). (Page 51)

56. **A** Growth funds usually don't pay dividends, but may increase share price over time. Thus, a younger person with risk tolerance could be suitable for this. (Page 64, 1.6.3)

57. **B** The Securities Act of 1934 is referred to as the People Act. The prospectus is not covered by the Act of 1934. (Page 173, 4.1.2)

58. **D** A pool of money and ownership of part of the pool describes an investment company. UITs (unit investment trusts), and mutual funds are organized as investment companies and use a pool of money for their investments and operation. (Page 78, 2.1)

59. **B** No taxable event occurs as a result of the change. However, if funds are withdrawn from the annuity, taxes will be due (LIFO—last in, first out). (Page 145, 3.1.2.3 and Page 149)

60. **A** Hot issues are issues that sell much above the initial public offering (IPO) price in the resale (secondary) market. Immediate family members, supported by the Registered Representative may not purchase a hot issue. (Page 179)

61. **B** Common stock, even though it is an ownership position in a company, is junior to all other securities. In liquidation of a company's asset's, the common stockholders come in last! (Page 9)

62. **D** The key to understanding this question is "mutual funds held in a cash account." This statement refers to nonretirement investments outside any tax favored account, such as an IRA, 401(k), etc. The fund may realize gains in any year, those gains are passed on to the investor to pay, and

a 1099 is issued. (Review the conduit theory.) (Page 114, 2.2.1.1)

63. **A** Regular way is the normal settlement time for securities, meaning either money is paid or securities are delivered. This must occur within three days after the trade date (T). Remember that regular way doesn't refer to government securities unless you are specifically told that in the question. (Page 36)

64. **C** A broker-dealer may act as either broker or dealer for a client transaction—but not both. Broker-dealers must disclose to the client in what capacity they operated on the trade confirmation. (Page 174, 4.1.2.1)

65. **B** Currency risk is a unique situation for a foreign stock. The other choices are strictly distracters! (Page 53)

66. **D** A bond's coupon rate and nominal rate mean the same thing. Yield to maturity (YTM) for a *discount bond* is higher than its coupon rate. (Page 40, Diagram is Key!)

67. **A** A need for highest income for life dictates some form of annuity. Of the choices listed, life only provides the highest income during the client's life. (Page 146)

68. **A** The Maloney Act set up the National Association of Securities Dealers (NASD) as the self-regulatory organization (SRO) for the over-the-counter (OTC) market. Remember the abbreviations! (Page 175, 4.1.2.2)

69. **D** Regulation T sets up basic guidelines for margin accounts, loan value of securities, settlement dates, and other areas. It also regulates initial public offerings (IPOs), stating that all new issues must be fully paid for when purchased (no borrowed money may be used). (Page 202, 4.4.2)

70. **C** From these choices, the only accurate answer is protecting customers from the default of their broker-dealer. If you know that the SIPC limits are $500,000 total and

$100,000 cash, you can eliminate choices I and IV. Market risk is certainly never protected in a regular securities account! (Page 183, 4.1.3 and Page 197, 4.3.3)

71. **B** The zero coupon bond does not have reinvestment risk. This is because a zero coupon bond is purchased at a deep discount from par (face) and builds in value (accretes) over time by compounding at a known percentage. Since they pay face value at maturity, there's no incentive for a company to call them early. (Page 16)

72. **C** Both the regulatory element and firm element must be met in order to maintain your Registered Representative status. Your broker-dealer will have the details. (Page 211, 4.5.4)

73. **D** The two phases are commonly called the accumulation and annuity phases. With many annuities, the annuity phase may be a periodic payment, systematic withdrawal, or other approach. (Page 147, 3.1.2.5)

74. **A** Stock distributed to investors is known as issued stock. (Page 4, 1.1.1.1)

75. **C** All choices are true for common stock. Par value assigned to common stock is printed on the stock certificate but has no meaning for the investor. Par value may be paid-in capital if money is actually collected from investors. Market price is supply and demand, and not connected to par value. (Page 5)

76. **B** Shares of open-end investment companies (mutual funds) are redeemable. This means shares are sold back directly to the company and not reissued. (Page 82 and Page 106, 2.1.12)

77. **C** Combination of growth in share price, plus a good dividend, is best suited to a growth and income fund. (Page 64, 1.6.4 and Page 93)

78. **D** Roth IRAs do not provide a tax deduction in the current tax year, but they do offer tax-deferred

growth and tax-exempt distribution. (Page 159, 3.2.1.8)

79. **A** A SEP (Simplified Employment Pension) plan is a qualified pension plan that is often used by small companies. (Page 159, 3.2.1.7)

80. **B** Regulatory element includes testing at a testing center at the end of your second year and every three years thereafter. (Page 211, 4.5.4)

81. **D** ERISA (Employee Retirement Income Security Act) provisions cover all of the areas mentioned in the question, plus communication and nondiscrimination. (Page 162)

82. **B** The declining sales charge is referred to as a contingent deferred sales charge (load). Since the charge only occurs if the client liquidates the fund during the declining sales charge period (i.e., after the purchase), it is known as a back-end load. (Page 101)

83. **D** The purpose of SIPC is consumer protection. It protects the consumer from brokerage firm default, but not market risk. (Page 183, 4.1.3)

84. **D** Antidilution means if stockholders want to keep a certain percentage of ownership in a company, they would have a preemptive right to purchase additional shares prior to a public offering of the shares. (Page 9)

85. **B** The custodian has responsibility for protection (safekeeping) of a fund's assets and other clerical functions. Safekeeping *does not mean* guarding against market loss! Also, with these types of Roman numeral questions with single correct answers, be sure to mark the answer below (B), and don't mistakenly mark (D), because your correct choice is the last Roman numeral answer. (Page 86, 2.1.2.5)

86. **A** Mid cap companies are defined as having a capitalization of $1 to $5 *billion.* (Page 92, 2.1.5.1—Growth funds part.)

87. **B** The low-grade corporate bond fund (also called a high-yield bond fund) would be the best choice from the

choices listed in the question. Remember—lower bond ratings mean higher yields! (Page 94, 2.1.5.2)

88. **C** GNMA and the Ginnie Mae pass-through certificates are a direct obligation of the U.S. government, backed by full faith and credit and taxing power of the government. (Page 23)

89. **D** Index funds would be the choice for limited realized gains, since they follow the index, such as the S&P 500. A broad index (like the S&P 500) will match the market results, while keeping trades within the fund at a minimum. (Page 95, 97, 115)

90. **C** The Securities and Exchange Commission (SEC) only *clears* an issue for distribution and does not make any judgment about the company or its quality. (Page 111, 2.1.13.2)

91. **B** Registered Representatives must have their broker-dealer's approval for any outside employment. (Page 180 and Page 211, 4.5.4)

92. **A** The death benefit for a variable life policy must be calculated at least once a year. (Page 156)

93. **C** Simplified arbitration may be used for disputes of $25,000 or less. It avoids personal appearances. (Page 210, 4.5.2.2)

94. **A** The Investment Company Act of 1940 requires semiannual (twice per year) financial reports. One of these reports (usually the "annual report") must be an audited report. (Page 98)

95. **A** The maximum allowable sales load in the first year is 8½%. Because of the competitive environment, though, very few charge the maximum. (Page 84)

96. **A** Turnover rate reflects what portion of the fund's assets are traded annu-

ally. This can affect the expense ratio as well because of the increased commissions that the fund must pay when making each portfolio trade. Another consideration is capital gains taxes. For instance, a turn rate of 100% means the fund replaces its portfolio once each year. This means the average holding period is one year, or less, and the gains are very likely taxed as short-term gains. (Page 84, 97, 115)

97. **C** The exempt issuers include all four choices listed in the question. U.S. territories include Guam, Puerto Rico, and U.S. Virgin Islands, and fall under the definition of municipalities just like state and city governments. Even if you were not sure about that, you can still answer the question relying on information that you did know. (Page 173, 4.1.1.1)

98. **A** Unless another method is chosen by the investor, the gains on mutual funds in a cash account (not sheltered by a retirement plan or annuity) are taxed by the IRS on the basis of FIFO (first in, first out) because this usually maximizes the tax liability. (Page 118, 2.2.2.4)

99. **D** Preferred stock is usually purchased for its dividend and the possibility of appreciation in share value. Preferred stock contains both the features of equity (ownership) and debt (income). It is used where moderate risk and reward is desired. (Page 9)

100. **B** Recruitment advertising is the only instance where broker-dealers do not need to identify themselves. (Page 192)

**End of Final Exam # 2**